Ukrainian for Speakers of English

Text

Roma Franko

Detselig Enterprises Ltd.
Calgary, Alberta

Ukrainian for Speakers of English: Text

Department of Languages
University of Saskatchewan
Saskatoon, Saskatchewan

Canadian Cataloguing in Publication Data

Franko, Roma Z.
Ukrainian for speakers of English : text

Includes index
ISBN 1-55059-095-2

1. Ukrainian language – Textbooks for second language learners.* 2. Ukrainian language – Study and teaching as a second language.* I. Title.
PG3827.3.F72 1994 491.7'982421 C94-910714-X

Detselig Enterprises Ltd.
210, 1220 Kensington Rd. N.W.
Calgary, Alberta T2N 3P5

Printed in Canada SAN 115-0324 ISBN 1-55059-095-2

PREFACE

Ukrainian for Speakers of English is intended for students who have no knowledge of Ukrainian. All of the material is presented from the point of view of a student who knows how to speak English, but who may not know the formal rules of English grammar. Thus, before a new point in Ukrainian grammar is introduced, students are first reminded about what they know, either formally or informally, about a similar structure in English.

In organizing the grammar points that are included in this program, an innovative approach has been used to assist students in making their way through the intricacies of a highly inflected language. Instead of presenting all of the inflected parts of speech simultaneously, they are introduced one at a time.

As an example, in Lessons 2-10, the focus is on learning how to conjugate Ukrainian verbs in the present tense. The adverbs and conjunctions that are included in these lessons are not inflected, and the pronouns that are presented are used only in the nominative case. This selective approach permits students to focus their attention fully on learning the endings that are used in conjugating verbs in the present tense.

The grammar explanations in the text are brief and simple; they convey only as much information as a student can be expected to assimilate in the early stages of learning a second language. Numerous examples, summaries, and charts are included to assist the learner in organizing the information that is being presented.

After a grammar point has been introduced and explained, the student is able to apply what has been learned about that particular structure by actively engaging in carefully co-ordinated oral exercises and mini-conversations that are to be practised in class, in the language lab, and at home. The written exercises provide both the student and the instructor with a means of checking how thoroughly the grammar structures have been learned.

There are either four or six pages of written exercises to accompany every lesson. The number of oral exercises varies according to the difficulty of the material that is being presented. An answer key is appended to *Oral Exercises.* There are fewer oral exercises in the later lessons; it is expected thatas students progress through the program they will be able to create more of their own conversations and dialogues based on the grammar and vocabulary that they have assimilated.

In deciding upon the vocabulary to be included in this text, a deliberate effort was made to select words that are useful both for illustrating the grammar points that are being made in a lesson, and for providing the student with a basic vocabulary for conversing about routine matters related to everyday living. While the intent was to adhere as closely as possible to standard literary Ukrainian, for a number of the words, mainly nouns, more than one Ukrainian equivalent is given. A few of these words may be considered dialectal, but they are used so commonly by speakers of Ukrainian in Canada, that it would be a disservice to the students to exclude them. The words that appear in slanted script are not used in the exercises, but students who are planning to travel to Ukraine should familiarize themselves with them as they are likely to hear them there.

This text and the accompanying workbooks have been piloted for two years in Introductory and Intermediate Ukrainian courses at the University of Saskatchewan, and for one year at the University of Regina. The response of the students to the carefully structured way of organizing the grammar has been enthusiastic, and the results have been most gratifying.

On the basis of this experience, it is recommended that the first twenty-two lessons be completed in an Introductory Course at the university level. In the Intermediate course, in which students from a variety of backgrounds may be enrolling, the first twenty-two lessons should be reviewed thoroughly before work is begun on the remaining sixteen.

At first glance, this suggested division of the lessons between the Introductory and the Intermediate courses may appear to be uneven; however, a closer examination of the text will reveal that there is less material, in terms of both vocabulary and grammar, in each of the first twenty-two lessons that in the later ones. For a broad overview of the content of this text, see the first four pages in Lesson 1.

At the high school level, Lessons 1-22 could be completed in a three-year program. In a four-year program, it should be possible to complete Lessons 1-25. The amount of material that can be covered depends, of course, on the number of hours that are allocated in a school to the teaching of a second language. It is more important to ensure that every grammar point is learned thoroughly before preceding to the next one than to try to move too quickly through the program in order to complete a given number of lessons.

By the end of Lesson 22, students have mastered approximately 100 verbs, 500 nouns and pronouns, and 100 adverbs, prepositions, and conjunctions. This functional vocabulary permits them to carry on a great variety of conversations about events occuring in the present. They are also able to use the basic verb **to be** in talking about the past and the future, Given the systematic and thorough structure of the program, students acquire the ability to use the language proficiently and competently and are motivated to continue their studies at the next level.

The Intermediate portion of the program enables students to speak the language in a more native-like manner. They learn how to use all the verbs in the past and future tenses, and in the imperative and conditional moods. They also acquire modifiers, i.e. adjectives and numbers, that enable them to speak more expressively. Their level of competency and their confidence in their language abilities makes it possible to introduce readings from a variety of sources: newspapers, magazines, Ukrainian readers, and letters from penpals in Ukraine. In sum, completion of the program lays the foundation for further formal and informal acquisition of the language, and for the study and enjoyment of Ukrainian literature.

① Купатся

② Куп И   Куп ся

③ Тап

④ пити

ВСТИВАТИ

⑤ УСТИВАТИ

⑥ Telefonyвати

⑦ сміятися

⑧ потім

спати

⑨

Letit.

Просити

летіти

сидіти

Во Б

Бояатися

ACKNOWLEDGEMENTS

I gratefully acknowledge the financial assistance of:

The Ukrainian Canadian Foundation of Taras Shevchenko
President's SSHRC Research Fund, University of Saskatchewan
University Publications Fund, University of Saskatchewan

I also gratefully acknowledge the assistance of:

The Division of Audio-Visual Services, University of Saskatchewan

I owe a special debt of gratitude to the following persons:

Mike Kaweski, a former student in one of my Ukrainian courses, for the patience, perseverance, attention to detail, excellent judgment,and good humour that he displayed in executing the demanding task of preparing camera-ready copy for publication.

Sonia Morris, my sister and sometime co-author, for her wise counsel and careful reading of all of the materials during both the pilot and final stages of this project.

Stefan Franko, my husband, for his unfailing encouragement, moral support, patience, and understanding.

I also wish to express my sincere thanks to everyone who assisted me in any way in the preparation of the various phases of this program: Dr. Earl Misanchuk, Prof. Maryna Romanets-Komolova, Natalka Karaieva, Frank Harrington, Roman Nemesh, Natalia Haiova, Albert Kachkowski, Ilariya Maximiuk, and Tanya Mysak.

This book is lovingly dedicated to the memory of my father, Roman F. Stratychuk (1902-1986), who learned to cherish Ukrainian in the burdey (sod hut) where he was born in what is now Saskatchewan, and who gently nurtured a love for the language and its literature in his children and grandchildren.

Detselig Enterprises Ltd. appreciates the financial assistance received for its 1994 publishing program from Canadian Heritage, Alberta Foundation for the Arts (a beneficiary of the Lottery Fund of the Government of Alberta), and Canada Council.

TABLE OF CONTENTS

LESSON 1

A. INTRODUCTION TO UKRAINIAN FOR SPEAKERS OF ENGLISH

In *Ukrainian for Speakers of English*, the structures of the Ukrainian language are introduced by building on your knowledge of spoken English. After a new structure has been explained, opportunities for practising it are provided in systematically co-ordinated oral and written exercises.

To make it easier for you to learn Ukrainian, carefully structured and sequenced oral and written exercises ensure mastery of one element before another is introduced. Earlier parts of the program are systematically reviewed and reinforced as new material is presented and each new structure is related to elements that you have already mastered. The order in which the structures are presented is described in A.2.

The vocabulary in this program is useful for carrying on everyday conversations with speakers of Ukrainian both in Ukraine and in North America. There are some differences in the words that are used by speakers of Ukrainian in Ukraine and those who speak it in North America. These minor differences are noted in the vocabularies.

A.1 Program Components

The program *Ukrainian for Speakers of English* consists of five components: three books, an introductory audio cassette, and a set of audio cassettes.

1. *Text*
2. *Oral Exercises*
3. *Written Exercises*
4. *Inroductory Audio Cassette*
5. *A Set of Audio Cassettes*

A.2 *Text*

The text consists of 38 lessons.

1. **Lessons 1-10**

   In the first lesson, you learn to read and write Ukrainian.

   The Introductory Audio Cassette accompanies this lesson.

In the next nine lessons, you learn how to talk about things that are happening at the present time.

To make it easier for you to begin speaking Ukrainian immediately, you learn only four parts of speech at the outset:

• verbs, used in the present tense	I **am reading**.
• pronouns, used as subjects	**They** remember.
• conjunctions	He **and** I are dancing.
• adverbs	They sing **very loudly**.

With the vocabulary that you learn in these ten lessons, you will be able to do all of the following:

• make simple statements	I live here.
• ask questions	Where do they live?
• make negative statements	I don't live here.
• use helping verbs	I want to live here.
• use subordinate clauses	I know that they live here.
• make a request	Please sit down.
• implement verbs of motion	I'm going there.

2. Lessons 11-22

As you progress through these lessons, you will greatly increase your speaking skills in Ukrainian by learning how to use words that name persons and objects:

• nouns	Where is the **poster**?
• pronouns	Do you see **it**?

To help you engage in interesting conversations about persons and objects, you will also learn how to use three additional parts of speech:

• prepositions	It's **on** the wall.
• adverbs of quantity	I see **many** posters.
• cardinal numbers	I see only **two** posters.

Midway through these lessons, you will learn more about the verb **to be** so that you will be able to use this verb in talking about something that happened in the past or that will happen in the future:

• past tense	He **was** at home.
• future tense	He **will be** at home.

3. **Lessons 23-25**

These three lessons are very important; after you have completed them, you will know how to use a variety of verbs to talk about events that have already occurred or that will occur in the future.

• past imperfective tense	She **was listening**.
• past perfective tense	She **paid** for the ticket.
• future imperfective tense	She **will be listening**.
• future perfective tense	She **will pay** for the ticket.

4. **Lessons 26-33**

After you have completed these lessons, you will be able to speak much more colorfully, because you will know how to describe people and objects.

To help you learn how to say more about persons and objects, the following parts of speech are introduced:

• adjectives	I have an **expensive** ring.
• interrogative pronouns	**Whose** watch is that?
• possessive pronouns	She has **my** wallet.
• substantives	Do you understand the **rich**?
• ordinal numerals	Where is the **second** taxi?
• demonstrative pronouns	Do you like **this** stereo?
• possessive adjectives	This is **mother's** necklace.

In addition, you will learn how to do the following:

• compare adjectives	My VCR is **newer**.
• compare adverbs	He gets up **later**.
• tell time	It's one o'clock.
• use dates, years, centuries	I'll be there on May 1.
• use impersonal constructions	It's snowing.

5. **Lessons 34-38**

In the final five lessons, you will learn additional structures that will help you sound even more like a native speaker of Ukrainian.

In these lessons you will learn how to do the following:

• give commands	Don't swim in the lake!
• implement the conditional mood	I would, if I could.
• use less common nouns	
• expand your use of numbers	

A.3 *Oral Exercises*

After the introduction of a new structure in the text, you are directed to specific exercises in *Oral Exercises.* To draw your attention to these exercises, the following symbol is used: 📼 .

You are strongly urged to practise the oral exercises at the time that they are introduced. **It is important to learn one structure well before another one is attempted**.

The oral exercises are designed to help you start communicating immediately in Ukrainian. Many of them are set up either as brief exchanges involving a question and an answer, or as slightly longer mini-conversations.

A.4 *Introductory Audio Cassette*

The introductory audio cassette accompanies Lesson 1 in Oral Exercises. It contains material that is intended to assist the student in learning to read Ukrainian.

A.5 *Audio Cassettes*

All of the oral exercises are recorded on cassettes. To help you use these cassettes, an index is provided.

If you want to learn to speak Ukrainian and to understand it when it is spoken, you must spend as much time as possible listening to these cassettes and repeating the structures.

The explanations in the text and the written exercises can give you a reading knowledge of Ukrainian; however, you have to hear Ukrainian spoken if you are going to learn to communicate orally.

Some students have found that the walkman is a valuable tool for learning a language; after they have practised an oral exercise, they are able to carry on with other activities as they listen to the cassettes over and over again.

A.6 *Written Exercises*

In the *Written Exercises,* the written work is systematically co-ordinated both with the new structures and with the oral exercises. This means that the written work should be done only after the oral work has been completed.

In the text, the written exercises are identified by the following symbol: ✍ .

The written exercises help you consolidate the structures that you have learned through doing the oral exercises. They are printed on perforated pages to make it more convenient for your instructor to mark them.

B. INTRODUCTION TO UKRAINIAN

You will begin your study of Ukrainian with the exciting and challenging task of learning a new alphabet!

In English, the Latin alphabet is used.

In Ukrainian, the Cyrillic alphabet is used.

B.1 The English Alphabet

When you first began to read and write English, you learned the 26 letters of the English alphabet.

1. five vowels: a, e, i, o, u
2. one semi-vowel: y
3. 20 consonants: b, c, d, f, g, h, j, k, l, m,
n, p, q, r, s, t, v, w, x, z

B.2 The Ukrainian Alphabet

In the Ukrainian alphabet, there are 33 letters.

1. six simple vowels: а, е, и, і, о, у
2. four iotized vowels: є, ї, ю, я
3. 22 consonants: б, в, г, ґ, д, ж, з, й, к, л, м,
н, п, р, с, т, ф, х, ц, ч, ш, щ
4. one "soft sign": ь

There are also two compound consonants that represent distinct sounds: дж, дз.

B.3 Similarities among English and Ukrainian Letters

As you examine the Ukrainian alphabet, you will notice that some of the letters look familiar.

You must keep in mind, however, that although the letters may **look** the same in the English and Ukrainian alphabets, they do not necessarily **sound** the same.

B.4 Spelling

Ukrainian is a highly phonetic language; most letters have only one sound, and words are usually written as they are pronounced. This means that there are far fewer problems with spelling in Ukrainian than in English.

In English, you have to learn how "to spell" words.

1. Words may look the same, but sound different: though, bough, cough, slough.

2. Words may sound the same but look different: meet, meat, mete.

In Ukrainian, similar situations do not arise. Indeed, there are no words for "spelling" or "to spell" in Ukrainian, nor is there a need for them.

B.5 Differences in Ukrainian Usage

Speakers of Ukrainian who live in Ukraine and those who live in other countries differ at times in their use of Ukrainian. Now that Ukraine is independent, scholars are working to resolve these differences. In the meantime, you should be aware of a few of them.

1. When Ukraine was part of the USSR, the letter **ґ** was removed from the Ukrainian alphabet; instead, the letter **г** was used to represent both the **h** and the **g** sounds. Speakers of Ukrainian who lived outside the USSR did use the letter **ґ** for the **g** sound, and **г** for the **h** sound.

2. In transliterating words from English into Ukrainian, the letter **х** is used in Ukraine to transcribe the English **h** sound (e.g. **хоке́й** for **h**ockey). In Canada and other Western countries, the letter **г** is used, because its sound is closer to the English **h** sound (e.g. **го́кей** for **h**ockey).

3. In a number of words, the iotized vowel **я** has been replaced in Ukraine by the simple vowel **а.**

Practise Oral Exercises 1.1, 1.2, 1.3, 1.4, 1.5, 1.6, 1.7

Do Written Exercises 1.1, 1.2, 1.3, 1.4, 1.5, 1.6

LESSON 2

A. VOCABULARY

Pronouns

he	він
I	я
it	вонó
she	вонá
they	вонú
we	ми
you	ти, ви

Verbs

to be	бýти

Adverbs

already	ужé/вже
also, too	такóж, теж
at home	удóма/вдóма
here	тут, ось
no	ні
now	тепéр
outdoors, outside	надвóрі
still	ще
there	там, он
where	де
yes	так

Vocabulary Notes

1. In the vocabulary lists in this text, words are presented in units according to the part of speech to which they belong: pronouns, verbs, adverbs, etc.

   Within these grammatical units, words are divided into smaller groups to make them easier to read and learn.

2. Unlike the English pronoun **I**, the Ukrainian pronoun **я** is capitalized **only** at the beginning of a sentence.

3. For an explanation about the pronouns **ти** and **ви** see B.2.

4. Some words that begin with **у**, have an alternate form that begins with **в**.

   уже́/вже

   удо́ма/вдо́ма

   The form that begins with **у** is used after words ending in consonants.

   Він **уже́** тут.

   Він **удо́ма**.

   The form that begins with **в** is used after words ending in vowels.

   Вона́ **вже** тут.

   Вони́ **вдо́ма**.

5. The adverbs **тако́ж** and **теж** are synonyms that may be used interchangeably.

   Ми вдо́ма. Вони́ **тако́ж** удо́ма.

   Ми вдо́ма. Вони́ **теж** удо́ма.

6. The adverbs **тут** (here) and **там** (there) are used to provide factual information that someone or something is either **here** or **there**.

   The adverbs **ось** (here) and **он** (there) are used to state **emphatically** that someone or something is either **here** or **there**.

   Both **ось** and **он** are often accompanied by a pointing gesture.

7. Two stress marks in one word indicate that you may hear either syllable stressed in spoken Ukrainian.

   If one of the stresses is preferred in literary Ukrainian, it is bolded: надво́рі́.

B. PRONOUNS: PERSONAL PRONOUNS

In both English and Ukrainian, personal pronouns are identified according to **person**.

B.1 First Person Pronouns

In English, we use the **singular** pronoun **I** when we refer to ourselves as a single person.

We use the **plural** pronoun **we** when we talk about ourselves as part of a group of two or more people.

These two personal pronouns, **I** and **we**, are known as first person pronouns.

In Ukrainian, the **singular** first person pronoun is **я**.

The **plural** first person pronoun in Ukrainian is **ми**.

	English	*Ukrainian*
First Person Singular	I	я
First Person Plural	we	ми

B.2 Second Person Pronouns

In English, we use the second person pronoun **you** when we speak to other people.

We use the pronoun **you** when we speak either to one person or to many people. This means that the pronoun **you** may be **either singular or plural** in meaning.

In Ukrainian, there are two second person pronouns: **ти** and **ви**.

1. The pronoun **ти** is **always singular** in meaning.

   Children use **ти** when they speak to one another.

   (In some families, children also use **ти** when they speak to a parent or to other adults in their immediate family.)

   As adults, we use **ти** when we speak to a child, a younger family member, a spouse, or a close adult friend.

2. The pronoun **ви**, like the English pronoun **you**, may be **either singular or plural** in meaning.

   Children and younger people always use the polite (formal) **ви** in its **singular** meaning when they are speaking to an adult outside their immediate family.

   As adults, we use the polite (formal) pronoun **ви** in its **singular** meaning when we speak to another adult with whom we are not on familiar terms.

   The pronoun **ви** in its **plural** meaning is used when we speak to more than one person.

   Although **ви** may be either singular or plural in meaning, it is always used with a plural verb form.

   In this text, and in the accompanying workbook, **you** *[s]* refers to the singular **ти**; **you** *[p]* refers to either the **p**olite (formal) singular **ви** or the **p**lural **ви**.

	English	***Ukrainian***
Second Person Singular	you *[s]*	ти
Second Person Plural	you *[p]*	ви

B.3 Third Person Pronouns

In English, when we talk about one person or thing, we use one of the **singular** third person pronouns: **he, she,** or **it**.

When we talk about two or more people or things in English, we use the **plural** third person pronoun: **they**.

In Ukrainian, when we talk about one person or thing, we use one of the following **singular** third person pronouns: **він, вона́,** or **воно́**.

When we talk about two or more people or things in Ukrainian, we use the **plural** third person pronoun: **вони́**.

	English	***Ukrainian***
Third Person Singular	he	він
	she	вона́
	it	воно́
Third Person Plural	they	вони́

B.4 Personal Pronouns: Summary

In both English and Ukrainian, personal pronouns are identified according to **person** (first, second, or third) and **number** (singular or plural).

English Personal Pronouns		
	Singular	*Plural*
First Person	I	we
Second Person	you	you
Third Person	he, she, it	they

Ukrainian Personal Pronouns		
	Singular	*Plural*
First Person	я	ми
Second Person	ти	ви
Third Person	він, вона́, воно́	вони́

✍ **Do Written Exercise 2.1**

C. VERBS: PRESENT TENSE

In both English and Ukrainian, when we talk about something that is happening **now**, we use a verb in the **present tense**.

Let's look at some of the ways in which the present tense is expressed in English.

I **am reading**.	We **remember**.
You *[s]* **understand**.	You *[p]* **are listening**.
She **does know**.	They **do sing**.
He **is dancing**.	It **is** here.

C.1 Conjugation of Verbs

When we **conjugate** a verb, we change its form so that it agrees with the personal pronoun that we're using.

Conjugating verbs in English in the present tense is easy; usually, only the verb form for the third person singular pronoun is changed.

Let's look at the verb **to read**. In the conjugation of this verb, only the verb form for **he**, **she**, and **it** changes: he, she, it **reads**.

	Singular	*Plural*
First Person	I read	we read
Second Person	you read	you read
Third Person	he reads she reads it reads	they read

As you will see in the next few lessons, conjugating verbs in the present tense in Ukrainian is a little more challenging; there are six different verb forms for almost all verbs.

C.2 To Be: Present Tense Conjugation

In English, the verb **to be** has three different verb forms (**am**, **is**, and **are**) when it is conjugated in the present tense.

	Singular	*Plural*
First Person	I am	we are
Second Person	you are	you are
Third Person	he is she is it is	they are

In spoken and written English today, these verb forms are often **contracted**.

	Singular	*Plural*
First Person	I'm	we're
Second Person	you're	you're
Third Person	he's she's it's	they're

In Ukrainian, the verb **to be** is **бýти**.

Бýти is the **only** Ukrainian verb that has the **same** present tense verb form for all the personal pronouns.

	Singular	*Plural*
First Person	я є	ми є
Second Person	ти є	ви є
Third Person	він є вонá є вонó є	вони́ є

C.3 бýти: Omission in the Present Tense

In English, the forms of the verb **to be** may be contracted, but they are never omitted.

I **am** here.	We **are** at home
I'**m** here.	We'**re** at home.
He **is** there.	They **are** outdoors.
He'**s** there.	They'**re** outdoors.

In Ukrainian, because **є** is used with all the personal pronouns in the present tense, it is usually omitted in Ukrainian sentences.

Where **is** he?	Де він?
He'**s** outdoors.	Він надвóрі.
Are they there?	Вони́ там?
No, they'**re** here.	Ні, вони́ тут.
Are you *[s]* here?	Ти тут?
Yes, **I'm** here.	Так, я тут.

Practise Oral Exercise 2.1

Do Written Exercise 2.2

C.4 бу́ти: Emphatic Use in the Present Tense

In English, when the forms of the verb **to be** are emphasized, they are not contracted.

I ***am*** outdoors.
She ***is*** here.
We ***are*** at home.
They ***are*** there.

In Ukrainian, when **є does** appear in a sentence, it adds emphasis to the statement that is being made.

I ***am*** here.	Я ***є*** тут.
It ***is*** there.	Воно́ ***є*** там.
We ***are*** outdoors.	Ми ***є*** надво́рі.
They ***are*** at home.	Вони́ ***є*** вдо́ма.

Practise Oral Exercise 2.2

C.5 бу́ти: Omission with Emphatic Adverbs

In English, when an emphatic statement is made with the adverbs **here** or **there,** the verb forms of the verb **to be** are used.

Here I **am**!
Here she **is**!
There they **are**!

In Ukrainian, when the emphatic adverbs **ось** and **он** are used, **є** is omitted.

Here she **is**!	Ось вона́!
Here they **are**!	Ось вони́!
There he **is**!	Он він!
There they **are**!	Он вони́!

Practise Oral Exercise 2.3

C.6 Summary

Compare the use of **to be** in English and **бýти** in Ukrainian in the following sentences:

1. **Statement of Fact**

He **is** here.	Він тут.
He**'s** here.	Він тут.
They **are** there.	Вони́ там.
They**'re** there.	Вони́ там.

2. **Emphatic Statement**

He ***is*** here.	Він ***є*** тут.
They ***are*** there.	Вони́ ***є*** там.

3. **Use with Emphatic Adverbs**

Here he **is**!	Ось він!
There they **are**!	Он вони́!

✍ **Do Written Exercise 2.3**

D. ADVERBS

In both English and Ukrainian, adverbs tell us **when**, **where**, **why,** or **how** something is happening.

Let's look at how adverbs are used in both these languages.

They are **outdoors now**.	Вони́ **тепе́р надво́рі**.
Is he **also there**?	Він **тако́ж там**?
No, he is **here**.	**Ні**, він **тут**.
Yes, she's **here already**.	**Так**, вона́ **вже тут**.

Practise Oral Exercise 2.4

✍ **Do Written Exercise 2.4**

E. INTERROGATIVE PARTICLE: ЧИ

In English, there is no interrogative particle.

In Ukrainian, the interrogative particle **чи** may be used to indicate a question.

Are they at home?
Чи вони́ вдо́ма?

Is he also here?
Чи він тако́ж тут?

The same question may be asked, however, without using **чи**.

Are they at home?
Вони́ вдо́ма?

Is he also here?
Він тако́ж тут?

Practise Oral Exercises 2.5, 2.6, 2.7

Do Written Exercises 2.5, 2.6

LESSON 3

A. VOCABULARY

Pronouns

what	що
who	хто

Adverbs

again	знов, зно́ву
always	за́вжди
not yet	ще ні
often, frequently	ча́сто
perhaps, maybe	мо́же, можли́во
probably	ма́бу́ть
seldom, rarely	рі́дко
sometimes	і́нколи, і́ноді, ча́сом
usually	звича́йно

Conjunctions

and	і/й, а
both … and	і … і
but	але́, а
either … or	або́ … або́
neither … nor	ні … ні
or	або́, чи

Vocabulary Notes

1. The conjunction **і** has an alternate form: **й.**

   The conjunction **і** is written as **і** when it is used between two consonants, or at the beginning of a sentence.

   Він і ми.

   І ми такóж тут.

   І ось вонó.

   The conjunction **і** is written as **й** when it is used between two vowels, or between a vowel and a consonant.

   Ти й я.

   Ми й вонú

   When you **say** a sentence that contains the conjunction **й**, you do not treat it as a separate word; instead, you attach it to the previous word.

   Тий я.

   Мий вонú.

2. The adverbs **знов** and **знóву** are synonyms that may be used interchangeably.

   Вонú **знов** надвóрі?

   Вонú **знóву** надвóрі?

3. The adverbs **мóже** and **можлúво** are synonyms that may be used interchangeably.

   Мóже вонú вдóма.

   Можлúво вонú вдóма.

4. The adverbs **íнколи, íноді** and **чáсом** are synonyms that may be used interchangeably.

   Вонú **íнколи** тут.

   Вонú **íноді** тут.

   Вонú **чáсом** тут.

B. CONJUNCTIONS

In both English and Ukrainian, conjunctions are used to connect words; they help us see how words are related to one another in a sentence.

B.1 And

The English conjunction **and** has its counterpart in the Ukrainian conjunction **і/й**.

He **and** she are at home.
Він **і** вона́ вдо́ма.

She **and** he are at home.
Вона́ **й** він удо́ма.

The Ukrainian conjunction **a** also means **and**; it is used in sentences in which a **contrast** is being made.

He is here **and** she is there.
Він тут, **а** вона́ там.

They are there, **and** we are at home.
Вони́ там, **а** ми вдо́ма.

When no contrast is being made in a sentence, **і/й** is used.

He is here, **and** she is here.
Він тут **і** вона́ тут.

You *[p]* are outdoors **and** they are outdoors.
Ви надво́рі **й** вони́ надво́рі.

Sometimes the conjunction **a** is used to begin a sentence.

He's here. **And** where is she?
Він тут. **А** де вона́?

Practise Oral Exercise 3.1

B.2 But

The English conjunction **but** has its counterpart in the Ukrainian conjunction **алé**.

He's seldom at home, **but** he's at home now.
Він рідко вдóма, **алé** він удóма тепéр.

We're home already, **but** they're still outdoors.
Ми вже вдóма, **алé** вони́ ще надвóрі.

Practise Oral Exercise 3.2

B.3 Or

The English conjunction **or** has its counterpart in the Ukrainian conjunction **абó**.

He's there, **or** maybe he's at home.
Він там, **абó** мóже він удóма.

When the conjunction **or** is found in a **question,** the Ukrainian counterpart for it is **чи**.

Is he here, **or** there?
Він тут, **чи** там?

Are they at home often **or** seldom?
Вони́ чáсто **чи** рідко вдóма?

Do not confuse the conjunction **чи** (**or**) with the interrogative particle ***чи*** which may be used to indicate a question, but which has no counterpart in English. (See Lesson 2, E.)

Is he here, **or** there?
Він тут, **чи** там?
Чи він тут, **чи** там?

Are they at home often **or** seldom?
Вони́ чáсто **чи** рідко вдóма?
Чи вони́ чáсто **чи** рідко вдóма?

Practise Oral Exercise 3.3

B.4 Either ... or

The English **either ... or** has its counterpart in the Ukrainian **абó ... абó**.

He is **either** here, **or** outside.
Він **абó** тут, **абó** надвóрі.

Either he **or** she is at home.
Абó він, **абó** вонá вдóма.

B.5 Neither ... nor

The English **neither ... nor** has its counterpart in the Ukrainian **ні ... ні**.

He's **neither** here, **nor** there.
Він **ні** тут, **ні** там.

She's **neither** here, **nor** at home.
Вонá **ні** тут, **ні** вдóма.

B.6 Both ... and

The English **both ... and** has its counterpart in the Ukrainian **і ... і**.

Both he **and** she are usually at home.
І він **і** вонá звичáйно вдóма.

Here are **both** he **and** she!
Ось **і** він **і** вонá!

Practise Oral Exercise 3.4

Do Written Exercises 3.1, 3.2

C. INTERROGATIVE PRONOUNS

Interrogative pronouns are used to ask questions about someone or something.

In English, the interrogative pronoun **who** is used to ask about a **person**, and **what** is used to ask about a **thing** or an object.

In Ukrainian, the interrogative pronoun **хто** is used to ask about a **person**, and **що** is used to ask about a thing or an object.

Who is at home? — **Хто** вдóма?
What is outside? — **Що** надвóрі?

	English	***Ukrainian***
Interrogative Pronoun (people)	who	хто
Interrogative Pronoun (things)	what	що

Practise Oral Exercises 3.5, 3.6, 3.7, 3.8, 3.9, 3.10

Do Written Exercises 3.3, 3.4

Practise Oral Exercise 3.11

Do Written Exercises 3.5, 3.6

LESSON 4

A. VOCABULARY

Verbs	**First Conjugation** ***(vowel stem 1)***
to ask, to inquire	пита́ти
to converse, to speak	розмовля́ти
to have breakfast	сні́дати
to have dinner *[noon meal]*	обі́дати
to have supper *[evening meal]*	вече́ряти
to hear	чу́ти
to know	зна́ти
to know how	умі́ти/вмі́ти
to listen	слу́хати
to read	чита́ти
to remember	пам'ята́ти
to sing	співа́ти
to think	ду́мати
to understand	розумі́ти
to wait	чека́ти

Adverbs

badly, poorly	пога́но
better	кра́ще, лі́пше
even	на́віть
excellently	прекра́сно
how	як
how much	скі́льки
less	ме́нше
little, not much	ма́ло, небага́то
more	бі́льше
much, a lot	бага́то
very	ду́же
well, fine	до́бре
worse	гі́рше

B. VERBS

The Ukrainian verb system differs in an important way from the English verb system: there are two Ukrainian infinitives for almost every English infinitive.

English Infinitive	*Ukrainian Infinitives*
to read	чита́ти, прочита́ти

In English, the various present, past and future tenses are all formed from a single infinitive: **to read**.

In Ukrainian, some tenses are formed from the **imperfective infinitive: чита́ти**. Other tenses are formed from the **perfective infinitive: прочита́ти**.

Imperfective and **perfective infinitives** are discussed later in this text when the past and future tenses of Ukrainian verbs are introduced.

For now, it is important to remember that the **present tense of Ukrainian verbs is formed from the imperfective infinitive**.

B.1 Present Tense in English

In English, **there are three ways of forming the present tense.**

Let's look at the three ways in which the verb **to read** may be conjugated in the present tense.

1. The Present Indefinite Tense

	Singular		*Plural*	
First Person	I	read	we	read
Second Person	you	read	you	read
Third Person	he	reads	they	read
	she	reads		
	it	reads		

2. The Present Progressive Tense

	Singular		Plural	
First Person	I	am reading	we	are reading
Second Person	you	are reading	you	are reading
Third Person	he	is reading	they	are reading
	she	is reading		
	it	is reading		

3. The Present Emphatic Tense

	Singular		Plural	
First Person	I	do read	we	do read
Second Person	you	do read	you	do read
Third Person	he	does read	they	do read
	she	does read		
	it	does read		

B.2 Present Tense in Ukrainian

***In Ukrainian,* there is only one way of forming the present tense.**

It is very important to keep this point in mind when you are translating from Ukrainian into English and vice versa.

Я читáю.	I read.
Я читáю.	I am reading. I'm reading.
Я читáю.	I do read.
Він читáє.	He reads.
Він читáє.	He is reading. He's reading.
Він читáє.	He does read.
Вони́ читáють.	They read.
Вони́ читáють.	They are reading. They're reading.
Вони́ читáють.	They do read.

B.3 Conjugation of Ukrainian Verbs in the Present Tense

Let's look at how the verb **to read** is conjugated in the present tense in Ukrainian.

First, you need to know the **imperfective infinitive** or the basic form of the verb.

When you look up a Ukrainian verb in a dictionary, the infinitive is the form that you are given.

The imperfective infinitive of the English verb **to read** in Ukrainian is **чита́ти.**

Second, you need to know how to form the **present tense stem** of the verb.

For **чита́ти** and verbs like it, the present tense stem is formed by **dropping the suffix -ти from the infinitive.**

Infinitive	*Present Tense Stem*
чита́ти (чита-**ти**)	чита**-**

To the present tense stem, which ends in a vowel, **a set of six different personal endings** is added.

	Singular		*Plural*	
First Person	я	чита́**ю**	ми	чита́**ємо**
Second Person	ти	чита́**єш**	ви	чита́**єте**
Third Person	він	чита́**є**	вони́	чита́**ють**
	вона́	чита́**є**		
	воно́	чита́**є**		

The vowel **-є** appears in four of the personal endings.

ти чита́**єш**
він чита́**є**
ми чита́**є**мо
ви чита́**є**те

The vowel **-ю** appears in the remaining two personal endings.

я чита́**ю**
вони́ чита́**ю**ть

B.4 Omission of Personal Pronouns in Ukrainian

The **personal endings** that are attached to the present tense stem of a Ukrainian verb readily identify **five** of the Ukrainian personal pronouns, even when the pronoun is omitted.

Розумі**ю**.	**I** understand.
Розумі**єш**?	Do **you** *[s]* understand?
Розумі**ємо**.	**We** understand.
Розумі**єте**.	**You** *[p]* understand.
Розумі**ють**.	**They** understand.

The **three** third person singular pronouns, **він**, **вонá**, and **вонó**, share a common ending; therefore, they may be omitted **only** if it is clear from the context who or what is meant.

In the example given below, the personal pronoun **він** appears in the question; therefore, it may be omitted in the answer.

Він розуміє?	Does **he** understand?
Так, розуміє.	Yes, **he** understands.

If the context is not known, **any one** of the three singular third person pronouns could be implied.

In the example given below, a specific personal pronoun is not stated in the question; therefore, it is unclear who is being referred to.

Розумі**є**?	Does he (she, it) understand?
Так, розумі**є**.	Yes, he (she, it) understands.

The interrogative pronouns **хто** and **що** may not be omitted. They are used with singular third person verb forms.

Хто розумі**є**?	Who understands?

B.5 Grouping Ukrainian Verbs into Conjugations

Imperfective infinitives are grouped into conjugations on the basis of the personal endings that they have in the present tense.

There are **three conjugations** of verbs in Ukrainian, but most verbs are found in the first two conjugations.

C. VERBS: FIRST CONJUGATION

The First Conjugation of Ukrainian verbs has **two patterns of personal endings**.

One pattern of personal endings is used when the present tense stem of a First Conjugation verb ends in a **vowel**.

The other pattern of personal endings is used when the present tense stem of a First Conjugation verb ends in a **consonant**.

C.1 Present Tense Stem Ends in a Vowel

There are two groups of verbs in the First Conjugation that have present tense stems ending in a vowel.

1. **Vowel Stem 1**
2. **Vowel Stem 2**

You will be learning the personal endings for these two groups of verbs in this lesson and in Lesson 5.

C.2 Present Tense Stem Ends in a Consonant

There are two groups of verbs in the First Conjugation that have present tense stems ending in a consonant.

1. **Consonant Stem 1**
2. **Consonant Stem 2**

You will learn the personal endings for these two groups of verbs in Lessons 6 and 7.

D. FIRST CONJUGATION: VOWEL STEM 1

The verbs presented in this lesson all belong to a group in the First Conjugation that in this text is referred to as the **vowel stem 1** group. This information about a verb is abbreviated as **[I,vs.1]**.

D.1 Present Tense Stems

The **present tense stem** of a verb that belongs to the **First Conjugation, vowel stem 1** group is formed by dropping the suffix **-ти** from the infinitive.

	Infinitive [I,vs.1]		***Present Tense Stem***
to ask	пита́ти	(пита-ти)	пита-
to converse	розмовля́ти	(розмовля-ти)	розмовля-
to have breakfast	сні́дати	(сніда-ти)	сніда-
to have dinner	обі́дати	(обіда-ти)	обіда-
to have supper	вече́ряти	(вечеря-ти)	вечеря-
to hear	чу́ти	(чу-ти)	чу-
to know	зна́ти	(зна-ти)	зна-
to know how	умі́ти	(умі-ти)	умі-
to listen	слу́хати	(слуха-ти)	слуха-
to read	чита́ти	(чита-ти)	чита-
to remember	пам'ята́ти	(пам'ята-ти)	пам'ята-
to sing	співа́ти	(співа-ти)	співа-
to think	ду́мати	(дума-ти)	дума-
to understand	розумі́ти	(розумі-ти)	розумі-
to wait	чека́ти	(чека-ти)	чека-

D.2 Present Tense Conjugation

All verbs that belong to the **vowel stem 1** group of the **First Conjugation** are conjugated like the verb **читáти**.

Infinitive: читáти	**Present Tense Stem: чита-**			
	Singular		*Plural*	
First Person	я	читá**ю**	ми	читá**ємо**
Second Person	ти	читá**єш**	ви	читá**єте**
Third Person	він	читá**є**	вонú	читá**ють**
	вонá	читá**є**		
	вонó	читá**є**		

Practise Oral Exercise 4.1

Do Written Exercises 4.1, 4.2, 4.3

E. NEGATIVE PARTICLE: НЕ

In English, the adverb **not** is used to change an affirmative statement into a negative one.

They are reading.
They are **not** reading.

In Ukrainian, the negative particle **не** is used in the same way.

Вонú читáють.	They are reading.
Вонú **не** читáють.	They are **not** reading.

In addition to negating verbs, the negative particle **не** may be positioned before other words in a sentence in order to negate them.

Він **не** тут, а вдóма
He isn't here, he's at home.

Не він читáє, а вонá
It isn't he who is reading, it's she.

Practise Oral Exercises 4.2, 4.3, 4.4, 4.5

Do Written Exercises 4.4, 4.5, 4.6

LESSON 5

A. VOCABULARY

Verbs

First Conjugation
(vowel stem 1)

to bathe oneself	купа́тися
to dress oneself	одяга́тися

First Conjugation
(vowel stem 2)

to buy	купува́ти
to dance	танцюва́ти
to drink	пи́ти
to get up	устава́ти/встава́ти
to joke	жартува́ти
to laugh	смія́тися
to marry, to get married	одру́жуватися
to sell	продава́ти
to telephone	телефонува́ти
to work	працюва́ти

Adverbs

afterwards, then	по́тім
early	ра́но
late	пі́зно
loudly	го́лосно
quickly	шви́дко
quietly	ти́хо
right now, at this moment	за́раз
slowly	пові́льно, пово́лі, пома́лу
then, at that time	тоді́
together	ра́зом
when	коли́

Vocabulary Notes

1. The adverbs **повíльно, повóлі** and **помáлу** are synonyms that may be used interchangeably.

   Вонú **повíльно** читáють.
   Вонú **повóлі** читáють.
   Вонú **помáлу** читáють.

2. The adverbs **пóтім** and **тодí** may both be translated by the English adverb **then**; however, their meanings are different.

   Він читáє, а **пóтім** він вечéряє.
   He reads and **then** (afterwards) he has supper.

   Ми зáвжди **тодí** вечéряємо.
   We always have supper **then** (at that time).

B. FIRST CONJUGATION: VOWEL STEM 2

In this lesson, Ukrainian verbs belonging to the **vowel stem 2** group **[I,vs.2]** of the First Conjugation are discussed.

B.1 Present Tense Stems

To form the present tense stem of a verb belonging to the **vowel stem 2** group of the First Conjugation, you **drop the suffix -ти *and* the syllable preceding it.**

	Infinitive [I,vs.2]		***Present Tense Stem***
to buy	купу**вá**ти	(купу-**ва**-ти)	купу-
to dance	танцю**вá**ти	(танцю-**ва**-ти)	танцю-
to get up	уста**вá**ти	(уста-**ва**-ти)	уста- (вста-)
to joke	жарту**вá**ти	(жарту-**ва**-ти)	жарту-
to sell	прода**вá**ти	(прода-**ва**-ти)	прода-
to telephone	телефону**вá**ти	(телефону-**ва**-ти)	телефону-
to work	працю**вá**ти	(працю-**ва**-ти)	працю-

B.2 Present Tense Conjugation

The same personal endings are attached to the present tense stems of verbs in both the vowel stem 1 and the vowel stem 2 groups of the First Conjugation.

Let's look at how the verb **працюва́ти** is conjugated in the present tense.

Infinitive: працюва́ти	**Present Tense Stem: працю-**			
	Singular		*Plural*	
First Person	я	працю́**ю**	ми	працю́**ємо**
Second Person	ти	працю́**єш**	ви	працю́**єте**
Third Person	він	працю́**є**	вони́	працю́**ють**
	вона́	працю́**є**		
	воно́	працю́**є**		

B.3 пи́ти

There are a few verbs like **пи́ти** that have to be learned as exceptions.

To form the present tense stem of **пи́ти**, the suffix **-ти** *and* the vowel preceding it are dropped; before the personal endings are added, an apostrophe is placed after the **п-**: **п'-**.

Infinitive: пи́ти	**Present Tense Stem: п'-**			
	Singular		*Plural*	
First Person	я	п'**ю**	ми	п'**ємо́**
Second Person	ти	п'**єш**	ви	п'**єте́**
Third Person	він	п'**є**	вони	п'**ють**
	вона	п'**є**		
	воно	п'**є**		

Practise Oral Exercise 5.1

Do Written Exercises 5.1, 5.2, 5.3

Practise Oral Exercise 5.2

Do Written Exercise 5.4

C. REFLEXIVE VERBS

In English, you know how to use verbs like **to dress oneself**.

	Singular	*Plural*
First Person	I dress **myself**	we dress **ourselves**
Second Person	you dress **yourself**	you dress **yourselves**
Third Person	he dresses **himself** she dresses **herself** it dresses **itself**	they dress **themselves**

In Ukrainian, the verb **to dress oneself** is **одяга́тися**. It is a **reflexive verb** that ends with the reflexive particle **-ся**.

C.1 Present Tense Stems

The present tense stem of a First Conjugation reflexive verb is formed in the usual way; however, the reflexive particle **-ся** remains after the suffix **-ти** is dropped.

1. Two of the reflexive verbs in this lesson belong to the **First Conjugation: vowel stem 1 group.**

	Infinitive [I,vs.1]		***Present Tense Stem***
to bathe	купа́тися	(купа-ти-ся)	купа-ся
to dress	одяга́тися	(одяга-ти-ся)	одяга-ся

2. The other two reflexive verbs belong to the **First Conjugation: vowel stem 2 group.**

	Infinitive [I,vs.2]		***Present Tense Stem***
to laugh	смія́тися	(смі-я-ти-ся)	смі-ся
to marry	одру́жуватися	(одружу-ва-ти-ся)	одружу-ся

C.2 Present Tense Conjugation

Let's look at how the reflexive verb **одяга́тися** is conjugated in the present tense.

Infinitive: одяга́тися	**Present Tense Stem: одяга-ся**			
	Singular		***Plural***	
First Person	я	одяга́**ю**ся	ми	одяга́**ємо**ся
Second Person	ти	одяга́**єш**ся	ви	одяга́**єте**ся
Third Person	він	одяга́**єть**ся	вони́	одяга́**ють**ся
	вона́	одяга́**єть**ся		
	воно́	одяга́**єть**ся		

There are two important points to keep in mind when you are conjugating reflexive verbs.

1. In all First Conjugation reflexive verbs, in both the **vowel stem 1** and the **vowel stem 2** groups, **-ть** must be added to the verb forms for the **singular third person pronouns *before*** the reflexive particle **-ся** is attached.

   він одяга́**єть**ся
   вона́ одяга́**єть**ся
   воно́ одяга́**єть**ся

2) The reflexive particle **-ся** may be contracted to **-сь** when it is attached to a verb form that ends in a vowel. You should be able to recognize the alternate forms ending in **-сь** when you hear or see them; however, in this text these contracted forms are not used.

одяга́т**и**ся	or	одяга́т**и**сь
одяга́**ю**ся	or	одяга́**ю**сь
одяга́є**мо**ся	or	одяга́є**мо**сь
одяга́є**те**ся	or	одяга́є**те**сь

✍ **Do Written Exercises 5.5, 5.6**

C.3 Usage of Reflexive Verbs

1. When verbs like **to dress oneself** are conjugated in English, the reflexive pronouns may or may not be used. If they **are** used, do not try to translate them into Ukrainian. The reflexive particle **-ся** in the Ukrainian verb makes it unnecessary to use a reflexive pronoun.

одяга́тися	**to dress (oneself)**
Я одяга́юся.	I am dressing (myself).
Ти одяга́єшся.	You *[s]* are dressing (yourself).
Він одяга́ється.	He is dressing (himself).
Вона́ одяга́ється.	She is dressing (herself).
Воно́ одяга́ється.	It is dressing (itself).
Ми одяга́ємося.	We are dressing (ourselves).
Ви одяга́єтеся.	You *[p]* are dressing (yourselves).
Вони́ одяга́ються.	They are dressing (themselves).

2. Some Ukrainian verbs that are conjugated with the reflexive particle **-ся** are not considered to be reflexive in English; therefore, they would never be used in English with reflexive pronouns.

   There are two such verbs in this lesson, **смія́тися** and **одру́жуватися**. The first one, **смія́тися**, is conjugated for you.

смія́тися	**to laugh**
Я сміюся.	I am laughing.
Ти смі́єшся.	You *[s]* are laughing.
Він смі́ється.	He is laughing.
Вона́ смі́ється.	She is laughing.
Воно́ смі́ється.	It is laughing.
Ми сміємо́ся.	We are laughing.
Ви сміється́ся.	You *[p]* are laughing.
Вони́ сміються.	They are laughing.

Practise Oral Exercises 5.3, 5.4, 5.5, 5.6, 5.7, 5.8

Do Written Exercises 5.7, 5.8

LESSON 6

A. VOCABULARY

Verbs	**First Conjugation** *(consonant stem 1)*
to be able	могти́
to carry	нести́
to go/come *[on foot]*	іти́
to grow	рости́
to haul, to transport	везти́
to live	жи́ти
to steal	кра́сти
to swim	плисти́

Pronouns

anyone, anybody	хтоне́будь
anything	щоне́будь
everyone, everybody	усі́/всі
everything	усе/все
no one, nobody	ніхто́
nothing	нішо́
some *[people]*	де́хто
some *[things]*	де́що
someone, somebody	хтось
something	щось

Adverbs

down, downwards	уни́з/вниз, удоли́ну/вдоли́ну
straight ahead	пря́мо
to the left	ліво́руч
to the right	право́руч
up, upwards	уго́ру/вго́ру
why	чому́

Conjunctions

because	бо, тому́ що

Vocabulary Notes

The verb **іти́** means **to go** or **to come** on foot.

Він іде́.	He is **going** *[on foot].*
Він іде́.	He is **coming** *[on foot].*

In some contexts, **іти́** may also mean to walk.

After a word ending in a vowel, the **і** of **іти́** changes to **й**.

Я йду́.	I'm going/coming *[on foot].*
Він **іде́.**	He's going/coming *[on foot].*
Вона **йде́.**	She's going/coming *[on foot].*

When you **say** words like **я йду́** and **вона йде́** you run them together to create one longer word.

Яйду́.
Вонайде́.

B. FIRST CONJUGATION: CONSONANT STEM 1

In Lessons 4 and 5, you learned how to conjugate verbs in the First Conjugation that have present tense stems ending in a **vowel**: [I,vs.1] and [I,vs.2].

In this lesson, you are introduced to verbs in the First Conjugation that have present tense stems ending in a **consonant**: [I,cs.1].

B.1 Present Tense Stems

To form the **present tense stem** of a First Conjugation verb belonging to the **consonant stem 1** group, the suffix **-ти** is dropped from the infinitive.

After the suffix **-ти** is dropped from the infinitive, the present tense stem ends in a consonant.

	Infinitive [I,cs.1]		*Present Tense Stem*
to carry	нести́	(нес-ти)	нес-
to haul	везти́	(вез-ти)	вез-

B.2 Present Tense Conjugation

All First Conjugation verbs with a present tense stem that ends in a consonant have exactly the same personal endings.

Let's look at how the verb **нести́** is conjugated.

Infinitive: нести́	**Present Tense Stem: нес-**	
	Singular	***Plural***
First Person	я нес**у́**	ми нес**емо́**
Second Person	ти нес**е́ш**	ви нес**ете́**
Third Person	він нес**е́** вона́ нес**е́** воно́ нес**е́**	вони́ нес**у́ть**

The vowel **е** appears in four of the personal endings.

ти нес**е́ш**
він нес**е́**
ми нес**емо́**
ви нес**ете́**

The vowel **у** appears in two of the personal endings.

я нес**у́**
вони́ нес**у́ть**

B.3 Irregular Present Tense Stems

Six verbs in this lesson have present tense stems that are formed irregularly. **Memorize the present tense stems of these verbs.**

	Infinitive [I,cs.1]	***Present Tense Stem***
to be able	могти́	мож-
to go, come *[on foot]*	іти́	ід-
to grow	рости́	рост-
to live	жи́ти	жив-
to steal	кра́сти	крад-
to swim	плисти́	плив-

Let's look at how the verb **могти́**, **жи́ти**, and **іти́** are conjugated.

Infinitive: могти́	**Present Tense Stem: мож-**			
	Singular		***Plural***	
First Person	я	мо́жу	ми	мо́жемо
Second Person	ти	мо́жеш	ви	мо́жете
Third Person	він	мо́же	вони́	мо́жуть
	вона́	мо́же		
	воно́	мо́же		

Infinitive: жи́ти	**Present Tense Stem: жи́в-**			
	Singular		***Plural***	
First Person	я	живу́	ми	живемо́
Second Person	ти	живе́ш	ви	живете́
Third Person	він	живе́	вони́	живу́ть
	вона́	живе́		
	воно́	живе́		

Infinitive: іти́	**Present Tense Stem: ід-**			
	Singular		***Plural***	
First Person	я	йду́	ми	йдемо́
Second Person	ти	йде́ш	ви	йдете́
Third Person	він	іде́	вони́	йду́ть
	вона́	йде́		
	воно́	йде́		

C. FIRST CONJUGATION VERBS: COMPARISON OF PERSONAL ENDINGS

By now you will have noticed that the present tense endings of First Conjugation verbs follow similar patterns.

First Conjugation: Vowel Stem 1 and Vowel Stem 2 Groups					
-ю	**-єш**	**-є**	**-ємо**	**-єте**	**-ють**
First Conjugation: Consonant Stem 1 Group					
-у	**-еш**	**-е**	**-емо**	**-ете**	**-уть**

It will help you to remember both sets of these personal endings if you recall what you learned about simple and iotized vowels in Lesson 1 in the *Oral Exercises*.

ю = й + у and є = й + е

Practise Oral Exercise 6.1

Do Written Exercises 6.1, 6.2, 6.3

D. VERBS: AUXILIARY (HELPING) VERBS

In English, we sometimes use two verbs in a sentence. One verb is the **main verb**, while the other one is an **auxiliary** or **helping verb**.

In the sentence that follows below, the main verb is the infinitive ***to read*** and the helping or auxiliary verb is **know how**.

I **know how *to read.***

In Ukrainian, verbs such as **умíти** and **могти́** are often used as auxiliary verbs with the infinitive of the main verb.

Do you **know how *to sing***?	Ти **вмíєш *співáти***?
Are you **able *to sing***?	Ти **мóжеш *співáти***?
Can you ***sing***?	Ти **мóжеш *співáти***?

Practise Oral Exercises 6.2, 6.3

Do Written Exercise 6.4

E. INDEFINITE PRONOUNS

In both English and Ukrainian, indefinite pronouns are used when the subject is not specified.

E.1 хтось, щось

The English indefinite pronouns **someone** and **something** have their Ukrainian counterparts in **хтось** and **щось**.

Notice that to form these two Ukrainian indefinite pronouns, **-сь** is added to the interrogative pronouns **хто** and **що: хтось** and **щось**.

Someone is swimming.	**Хтось** пливé.
Something is growing.	**Щось** ростé.

Practise Oral Exercise 6.4

E.2 хтонéбудь, щонéбудь

The English indefinite pronouns **anyone (anybody)** and **anything** have their Ukrainian counterparts in **хтонéбудь** and **щонéбудь**.

Notice that to form these two Ukrainian indefinite pronouns, **-нéбудь** is added to the interrogative pronouns **хто** and **що: хтонéбудь** and **щонéбудь.**

Is **anyone (anybody)** working?	**Хтонéбудь** працює?
Does **anything** grow here?	**Щонéбудь** тут росте?

The pronoun **хтонéбудь** may also be written as **хто-нéбудь, хтобýдь, хто-бýдь, будь-хтó.**

The pronoun **щонéбудь** may also be written as **що-нéбудь, щобýдь, що-бýдь, будь-щó.**

There is no difference in meaning among these forms and you should be able to recognize them when you see them as they are quite similar; however, in this text, only the forms given in the vocabulary are used.

Practise Oral Exercise 6.5

E.3 де́хто, де́що

The Ukrainian indefinite pronouns **де́хто** and **де́що** imply that only a few persons or things are being referred to out of a larger number of people or things.

Notice that to form these two Ukrainian indefinite pronouns, **де** is added to the interrogative pronouns **хто** and **що: <u>де́</u>хто** and **<u>де́</u>що**.

In English, the indefinite pronoun **some** is used with a **plural** verb.

> **Some** *[people]* are thinking, and **some** are conversing.
> **Some** *[things]* are growing, and **some** aren't growing.

In Ukrainian, the indefinite pronouns **де́хто** and **де́що** are used with **singular** verbs.

> **Де́хто** ду́має, а **де́хто** розмовля́є.
> **Some** *[people]* are thinking, and **some** are conversing.
>
> **Де́що** росте́, а **де́що** не росте́.
> **Some** *[things]* are growing, and **some** aren't growing.

Practise Oral Exercise 6.6

E.4 ніхто́, нішо́

The English negative pronouns **nobody (no one)** and **nothing** have their Ukrainian counterparts in **ніхто́** and **нішо́**.

Notice that to form these two Ukrainian indefinite pronouns, **ні** is added to the interrogative pronouns **хто** and **що: <u>ні</u>хто́** and **<u>ні</u>що́**.

In English, the verb may not be negated when a negative pronoun is the subject, as there may not be two negative words in a single sentence.

> **Nobody** is waiting.
> **Nothing** grows here.

In Ukrainian, the negative word **не** must be used to negate the verb when the subject is a negative pronoun.

> **Ніхто́** <u>**не**</u> чека́є.
> Тут **нішо́** <u>**не**</u> росте́.

Practise Oral Exercise 6.7

E.5 усí

The Ukrainian pronoun **усí** has two equivalents in English.

1. everyone, everybody
2. all

In English, the pronoun **everyone** is used with a **singular** verb, while the pronoun **all** is used with a **plural** verb.

Everyone (Everybody) is asking.
All are asking.

In Ukrainian, the pronoun **усí** is used with a plural verb.

Everyone (Everybody) is asking.	**Усí** питáють.
All are asking.	**Усí** питáють.

If a personal pronoun precedes **усí**, the verb form in Ukrainian agrees with it.

We're all asking.	**Ми всі** питáємо.
All of us are asking.	**Ми всі** питáємо.
You're*[p]* **all** asking.	**Ви всі** питáєте.
All of you are asking.	**Ви всі** питáєте.
They're all asking.	**Вонú всі** питáють.
All of them are asking.	**Вонú всі** питáють.

Practise Oral Exercise 6.8

E.6 усé

The Ukrainian pronoun **усé** has two equivalents in English.

1. everything
2. all

Everything is working.	**Усé** працю́є.
It's all working.	**Усé** працю́є.
All of it is working.	**Усé** працю́є.

Practise Oral Exercises 6.9, 6.10, 6.11, 6.12

Do Written Exercises 6.5, 6.6

LESSON 7

A. VOCABULARY

Verbs

First Conjugation
(consonant stem 2)

to cry	пла́кати
to groan	стогна́ти
to lie, to tell a lie	бреха́ти
to go/come *[by vehicle]*	ї́хати
to say	каза́ти
to take	бра́ти
to want	хоті́ти
to whisper	шепта́ти
to write	писа́ти

First Conjugation
(mixed group)

to fight, to struggle	боро́тися
to plough (plow)	ора́ти

Adverbs

everywhere	усю́ди/всю́ди
here *[**towards** this place]*	сюди́
home *[**towards** home, homewards]*	додо́му
never	ніко́ли
nowhere *[**at** no place]*	ніде́
nowhere *[**towards** no place]*	ніку́ди
outdoors *[**towards** the outdoors]*	надві́р
somewhere, someplace *[**at** some place]*	десь
somewhere, someplace *[**towards** some place]*	куди́сь
there *[**towards** that place]*	туди́
where to *[**towards** which place]*	куди́

Vocabulary Notes

The verb **ї́хати** means either **to go** or **to come** by vehicle.

Вони́ ї́дуть.	They are **going** ***[by vehicle].***
Вони́ ї́дуть.	They are **coming** ***[by vehicle].***

In some contexts, **ї́хати** may also mean **to drive** or **to ride.**

B. FIRST CONJUGATION: CONSONANT STEM 2

In this lesson, First Conjugation verbs belonging to the **consonant stem 2** group **[I,cs.2]** are introduced.

B.1 Present Tense Stems

To form the present tense stem of a First Conjugation verb belonging to the consonant stem 2 group, **the suffix -ти *and* the vowel preceding it are dropped**.

	Infinitive [I,cs.2]		*Present Tense Stem*
to groan	стогна́ти	(стог**н**-а-ти)	стог**н**-

B.2 Present Tense Conjugation

The same personal endings are added to the present tense stems of verbs belonging to the consonant stem 1 and the consonant stem 2 groups.

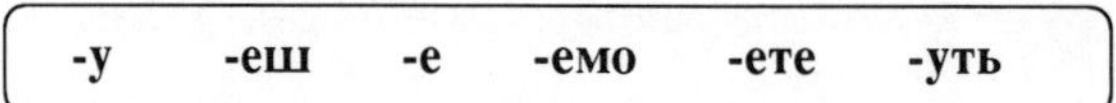

-у	-еш	-е	-емо	-ете	-уть

Let's look at how the verb **стогна́ти** is conjugated.

Infinitive: стогна́ти	**Present Tense Stem: стогн-**	
	Singular	*Plural*
First Person	я сто́гн**у**	ми сто́гн**емо**
Second Person	ти сто́гн**еш**	ви сто́гн**ете**
Third Person	він сто́гн**е** вона́ сто́гн**е** воно́ сто́гн**е**	вони́ сто́гн**уть**

B.3 Altered Present Tense Stems

In some verbs in the consonant stem 2 group, **the final consonant of the present tense stem is changed** before the personal endings are added to it.

In this lesson, there are six verbs in which a change occurs in the present tense stem.

	Infinitive [I,cs.2]		*Present Tense Stem*
to cry	пла́кати	(плак-а-ти)	плач-
to lie, tell a lie	бреха́ти	(брех-а-ти)	бреш-
to say	каза́ти	(каз-а-ти)	каж-
to want	хоті́ти	(хот-і-ти)	хоч-
to whisper	шепта́ти	(шепт-а-ти)	шепч-
to write	писа́ти	(пис-а-ти)	пиш-

The changes in the present tense stems of verbs in the **consonant stem 2** group in this lesson are summarized below.

с, х	become	**ш**
к, т	become	**ч**
з	becomes	**ж**

The change that occurs in the final consonant in the present tense stem is maintained throughout the conjugation of the verb.

Let's look at how the verb **писа́ти** is conjugated.

Infinitive: писа́ти	**Present Tense Stem: пиш-**	
	Singular	*Plural*
First Person	я пишу́	ми пи́шемо
Second Person	ти пи́шеш	ви пи́шете
Third Person	він пи́ше вона́ пи́ше воно́ пи́ше	вони́ пи́шуть

B.4 Irregular Present Tense Stems

1. In the verb **ї́хати,** the **х** changes to a **д.**

	Infinitive [I,cs.2]		*Present Tense Stem*
to go *[by vehicle]*	ї́хати	(їх-а-ти)	їд-

This change in the present tense stem is maintained throughout the conjugation of the verb.

Infinitive: ї́хати		**Present Tense Stem: їд-**	
	Singular		***Plural***
First Person	я	ї́ду	ми ї́демо
Second Person	ти	ї́деш	ви ї́дете
Third Person	він	ї́де	вони́ ї́дуть
	вона́	ї́де	
	воно́	ї́де	

2. One verb in this lesson has **the vowel -е inserted between the two consonants in its present tense stem.**

	Infinitive [I,cs.2]		*Present Tense Stem*
to take	бра́ти	(б**р**-а-ти)	**бер-**

This change in the present tense stem is maintained throughout the conjugation of the verb.

Let's look at how the verb **бра́ти** is conjugated.

Infinitive: бра́ти		**Present Tense Stem: бер-**	
	Singular		***Plural***
First Person	я	беру́	ми беремо́
Second Person	ти	бере́ш	ви берете́
Third Person	він	бере́	вони́ беру́ть
	вона́	бере́	
	воно́	бере́	

C. FIRST CONJUGATION: MIXED GROUP

There are a few (very few!) verbs that belong to a third group in the First Conjugation that is aptly called the **mixed group** [I,mixed].

C.1 Present Tense Stems

The **present tense stem** of a verb that belongs to the **mixed group** ends in either the consonant **р** or **л** after the suffix **-ти** *and* the vowel preceding it are dropped.

	Infinitive [I,mixed]		*Present Tense Stem*
to plow	ора́ти	(**ор**-а-ти)	**ор-**
to fight	боро́тися	(**бор**-о-ти-ся)	**бор**-ся

C.2 Present Tense Conjugation

The present tense **personal endings** for **я** and **вони́** are like the ones for the First Conjugation **vowel** groups: **-ю, -ють.**

The present tense **personal endings** for the remaining pronouns (**ти, він, вона́, воно́, ми, ви**) are like the ones for the First Conjugation **consonant** groups: **-еш, -е, -емо, -ете.**

Let's look at how the verb **ора́ти** is conjugated.

Infinitive: ора́ти	**Present Tense Stem: ор-**	
	Singular	*Plural*
First Person	я **орю́**	ми **о́ремо**
Second Person	ти **о́реш**	ви **о́рете**
Third Person	він **о́ре** вона́ **о́ре** воно́ **о́ре**	вони́ **о́рють**

C.3 Conjugation of Reflexive Verbs

The reflexive verb **боро́тися** is conjugated like **ора́ти**.

You must remember, however, that because it is a reflexive verb, **-ть** is inserted **in the singular third person verb forms: він (вона́, воно́) бо́реться.**

D. SUMMARY: PERSONAL ENDINGS OF FIRST CONJUGATION VERBS

Group	я	ти	він	ми	ви	вони́
Vowel	-ю	-єш	-є	-ємо	-єте	-ють
Consonant	-у	-еш	-е	-емо	-ете	-уть
Mixed	-ю	-еш	-е	-емо	-ете	-ють

Practise Oral Exercises 7.1, 7.2, 7.3

Do Written Exercises 7.1, 7.2, 7.3, 7.4

E. ADVERBS: LOCATION AND DIRECTIONAL MOTION

Adverbs that indicate the **location** of someone or something, and those that imply the **movement** of someone or something, are viewed quite differently in English and Ukrainian. In this lesson, you are introduced to some of the basic differences.

E.1 The Difference between де and куди́

In English, no distinction is made between adverbs of **location** and adverbs indicating **directional motion.**

The adverb **where** is used to ask both about **location** (**in** what place someone or something is) *and* about **directional motion** (**towards** what place someone or something is going).

Location:	**Where** is he?	(**In** what place is he?)
Directional Motion:	**Where** is he going?	(**Towards** what place is he going?)

In Ukrainian, a distinction is made between being in a place (**де**), and going towards a place (**куди́**).

Location:	**Де** він?	Where (**in** what place) is he?
Directional Motion:	**Куди́** він іде́?	Where (**towards** what place) is he going?

E.2 Adverbs like де and куди́

Let's look at other adverbs of location and directional motion.

English			
Location or Directional Motion			
here	**at** this place	or	**towards** this place
there	**at** that place	or	**towards** that place
nowhere	**at** no place	or	**towards** no place
somewhere	**at** some place	or	**towards** some place

Ukrainian			
Location		*Directional Motion*	
тут	**at** this place	**сюди́**	**towards** this place
там	**at** that place	**туди́**	**towards** that place
ніде́	**at** no place	**ніку́ди**	**towards** no place
десь	**at** some place	**куди́сь**	**towards** some place

Compare the following sets of sentences.

He is **here**.	Він **тут**.
He is coming **here**.	Він іде́ **сюди́**.
He is **there**.	Він **там**.
He is going **there**.	Він іде́ **туди́**.

E.3 More Adverbs like де and куди́

The adverbs **удо́ма** (at home) and **надво́рі** (outdoors, outside) are used to indicate location.

Where is he?	He's either **at home** or **outdoors**.
Де він?	Він або́ **вдо́ма** або́ **надво́рі**.

When the ideas of **going home** or **going outside** are being expressed, you must use **додо́му** and **надві́р** respectively to convey the directional motion that is implied.

Where is he going?	He's either going **home** or **outdoors**.
Куди́ він іде́?	Він іде́ або́ **додо́му**, або́ **надві́р**.

E.4 Summary

Location	*English*	*Ukrainian*
at what place?	where	де
at this place	here	тут
at that place	there	там
at no place	nowhere	ніде́
at some place	somewhere	десь
at home	at home	удо́ма/вдо́ма
in the outdoors	outdoors	надво́рі

Directional Motion	*English*	*Ukrainian*
towards what place? (whither?)	where	куди́
towards this place (hither)	here	сюди́
towards that place (thither)	there	туди́
towards no place	nowhere	ніку́ди
towards some place	somewhere	куди́сь
towards home, homewards	homewards	додо́му
towards the outdoors	outdoors	надві́р

Practise Oral Exercise 7.4

F. NEGATION

In English, there may be only **one** negative word in a sentence.

I **never** sing.
Nobody ever rides anywhere.

In Ukrainian, sentences with **two** or **more** negative words are grammatically correct.

I **never** sing.	Я **ніко́ли не** співа́ю.
Nobody ever rides anywhere.	**Ніхто́ ніко́ли ніку́ди не** ї́де.

Practise Oral Exercises 7.5, 7.6, 7.7

Do Written Exercises 7.5, 7.6

LESSON 8

A. VOCABULARY

Verbs

Second Conjugation
(consonant stem лнр)

to shave oneself	голи́тися
to smoke	кури́ти
to talk, to speak	говори́ти
to worry	жури́тися

Second Conjugation
(consonant stem жчшщ)

to be glad, to be delighted	тішитися
to be silent	мовча́ти
to complain	ска́ржитися
to hurry	спіши́ти
to learn, to study	учи́тися/вчи́тися
to lie, to be lying down	лежа́ти
to run	бігти
to see	ба́чити
to shout, to scream	крича́ти
to weigh	ва́жити

Adverbs

at night	уночі́/вночі́
during the day	уде́нь/вдень
in the afternoon	пополу́дні, після обі́ду
in the evening	уве́чорі/вве́чорі, уве́чері/вве́чері
in the fall	восени́
in the morning	ура́нці/вра́нці
in the spring	навесні́
in the summer	улі́тку/влі́тку
in the winter	узи́мку/взи́мку
so, in such a manner	так

Conjunctions

if, whether	чи
that	що

B. VERBS: SECOND CONJUGATION

In the Second Conjuation, there are **two groups of verbs that are identified in this text by their present tense stems.**

1. **Present tense stems ending in a *consonant***
2. **Present tense stems ending in a *vowel***

Most verbs in the Second Conjugation belong to the consonant stem group; only a few verbs belong to the vowel stem group.

B.1 Consonant Stem Group

To form the present tense stem of a verb in the consonant stem group of the Second Conjugation both the suffix -ти *and* the vowel preceding it are dropped.

B.2 Consonant Stem Subgroups

All verbs in the consonant stem group of the Second Conjugation have the same present tense endings for **ти, він, вона́, воно́, ми, ви.**

Personal Endings		
	Singular	***Plural***
First Person		**ми** (stem) **-имо**
Second Person	**ти** (stem) **-иш**	**ви** (stem) **-ите**
Third Person	**він** (stem) **-ить** **вона́** (stem) **-ить** **воно́** (stem) **-ить**	

There are, however, some slight differences in the endings of the verb forms for the pronouns **я** and **вони́**.

To help you remember these differences, **the consonant group of the Second Conjugation is divided into four subgroups in this text.**

1. Present tense stems ending in one of **л, н, р**
2. Present tense stems ending in one of **ж, ч, ш, щ**
3. Present tense stems ending in one of **б, в, м, п, ф**
4. Present tense stems ending in one of **д, з, с, т**

The first two subgroups are discussed in this lesson; the third and fourth subgroups are discussed in Lesson 9.

C. SECOND CONJUGATION: CONSONANT STEM Л, Н, Р

All verbs belonging to the subgroup **[II,лнр]** have a present tense stem ending in one of **л, н,** or **р.**

C.1 Present Tense Stems

In this lesson, there are four verbs that have present tense stems ending in one of **л, н,** or **р** after **the suffix -ти *and* the vowel preceding it are dropped.**

	Infinitive [II,лнр]		***Present Tense Stem***
to shave oneself	голи́тися	(гол-и-ти-ся)	гол-ся
to smoke	кури́ти	(кур-и-ти)	кур-
to talk	говори́ти	(говор-и-ти)	говор-
to worry	жури́тися	(жур-и-ти-ся)	жур-ся

C.2 Present Tense Conjugation

Let's look at how the verb **говори́ти** is conjugated.

Infinitive: говори́ти	**Present Tense Stem: говор-**			
	Singular		***Plural***	
First Person	я	говорю́	ми	гово́римо
Second Person	ти	гово́риш	ви	гово́рите
Third Person	він	гово́рить	вони́	гово́рять
	вона́	гово́рить		
	воно́	гово́рить		

As stated previously, the present tense endings of the verb forms for **ти, він (вона́, воно́), ми,** and **ви** all contain the vowel **и: -иш, -ить, -имо, -ите.**

The personal endings for the **я** and **вони́** verb forms are, respectively, **-ю** and **-ять.**

D. SECOND CONJUGATION: REFLEXIVE VERBS

In the Second Conjugation, the singular third person verb form ends in a **-ть**; therefore, in reflexive verbs it is **not** necessary to insert another **-ть** before the reflexive particle **-ся** is added.

Він гóлиться.
He is shaving himself.

Practise Oral Exercises 8.1, 8.2

Do Written Exercise 8.1

E. SECOND CONJUGATION: CONSONANT STEM Ж, Ч, Ш, Щ

All verbs belonging to the subgroup **[II,жчшщ]** have a present tense stem ending in one of **ж, ч, ш,** or **щ.**

E.1 Present Tense Stems

In this lesson there are nine Second Conjugation verbs that have a present tense stem ending in one of **ж, ч, ш,** or **щ**.

	Infinitive *[II,жчшщ]*		*Present Tense Stem*
to be glad	тíшитися	(тіш-и-ти-ся)	тіш-ся
to be lying down	лежáти	(леж-а-ти)	леж-
to be silent	мовчáти	(мовч-а-ти)	мовч-
to complain	скáржитися	(скарж-и-ти-ся)	скарж-ся
to hurry	спішúти	(спіш-и-ти)	спіш-
to learn	учúтися	(уч-и-ти-ся)	уч-ся
to see	бáчити	(бач-и-ти)	бач-
to shout	кричáти	(крич-а-ти)	крич-
to weigh	вáжити	(важ-и-ти)	важ-

E.2 Present Tense Conjugation

Let's look at how the verb **ба́чити** is conjugated.

Infinitive: ба́чити	**Present Tense Stem: бач-**	
	Singular	*Plural*
First Person	я ба́чу	ми ба́ч**имо**
Second Person	ти ба́ч**иш**	ви ба́ч**ите**
Third Person	він ба́ч**ить** вона́ ба́ч**ить** воно́ ба́ч**ить**	вони́ ба́ч**ать**

As stated previously, the present tense endings of the verb forms for **ти, він (вона́, воно́), ми,** and **ви** all contain the vowel **и**: **-иш, -ить, -имо, -ите.**

The endings for the **я** and **вони́** verb forms are, respectively, **-у** and **-ать**.

E.3 Altered Present Tense Stem: бігти

There is a consonant change in the present tense stem of **бі́гти** (**г** → **ж**) that stays throughout its conjugation. Because its present tense stem ends in **ж**, **бі́гти** is assigned to the **consonant жчшщ** group of the Second Conjugation.

Let's look at how the verb **бі́гти** is conjugated.

Infinitive: бі́гти	**Present Tense Stem: біж-**	
	Singular	*Plural*
First Person	я біжу́	ми біж**имо́**
Second Person	ти біж**и́ш**	ви біж**ите́**
Third Person	він біж**и́ть** вона́ біж**и́ть** воно́ біж**и́ть**	вони́ біж**а́ть**

Practise Oral Exercises 8.3, 8.4, 8.5

Do Written Exercises 8.2, 8.3

F. SUBORDINATE CLAUSES

In both English and Ukrainian, subordinate clauses are used extensively. Even if you are not sure what subordinate clauses are, you need not be intimidated by them because you use them all the time!

In English, all of the following sentences consist of a **principal clause** (I see, I think, I read, I know, who knows) and a *subordinate clause* that has been italicized.

I see *where he's going.*	**I read** *when I eat breakfast.*
I remember *where it is.*	**I know** *why she's here.*
I think *that he's at home.*	**Who knows** *if he's at home?*

In Ukrainian, both **principal clauses** and *subordinate clauses* are used in the same way as they are in English, except that when they are written down in Ukrainian, **they are always separated by a comma.**

I see *where he's going.* **Я ба́чу,** *куди́ він іде́.*	**I read** *when I eat breakfast.* **Я чита́ю,** *коли́ я сні́даю.*
I remember *where it is.* **Я пам'ята́ю,** *де воно́.*	**I know** *why she's here.* **Я зна́ю,** *чому́ вона́ тут.*
I think *that he's at home.* **Я ду́маю,** *що він удо́ма.*	**Who knows** *whether he's at home?* **Хто зна́є,** *чи він удо́ма?*

There is one important point that you must keep in mind when you are translating sentences with subordinate clauses from English into Ukrainian.

In English, the conjunction **that** may be omitted in a sentence.

I know that he's at home.
I know (that) he's at home.

In Ukrainian, the conjunction **що must** be used.

I know (that) he's at home.
Я зна́ю, **що** він удо́ма.

We think (that) she's studying.
Ми ду́маємо, **що** вона́ вчи́ться.

Practise Oral Exercises 8.6, 8.7

Do Written Exercises 8.4, 8.5

LESSON 9

A. VOCABULARY

Verbs

Second Conjugation
(consonant stem бвмпф)

to do	роби́ти
to look at	диви́тися
to love, to like	люби́ти
to sleep	спа́ти

Second Conjugation
(consonant stem дзст)

to fly	леті́ти
to have to	му́сити
to pay	плати́ти
to request, to plead	проси́ти
to sit, to be sitting	сиді́ти

Second Conjugation
(vowel stem)

to fear, to be frightened	боя́тися
to stand, to be standing	стоя́ти

Adverbs

almost	ма́йже
for a long time	до́вго
for a longer time	до́вше
from here	зві́дси
from there	зві́дти
from where	зві́дки
not at all	зо́всім не
only	ті́льки, лише́
this evening, tonight	сьогóдні ввéчорі, сьогóдні ввéчері
this morning	сьогóдні врáнці
today	сьогóдні, ни́ні

B. SECOND CONJUGATION: CONSONANT STEM Б, В, М, П, Ф

Verbs belonging to the subgroup [II,бвмпф] have a present tense stem ending in one of **б, в, м, п,** or **ф**.

B.1 Present Tense Stems

In this lesson, four verbs have present tense stems ending in one of **б, в, м, п,** or **ф**.

	Infinitive [II,бвмпф]		*Present Tense Stem*
to do	роби́ти	(роб-и-ти)	роб-
to look at	диви́тися	(див-и-ти-ся)	див-ся
to love	люби́ти	(люб-и-ти)	люб-
to sleep	спа́ти	(сп-а-ти)	сп-

B.2 Present Tense Conjugation

In the verb forms for **я** and **вони́,** the letter **л** is inserted before the personal endings are added to the present tense stem:

я люблю́, вони́ лю́блять

Let's look at how the verb **люби́ти** is conjugated.

Infinitive: люби́ти	**Present Tense Stem: люб-**	
	Singular	*Plural*
First Person	я **люблю́**	ми **лю́бимо**
Second Person	ти **лю́биш**	ви **лю́бите**
Third Person	він **лю́бить** вона́ **лю́бить** воно́ **лю́бить**	вони́ **лю́блять**

Practise Oral Exercises 9.1, 9.2

Do Written Exercise 9.1

C. SECOND CONJUGATION: CONSONANT STEM Д, З, С, Т

Verbs belonging to the subgroup [II,дзст] have a present tense stem ending in one of **д, з, с,** or **т**.

C.1 Present Tense Stems

In this lesson, five verbs have present tense stems ending in one of the following consonants: **д, з, с, т**.

In all of these verbs there is a change in the present tense stem of the verb form for **я**.

	Infinitive [II,дзст]		*Present Tense Stem*	
to fly	леті́ти	(ле**т**-і-ти)	лет-	(я ле**ч**у́)
to have to	му́сити	(му**с**-и-ти)	мус-	(я му́**ш**у)
to pay	плати́ти	(пла**т**-и-ти)	плат-	(я пла**ч**у́)
to request	проси́ти	(про**с**-и-ти)	прос-	(я про**ш**у́)
to sit	сиді́ти	(си**д**-і-ти)	сид-	(я си**дж**у́)

The changes in the present tense stems of the verb forms for **я** in the verbs in this lesson are summarized below.

с	becomes	**ш**
т	becomes	**ч**
д	becomes	**дж**

It is important to remember that the change in the present tense stem of a verb in the **д, з, с, т subgroup of the Second Conjugation** occurs ***only*** in the verb form for the pronoun **я**.

C.2 Present Tense Conjugation

All verbs belonging to the **д, з, с, т subgroup** are conjugated like **сидíти**.

Infinitive: сидíти	**Present Tense Stem: сид-**	
	Singular	***Plural***
First Person	я **сиджý**	ми **сидимó**
Second Person	ти **сидúш**	ви **сидитé**
Third Person	він **сидúть** вонá **сидúть** вонó **сидúть**	вонú **сидя́ть**

C.3 Consonant Stem Changes: First and Second Conjugations

It is important to remember that the present tense stem of a verb in the **д, з, с, т subgroup of the Second Conjugation** changes ***only*** in the verb form for the pronoun **я**.

You will recall that in the consonant stem 2 group of the First Conjugation, the change in the stem of the present tense is maintained throughout the conjugation of the verb.

If you learn the verb forms for both **я** and **ти**, it will help you to remember whether a verb belongs to the First or Second Conjugation,

If the consonant change remains in the verb form for **ти,** the verb belongs to the First Conjugation: я пи**ш**ý, ти пú**ш**еш.

If the consonant change is **not** maintained in the verb form for **ти**, the verb belongs to the Second Conjugation: я си**дж**ý, ти си**д**úш.

Practise Oral Exercises 9.3, 9.4

Do Written Exercise 9.2

D. SECOND CONJUGATION: VOWEL STEM

There are some verbs (but not very many) that belong to the **vowel stem group** of the Second Conjugation [II,vs].

D.1 Present Tense Stems

To form the present tense stem of a verb in the vowel stem group, **the suffix -ти** ***and*** **the vowel preceding it are dropped. The stem that is left ends in a vowel.**

In this lesson, there are only two verbs that belong to the **vowel stem** group of the Second Conjugation.

	Infinitive [II,vs]		*Present Tense Stem*
to fear	боя́тися	(бо-я-ти-ся)	бо-ся
to stand	стоя́ти	(сто-я-ти)	сто-

D.2 Present Tense Conjugation

Verbs in the vowel stem group have the vowel **-ї** in their personal endings where those in the consonant stem group have the vowel **-и**: **-їш, -їть, -їмо, -їте**.

The personal endings of the verb forms for **я** and **вони́** are **-ю** and **-ять** respectively.

All verbs in this subgroup are conjugated like **стоя́ти**.

Infinitive: стоя́ти	**Present Tense Stem: сто-**	
	Singular	*Plural*
First Person	я сто**ю́**	ми сто**їмо́**
Second Person	ти сто**́їш**	ви сто**їте́**
Third Person	він сто**́їть** вона́ сто**́їть** воно́ сто**́їть**	вони́ сто**я́ть**

Remember that **боя́тися** is a reflexive verb; therefore, the reflexive particle **-ся** must be included in its conjugation.

Practise Oral Exercise 9.5

Do Written Exercise 9.3

E. SUMMARY: PERSONAL ENDINGS OF SECOND CONJUGATION VERBS

Group	я	ти	він	ми	ви	вони́
ж,ч,ш,щ	**-у**	-иш	-ить	-имо	-ите	**-ать**
л,н,р	**-ю**	-иш	-ить	-имо	-ите	**-ять**
б,в,м,п,ф	**-лю**	-иш	-ить	-имо	-ите	**-лять**
д,з,с,т	**-у**	-иш	-ить	-имо	-ите	**-ять**
vowel	**-ю**	-їш	-їть	-їмо	-їте	**-ять**

Practise Oral Exercises 9.6, 9.7

Do Written Exercise 9.4

F. IMPERSONAL SENTENCES

In both English and Ukrainian, there are impersonal sentences in which the subject is either unspecified or absent.

F.1 Unspecified Subject

In English, an indefinite or unspecified subject is often expressed by using the pronoun **they**, as in **they** say.

> **They** say she dances excellently.
> **They** say he doesn't know how to work.

In Ukrainian, this indefinite or nebulous subject is expressed by using the third person plural form of the verb **каза́ти** ***without the pronoun*** **вони́**.

> **Ка́жуть,** що вона́ прекра́сно танцю́є.
> **They say** she dances excellently.

> **Ка́жуть,** що він не вмі́є працюва́ти.
> **They say** he doesn't know how to work.

Practise Oral Exercise 9.8

F.2 тре́ба

In Ukrainian, the word **тре́ба and the infinitive of a verb** are used to express the idea that it is necessary to do something.

Чи тут **тре́ба** шепта́ти?
Is it necessary to whisper here?
(Does one have to whisper here?)

Тут **тре́ба** стоя́ти.
It's necessary to stand here.
(One has to stand here.)

In a negative sentence, the adverb **не** precedes **тре́ба.**

Тут **не тре́ба** плати́ти.
It's not necessary to pay here.
(One doesn't have to pay here.)

Не **тре́ба** тут шепта́ти.
It's not necessary to whisper here.
(One doesn't have to whisper here.)

Practise Oral Exercise 9.9

F.3 мо́жна

In Ukrainian, the word **мо́жна and the infinitive of a verb** are used to express the idea that it is permissible or possible to do something.

Тут **мо́жна** кури́ти.
Smoking is permitted here.
(One is allowed to smoke here.)

Чи тут **мо́жна** танцюва́ти?
Is dancing permitted here?
(Is one allowed to dance here?)

In a negative sentence, the adverb **не** precedes **мо́жна**.

Тут **не мо́жна** крича́ти.
Shouting isn't permitted here.
(One isn't allowed to shout here.)

Чому́ тут **не мо́жна** співа́ти?
Why isn't singing permitted here?
(Why isn't one allowed to sing here?)

Practise Oral Exercise 9.10

F.4 про́шу

In Ukrainian, there is an impersonal (and very polite) way of giving commands that you can learn to use now by using **про́шу** ***and the infinitive of a verb.***

You will learn how to give commands in other ways later in the text.

Про́шу слу́хати.
Please listen.

Про́шу співа́ти.
Please sing.

In a negative sentence, the adverb **не** precedes the infinitive.

Про́шу не крича́ти.
Please don't shout.

Про́шу не стогна́ти.
Please don't groan.

Practise Oral Exercises 9.11, 9.12, 9.13

Do Written Exercises 9.5, 9.6

G. EMPHATIC PARTICLE: Ж (ЖЕ)

In Ukrainian, you may place additional emphasis on a word when you are speaking by using the emphatic particle **ж (же)** after it. If the word that the emphatic particle follows ends in a consonant, **ж** is used; if it ends in a vowel, **же** is used.

Let's look at a few examples.

Чому́ **ж** ти пла́чеш?
But *why* are you *[s]* crying?

Куди́ **ж** вони́ йду́ть?
But *where* are they going?

Він **же** тут, не вона́.
But it's *he* who's here, not she.

Ми тут **же**, а ви там.
But we're *here,* and you're there.

LESSON 10

A. VOCABULARY

Verbs

First Conjugation
(vowel stem 1)

to fly	літáти
to run	бíгати
to swim	плáвати

Second Conjugation
(consonant stem дзст)

to carry, to wear	носи́ти
to go/to come *[on foot]*	ходи́ти
to go/to come *[by vehicle]*	ї́здити
to haul, to transport	вози́ти

Third Conjugation

to eat	ї́сти

Adverbs

earlier	ранíше
every day	щодня́
every evening	щовéчора
every hour	щогоди́ни
every minute	щохвили́ни
every month	щомíсяця
every morning	щорáнку
every night	щонóчі
every week	щоти́жня
every year	щорóку
how often	як чáсто
later	пізнíше

Vocabulary Notes

Remember that present tense stems of verbs belonging to the **д, з, с, т** subgroup of the Second Conjugation **[II,дзст]** undergo a change **only** in the verb form for **я**.

вози́ти	я во**ж**у́	ти во́з-иш
ї́здити	я ї́**жд**жу	ти ї́зд-иш
носи́ти	я но**ш**у́	ти но́с-иш
ходи́ти	я хо**дж**у́	ти хо́д-иш

B. THIRD CONJUGATION

At this time you will be learning only one verb that belongs to the Third Conjugation: **ї́сти** (to eat).

Infinitive: ї́сти	**Present Tense Stem: ї-**	
	Singular	*Plural*
First Person	я **їм**	ми **їмо́**
Second Person	ти **їси́**	ви **їсте́**
Third Person	він **їсть** вона́ **їсть** воно́ **їсть**	вони́ **їдя́ть**

Be prepared to understand speakers of Ukrainian in Canada who say **ти їш** instead of **ти їси́**.

Remember, however, that you are expected to use the correct form: **ти їси́**.

Practise Oral Exercises 10.1, 10.2, 10.3

Do Written Exercises 10.1, 10.2

C. SUMMARY: PRESENT TENSE ENDINGS OF UKRAINIAN VERBS

You now know the present tense personal endings for all three conjugations of Ukrainian verbs. This means that you should be able to use correctly, in the present tense, any Ukrainian verb that you encounter.

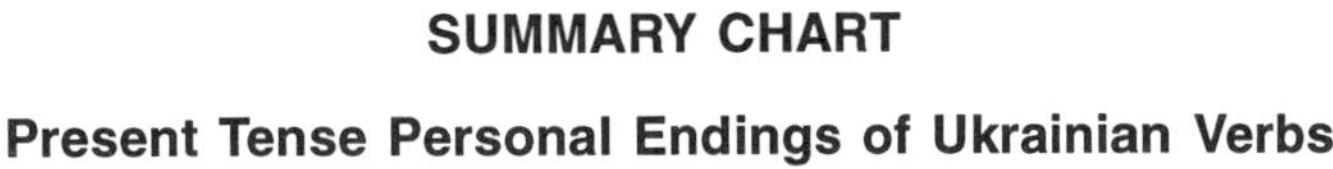

SUMMARY CHART

Present Tense Personal Endings of Ukrainian Verbs

First Conjugation						
Group	**я**	**ти**	**він**	**ми**	**ви**	**вони́**
Vowel	**-ю**	-єш	-є	-ємо	-єте	**-ють**
Consonant	**-у**	-еш	-е	-емо	-ете	**-уть**
Mixed	**-ю**	-еш	-е	-емо	-ете	**-ють**

Second Conjugation						
Group	**я**	**ти**	**він**	**ми**	**ви**	**вони́**
ж,ч,ш,щ	**-у**	-иш	-ить	-имо	-ите	**-ать**
л,н,р,	**-ю**	-иш	-ить	-имо	-ите	**-ять**
б,в,м,п,ф	**-лю**	-иш	-ить	-имо	-ите	**-лять**
д,з,с,т	**-у**	-иш	-ить	-имо	-ите	**-ять**
Vowel	**-ю**	-їш	-їть	-їмо	-їте	**-ять**

Third Conjugation						
Group	**я**	**ти**	**він**	**ми**	**ви**	**вони́**
ї́сти	**-м**	-си	-сть	-мо	-сте	**-дять**

D. VERBS OF MOTION

In this lesson, a few of the verbs of motion are introduced. You will learn more about these verbs later.

D.1 Durative and Iterative Verbs

In English, different kinds of movement or motion may be indicated by the same verb of motion.

Let's look at the verb **to go/come*[on foot]*.**

1. The verb **to go** may be used to express an ongoing, one-time, or unidirectional movement.

   He's **going** home now.

2. The same verb, **to go,** may also be used to express repeated, habitual, or multidirectional movements.

   He often **goes** there.

In Ukrainian, the same verb of motion may **not** be used to express these different ideas. To translate the sentences in the above two examples, you have to use two verbs: **іти́** in the first example; and **ходи́ти** in the second one.

1. The verb **іти́** expresses an ongoing, one-time, or unidirectional movement.

   He's going home now.
   Він тепе́р **іде́** додо́му.

   The verb **іти́** is a **durative** verb. A durative verb refers to an action that is continuous or of some duration.

2. The verb **ходи́ти** expresses repeated, habitual, or multidirectional movements.

   He often goes there.
   Він ча́сто **хо́дить** туди́.

   The verb **ходи́ти** is an **iterative** verb. An iterative verb refers to an action that is repeated or reiterated.

D.2 List: Verbs of Motion

At this time you will learn **seven pairs of durative and iterative verbs of motion.**

Half of these verbs were introduced in previous lessons, but were not identified as being either durative or iterative at the time. The remaining seven verbs are listed in the vocabulary for this lesson.

	Durative	*Iterative*
to carry	нести́	носи́ти
to fly	леті́ти	літа́ти
to go/come *[by vehicle]*	ї́хати	ї́здити
to go/come *[on foot]*	іти́	ходи́ти
to haul/transport	везти́	вози́ти
to run	бі́гти	бі́гати
to swim	плисти́	пла́вати

D.3 Using Verbs of Motion in Sentences

In order to decide which verb of motion to use in a sentence, the durative or the iterative, you must determine the kind of action that is being implied.

When you encounter a verb of motion, you should ask yourself if the action is an ongoing one (use the durative verb) or if it is one that is being repeated (use the iterative verb).

It is especially helpful to be on the lookout for adverbs that imply habitual or repeated actions as these signal that the iterative verb of motion is required.

The context in which a verb is being used usually provides a clear indication which verb of motion should be chosen.

When sentences are presented out of context, it is sometimes difficult to decide which verb of motion should be used; indeed, in some exercises, two interpretations of the same sentence may be possible.

Read through the following sentences and think carefully about the verbs that are used in them.

Iterative Verbs

1. Він за́вжди **ї́здить** додо́му.
   He always goes *[by vehicle]* home.

2. Він ка́же, що вона́ щодня́ му́сить **ходи́ти.**
   He says that she has to walk every day.

3. Чи ти лю́биш **пла́вати**?
   Do you[s] like to swim?

4. Вони́ ча́сто **літа́ють**.
   They often fly.

5. Ми хо́чемо **бі́гати** надво́рі.
   We want to run around outdoors.

6. Він мо́же ду́же шви́дко **бі́гати**.
   He can run very quickly.

Durative Verbs

1. Хто за́раз **ї́де** додо́му?
   Who is going home right now?

2. Вона́ **йде́** туди́, а він **іде́** сюди́.
   She is going there, and he is going there.

3. Куди́ ти так бага́то **несе́ш**?
   Where are you[s] carrying so much?

4. Коли́ ви **летите́** додо́му?
   When are you[p] flying home?

5. Зві́дки вони́ **біжа́ть**?
   Where are they running from?

6. Чому́ він так ма́ло **везе́** додо́му?
   Why is he hauling home so little?

Practise Oral Exercises 10.3, 10.4, 10.5

Do Written Exercises 10.3, 10.4, 10.5

Practise Oral Exercises 10.6, 10.7

Do Written Exercise 10.6

Practise Oral Exercises 10.8, 10.9

Do Written Exercises 10.7, 10.8

LESSON 11

A. VOCABULARY

Nouns

assignment, homework	завда́ння *[n]*
book	кни́жка
briefcase	те́чка, *портфе́ль*
chalk	кре́йда *[sg]*
chalkboard	табли́ця, *до́шка*
class, classroom	кля́са, *клас*
computer	комп'ю́тер
corridor	коридо́р
dictionary	словни́к
door	две́рі *[pl]*
eraser	ґу́мка
friend	това́риш; това́ришка
genius	ге́ній
knapsack	напле́чник, *рюкза́к*
lesson, lecture	ле́кція, *уро́к*
man	чолові́к
museum	музе́й
notebook	зо́шит
pen	перо́, *ру́чка*
pencil	олivéць
place, location	мі́сце
poster	афі́ша
professor	профе́сор
pupil	у́чень, школя́р; учени́ця, школя́рка
school	шко́ла
stairs	схо́ди *[pl]*
student	студе́нт; студе́нтка
surname	прі́звище
teacher	учи́тель/вчи́тель; учи́телька/вчи́телька
textbook	підру́чник
university	університе́т
woman	жі́нка

Demonstrative Pronouns

that	то
this	це

Conjunction

and	та

Vocabulary Notes

1. Two or more Ukrainian equivalents are given for a few of the nouns. Some are synonyms that are used both in Canada and in Ukraine. Words printed in slanted type are used mainly in Ukraine; these words are not included in the exercises, but students are encouraged to learn them if they plan to travel to Ukraine.

2. ***In Ukrainian***, some feminine nouns are formed by adding a suffix to a masculine noun. In the Vocabularies, a feminine noun formed in this way is placed after the masculine noun, and is separated from it by a semi-colon.

   friend – **товáриш; товáришка**

   When an English word like **friend** is used in the exercises in this course, it is followed by *[m]* if the Ukrainian masculine noun is to be used, and by *[f]* if the Ukrainian feminine noun is to be used. (See E.4.)

   friend *[m]* – **товáриш**
   friend *[f]* – **товáришка**

4. ***In both English and Ukrainian***, some nouns are always plural, while other nouns are almost always singular. In the Vocabularies, plural nouns are noted as: **stairs** – **схóди** *[pl]*; nouns that are usually singular are noted as: **chalk** – **крéйда** *[sg]*.

5. Nouns that are always plural, like **двéрі** and **схóди**, have no gender. (See B.3 for a discussion of gender.)

6. Neuter nouns ending in the vowel **я** are identified as being neuter: **завдáння** *[n]* (See B.3 for a discussion of gender.)

7. In Ukraine, the terms **студéнт** and **студéнтка** are used only for university students, while **ýчень** and **учени́ця,** and **школя́р** and **школя́рка** are used interchangeably for both elementary and high school pupils.

Shortcuts to Learning Vocabulary!

If you are like most students who set out to learn a new language, you are probably experiencing some frustration by now: you are eager to speak the language, but you are finding the challenge of learning new vocabulary a bit overwhelming!

The following suggestions will help you learn new words.

1. List the words that resemble their English counterparts.

   комп'ютер – computer, коридóр – corridor

2. Find words in the list that appear to be related.

   шкóла, школя́р, школя́рка

3. Try to see similarities between words you are learning and words you already know.

   учи́тися – учи́тель, учи́телька, у́чень, учени́ця

4. Start a list of opposites (antonyms) to which you can keep adding as you progress through the lessons.

   жíнка – чоловíк

5. Classify the words according to categories that you can update with every new lesson (e.g. the classroom, the home, the city, foods, the professions, travel, nature, sports, etc.).

6. Finally, resign yourself to the fact that some words may not fit into any of the above categories!

B. NOUNS

In both English and Ukrainian, a noun names a person, place, thing, animal, action, idea, quality, or emotional state.

A noun may be classified according to its number, gender, and declension.

1. **Number** – A noun may be either singular or plural.
2. **Gender** – A noun may be feminine, masculine, or neuter.
3. **Declension** – The ending of a noun may change to show how it is related to other words in a sentence.

The **number** and **gender** of nouns is discussed in this lesson.

The **declension** of Ukrainian nouns, that is, changing the endings of nouns in accordance with their use in a sentence, is introduced in Lesson 12.

B.1 Number

In both English and Ukrainian, most nouns may be either **singular** or **plural**.

When we refer to only **one** person, **one** thing, **one** animal, etc., we are using the **singular** form of a noun.

When we refer to **two or more** persons, things, animals, etc., we are using the **plural** form of a noun.

B.2 Gender

In English, nouns are classified according to their **natural gender**.

Nouns that refer to **animate** (living) beings are either **masculine** or **feminine.**

Nouns that refer to **inanimate** (nonliving) things or objects are usually **neuter**.

Gender: English Nouns			
	Masculine	***Feminine***	***Neuter***
Animate Nouns	man	woman	—
Inanimate Nouns	—	—	book

In Ukrainian, nouns are not always classified according to their natural gender.

Most Ukrainian **animate** (living) nouns, like English animate nouns, are either **feminine or masculine**.

Unlike English, however, in which almost all inanimate nouns are neuter, Ukrainian **inanimate** (nonliving) nouns may be **feminine, masculine**, or **neuter**.

To determine whether an inanimate Ukrainian noun is feminine, masculine, or neuter, you have to look at the **consonant** or **vowel** in which it ends when it is in its basic form.

The basic form of a noun is the one that you find when you look up a noun in a dictionary.

Languages, like Ukrainian, in which nouns are classified according to their endings, are said to have **grammatical gender**.

✍ **Do Written Exercises 11.1, 11.2**

B.3 Gender-Marked Endings of Ukrainian Nouns

Most feminine, masculine, and neuter Ukrainian nouns, both animate and inanimate, are readily identifiable by their endings.

1. **Feminine Nouns**: most end in the vowels **а (кни́жка)**, and **я (ле́кція)**.
2. **Masculine Nouns**: most end in a consonant (**зо́шит**), including **й (музе́й)**, and **ь (оліве́ць)**.
3. **Neuter Nouns**: most end in the vowels **о (перо́)**, and **е (мі́сце)**; some end in **я (завда́ння)**.

The word "most" has been used because not all the categories of Ukrainian nouns are being presented at this time.

Gender: Ukrainian Nouns			
	Feminine	*Masculine*	*Neuter*
Animate Nouns	жі́нка учени́ця Марі́я	чолові́к у́чень ге́ній	—
Inanimate Nouns	ґу́мка табли́ця ле́кція	словни́к оліве́ць музе́й	перо́ мі́сце завда́ння

✍ **Do Written Exercises 11.3, 11.4**

C. DEFINITE AND INDEFINITE ARTICLES

In English, there are definite and indefinite articles.

The definite article **the** is used to indicate **specific** persons or things.

The man is writing.	I see **the** eraser.
The men are writing.	I see **the** erasers.

The indefinite articles **a** and **an** are used when reference is being made to **unspecified** persons or things.

A is used before a noun beginning in a consonant; **an** is used before a word beginning in a vowel.

A man is writing.	I see **an** eraser.

In Ukrainian, there are no equivalents for the English definite article **the**, or for the indefinite articles **a** and **an**. These articles must be supplied or omitted as required in translation exercises.

In the third example given below, the plural noun **чоловíки** is used. You will learn how to form the plurals of Ukrainian nouns in the next lesson.

Чоловíк пи́ше.	**A man** is writing.
Чоловíк пи́ше.	**The man** is writing
Чоловíки пи́шуть.	**The men** are writing.

D. DEMONSTRATIVE PRONOUNS: ЦЕ, ТО

In Ukrainian, the interrogative pronouns **хто** and **що** are used along with the demonstrative pronouns **це** (this) and **то** (that) to ask about unfamiliar people or things.

1. The questions **Хто це**? and **Хто то**? are used to ask about one person or about many people.

Хто це?	**Who is this**?
Це чоловíк.	**This is** a man.
Це чоловíки.	**These are** men.
Хто то?	**Who is that**?
То жíнка.	**That's** a woman.
То жінки́.	**Those are** women.

2. The questions **Що це**? and **Хто то**? are used to ask about one thing or about many things.

Що це?	**What's this**?
Це комп'ютер.	**This is** a computer.
Це книжка.	**This is** a book.
Це перо́.	**This is** a pen.
Це схо́ди.	**These are** stairs.

Що то?	**What's that**?
То музе́й.	**That's** a museum.
То табли́ця.	**That's** a chalkboard.
То прі́звище.	**That's** a surname.
То схо́ди.	**Those are** stairs.

3. To construct a negative sentence, **не** is placed before the word that is being negated.

Це не у́чень.	**This isn't** a pupil *[m]*.
Це не те́чка.	**This isn't** a briefcase.
То не учени́ця.	**That's not** a pupil *[f]*.
То не наплі́чник.	**That's not** a knapsack.

Practise Oral Exercise 11.1

Do Written Exercise 11.5

E. SUBSTITUTION OF PRONOUNS FOR NOUNS

In both English and Ukrainian, pronouns may be substituted for nouns.

The **man** is writing.	**He** is writing.
The **stairs** are there.	**They** are there.

E.1 Singular Nouns

In English, because nouns are classified according to their **natural gender**, all **animate** nouns are either **masculine** or **feminine,** and the pronouns **he** or **she** are substituted for them.

The **man** is writing.	**He** is writing.
The **woman** is writing.	**She** is writing.

English **inanimate** nouns are **neuter**, and the pronoun **it** is substituted for them.

The **notebook** is here.	**It** is here.

In Ukrainian, however, because nouns have **grammatical gender**, you must be careful when you substitute pronouns for them.

The pronoun **він** is substituted for **all masculine nouns, animate and inanimate.**

Animate:	**Чоловік** пи́ше.	**Він** пи́ше.
Inanimate:	**Зо́шит** тут.	**Він** тут.

The pronoun **вона́** is substituted for **all feminine nouns, animate and inanimate**.

Animate:	**Жі́нка** пи́ше.	**Вона́** пи́ше.
Inanimate:	**Те́чка** тут.	**Вона́** тут.

The pronoun **воно́** is substituted for **all neuter nouns**.

Inanimate:	**Завда́ння** тут.	**Воно́** тут.

Remember that, unlike English inanimate nouns which are always neuter, **Ukrainian inanimate nouns may be feminine, masculine, or neuter**; therefore, the pronouns that are substituted for Ukrainian nouns must agree with them in gender.

The **notebook** is here.	**It** is here.
Зо́шит тут.	**Він** тут.
The **book** is here.	**It** is here.
Кни́жка тут.	**Вона́** тут.
The **assignment** is here.	**It** is here.
Завда́ння тут.	**Воно́** тут.

E.2 Plural Nouns

In both English and Ukrainian, the pronoun **they (вони́)** is substituted for all plural nouns. (Remember that you will learn how to form the plurals of Ukrainian nouns in the next lesson.)

The **men** are here.	**They** are here.
Чолові́ки тут.	**Вони́** тут.
The **women** are here.	**They** are here.
Жінки́ тут.	**Вони́** тут.
The **pens** are here.	**They** are here.
Пе́ра тут.	**Вони́** тут.

If a noun that is always plural in Ukrainian (**две́рі**) is a singular noun in English (**door**), the appropriate pronoun must be used in both languages.

The **door** is there.	**It** is there.
Две́рі там.	**Вони́** там.

Practise Oral Exercises 11.2, 11.3

Do Written Exercise 11.6

E.3 Nouns without Distinctive Gender

In both English and Ukrainian, some nouns may refer to **either a man or a woman: professor – профе́сор**.

If you have no way of knowing, for example, if reference is being made to a male or female professor, then either **he** or **she** may be substituted for the word.

The **professor** is here.	**He/She** is here.
Профе́сор тут.	**Він/Вона́** тут.

If, however, the gender of the professor is made clear, there is no problem in determining which pronoun to use.

Who is **she**?	**She** is a **professor.**
Хто **вона́**?	**Вона́ профе́сор.**
Who is **he**?	**He** is a **professor.**
Хто **він**?	**Він профе́сор.**

E.4 Ukrainian Nouns with Distinctive Gender

In English, it is not clear in the following sentence if reference is being made to a male or a female student.

The **student** is outdoors.	**He/She** is outdoors.

In Ukrainian, there are distinctive words for a **male** student (**студéнт**) and for a **female** student (**студéнтка**).

Студéнт надвóрі.	**Він** надвóрі.
Студéнтка надвóрі.	**Вонá** надвóрі.

When a nondistinctive English word like **student** is used in the exercises in this course, the gender that is being asked for is stated in brackets so that you will know which Ukrainian noun to use: **student***[m]* for **студéнт**, and **student***[f]* for **студéнтка**.

The **student***[m]* is outdoors.	**He** is outdoors.
Студéнт надвóрі.	**Він** надвóрі.
The **student***[f]* is outdoors.	**She** is outdoors.
Студéнтка надвóрі.	**Вонá** надвóрі.

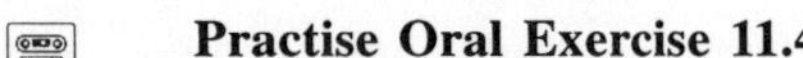

Practise Oral Exercise 11.4

Do Written Exercise 11.7

F. CONJUNCTION: TA

The conjunction **та** has the same meaning as the conjunction **і/й**; however, the use of **та** is usually limited to joining words, phrases, or clauses of equal importance.

Let's look at a few examples.

Жíнка **та** чоловíк удóма.
Ось ýчень **та** ученúця.
Школя́рка **та** школя́р надвóрі.
Де студéнт **та** студéнтка?

Вонú жартýють **та** смíються.
Де ви обíдаєте **та** вечéряєте?
Хто вмíє читáти **та** писáти?
Ми всі хóчемо співáти **та** танцювáти.

LESSON 12

A. VOCABULARY

Nouns

apartment	поме́шкання *[n]*, *кварти́ра*
boss, manager	нача́льник; нача́льниця
building	буди́нок (будинк-)
cafeteria	кафете́рія, кафете́рій
car	а́вто, *маши́на*
chair	крі́сло, стіле́ць (стільц-)
chauffeur	шофе́р *[h]*
city, town	мі́сто
doctor	лі́кар *[s]*, до́ктор *[h]*; лі́карка, до́кторка
driver	воді́й
garage	ґара́ж, гара́ж
home	дім (дом-)
hospital	ліка́рня, шпита́ль
hotel	готе́ль
house	ха́та, *буди́нок (будинк-)*
intersection	перехре́стя *[n]*
labourer	робітни́к; робітни́ця
library	бібліоте́ка
librarian	бібліоте́кар *[s]*; бібліоте́карка
mechanic	меха́нік
motel	моте́ль
nurse	медбра́т; медсестра́
office	канцеля́рія, *кабіне́т*
patient	пацієнт; пацієнтка
police officer	поліца́й, *міліціоне́р [h]*
restaurant	рестора́н
secretary	секрета́р *[s]*; секрета́рка
table	стіл (стол-)
taxi, cab	таксі́вка, таксі́ *[indecl.]*
thief	зло́дій; зло́дійка
tourist	тури́ст; тури́стка
village, small town	село́
worker, employee	працівни́к; працівни́ця

Vocabulary Notes

1. Masculine nouns ending in **-р** are identified as being **hard***[h]*, **mixed***[mx]*, or **soft***[s]*. These terms (hard, mixed, and soft) are explained in section C.

   In Lesson 11 there are four masculine nouns that end in **-р**: **комп'ю́тер***[h]*, **коридо́р***[h]*, **профе́сор***[h]*, **школя́р***[mx]*.

2. If the stem of a masculine noun changes when it is declined, the altered stem is given in parentheses: **стіл (стол-)**; **буди́нок (будинк-)**.

   The formation of noun stems is discussed in section E.

3. ***In Ukrainian***, some nouns never change; they are the same in the singular and in the plural, and their endings do not change regardless of how they are used in a sentence. Such nouns are called **indeclinable nouns**. In this text they are identified for you in the following manner in the Vocabularies: **таксі́***[indecl.]*.

B. DECLENSION

In English, most nouns are changed in only two ways in order to convey meaning in a sentence: either **-s** or **-es** is added to form the plural of a noun; and, either **-'s** or **-s'** is added to form, respectively, the possessive singular or plural.

It is because noun endings change so infrequently in English that the order in which nouns are used in a sentence is very important in conveying meaning.

Let's look at the following sentence in which there are two nouns: **woman** and **child**.

> The **woman** is carrying the **child**.

In this sentence, the word order makes it clear that the woman is doing the carrying, and that the child is being carried.

If you use the same two nouns, **woman** and **child**, but exchange their positions in the sentence, you get quite a different meaning.

> The **child** is carrying the **woman**.

In Ukrainian, the endings of nouns change much more frequently than they do in English, and these endings indicate how words are related to one another in a sentence.

Let's look at the example about the **woman** and the **child**.

In Ukrainian, the basic (dictionary) forms of the two nouns are: **жі́нка** for **woman**, and **дити́на** for **child**.

When the English sentence in the example is translated into Ukrainian, the ending of the word for child must be changed: **дити́на** becomes **дити́ну**.

> The **woman** is carrying the **child**.
> **Жі́нка** несе́ **дити́ну**.

The ending **-у** on the noun **дити́ну** makes it clear that it is the **child** who is being carried; therefore, reordering the words in the Ukrainian sentence may produce a shift in emphasis, but it does not change the basic meaning of the sentence.

Ukrainian Sentence	*English Translation*
Жі́нка несе́ дити́ну.	The woman is carrying the child.
Жі́нка дити́ну несе́.	The woman is carrying the child.
Дити́ну жі́нка несе́.	The woman is carrying the child.
Дити́ну несе́ жі́нка.	The woman is carrying the child.
Несе́ жі́нка дити́ну.	The woman is carrying the child.
Несе́ дити́ну жі́нка.	The woman is carrying the child.

Changing the endings of nouns is known as declining nouns, and nouns are grouped, according to sets of endings, into **declensions**.

C. THREE DECLENSIONS OF UKRAINIAN NOUNS

In this text, Ukrainian nouns are grouped, according to the endings of their basic form, into three declensions: **hard**, **mixed**, and **soft**.

C.1 Hard Declension Nouns

Feminine Nouns	end in **-а** (кни́жка)
Masculine Nouns	end in consonants (зо́шит, стіл, словни́к) – except **-ж,-ч**, **-ш,-щ**, **-ь**, **-й**, and some in **-р** (a few masculine **animate** nouns end in **-о**)
Neuter Nouns	end in **-о** (крі́сло)

C.2 Mixed Declension Nouns

Feminine Nouns	end in **-жа, -ча, -ша,** or **-ща** (афі́ша)
Masculine Nouns	end in **-ж, -ч, -ш,** or **-щ** (**това́риш**); – some end in **-р** (школя́р)
Neuter Nouns	end in **-же, -че, -ше**, or **-ще** (пру́звище)

C.3 Soft Declension Nouns

Feminine Nouns	**Soft 1 nouns** – end in a **consonant** and **-я** (учени́ця) **Soft 2 nouns** – end in a **vowel** and **-я** (ле́кція)
Masculine Nouns	**Soft 1 nouns** – end in **-ь** (оліве́ць), – some end in **-р** (секрета́р) **Soft 2 nouns** – end in **-й** (музе́й)
Neuter Nouns	**Soft 1 nouns** – end in the vowel **-е** (мі́сце) **Soft 2 nouns** – end in **two consonants, doubled or different**, and **-я** (завда́ння, перехре́стя)

C.4 Summary Chart: Three Declensions of Ukrainian Nouns

Summary: Three Declensions of Ukrainian Nouns				
	Hard	*Mixed*	*Soft 1*	*Soft 2*
Feminine Nouns	**-а**	**-жа, -ча, -ша, -ща**	**-я**	**-я**
Masculine Nouns	consonant (except: **-ж, -ч, -ш, -щ, -ь, -й**) some in **-р**	**-ж, -ч, -ш, -щ** some in **-р**	**-ь** some in **-р**	**-й**
Neuter Nouns	**-о**	**-же, -че, -ше, -ще**	**-е**	**-я**

Practise Oral Exercise 12.1

Do Written Exercise 12.1

12.1 + 12.2 written for Hwk.

D. NOMINATIVE CASE

When a noun is in its basic (dictionary) form, it is in the **nominative case**.

In both English and Ukrainian, there are three ways in which singular and plural nouns are used in the nominative case.

1. As the **subject** of a sentence
2. As a **complement** of the verb **to be**
3. In **apposition** to the **subject** or **complement**

D.1 Subject

In English, a simple sentence consists of a **subject** and a **predicate.**

The **subject** indicates **who** is doing something.

The **predicate** indicates **what is being done**.

Let's examine the following sentence.

The man is writing.

Subject:	(Who is writing?)	**The man**.
Predicate:	(What is he doing?)	He **is writing**.

In Ukrainian, when the same simple sentence is written, the subject, **чоловíк**, is in the nominative case.

Чоловíк пи́ше.

Subject:	(Хто пи́ше?)	**Чоловíк**.
Predicate:	(Що чоловíк рóбить?)	Він **пи́ше**.

D.2 Complement (Predicate Noun)

In English, nouns in the nominative case are also used as **complements**; these nouns give more information about the subject, and complete the predicate when the verb **to be** is used.

Let's look at the following sentence:

Petro Kozak is a teacher.

Subject:	(Who is a teacher?)	**Petro Kozak**.
Predicate:	(What is he doing?)	He **is**.
Complement:	(Who is Petro Kozak?)	He is **a teacher**.

In Ukrainian, **complements** are also used with the verb to be: **бу́ти**. You have to remember, of course, that in Ukrainian the verb **бу́ти** is often omitted in the present tense.

In both of the following sentences, **учи́тель** serves as a **complement**. The dash in the second sentence indicates that there is a slight pause between the two words in spoken Ukrainian.

1. **Петро́ Коза́к (є) учи́тель.**
2. **Петро́ Коза́к – учи́тель.**

Subject:	(Хто вчи́тель?)	**Петро́ Коза́к.**
Predicate:	("є" is omitted)	
Complement:	(Хто Петро́ Коза́к?)	Він **учи́тель.**

D.3 Noun in Apposition

In English, nouns may be used to provide more information about the subject or the complement; such nouns are called **appositives** as they stand next to, or are "in apposition to", the subject or the complement.

1. Noun in apposition to the subject

The teacher, Maria Sawchuk, is reading.

Subject:	(Who is reading?)	**The teacher** is reading.
Appositive:	(Who is the teacher?)	**Maria Sawchuk.**
Predicate:	(What is she doing?)	She **is reading.**

2. Noun in apposition to the complement

She is the teacher, Maria Sawchuk.

Subject:	(Who is?)	**She** is.
Predicate:	(What is she doing?)	She **is.**
Complement:	(Who is she?)	She is the **teacher.**
Appositive:	(Who is the teacher?)	**Maria Sawchuk.**

In Ukrainian, nouns are also used in apposition both to the subject and to the complement, and, like the subject and the complement, they too are in the nominative case.

1. Noun in apposition to the subject

Учи́телька, Марі́я Савчу́к, чита́є.

Subject:	(Хто чита́є?)	**Учи́телька** чита́є.
Appositive:	(Хто вчи́телька?)	**Марі́я Савчу́к.**
Predicate:	(Що вона́ ро́бить?)	Вона́ **чита́є.**

2. Noun in apposition to the complement

Вона́ – вчи́телька, Марі́я Савчу́к.

Subject:	(Хто?)	**Вона́.**
Predicate:	("є" is omitted.)	
Complement:	(Хто вона́?)	Вона́ **вчи́телька.**
Appositive:	(Хто вчи́телька?)	**Марі́я Савчу́к.**

✍ **Do Written Exercise 12.2**

E. FORMATION OF NOUN STEMS

In English, either **-s** or **-es** is added to singular nouns to form their plurals: boy – boy**s**, box – box**es**. There are some exceptions, of course: man – men, child – children.

In Ukrainian, before you can form the nominative plural case of a noun, you have to know the following:

1. the **gender** of the noun;
2. the **declension** to which the noun belongs; and
3. the **stem** of the noun.

The stem of a noun is formed from its nominative singular form.

E.1 Feminine and Neuter Nouns

For all feminine and neuter nouns, the noun stem is formed by dropping the final vowel from the nominative singular form.

		Nominative Singular	*Stem*
Feminine	***Hard***	кни́жка	книжк-
	Mixed	афі́ша	афіш-
	Soft 1	ліка́рня	лікарн-
	Soft 2	ле́кція	лекці-
Neuter	***Hard***	а́вто	авт-
	Mixed	прі́звище	прізвищ-
	Soft 1	мі́сце	місц-
	Soft 2	завда́ння	завданн-

E.2 Masculine Nouns

1. **Masculine Hard and Mixed Declension Nouns**: the stem is the nominative singular form. For masculine animate nouns ending in the vowel **-о,** this final **-о** is dropped.

		Nominative Singular	*Stem*
Masculine	***Hard***	рестора́н	ресторан-
		Марко́	Марк-
	Mixed	ґара́ж	ґараж-

2. **Masculine Soft 1 and Soft 2 Declension Nouns**: **-ь, -й** are dropped.

		Nominative Singular	*Stem*
Masculine	***Soft 1***	учи́тель	учител-
	Soft 2	музе́й	музе-

3. In some masculine nouns there are additional changes when the noun stem is formed. These changes are noted in the Vocabularies: **стіл (стол-)**

   1) In some nouns, **-і** in the stem becomes **-о**.

Nominative Singular	*Stem*
стіл	стол-

This change is based on differences between **closed** and **open syllables**. A closed syllable ends in a **consonant** (так); an open syllable ends in a **vowel** (ні).

The word **стіл** is a closed syllable. When an ending is added to it, **стіл** changes into a two-syllable word; when this happens, the **і** of the closed syllable changes to an **о** in the open syllable: сто-ли́.

   2) In some nouns, **-е** or **-о** before the final consonant is dropped when the stem is formed.

Nominative Singular	*Stem*
у́чень	учн-
оліве́ць	олівц-
буди́нок	будинк-

3) In a few nouns, **-е** before the final consonant is replaced by **-ь**.

Nominative Singular	*Stem*
стіле́ць	стільц-

✍ **Do Written Exercise 12.3**

F. NOMINATIVE PLURAL ENDINGS

Nominative plural endings are added to the **stem** of the noun.

F.1 Feminine and Masculine Nouns

The nominative plural endings are identical for feminine and masculine nouns.

Hard Declension: **-и**
Mixed and Soft 1 Declensions: **-і**
Soft 2 Declension: **-ї**

Feminine Nouns: Nominative Plural Endings				
Declension	*Endings*	*Nominative Singular*	*Stem*	*Nominative Plural*
Hard	**-и**	кля́са	кляс-	кля́с**и**
Mixed	**-і**	афі́ша	афіш-	афі́ш**і**
Soft 1	**-і**	ліка́рня	лікарн-	ліка́рн**і**
Soft 2	**-ї**	ле́кція	лекці-	ле́кці**ї**

Masculine Nouns: Nominative Plural Endings				
Declension	*Endings*	*Nominative Singular*	*Stem*	*Nominative Plural*
Hard	**-и**	зо́шит	зошит-	зо́шит**и**
Mixed	**-і**	ґара́ж	ґараж-	ґараж**і́**
Soft 1	**-і**	у́чень	учн-	у́чн**і**
Soft 2	**-ї**	музе́й	музе-	музе́**ї**

Nouns like **студе́нтка** and **студе́нт** have their own plural forms; however, if both genders are being referred to, the **masculine** plural form is used.

студе́нтки	female students
студе́нти	male students **or** male and female students

Practise Oral Exercise 12.2

F.2 Neuter Nouns

Hard and Mixed Declensions: **-а**

Soft 1 and Soft 2 Declensions: **-я**

For Soft 2 Declension neuter nouns, the nominative singular and plural forms are identical. In order to determine whether one of these nouns is being used in the singular or plural, you have to look at the context in which it is being used.

Neuter Nouns: Nominative Plural Endings

Declension	*Endings*	*Nominative Singular*	*Stem*	*Nominative Plural*
Hard	**-а**	мі́сто	міст-	**міста́**
Mixed	**-а**	прі́звище	прізвищ-	**прі́звища**
Soft 1	**-я**	мі́сце	місц-	**місця́**
Soft 2	**-я**	завда́ння	завданн-	**завда́ння**

Practise Oral Exercise 12.3

F.3 Summary Chart: Nominative Plural Endings

Summary: Nominative Plural Endings

	Hard	*Mixed*	*Soft 1*	*Soft 2*
Feminine	**-и**	**-і**	**-і**	**-ї**
Masculine	**-и**	**-і**	**-і**	**-ї**
Neuter	**-а**	**-а**	**-я**	**-я**

Practise Oral Exercises 12.4, 12.5, 12.6

Do Written Exercises 12.4, 12.5, 12.6

LESSON 13

A. VOCABULARY

Nouns

aunt	ті́тка
boy	хло́пець (хлопц-)
brother	брат
child	дити́на; *pl.* ді́ти
cousin	кузе́н; кузи́на, кузи́нка
daughter	дочка́
daughter-in-law	неві́стка
family *[extended]*	рідня́
family *[immediate]*	роди́на, *сім'я́*
farm	фа́рма, *фе́рма*
farmer	фа́рмер *[h]*, *фе́рмер [h]* фа́рмерка, *фе́рмерка*
father, dad	ба́тько (батьк-), та́то (тат-)
father-in-law *[man's]*	тесть
father-in-law *[woman's]*	све́кор (свекр-)
girl	ді́вчина; *pl.* дівча́та
granddaughter	ону́ка, ву́нка
grandfather, grandpa	дід, діду́сь
grandmother, granny	ба́ба, бабу́ся
grandson	ону́к, внук
great granddaughter	пра́внука
great grandfather	пра́дід
great grandmother	праба́ба
great grandson	пра́внук
husband	чолові́к, муж
Miss	па́нна
mother, mom	ма́ма
mother-in-law *[man's]*	те́ща
mother-in-law *[woman's]*	свекру́ха
Mr., sir	пан
Mrs., madam	па́ні *[indecl.]*

nephew	племі́нник
niece	племі́нниця
parents	батьки́ *[pl]*, ро́дичі *[pl]*
person	люди́на; *pl.* лю́ди
relative	ро́дич; ро́дичка
sister	сестра́
son	син
son-in-law	зять
uncle	дя́дько (дядьк-)
waiter	офіція́нт, *офіціа́нт*
waitress	офіція́нтка, *офіціа́нтка*
wife	дружи́на, жі́нка

Vocabulary Notes

1. ***In English***, **Mr.**, **Mrs.**, and **Miss** are always capitalized.

   In Ukrainian, **пан, па́ні**, and **па́нна** are capitalized only when they appear at the beginning of a sentence.

2. The feminine nouns **дити́на** and **люди́на** are used in the singular for both male and female human beings.

Він – дити́на (люди́на).	He is a child (a person).
Вона́ – дити́на (люди́на).	She is a child (a person).

3. The nouns **дити́на, ді́вчина**, and **люди́на** are used only in the singular; the plural forms are, respectively, **ді́ти**, **дівча́та**, and **лю́ди**. In the Vocabularies, such words are separated by a semi-colon, and *pl.* precedes the plural form: **дити́на;** ***pl.*** **ді́ти**.

Nominative Singular	*Nominative Plural*
дити́на	ді́ти
ді́вчина	дівча́та
люди́на	лю́ди

4. **Сім'я́** is a feminine, Soft 2 Declension noun.

Nominative Singular	*Stem*	*Nominative Plural*
сім'**я́**	сім'-	сі́м'ї

5. **Terms of Kinship**

In this lesson you are introduced to the most basic terms of kinship. Later, you will learn synonyms for these words. You will also learn that, in some instances, kinship is viewed differently in Ukrainian than in English.

1) **Мáма** is the English **mom**; the more formal word is **мáти**. Only **мáма** will be used now, as **мáти** belongs to a declension that is introduced later in this text.

2) **Тáто** is the English **dad** or **daddy**; the more formal **father** is **бáтько**.

3) The word **батьки́** is usually used for **parents**. In Canada, the term **рóдичі** is also used for **parents**; in Ukraine, **рóдичі** means **relatives**.

4) There are many terms for **grandmother (grandma, granny)**and **grandfather (granddad, grandpa)** but **бáба/бабýся** and **дід/дідýсь** are most commonly used. **Дід** is sometimes **ді́до** in the nominative singular case.

   There is no Ukrainian word for **grandparents**.

5) Both **внýк** and **внýка** have alternate forms: **у̲нýк** and **у̲нýка**; however, these form are rarely used. There is also a word in Ukrainian for a very young **grandchild** that you will learn later in this text.

   The Ukrainian word for **granchildren** of any age is **онýки (внýки)**, the nominative plural form for both **онýк (внук)** and **онýка (внýка)**.

6) The prefix **пра-** is used in Ukrainian to convey the relationship between **great grandparents** and **great grandchildren**.

   There is no Ukrainian word for **great grandparents**; **прáдіди** is one of the words that is used for **ancestors**.

7) **Ті́тка (aunt)**, **дя́дько (uncle)**, **племі́нниця (niece)** and **племі́нник (nephew)** may be viewed as "generic" terms; there are different words for these relatives if they are on your mother's or your father's side of the family, and, even more specifically, if they are blood relatives or related through marriage.

8) There are other terms for both male and female cousins, but the terms **кузéн**, and **кузи́на, кузи́нка** are the easiest to use and remember.

9) A **man's** father-in-law is **тесть**; his mother-in-law is **тéща**.

   A **woman's** father-in-law is **свéкор**; her mother-in-law is **свекрýха**.

10) The word **чолові́к** is used both for **man** and for **husband**.

   The word **жі́нка** is used both for **woman** and for **wife**.

B. VOCATIVE CASE

In English, when you use someone's name in speaking directly to him or her, you do not make any changes in it. When you write down what you have said, you simply set off the name from the rest of the sentence with a comma.

> **Ivan**, are you *[s]* at home?
>
> Where are you *[s]* going, **Tamara**?

In Ukrainian, you also use a comma to set off the name from the rest of the sentence; in addition, however, you have to change the ending of the noun.

The nominative singular forms of **Ivan** and **Tamara** in Ukrainian are, respectively, **Іва́н** and **Тама́ра**. Let's see how the two English sentences given above are translated into Ukrainian.

> **Ivan**, are you *[s]* at home?
>
> **Іва́не**, ти вдо́ма?
>
> Where are you *[s]* going, **Tamara**?
>
> Куди́ ти йде́ш, **Тама́ро**?

In the two English sentences, when you speak directly to either Ivan or Tamara, you do not make any changes in their names: **Ivan** remains **Ivan**, and **Tamara** remains **Tamara.**

In the two Ukrainian sentences, the endings of the nouns do change: from **Іва́н** to Іва́не; and from **Тама́ра** to **Тама́ро**. With the change in their endings, these nouns are no longer in the nominative case; they are now in the **vocative case**.

In this lesson you will learn all the endings that are attached to the stems of Ukrainian nouns to form both the vocative singular and the vocative plural cases.

In theory, both animate and inanimate nouns may be in the vocative case in Ukrainian; however, it is highly unlikely that you will ever have the occasion to speak directly to an inanimate object.

> **Ґу́мко**, де ти?
>
> **Eraser**, where are you *[s]*? (!)

C. VOCATIVE PLURAL ENDINGS

The vocative plural endings are added to the **stem** of a noun.

C.1 All Genders

The vocative plural endings for almost all nouns are the same as the nominative plural endings. (Check the charts in Lesson 12, F.)

Feminine Nouns: Vocative Plural Endings				
Declension	***Endings***	***Nominative Singular***	***Stem***	***Vocative Plural***
Hard	**-и**	сестрá	сестр-	сéстр**и**
Mixed	**-і**	тéща	тещ-	тéщ**і**
Soft 1	**-і**	бабýся	бабус-	бабýс**і**
Soft 2	**-ї**	Марíя	Марі-	Марí**ї**

Masculine Nouns: Vocative Plural Endings				
Declension	***Endings***	***Nominative Singular***	***Stem***	***Vocative Plural***
Hard	**-и**	брат	брат-	брат**и́**
Mixed	**-і**	товáриш	таовариш-	товариш**í**
Soft 1	**-і**	ýчень	учн-	ýчн**і**
Soft 2	**-ї**	водíй	воді-	воді**ї́**

Neuter Nouns: Vocative Plural Endings				
Declension	***Endings***	***Nominative Singular***	***Stem***	***Vocative Plural***
Hard	**-а**	мíсто	міст-	міст**á**
Mixed	**-а**	прíзвище	прізвищ-	прíзвищ**а**
Soft 1	**-я**	мíсце	місц-	місц**я́**
Soft 2	**-я**	завдáння	завданн-	завдáнн**я**

Learn the plural nominative and vocative forms for the nouns **ді́вчина, дити́на**, and **люди́на**.

Nominative Singular	*Nominative Plural*	*Vocative Plural*
ді́вчина	дівча́та	дівча́та
дити́на	ді́ти	ді́ти
люди́на	лю́ди	лю́ди

The vocative plural form for **пан** is **пано́ве**, and the phrase "Ladies and Gentlemen!" is "**Пані́ й пано́ве**!".

To form the vocative case of inanimate nouns that are always plural, you simply use their nominative forms.

C.2 Summary Chart: Vocative Plural Endings

In the charts in this text, the following notation is used to indicate that the vocative plural endings are the same as the nominative plural endings: [=Npl]

Summary: Vocative Plural Endings				
	Hard	*Mixed*	*Soft 1*	*Soft 2*
Feminine	**-и** [=Npl]	**-і** [=Npl]	**-і** [=Npl]	**-ї** [=Npl]
Masculine	**-и** [=Npl]	**-і** [=Npl]	**-і** [=Npl]	**-ї** [=Npl]
Neuter	**-а** [=Npl]	**-а** [=Npl]	**-я** [=Npl]	**-я** [=Npl]

Practise Oral Exercise 13.1

Do Written Exercise 13.1

D. VOCATIVE SINGULAR ENDINGS

Vocative singular endings are added to the **stem** of a noun.

D.1 Feminine Nouns

The vocative singular endings for feminine nouns are quite straightforward. Three of the Declensions, the Hard, Mixed, and Soft 2, have their own distinctive endings.

There are, however, two possible endings for feminine Soft 1 Declension nouns in the vocative singular case: **-е** and **-ю.**

You will probably use the ending **-ю** much more frequently than the ending **-е,** as **-ю** is used for most personal names that end in **-я,** such as **Лéся,** and to express affection in terms of endearment, such as **бабýсю.**

Hard Declension: **-о**

Mixed Declension: **-е**

Soft 1 Declension: **-е** or **ю**

Soft 2 Declension: **-є**

Feminine Nouns: Vocative Singular Endings				
Declension	***Endings***	***Nominative Singular***	***Stem***	***Vocative Singular***
Hard	**-о**	сестрá	сестр-	сéстр**о**
Mixed	**-е**	тéща	тещ-	тéщ**е**
Soft 1	**-е** **-ю**	ученúця бабýся	учениц- бабус-	ученúц**е** бабýс**ю**
Soft 2	**-є**	Марíя	Марі-	Марí**є**

Practise Oral Exercise 13.2

D.2 Masculine Nouns

All masculine Hard Declension nouns, except those that have **-к** for a final consonant, take the ending **-е** in the singular vocative case.

Masculine Hard Declension nouns that end in **-к**, and all Mixed Declension nouns, except those that end in **-р** (only **школя́р** thus far in this text), take the vocative singular ending **-у**.

All masculine Soft Declension nouns, except Soft 1 Declension nouns that end in **-ець**, take the ending **-ю** in the vocative singular case.

For Soft 1 Declension nouns ending in **-ець**, the vowel **-е** is dropped when the stem is formed, and the final consonant **-ц** changes to **-ч** before the vocative singular ending **-е** is added.

Hard Declension: **-е, -ку**

Mixed Declension: **-у, -ре**

Soft 1 Declension: **-ю, -ець → -че**

Soft 2 Declension: **-ю**

Masculine Nouns: Vocative Singular Endings				
Declension	***Endings***	***Nominative Singular***	***Stem***	***Vocative Singular***
Hard	**-е**	кузе́н	кузен-	кузе́**не**
	-у	ба́тько	бать**к**-	ба́ть**ку**
Mixed	**-у**	ро́дич	родич-	ро́дич**у**
	-е	школя́р	школя**р**-	школя́**ре**
Soft 1	**-ю**	у́чень	учн-	у́чн**ю**
	-е	хло́п**ець**	хлоп**ц**-	хло́п**че**
Soft 2	**-ю**	водí**й**	водí-	водí**ю**

Learn these exceptions to the rules given above.

Nominative Singular	*Stem*	*Vocative Singular*
та́то	тат-	та́**ту**
син	син-	си́**ну**
дід	дід-	ді́**ду**
чоловí**к**	чоловí**к**-	чоловí**че**

D.3 Neuter Nouns

The vocative singular and the nominative singular endings are identical for all neuter nouns. In the Summary Chart (D.4), this is noted as: [=Nsg].

You will rarely (if ever!) have the opportunity to use neuter nouns in the vocative case.

Hard Declension: **-o**

Mixed Declension: **-e**

Soft 1 Declension: **-e**

Soft 2 Declension: **-я**

Neuter Nouns: Vocative Singular Endings				
Declension	***Endings***	***Nominative Singular***	***Stem***	***Vocative Singular***
Hard	**-o**	перó	пер-	пер**ó**
Mixed	**-e**	прíзвище	прізвищ-	прíзвищ**е**
Soft 1	**-e**	мíсце	місц-	мíсц**е**
Soft 2	**-я**	завдáння	завданн-	завдáнн**я**

D.4 Summary Chart: Vocative Singular Endings

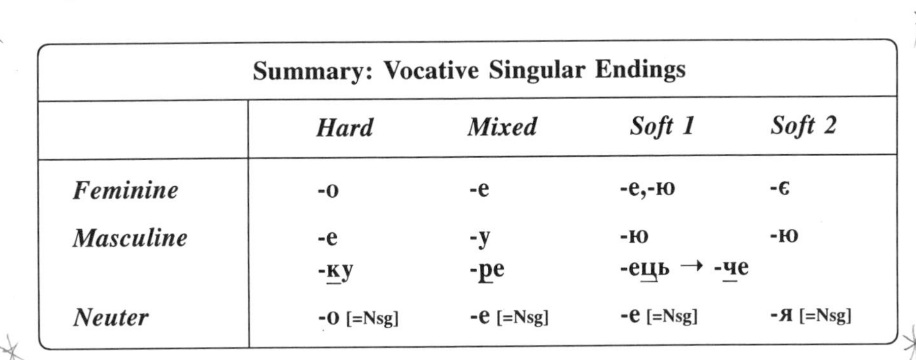

Summary: Vocative Singular Endings				
	Hard	***Mixed***	***Soft 1***	***Soft 2***
Feminine	**-o**	**-e**	**-е,-ю**	**-є**
Masculine	**-e** **-ку**	**-у** **-ре**	**-ю** **-ець → -че**	**-ю**
Neuter	**-o** [=Nsg]	**-e** [=Nsg]	**-e** [=Nsg]	**-я** [=Nsg]

Practise Oral Exercises 13.3, 13.4

Do Written Exercise 13.2

E. VOCATIVE CASE: PERSONAL NAMES

In English, Ukrainian names are either left as they are (e.g. "Андрíй" is transliterated as "Andriy"), or English names are selected as equivalents (e.g."Андрíй" – "Andrew").

In Ukrainian, English personal names that end like Ukrainian feminine and masculine nouns are declined. In the following examples, the name **Diana** ends in the vowel **-a** like Ukrainian feminine nouns, and the name **Edward** ends in a consonant like Ukrainian masculine nouns; therefore, both these names may be declined.

	Nominative Singular	*Stem*	*Vocative Singular*
Diana	Дія́на	Діян-	Дія́но
Edward	Е́двард	Едвард-	Е́дварде

English names that end differently than Ukrainian nouns are treated as **indeclinable nouns** (their endings do not change). Unlike Ukrainian feminine nouns that end in either **-a** or **-я**, the name **Sharon** ends in a consonant; and, unlike Ukrainian masculine nouns that end in a consonant, the name **Ronny** ends in the vowel **-i** when it is transliterated into Ukrainian. These two names, therefore, are not declined in Ukrainian.

	Nominative Singular	*Stem*	*Vocative Singular*
Sharon	Ше́рон	—	Ше́рон
Ronny	Ро́нні	—	Ро́нні

There are a few Ukrainian **masculine** personal names that end in **-a**; these names are declined like Ukrainian feminine nouns.

	Nominative Singular	*Stem*	*Vocative Singular*
Mykola	Мико́ла	Микол-	Мико́ло

Ukrainian masculine and feminine personal names that are used in this text are listed in the Appendix E. This Appendix also includes a list of Ukrainian surnames included in the text.

Usually, there is more than one way in which Ukrainian personal names and surnames are written in English; some of these alternate spellings are provided in the lists.

Practise Oral Exercise 13.5

Do Written Exercise 13.3

F. POLITE FORMS OF ADDRESS

In Ukraine, the preferred form of polite address is to use a person's first name along with his or her patronymic. The patronymic is formed from the first name of one's father.

The patronymic of a son whose father is named **Ivan** is **Ivanovych** (son of Ivan); the patronymic of the daughter is **Ivanivna** (daughter of Ivan).

When this form of address is used, both the personal name and the patronymic are in the vocative case.

Куди́ **ви** йдете́, **Рома́не Іва́новичу**?
Where are you *[pl]* going, Roman Ivanovych?

Де **ви** живете́, **Тама́ро Іва́нівно**?
Where do you *[pl]* live, Tamara Ivanivna?

In Canada, the patronymic is not widely used. Depending on how well they know one another, most Ukrainian-speaking Canadians address each other politely in a number of ways.

1. The vocative case of **пан** or **па́нна** is used with a person's surname. The surname is not declined, and, as you were told in the Vocabulary Notes, **па́ні** is not declined. This is the most formal way of addressing people politely.

   Куди́ **ви** йдете́, **па́не Коза́к**?
   Where are you *[pl]* going, Mr. Kozak?

   Па́нно Гонча́р, ви вчите́ся?
   Miss Honchar, are you *[pl]* studying?

   Де **ви** живете́, **па́ні Савчу́к**?
   Where do you *[pl]* live, Mrs. Sawchuk?

2. The vocative case of **пан** or **па́нна** is used with a personal name. **Па́ні** is not declined. This form of polite address is more familiar than the previous one presented above, which uses the surname.

   Па́не Е́дварде, ви лю́бите танцюва́ти?
   (Mr.) Edward, do you *[pl]* like to dance?

   Ви прекра́сно співа́єте, **па́нно Суза́нно**!
   You *[pl]* sing beautifully, (Miss) Susanna!

   Пані Мари́но, чому́ **ви** не смієте́ся?
   (Mrs.) Maryna, why aren't you *[pl]* laughing?

3. The polite/formal pronoun **ви** is used with the vocative case of a personal name (without пан, пáнна, or пáні). This form of polite address is used with people whom one knows quite well. (For very close friends, as explained in Lesson 2, the pronoun **ти** is used.)

   Ви хóчете обíдати, **Богдáне**?
   Do you *[pl]* want to have dinner, Bohdan?

   Чомý **ви** смієтéся, **Мáрто**?
   Why are you *[pl]* laughing, Martha?

4. If you do not know the name of the person whom you wish to address politely, it is proper to use only **пан** or **пáнна** in the vocative case, or **пані**.

   Пáне, **ви** знáєте, де канцелярíя?
   (Mr.) Sir, do you *[pl]* know, where the office is?

   Пáнно, **ви** знáєте, хто тут сидúть?
   Miss, do you *[pl]* know who is sitting here?

   Пáні, **ви** тут працю́єте?
   (Mrs.) Madam, do you *[pl]* work here?

5. Occasionally you will hear **пан** or **пáнна** in the vocative case, or **пáні**, used with the title that indicates the occupation of the person who is being addressed.

   Пáне поліцáю, чомý **ви** спішитé?
   (Mr. Police Officer) Sir, why are you *[pl]* hurrying?

   Пáнно бібліотéкарко, чи **ви** тут працю́єте?
   (Miss Librarian) Miss, do you *[pl]* work here?

   Пáні вчúтелько, **ви** вже йдетé додóму?
   (Mrs. Teacher) Madam, are you *[pl]* going home already?

Practise Oral Exercises 13.6, 13.7

Do Written Exercises 13.4, 13.5, 13.6, 13.7

LESSON 14

A. VOCABULARY

Nouns

balcony	бальќон, балќон,
bank *[building]*	банк
basement	пивни́ця, підвáл
bathroom	лазни́чка, умивáльня, *туалéт*
bed	лíжко
bedroom	спáльня
bookstore	книгáрня
cashier	каси́р *[h]*; каси́рка
cash register	кáса
couch	канáпа
cupboard, closet	шáфа
customer	покупéць (покупц-); покупни́ця
dining room	їдáльня
drawer	шухля́да
floor	підлóга
furniture	мéблі *[pl]*
kitchen	кýхня
living room	вітáльня
money	грóші *[pl]*
pantry, storage room	комóра
road	дорóга
room	кімнáта
rug, tapestry, kylym	ки́ли́м
salesclerk	продавéць (продавц-); продавни́ця, *продавщи́ця*
shelf	поли́ця
showcase, display window	вітри́на
sidewalk	хідни́к, *тротуáр [h]*
store	крамни́ця, склеп, *магази́н*
street	вýлиця
study	кабінéт
veranda	верáнда
wall	стінá

Prepositions

in	у/в
on, at	на

Vocabulary Notes

1. ***In Ukraine***, the word **ки́лим** is used both for a decorative wall hanging or tapestry that is woven out of wool, and for an area rug. ***In Canada***, **ки́лим** is also used for wall-to-wall carpeting.

2. ***In Ukraine***, a public washroom is called a **туале́т**. The bathroom in a home is divided into two parts that are often separated into two small rooms: the sink and bathtub are in the part/room referred to as a **ва́нна кімна́та**, while the toilet is in the part/room that is called a **туале́т**.

B. LOCATIVE CASE

In English, we often use sentences that indicate the location of someone or something.

In the two sentences that follow, the bolded words tell us **where** someone or something is; in other words, they indicate the **location** of someone or something.

1. The child is **in the bedroom**.
2. The knapsack is **on the chair**.

If you look carefully at the bolded words in these two sentences, you will see that there is a pattern to them: they both begin with **in** or **on**, and end with a noun.

The words **in** and **on** are known as **prepositions** and, together with the nouns that follow them, they form **prepositional phrases**.

Prepositional phrases provide us with more information about another part of speech in a sentence. In the examples used above, they tell us **where** something or someone is.

In Ukrainian, prepositional phrases are also used to indicate location.

Let's look at how the two English sentences presented above are translated into Ukrainian.

1. The child is **in the bedroom**.
   Дити́на **у спа́льні.**

2. The knapsack is **on the chair.**
   Наплє́чник **на крі́слі**.

In both the English and Ukrainian sentences, the bolded words form **prepositional phrases** that begin with a preposition and end with a noun.

Like their English counterparts, the Ukrainian phrases, beginning with the prepositions **на** or **у**, provide information about the **location** of the subject; in other words, they tell us **where** someone or something is.

In the Ukrainian sentences, however, the endings of the noun in the prepositional phrases are changed from their nominative singular endings.

Whenever a noun is used after the prepositions **на** or **у** to indicate **location** in Ukrainian, its ending must be changed so that it is in the **locative case**.

Different endings are added to the **stems** of nouns to form the singular locative case and the plural locative case.

C. LOCATIVE PLURAL ENDINGS

The same endings are used to form the locative plural case of nouns of all genders.

C.1 All Genders

The locative case is always used with prepositions; therefore, in the charts in this text, nouns and pronouns in the locative case are preceded by ellipsis periods (**...**) to remind you that a preposition has been omitted.

Hard and Mixed Declensions: **-ах**

Soft 1 and Soft 2 Declensions: **-ях**

Feminine Nouns: Locative Plural Endings				
Declension	***Endings***	***Nominative Singular***	***Stem***	***Locative Plural***
Hard	**-ах**	кля́са	кляс-	... кля́с**ах**
Mixed	**-ах**	афі́ша	афіш-	... афі́ш**ах**
Soft 1	**-ях**	ку́хня	кухн-	... ку́хн**ях**
Soft 2	**-ях**	ле́кція	лекці-	... ле́кці**ях**

Masculine Nouns: Locative Plural Endings				
Declension	***Endings***	***Nominative Singular***	***Stem***	***Locative Plural***
Hard	**-ах**	банк	банк-	... ба́нк**ах**
Mixed	**-ах**	ро́дич	родич-	... ро́дич**ах**
Soft 1	**-ях**	у́чень	учн-	... у́чн**ях**
Soft 2	**-ях**	музе́й	музе-	... музе́**ях**

Neuter Nouns: Locative Plural Endings				
Declension	***Endings***	***Nominative Singular***	***Stem***	***Locative Plural***
Hard	**-ах**	лі́жко	ліжк-	... лі́жк**ах**
Mixed	**-ах**	прі́звище	прізвищ-	... прі́звищ**ах**
Soft 1	**-ях**	мі́сце	місц-	... місц**я́х**
Soft 2	**-ях**	завда́ння	завданн-	... завда́нн**ях**

Learn the locative forms of the following nouns that are always plural.

	Nominative Plural	***Locative Plural***	***Nominative Plural***	***Locative Plural***
Animate	батьки́	... батьк**а́х**	лю́ди	... лю́д**ях**
	дівча́та	... дівча́т**ах**	ді́ти	... ді́т**ях**
Inanimate	схо́ди	... схо́д**ах**	две́рі	... две́р**ях**
	гро́ші	... гро́ш**ах**	ме́блі	... ме́бл**ях**

C.2 Summary Chart: Locative Plural Endings

Summary: Locative Plural Endings				
	Hard	*Mixed*	*Soft 1*	*Soft 2*
Feminine	**-ах**	**-ах**	**-ях**	**-ях**
Masculine	**-ах**	**-ах**	**-ях**	**-ях**
Neuter	**-ах**	**-ах**	**-ях**	**-ях**

Practise Oral Exercises 14.1, 14.2, 14.3

Do Written Exercises 14.1, 14.2

D. LOCATIVE SINGULAR ENDINGS

Except for masculine animate (human) nouns, the locative singular endings are similar for all genders.

D.1 Feminine Nouns

The stems of feminine Hard Declension nouns ending in **-г, -к, -х** are changed before the locative singular ending **-і** is added to them; stems ending in **г**: **г → з**; stems ending in **к**: **к → ц**; stems ending in **х**: **х → с**.

Hard, Mixed, and Soft 1 Declensions: **-і**

Soft 2 Declension: **-ї**

Feminine Nouns: Locative Singular Endings				
Declension	*Endings*	*Nominative Singular*	*Stem*	*Locative Singular*
Hard	-і	ша́фа	шаф-	... ша́фі
		доро́га	дорог-	... доро́зі
		те́чка	течк-	... течці
		свекру́ха	свекрух-	... свекру́сі
Mixed	-і	афі́ша	афіш-	... афі́ші
Soft 1	-і	ку́хня	кухн-	... ку́хні
Soft 2	-ї	ле́кція	лекці-	... ле́кції

Practise Oral Exercise 14.4

D.2 Masculine Nouns

The locative singular endings for masculine animate (human) nouns differ from those of masculine animate (animals) and masculine inanimate nouns.

1. Animate Nouns (Humans)

Masculine animate nouns that refer to humans have a distinctive set of endings.

Hard Declension: **-ові**

Mixed and Soft 1 Declensions: **-еві**

Soft 2 Declension: **-єві**

Masculine Animate (Human) Nouns: Locative Singular Endings				
Declension	***Endings***	***Nominative Singular***	***Stem***	***Locative Singular***
Hard	**-ові**	син	син-	... си́**нові**
Mixed	**-еві**	ро́дич	родич-	... ро́дич**еві**
Soft 1	**-еві**	у́чень	учн-	... у́чн**еві**
Soft 2	**-єві**	воді́й	воді-	... воді́**єві**

Practise Oral Exercise 14.5

2. Inanimate Nouns and Animate (Animals) Nouns

Masculine animate nouns that refer to animals (you haven't learned any thus far in this text) usually take the same locative singular endings as inanimate nouns; however, you will find that some animals (especially domesticated ones) may take the same locative singular endings as human nouns,

Masculine Hard Declension nouns ending in **-к** usually take the ending **-у** in the locative singular case.

A few masculine Hard Declension nouns that end in **-г**, **-к**, and **-х**, undergo the same change in their stems as feminine nouns before the locative singular ending **-і** is added; stems ending in **г**: **г** → **з**; stems ending in **к**: **к** → **ц**; stems ending in **х**: **х** → **с**. When a noun like this is introduced in this text, this change will be noted for you in the Vocabulary Notes.

Hard Declension: **-і**
-у for stems ending in **-к**

Mixed and Soft 1 Declensions: **-і**

Soft 2 Declension: **-ї**

Masculine Inanimate and Animate (Animals) Nouns: Locative Singular Endings				
Declension	***Endings***	***Nominative Singular***	***Stem***	***Locative Singular***
Hard	**-і**	зо́шит	зошит-	... зо́шит**і**
	-у	банк	банк-	... ба́нк**у**
Mixed	**-і**	ґара́ж	ґараж-	... ґара́ж**і**
Soft 1	**-і**	готе́ль	готел-	... готе́л**і**
Soft 2	**-ї**	музе́й	музе-	... музе́**ї**

Practise Oral Exercise 14.6

D.3 Neuter Nouns

Neuter Hard Declension nouns that have a stem ending in **a consonant and -к** take the locative singular ending **-у**. For all other neuter nouns, the ending is **-і**.

Hard Declension: **-і**
-у for stems ending in **consonant + к**

Mixed, Soft 1, and Soft 2 Declensions: **-і**

Neuter Nouns: Locative Singular Endings				
Declension	***Endings***	***Nominative Singular***	***Stem***	***Locative Singular***
Hard	-і	крі́сло	крісл-	... крі́сл**і**
	-у	лі́жко	ліжк-	... лі́жк**у**
Mixed	-і	прі́звище	прізвищ-	... прі́звищ**і**
Soft 1	-і	мі́сце	місц-	... мі́сц**і**
Soft 2	-і	завда́ння	завда́нн-	... завда́нн**і**

Practise Oral Exercise 14.7

D.4 Summary Chart: Locative Singular Endings

Summary: Locative Singular Endings				
	Hard	*Mixed*	*Soft 1*	*Soft 2*
Feminine	-і	-і	-і	-ї
Masculine				
– Animate: Human	-ові	-еві	-еві	-єві
– Animate: Animals	-і -ку	-і	-і	-ї
– Inanimate	-і -ку	-і	-і	-ї
Neuter	-і -ку	-і	-і	-і

Practise Oral Exercises 14.8, 14.9

Do Written Exercises 14.3, 14.4

E. LOCATIVE CASE: DECLENSION OF PRONOUNS

In Ukrainian, pronouns, like nouns, are declined when they are used in the locative case. Unlike nouns, however, pronouns look quite different when they are in the locative case!

E.1 Interrogative Pronouns

In English, the interrogative pronoun **who** changes when it is used with a preposition. The interrogative pronoun **what** does not change.

who	On **whom** do you see something?
what	On **what** do you see something

In Ukrainian, both **хто** and **що** change when they are used in the locative case.

Nominative Case	*Locative Case*
хто	**... кóму**
що	**... чóму**

Let's look at how the English sentences are translated into Ukrainian.

On **whom** do you *[s]* see something?
На **кóму** ти щось бáчиш?

On **what** do you *[s]* see something?
На **чóму** ти щось бáчиш?

E.2 Personal Pronouns

In English, five personal pronouns change when they are used with prepositions. Three personal pronouns do not change.

Singular Pronouns		*Plural Pronouns*	
I	Is it on **me**?	**we**	Is it on **us**?
you *[s]*	Is it on you?	you *[p]*	Is it on you?
he	Is it on **him**?	**they**	Is it on **them**?
she	Is it on **her**?		
it	Is it on it?		

Singular Pronouns		***Plural Pronouns***	
I	**me**	**we**	**us**
you *[s]*	you	you *[p]*	you
he	**him**	**they**	**them**
she	**her**		
it	it		

In Ukrainian, all the personal pronouns change when they are used with prepositions in the locative case.

Singular Pronouns		**Plural Pronouns**	
Nominative Case	***Locative Case***	***Nominative Case***	***Locative Case***
я	... **мéні**	**ми**	... **нас**
ти	... **тóбі**	**ви**	... **вас**
вонá	... **ній**	**вони́**	... **них**
він	... **ньóму**		
вонó	... **ньóму**		

Practise Oral Exercise 14.10

Do Written Exercise 14.5

F. WORD ORDER IN UKRAINIAN

In English, definite and indefinite articles are used to distinguish between a specific person or object and one that is not specified.

Compare the following two sets of questions and answers.

In the first example, reference is being made to **the book** for which someone is looking.

In the second example, reference is being made to the fact that the object on the floor happens to be **a book.** This response is introduced by the words **there is (there's)**.

1. Where is **the book**?
   The book is on the floor.

2. **What's** on the floor?
   There's a book on the floor.

In Ukrainian, because there are no definite or indefinite articles, **the difference in meaning may be expressed by changing the word order in a sentence.**

Where is **the book**?	Де **кни́жка**?
The book is on the floor.	**Кни́жка** на підло́зі.
What's on the floor?	**Що** на підло́зі?
There's a book on the floor.	На підло́зі **кни́жка**.

Notice that the words **there is (there's)**, in the second English example, do not appear in the Ukrainian response. It is important to remember this when you are translating sentences from English into Ukrainian.

Let's look at examples with a plural noun.

In English, using a plural noun does not change the way in which the first response is structured; however, in the second English response, the indefinite article **a** disappears, and the sentence is introduced with the words **there are**.

In Ukrainian, the same sentence structure is used in the responses for both singular and plural nouns.

Where are **the books**?	Де **книжки́**?
The books are on the floor.	**Книжки́** на підло́зі.
What's on the floor?	**Що** на підло́зі?
There are books on the floor.	На підло́зі **книжки́**.

Practise Oral Exercises 14.11, 14.12

Do Written Exercise 14.6

LESSON 15

A. VOCABULARY

Nouns

apple	я́блуко
banana	бана́н
baseball *[game]*	бейсбо́л
basketball *[game]*	баскетбо́л
beer	пи́во
breakfast	сніда́нок (сніданк-)
cards *[playing cards]*	ка́рти *[pl]*
checkers	ша́шки *[pl]*
chess	ша́хи *[pl]*
cocktail	builtin коктейль
coffee	ка́ва
concert	конце́рт
football, soccer *[game]*	футбо́л
formal dance, ball	заба́ва, баль
golf	ґольф, *гольф*
hockey	го́кей, *хоке́й*
juice	сік (сок-)
lunch, dinner *[meal at noon]*	обі́д
milk	молоко́
movies, movie theatre	кіно́ *[indecl.]*
orange	помара́нча, *апельси́н*
party, evening social	вечі́рка
punch *[drink]*	пунш
snack, light lunch	пере́куска
stadium	стадіо́н
supper, dinner *[evening meal]*	вече́ря
tea	чай
tennis	те́ніс
theatre	теа́тр *[h]*
ticket	квито́к (квитк-)
volleyball *[game]*	волейбо́л
water	вода́
wine	вино́

Prepositions

about	про
for	за, на
into	у/в

Verbs

to enter, to come into	вхóдити: вхóджу, вхóд-иш
to have	мáти: мá-ю, -єш
to play	грáти: грá-ю, -єш
to prepare	готувáти: готý-ю, -єш
to put, to place	клáсти: клад-ý, -éш

Vocabulary Notes

1. There are Ukrainian terms for the various sports; however, the international terms are usually used now, both in Ukraine and in Canada. In Ukraine, **футбóл** means soccer, and **америкáнський футбóл** (American football) is used for football.

2. The word **кінó** is used for a movie theatre; **теáтр** is used for live stage productions.

B. ACCUSATIVE CASE: DIRECT OBJECT

The main function of the accusative case is to serve as the direct object in a sentence.

In English, many sentences have a **direct object**.

1. **The woman loves the child.**

Subject:	(Who loves?)	**The woman**.
Predicate:	(What does she do?)	She **loves.**
Direct Object:	(Whom does she love?)	She loves **the child.**

2. **The boy is buying a poster.**

Subject:	(Who is buying?)	**The boy**.
Predicate:	(What is he doing?)	He **is buying**.
Direct Object:	(What is he buying?)	He is buying **a poster**.

In both sentences, someone else or something else is being directly affected by the action of the subject: the child is loved by the woman; the poster is being bought by the boy.

The person or thing affected by the action of the subject is known as the **direct object**.

In Ukrainian, there also are many sentences that have a direct oject.

There is a difference, however, in the endings that nouns have when they are the direct object of a negated verb (a verb that **is** negated) and when they are the direct object of an affirmative verb (a verb that **is not** negated).

In this text, a verb that **is** negated is called a **negated verb**; a verb that **is not** negated is called an **affirmative verb**.

Negated Verb:	Ми **не читáємо**.
Affirmative Verb:	Ми **читáємо**.

When a noun is the direct object of an affirmative verb, it is in the **accusative case**.

Let's look at how the English sentences presented above are translated into Ukrainian.

1. **Жíнка лю́бить дити́ну.**

Subject:	(Хто лю́бить?)	**Жíнка** лю́бить.
Predicate:	(Що жíнка рóбить?)	Вонá **лю́бить**.
Direct Object:	(Когó вонá лю́бить?)	Вонá лю́бить **дити́ну**.

2. **Хлóпець купу́є афíшу.**

Subject:	(Хто купу́є?)	**Хлóпець**.
Predicate:	(Що хлóпець робить?)	Він **купу́є**.
Direct Object:	(Що він купу́є?)	Він купу́є **афíшу**.

In the English sentences, the nouns **child** and **poster** do not change when they are used as direct objects and neither does the interrogative pronoun **what**.

The interrogative pronoun **who** changes to **whom**.

In the Ukrainian sentences, the endings of the feminine nouns that are used as direct objects do change: **дити́на** → **дити́ну**, and **афíша** → **афíшу**. These two nouns are no longer in the nominative case; now that they are direct objects of affirmative verbs, they are in the accusative case.

The interrogative pronoun **хто** becomes **когó**; **що** does not change.

Not all Ukrainian nouns change their endings when they are used as direct objects of affirmative verbs; however, if they have this function in a sentence, they are considered to be in the accusative case.

C. ACCUSATIVE SINGULAR ENDINGS

The accusative singular endings are attached to the **stems** of nouns.

C.1 Feminine Nouns

The accusative singular endings are the same for feminine animate and inanimate nouns.

Hard and Mixed Declensions: **-у**

Soft 1 and Soft 2 Declensions: **-ю**

Feminine Nouns: Accusative Singular Endings				
Declension	***Endings***	***Nominative Singular***	***Stem***	***Accusative Singular***
Hard	**-у**	вода́	вод-	**во́ду**
Mixed	**-у**	помара́нча	памаранч-	**помара́нчу**
Soft 1	**-ю**	вече́ря	вечер-	**вече́рю**
Soft 2	**-ю**	ле́кція	лекці-	**ле́кцію**

Practise Oral Exercise 15.1

C.2 Masculine Nouns

The accusative singular endings are different for masculine animate and inanimate nouns.

1. Animate Nouns

Masculine animate nouns take one of two endings: **-а** or **-я**.

Hard and Mixed Declensions: **-а**

Soft 1 and Soft 2 Declensions: **-я**

Masculine (Animate) Nouns: Accusative Singular Endings				
Declension	***Endings***	***Nominative Singular***	***Stem***	***Accusative Singular***
Hard	**-а**	брат	брат-	**бра́та**
Mixed	**-а**	ро́дич	родич-	**ро́дича**
Soft 1	**-я**	продаве́ць	прдавц-	**продавця́**
Soft 2	**-я**	поліца́й	поліца-	**поліца́я**

2. Inanimate Nouns

For inanimate masculine nouns, the accusative singular form is the same as the nominative singular form: [=Nsg].

Hard, Mixed, Soft 1, and Soft 2 Declensions: [=Nsg]

Masculine (Inanimate) Nouns: Accusative Singular Endings				
Declension	***Endings***	***Nominative Singular***	***Stem***	***Accusative Singular***
Hard	**[consonant]**	буди́нок	будинок-	буди́н**ок**
Mixed	**[жчшщ]**	ґара́ж	ґараж-	ґара́**ж**
Soft 1	**-ь**	готе́ль	готел-	готе́л**ь**
Soft 2	**-й**	музе́й	музе-	музе́**й**

C.3 Neuter Nouns

For neuter nouns, the accusative singular form is the same as the nominative form: [=Nsg].

Hard, Mixed, Soft 1, and Soft 2 Declensions: [=Nsg]

Neuter Nouns: Accusative Singular Endings				
Declension	***Endings***	***Nominative Singular***	***Stem***	***Accusative Singular***
Hard	**-о**	а́вто	авт-	а́вт**о**
Mixed	**-е**	прі́зище	прізвищ-	прі́звищ**е**
Soft 1	**-е**	мі́сце	місц-	мі́сц**е**
Soft 2	**-я**	завда́ння	завданн-	завда́нн**я**

Practise Oral Exercises 15.2, 15.3

C.4 Summary Chart: Accusative Singular Endings

Summary: Accusative Singular Endings				
	Hard	*Mixed*	*Soft 1*	*Soft 2*
Feminine	**-у**	**-у**	**-ю**	**-ю**
Masculine				
– Animate	**-а**	**-а**	**-я**	**-я**
– Inanimate	[=Nsg]	[=Nsg]	[=Nsg]	[=Nsg]
Neuter	[=Nsg]	[=Nsg]	[=Nsg]	[=Nsg]

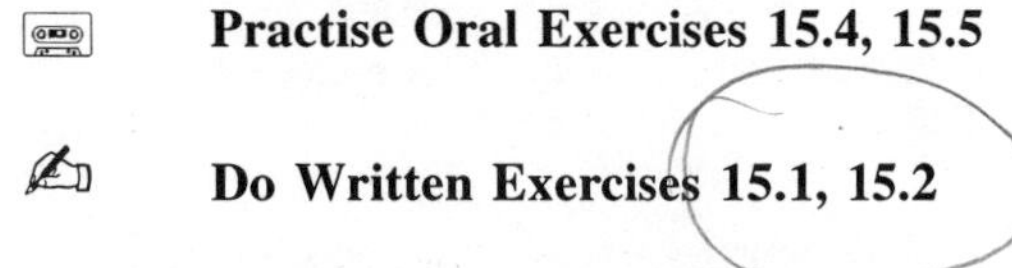

Practise Oral Exercises 15.4, 15.5

Do Written Exercises 15.1, 15.2

D. ACCUSATIVE PLURAL ENDINGS

The only new endings that you have to learn for the accusative plural endings are the ones for **feminine and masculine animate nouns**.

D.1 Feminine Nouns

The accusative plural endings are different for feminine **animate** and **inanimate** nouns.

1. **Animate Nouns**

   For Hard and Mixed Declension nouns, the **stem** of the noun is used for the accusative plural case. For Soft 1 Declension nouns **-ь** is added to the stem, and for Soft 2 Declension nouns, **-й** is added.

   If the stem of a Hard Declension noun ends in **a consonant and -к**, the vowel **о** is inserted between the consonant and **-к** (**учительо́к**); if the stem ends in **a consonant and one of -л, -н**, or **-р**, the vowel **е** is inserted between the consonant and **-л, -г**, or **-р** (**медсесте́р**).

Hard Declension: **stem**
– stems ending in **a consonsant and к,** insert **о** before **к**
– stems ending in **a consonant and н, р,** or **л,** insert **е** before **н, р, л**

Mixed Declension: **stem**

Soft 1 Declension: **-ь**

Soft 2 Declension: **-й**

Feminine Animate Nouns: Accusative Plural Endings				
Declension	***Endings***	***Nominative Singular***	***Stem***	***Accusative Plural***
Hard	**stem**	дружи́на	дружин-	дружи́н
		каси́рка	касирк-	каси́рок
		сестра́	сестр-	сесте́р
Mixed	**stem**	те́ща	тещ-	тещ
Soft 1	**-ь**	продавни́ця	продавниц-	продавни́ць
Soft 2	**-й**	Марі́я	Марі-	Марі́й

A few animate feminine nouns, like **ма́ма**, **ба́ба**, and **па́нна**, have the same accusative plural endings as masculine animate nouns: **мамі́в**, **бабі́в** and **паннів**. (These masculine endings are given in D.2.)

Practise Oral Exercise 15.6

2. Inanimate Nouns

For inanimate feminine nouns, the accusative plural endings are the same as the nominative plural endings: [=Npl]. (See Lesson 12, F.)

Hard, Mixed, Soft 1, and Soft 2 Declensions: [=Npl]

Feminine Inanimate Nouns: Accusative Plural Endings				
Declension	***Endings***	***Nominative Singular***	***Stem***	***Accusative Plural***
Hard	**-и**	кля́са	кляс-	кля́си
Mixed	**-і**	афі́ша	афіш-	афі́ші
Soft 1	**-і**	ліка́рня	лікарн-	ліка́рні
Soft 2	**-ї**	кафете́рія	кафетері-	кафете́рії

Practise Oral Exercise 15.7

D.2 Masculine Nouns

The accusative plural endings are different for masculine animate and inanimate nouns.

1. Animate Nouns

Masculine animate nouns have distinctive endings in the accusative plural case.

Hard, Mixed, and Soft 1 Declensions: **-ів**

Soft 2 Declension: **-їв**

Masculine Animate Nouns: Accusative Plural Endings				
Declension	*Endings*	*Nominative Singular*	*Stem*	*Accusative Plural*
Hard	-ів	брат	брат-	братів
Mixed	-ів	рóдич	родич-	рóдичів
Soft 1	-ів	продавéць	продавц-	продавців
Soft 2	-їв	поліцáй	поліца-	поліцáїв

Practise Oral Exercise 15.8

2. Inanimate Nouns

For inanimate masculine nouns, the accusative plural endings are the same as the nominative plural endings: [=Npl]. (See Lesson 12, F.)

Hard, Mixed, Soft 1, and Soft 2 Declensions: **[=Npl]**

Masculine Inanimate Nouns: Accusative Plural Endings				
Declension	*Endings*	*Nominative Singular*	*Stem*	*Accusative Plural*
Hard	-и	будúнок	будинк-	будúнки
Mixed	-і	ґарáж	ґараж-	ґарáжі
Soft 1	-і	готéль	готел-	готéлі
Soft 2	-ї	музéй	музе-	музéї

D.3 Neuter Nouns

For neuter nouns, the accusative plural endings are the same as the nominative plural endings: [=Npl]. (See Lesson 12, F.)

Hard, Mixed, Soft 1, and Soft 2 Declensions: **[=Npl]**

Neuter Nouns: Accusative Plural Endings				
Declension	***Endings***	***Nominative Singular***	***Stem***	***Accusative Plural***
Hard	**-а**	ліжко	ліжк-	ліжк**а**
Mixed	**-а**	прі́звище	прізвищ-	прі́звищ**а**
Soft 1	**-я**	мі́сце	місц-	місц**я́**
Soft 2	**-я**	завда́ння	завданн-	завда́нн**я**

D.4 Nouns That Are Always Plural

Learn the accusative endings for the **animate** nouns that are always plural.

Nominative Plural	***Stem***	***Accusative Plural***
батьки́	батьк-	батьк**і́в**
дівча́та	дівчат-	дівча́т
ді́ти	діт-	діт**е́й**
лю́ди	люд-	люд**е́й**

For **inanimate** nouns that are always plural, the nominative and accusative forms are the same.

Nominative Plural	***Stem***	***Accusative Plural***
гро́ш**і**	грош-	гро́ш**і**
две́р**і**	двер-	две́р**і**
ме́бл**і**	мебл-	ме́бл**і**
ка́рт**и**	карт-	ка́рт**и**
схо́д**и**	сход-	схо́д**и**
ша́шк**и**	шашк-	ша́шк**и**
ша́х**и**	шах-	ша́х**и**

D.5 Summary Chart: Accusative Plural Endings

Summary: Accusative Plural Endings				
	Hard	*Mixed*	*Soft 1*	*Soft 2*
Feminine				
– ***Animate***	**stem**	**stem**	**-ь**	**-й**
– ***Inanimate***	**-и** [=Npl]	**-і** [=Npl]	**-і** [=Npl]	**-ї** [=Npl]
Masculine				
– ***Animate***	**-ів**	**-ів**	**-ів**	**-їв**
– ***Inanimate***	**-и** [=Npl]	**-і** [=Npl]	**-і** [=Npl]	**-ї** [=Npl]
Neuter	**-а** [=Npl]	**-а** [=Npl]	**-я** [=Npl]	**-я** [=Npl]

Practise Oral Exercises 15.9, 15.10, 15.11

Do Written Exercises 15.3, 15.4

E. PREPOSITIONS AND CASES

In addition to serving as direct objects of affirmative verbs, nouns are also used in the accusative case after a number of prepositions.

E.1 у/в

The preposition **у/в** governs two cases: the **locative** (see Lesson 14) and the **accusative**.

When **location** is indicated (in answer to the question **де**), **у/в** is followed by the **locative case**.

Де дівча́та?	**Where** are the girls?
Вони́ **в теа́трі**.	They're **in the theatre**.

When **directional motion towards or into** is suggested (in answer to the question **куди́**), the **accusative case** is used.

Куди́ ви йдете́?	**Where** are you *[p]* going?
Ми йдемо́ **в теа́тр**.	We're going **to the theatre**.

In addition, when nouns that indicate **a sport** or **a game** are used with the verb **гра́ти**, they must be in the **accusative case** after the preposition **у/в**.

У що ви гра́єте?	**What sport** do you play?
Ми гра́ємо **в те́ніс**.	We're play **tennis**.
У що ви гра́єте?	**What game** are you playing?
Ми гра́ємо **в ша́хи**.	We're playing **chess**.

Practise Oral Exercise 15.12

E.2 на

The preposition **на** governs two cases: the **locative** (see Lesson 14) and the **accusative**.

When **location** is indicated (in answer to the question **де**), **на** is followed by the **locative case**.

Де хло́пці?	**Where** are the boys?
Вони́ **на вечі́рці**.	They're **at a party**.
Де книжки́?	**Where** are the books?
Вони́ **на столі́**.	They're **on the table**.

When **directional motion towards** or **into** is suggested (in answer to the question **куди́**), **на** is followed by the **accusative case**.

Куди́ ви йдете́?	**Where** are you *[p]* going?
Ми йдемо́ **на вечі́рку**.	We're going **to a party**.
Що ти кладе́ш **на стіл**?	What are you *[s]* putting **on the table**?
Я кладу́ книжки́ **на стіл**.	I'm putting the books **on the table**.

The preposition **на** can also mean **for** when it is used with nouns in the **accusative** case after some Ukrainian verbs.

Що ти готу́єш **на сніда́нок**?	What are you *[s]* **preparing for breakfast**?
Я готу́ю ка́ву **на сніда́нок**.	I'm preparing coffee **for breakfast**.
Що ти їси́ **на пере́куску**?	What do you *[s]* eat **for a snack**?
Я їм я́блуко **на пере́куску**.	I eat an apple **for a snack**.
Що ви купу́єте **на вече́рю**?	What are you *[p]* buying **for supper**?
Я купу́ю вино́ **на вече́рю**.	I'm buying wine **for supper**.

Practise Oral Exercise 15.13

E.3 за

To express the idea of **paying** for something, the verb **плати́ти** is followed by the preposition **за** and the **accusative case**.

Чи хтось **пла́тить за ка́ву?**	Is someone **paying for the coffee**?
Ні, ніхто́ не **пла́тить за ка́ву**.	No, no one is **paying for the coffee**.
За що тре́ба **плати́ти**?	**For what** does one have **to pay**?
Треба **плати́ти за пунш**.	One has **to pay for the punch**.
За що ти му́сиш плати́ти?	**For what** do you *[s]* have **to pay**?
Я му́шу **плати́ти за квитки́.**	I have **to pay for the tickets**.

Practise Oral Exercise 15.14

E.4 про

The preposition **про** always governs the **accusative case**.

Про що ви ду́маєте?	**About what** are you *[p]* thinking?
Ми ду́маємо **про пере́куску**.	We're thinking **about lunch**.
Про ко́го ви розмовля́єте?	**About whom** are you *[p]* talking?
Ми розмовля́ємо **про медсестру́**.	We're talking **about the nurse**.

Practise Oral Exercises 15.15, 15.16, 15.17

Do Written Exercises 15.5, 15.6

LESSON 16

A. VOCABULARY

Nouns

accordion	акордіо́н, акордео́н
band *[musical]*	ба́нда, анса́мбль
bandura	банду́ра
drum	бараба́н
guitar	ґіта́ра, *гіта́ра*
orchestra	орке́стра, *орке́стр [h]*
piano	піяні́но, *піані́но [indecl.]*
sopilka	сопі́лка
tsymbaly, dulcimer	цимба́ли *[pl]*
violin	скри́пка
autumn, fall	о́сінь *[f]* (осен-)
day	день (дн-)
east	схід (сход-)
month, moon	мі́сяць
north, midnight	пі́вніч *[f]* (півноч-)
season *[time of year]*	пора́
south, noon	пі́вдень (півдн-)
spring	весна́
summer	лі́то
week	ти́ждень (тижн-)
west	за́хід (заход-)
winter	зима́
year	рік (рок-), *l.sg.* … ро́ці
January	сі́чень (січн-)
February	лю́тий
March	бе́резень (березн-)
April	кві́тень (квітн-)
May	тра́вень (травн-)
June	че́рвень (червн-)
July	ли́пень (липн-)
August	се́рпень (серпн-)
September	ве́ресень (вересн-)
October	жо́втень (жовтн-)
November	листопа́д
December	гру́день (грудн-)

Monday	понеді́лок (понеділк-)
Tuesday	вівто́рок (вівтірк-)
Wednesday	середа́
Thursday	четве́р *[h]* (четверг-)
Friday	п'я́тниця
Saturday	субо́та
Sunday	неді́ля

Adverbs

tomorrow	за́втра
day after tomorrow	післяза́втра
yesterday	учо́ра/вчо́ра
day before yesterday	позавчо́ра

Verbs

to lie down, to lay oneself down	ляга́ти: ляга́-ю, -єш
to sit down, to sit oneself down	сіда́ти: сіда́-ю, -єш

Vocabulary Notes

1. ***In English***, the names of the months and of the days are always capitalized.

   In Ukrainian, the names of the months and of the days are capitalized only when they appear at the beginning of a sentence.

   You will learn how to decline **лю́тий** later in this text when the declension of adjectives is introduced. The locative singular form for **лю́тий** is **... лю́тому.**

2. You will learn how to decline the feminine nouns **о́сінь** and **пі́вніч** later in this text. For now, you need to know that they have the same form in the nominative and accusative singular cases, and that the locative singular of **пі́вніч** is **... пі́вночі**.

3. The expression **ляга́ти спа́ти** means **to go to sleep**.

   Коли́ ти ляга́єш спа́ти? When do you *[s]* go to sleep?

4. Three Ukrainian musical instruments are included in this vocabulary.

   The **sopilka** is an end-blown wooden flute with six apertures (like a recorder). It ranges in length from 20-40 centimeters.

   The **bandura** is a multi-stringed instrument that is held upright on one's lap and is plucked like a harp.

   The **tsymbaly** (**dulcimer**) is a multi-stringed instrument that sits on its own stand and is struck with little wooden mallets.

B. ACCUSATIVE CASE: DECLENSION OF PRONOUNS

Pronouns, like nouns, may serve as direct objects in sentences. They are also used with prepositions that govern the accusative case.

B.1 Interrogative Pronouns

In both English and Ukrainian, only the interrogative pronoun **who** (**хто**) changes when it is in the accusative case; **what** (**що**) does not change.

who	**Whom** do you *[s]* see? **About whom** is he thinking?	**хто**	**Когó** ти бáчиш? **Про кóго** він дýмає?
what	**What** do you *[s]* see? **About what** is he thinking?	**що**	**Що** ти бáчиш? **Про що** він дýмає?

B.2 Personal Pronouns

In English, as you learned in Lesson 14, five personal pronouns change when they are used with prepositions. The same changes occur in these pronouns when they are used as direct objects in a sentence.

Singular Pronouns		*Plural Pronouns*	
I	Do you see **me**?	**we**	Do you see **us**?
he	Do you see **him**?	**they**	Do you see **them**?
she	Do you see **her**?		

Three personal pronouns do not change when they are used either with prepositions or as direct objects.

Singular Pronouns		*Plural Pronouns*	
it	Do you see **it**?		
you *[s]*	Who sees **you**?	**you** *[p]*	Who sees **you**?

In Ukrainian, all the personal pronouns change when they are used as direct objects.

In addition, as indicated in the chart that follows, third person personal pronouns undergo another change when they come after a preposition: the consonant **н-** is prefixed to them.

After a preposition, the stress in a two-syllable pronoun shifts to the first syllable: **про кóго, про мéне, про тéбе, про ньóго, про нéї.**

	Direct Object	*After a Preposition*
я	Хто ба́чить **мене́**?	Він гово́рить **про ме́не**.
ти	Хто ба́чить **тебе́**?	Він гово́рить **про те́бе**.
вона́	Хто ба́чить **її́**?	Він гово́рить **про не́ї**.
він	Хто ба́чить **його́**?	Він гово́рить **про ньо́го**.
воно́	Хто ба́чить **його́**?	Він гово́рить **про ньо́го**.
ми	Хто ба́чить **нас**?	Він гово́рить **про нас**.
ви	Хто ба́чить **вас**?	Він гово́рить **про вас**.
вони́	Хто ба́чить **їх**?	Він гово́рить **про них**.

Practise Oral Exercises 16.1, 16.2

Do Written Exercise 16.1

C. VERBS

Some ideas are expressed in Ukrainian by using a verb along with a preposition and a noun or pronoun in a specific case.

Different cases may be used with the same preposition to express different ideas.

C.1 гра́ти

1. **гра́ти у/в + the accusative case: to play a sport or a game** (See Lesson 15.)

   When nouns that indicate either a **sport** or a **game** are used with the verb **гра́ти**, they must be in the **accusative** case after the preposition **у/в**.

У що ви гра́єте?	**What** (**sport**, **game**) do you play?
Ми гра́ємо **в те́ніс**.	We play **tennis**.
Ми гра́ємо **в ша́хи**.	We play **chess**.

2. **гра́ти на + the locative case: to play an instrument**

   When nouns that indicate a **musical intrument** are used with the verb **гра́ти**, they must be in the **locative** case after the preposition **на**.

На чо́му вона́ гра́є?	(**On**) **what** does she play?
Вона́ гра́є **на скри́пці**.	She plays (**on**) **the violin**.

Practise Oral Exercise 16.3

C.2 лягáти, лежáти

1. **лягáти на + the accusative case: to lie down on something** (to lay oneself down upon something)

   The verb **лягáти** involves **directional motion**. It is used with the preposition **на** and the **accusative case**.

На що він лягáє?	**On what** is he lying down?
Він лягáє **на ліжко**.	He's lying down **on the bed**. (He's laying himself down upon the bed.)

2. **лежáти на + the locative case: to be lying on something**

   The verb **лежáти** indicates **location**. It is used with the preposition **на** and the **locative case**.

На чóму він лежúть?	**On what (Where)** is he lying?
Він лежúть **на ліжку**.	He's lying **on the bed**.

Practise Oral Exercise 16.4

C.3 сідáти, сидíти

1. **сідáти на + the accusative case: to sit down on something** (to seat oneself on something)

   The verb **сідáти** involves **directional motion**. It is used with the preposition **на** and the **accusative case**.

На що він сідáє?	**On what** is he sitting down? (**On what** is he seating himself?)
Він сідáє **на крíсло**.	He's sitting down on a chair. (He's seating himself **on a chair**.)

2. **сидíти на + the locative case**: to be sitting on something

   The verb **сидíти** indicates **location**. It is used with the preposition **на** and the **locative case**.

На чóму він сидúть?	**On what** (**Where**) is he sitting?
Він сидúть **на крíслі**.	He's sitting **on a chair**.

Practise Oral Exercise 16.5

C.4 диви́тися

The verb **диви́тися** is used with either the preposition **на** or **у/в** and a noun in the **accusative case**.

1. **диви́тися на + the accusative case: to look at**

На що ти ди́вишся? Я дивлю́ся **на вітри́ну**.	**At what** are you*[s]* looking? I'm looking **at the showcase**.
На ко́го ви ди́витеся? Ми ди́вимося **на студе́нтку**.	**At whom** are you*[p]* looking? We're looking **at the student***[f]*.
На ко́го ти ди́вишся? Я дивлю́ся **на діте́й**.	**At whom** are you*[s]* looking? I'm looking **at the children**.

2. **диви́тися у/в + the accusative case: to look into**

У що (**Куди́**) ти ди́вишся? Я дивлю́ся **у во́ду**.	**Where** are you*[s]* looking? I'm looking **into the water**.

Practise Oral Exercise 16.6

C.5 чека́ти

The idea **to wait for** is expressed in Ukrainian by using the verb **чека́ти** and the preposition **на** followed by the accusative case.

чека́ти на + the accusative case: to wait for

На ко́го ти чека́єш? Я чека́ю **на сестру́**.	**For whom** are you*[s]* waiting? I'm waiting **for** (my) **sister**.
На ко́го ви чека́єте? Ми чека́ємо **на батькі́в**.	**For whom** are you*[p]* waiting? We're waiting **for** (our) **parents**.
На що ви чека́єте? Ми чека́ємо **на таксі́вку**.	**For what** are you*[p]* waiting? We're waiting for **a taxi**.

Practise Oral Exercise 16.7

C.6 іти́/ходи́ти, ї́хати/ї́здити

It is important to remember when to use the prepositions **у/в** and **на** with verbs of motion.

1. **іти́/ходи́ти в + the accusative case: to go to** ***[on foot]***
   ї́хати/ї́здити в + the accusative case: to go to ***[by vehicle]***

   When **directional motion to a building** is implied, the verbs **іти́/ходи́ти** or **ї́хати/ї́здити** are usually used with the preposition **у/в + the accusative case** of that noun.

   Directional Motion

Куди́ ти йде́ш?	**Where** are you *[s]* going *[on foot]*?
Я йду́ **в теа́тр**.	I'm going *[on foot]* **to the theatre**.
Я ча́сто ходжу́ **в теа́тр**.	I often go *[on foot]* **to the theatre**.
Куди́ ви ї́дете?	**Where** are you *[p]* going *[by vehicle]*?
Ми ї́демо **в теа́тр**.	We're going *[by vehicle]* **to the theatre**.
Ми ча́сто ї́здимо **в теа́тр**.	We often go *[by vehicle]* **to the theatre**.

   These same nouns are in the **locative case** after the preposition **у/в** when **location** is being indicated.

   Location

Я **в теа́трі**.	I'm **in the theatre**.

2. **іти́/ходи́ти на + the accusative case: to go to** ***[on foot]***
   ї́хати/ї́здити на + the accusative case: to go to ***[by vehicle]***

   When **directional motion to an event, an open space, or an open-air structure** is implied, the verbs **іти́/ходи́ти** or **ї́хати/ї́здити** are usually used with the preposition **на + the accusative case** of that noun.

   Directional Motion

Куди́ ти йде́ш?	**Where** are you *[s]* going *[on foot]*?
Я йду́ **на футбо́л**.	I'm going *[on foot]* **to the football game**.
Я ча́сто ходжу́ **на футбо́л**.	I often go *[on foot]* **to football games**.
Куди́ ви ї́дете?	**Where** are you *[p]* going *[by vehicle]*?
Ми ї́демо **на конце́рт**.	We're going *[by vehicle]* **to the concert**.
Ми ча́сто ї́здимо **на конце́рти**.	We often go *[by vehicle]* **to concerts**.

   These same nouns are in the **locative** case after the preposition **на** when **location** is being indicated.

   Location

Я **на конце́рті**.	I'm **at the concert**.

It is important to remember which nouns are used with the preposition **на**; therefore, the nouns from previous lessons that fall into this category are listed alphabetically for you now in columns:

балько́н	вера́нда	го́кей	ле́кція	стадіо́н
баскетбо́л	вече́ря	ґольф	обі́д	те́ніс
бейсбо́л	вечі́рка	доро́га	пере́куска	фа́рма
	волейбо́л	заба́ва	перехре́стя	футбо́л
	ву́лиця	конце́рт	сніда́нок	хідни́к

Practise Oral Exercises 16.8, 16.9

Do Written Exercise 16.2

D. БУ́ТИ: FUTURE AND PAST TENSES

The future and past tenses of Ukrainian verbs are introduced in Lessons 23-25. Until then, the verb **бу́ти** is the only verb that you will be using in the future and past tenses.

D.1 Future Tense

In English, the verb **to be** is conjugated as follows in the future tense.

	Singular		*Plural*	
First Person	I	shall	we	shall
Second Person	you	will	you	will
Third Person	he	will	they	will
	she	will		
	it	will		

In Ukrainian, the conjugation of the verb **бу́ти** in the future tense does not require you to learn any new endings.

The future tense stem of **бу́ти** is **буд-**.

The personal endings that are added to the future tense stem are identical to the present tense endings in the consonant stem groups of the First Conjugation:

-у	**-еш**	**-е**	**-емо**	**-ете**	**-уть**

Infinitive: **бу́ти**	Future Tense Stem: **буд-**	
	Singular	*Plural*
First Person	я **бу́ду**	ми **бу́демо**
Second Person	ти **бу́деш**	ви **бу́дете**
Third Person	він **бу́де** вона́ **бу́де** воно́ **бу́де**	вони́ **бу́дуть**

Practise Oral Exercise 16.10

Do Written Exercise 16.3

D.2 Past Tense

In English, the verb forms **was** and **were** are used when the verb **to be** is conjugated in the past tense.

	Singular	*Plural*
First Person	I was	we were
Second Person	you were	you were
Third Person	he was she was it was	they were

In Ukrainian, the past tense stem of **бу́ти** is **бу-**.

The endings used in the verb forms for the singular personal pronouns are marked by **gender**.

Singular Past Tense Personal Endings

Masculine personal ending: **-в**

Feminine personal ending: **-ла**

Neuter personal ending: **-ло**

There is only one ending for all the plural pronouns.

Plural Past Tense Personal Ending

All genders: **-ли**

Let's look at the past tense conjugation of **бу́ти**.

Infinitive: бу́ти		**Past Tense Stem: бу-**		
	Masculine	***Feminine***	***Neuter***	***All Genders***
First Person	я бу**в**	я бу**ла́**	я бу**ло́**	ми бу**ли́**
Second Person	ти бу**в**	ти бу**ла́**	ти бу**ло́**	ви бу**ли́**
Third Person	він бу**в**	вона́ бу**ла́**	воно́ бу**ло́**	вони́ бу**ли́**

Exaamine the following sentences carefully.

Де **ти був**, Ада́ме?	Where **were you** *[s]*, Adam?
Я був на фа́рмі.	**I was** at the farm.
Де **ти була́**, Окса́но?	Where **were you** *[s]*, Oksana?
Я була́ в теа́трі.	**I was** at the theatre.
Де **ви були́**, ді́ти?	Where **were you** *[p]*, children?
Ми були́ в шко́лі.	**We were** at school.

Practise Oral Exercise 16.11

Do Written Exercise 16.4

E. DAYS OF THE WEEK

In English, we use the preposition **on** with the days of the week to indicate when something happens.

In Ukrainian, the days of the week are in the **accusative case** after the preposition **у/в** to indicate when something happens.

Where were you *[s]* **on Tuesday**, David?
Де ти був **у вівто́рок**, Дави́де?

Where were you *[p]* **on Sunday**, Diana?
Де ви були́ **в неді́лю**, Ді́яно?

On Thursday I'm going to the movies.
У четве́р я йду́ в кіно́.

Practise Oral Exercises 16.12, 16.13

F. MONTHS OF THE YEAR

In English, we use the preposition **in** to indicate the month when something happens.

In Ukrainian, a month is in the **locative** case after the preposition **у/в** to indicate when something happens.

Where were you *[s]* **in May**, Oksana?
Де ти була́ **в тра́вні**, Окса́но?

Where will you *[p]* be **in February**, Sophia?
Де ви бу́дете **в лю́тому,** Софі́є?

Practise Oral Exercises 16.14, 16.15

Do Written Exercise 16.5

G. SEASONS

In English, the seasons are indicated by using the name of the season in a prepositional phrase.

I'm going there **in the spring**.

In Ukrainian, an adverb is used instead of a prepositional phrase.

Я ї́ду туди́ **навесні́**.
I'm going there **in the spring**.

In English, the months that are included in the four seasons vary in the different countries in which English is spoken.

In Ukrainian, the four seasons in Ukraine all consist of three months.

It will be easier for you to remember the seasons in Ukrainian if you think about the adverbs that you learned in Lesson 8.

весна́ (**навесні́**)	**лі́то** (**улі́тку**)	**о́сінь** (**восени́**)	**зима́** (**узи́мку**)
бе́резень	че́рвень	ве́ресень	гру́день
кві́тень	ли́пень	жо́втень	сі́чень
тра́вень	се́рпень	листопа́д	лю́тий

Practise Oral Exercise 16.16

H. DIRECTIONS

In English, a **preposition** is used to distinguish between **location** and **directional motion** when you are speaking about directions; the noun does not change.

Location
He lives **in the west**.

Directional Motion
He's travelling **to the west**.

In Ukrainian, the noun must be in the correct case after the preposition **на** to indicate either **location** and **directional motion** when you are speaking about directions.

1. на + locative case to indicate location

Location	*Location*
Він живé **на схóді**.	He lives **in the east**.
Він живé **на зáході**.	He lives **in the west**.
Він живé **на півдні**.	He lives **in the south**.
Він живé **на півночі**.	He lives **in the north**.

2. на + accusative case to indicate directional motion

Directional Motion	*Directional Motion*
Він ї́де **на схід**.	He's travelling **to the east**.
Він ї́де **на зáхід**.	He's travelling **to the west**.
Він ї́де **на південь**.	He's travelling **to the south**.
Він ї́де **на північ**.	He's travelling **to the north**.

Practise Oral Exercises 16.17, 16.18

Do Written Exercise 16.6

LESSON 17

A. VOCABULARY

Nouns

bowl, soup bowl	ми́ска
clock, watch	годи́нник
coffee table, end table	сто́лик
coffee pot, percolator	ка́вник
corner	куто́к (кутк-)
cup	горня́тко, ча́шка
curtain	фіра́нка
deep freeze, freezer	морози́льник
dishes	по́суд *[sg]*
dishwasher	посудоми́йка
fork	виде́лка
glass *[for drinking]*	скля́нка
knife	ні́ж (нож-)
lamp	ля́мпа, *ла́мпа*
magazine, journal	журна́л
mirror	дзе́ркало
newspaper	газе́та, ґазе́та
painting, picture	карти́на, о́браз
plant *[potted]*, house plant	вазо́нок (вазонк-)
plate	тарі́лка
radio	ра́діо *[n, indecl.]*
refrigerator, fridge	холоди́льник
scissors	но́жиці *[pl]*
spoon	ло́жка
stereo	сте́рео *[n, indecl.]*
teapot, kettle	ча́йник
teaspoon	ло́жечка
telephone	телефо́н
television set, TV	телеві́зор *[h]*
vacuum cleaner	пилосмо́к, пилосо́с
vase	ва́за
videoplayer, VCR	ві́део *[n, indecl.]*
window	вікно́

Verbs

to choose, to select	вибирáти: вибирá-ю, -єш
to cost	коштувáти: коштý-ю, -єш
to order	замовля́ти: замовля́-ю, -єш

Vocabulary Notes

1. Now that you know how to use the verb **бýти** in the past tense, it is important that you use the correct verb form with indeclinable nouns. Most singular indeclinable nouns are considered to be **neuter** in gender; however, because there are exceptions (e.g. **пáні** is considered to be a feminine noun), from now on, the gender of indeclinable nouns will be indicated in the Vocabularies: **рáдіо** ***[n, indecl.]***

   Рáдіо **булó** на столí.
   The radio was on the table.

2. The word **óбраз** can also be used in reference to an **icon**; however, in Canada, the Ukrainian word for **icon** is usually **ікóна**.

B. GENITIVE CASE

In Ukrainian, the genitive case is used in a number of ways. In this lesson you will learn two of these uses. In the next two lessons, you will learn several more ways of using this important case.

B.1 Possession

In English, possession is expressed either by **an apostrophe**, or by a prepositional phrase beginning with the preposition **of**.

1. **The professor's son is playing.**
   or
   The son of the professor is playing.

Subject:	(Who is playing?)	**The son**.
Predicate:	(What is he doing?)	He **is playing**.
Possessive:	(Whose son is playing?)	**The professor's** son. The son **of the professor**.

2. **Tamara knows the professor's wife.**
   or
   Tamara knows the wife of the professor.

Subject:	(Who knows?)	**Tamara** knows.
Predicate:	(What does she do?)	She **knows**.
Direct Object:	(Whom does she know?)	She knows **the wife**.
Possessive:	(Whose wife does she know?)	**The professor's** wife. The wife **of the professor**.

As these two examples indicate, the possessive noun provides us with more information about another noun in the sentence.

In Ukrainian, a noun that shows possession is in the genitive case. When a noun is used in the genitive case, its ending changes.

Here are the two above English sentences translated into Ukrainian.

1. **Син профе́сора гра́є.**

Subject:	(Who is playing?)	**Син**.
Predicate:	(What is he doing?)	Він **гра́є**.
possessive:	(Whose son is playing?)	Син **профе́сора**.

2. **Тама́ра зна́є дружи́ну профе́сора.**

Subject:	(Who knows?)	**Тама́ра** зна́є.
Predicate:	(What does she do?)	Вона́ **зна́є**.
Direct Object:	(Whom does she know?)	Вона́ зна́є **дружи́ну**.
Possessive:	(Whose wife does she know?)	Дружи́ну **профе́сора**.

B.2 Direct Object of a Negated Verb

In English, a noun that is the direct object in a sentence remains the same irrespective of whether it is the direct object of an affirmative verb or a negated one. In the following two sentences, the direct object, **book**, does not change.

1. Danylo **is** buying **a book**.
2. Danylo **is not** buying **a book**.

***In Ukrainian*, a direct object is in either the accusative or the genitive case.**

When a noun is the direct object of **an affirmative verb**, it is usually in the **accusative** case.

When a noun is the direct object of **a negated verb**, it is usually in the **genitive** case.

Let's see how the two English sentences are translated into Ukrainian.

In the first sentence, the verb **купу́є** is not negated; therefore, the direct object is in the **accusative** case: **кни́жку**.

1. Danylo is buying **a book**.
   Дани́ло купу́є **кни́жку**.

In the second sentence, the verb **не купу́є** is negated; therefore, the direct object is in the **genitive** case: **кни́жки**.

2. Danylo is **not** buying **a book**.
   Дани́ло **не** купу́є **кни́жки**.

C. GENITIVE SINGULAR ENDINGS

You will now learn the endings that are attached to the stems of nouns when they are used in the genitive singular case.

C.1 Feminine Nouns

For almost all feminine nouns, both animate and inanimate, the genitive singular endings are the same as the nominative plural endings.

Although the two forms look identical, it is easy to tell if a word is in the genitive singular case or the nominative plural case from the context in which it is used. In addition, in some feminine nouns the stress is different in these two cases.

Hard, Mixed, Soft 1, and Soft 2 Declensions: [=Npl]

Feminine Nouns: Genitive Singular Endings				
Declension	*Endings*	*Nominative Singular*	*Stem*	*Genitive Singular*
Hard	**-и**	банду́ра	бандур-	банду́р**и**
Mixed	**-і**	те́ща	тещ-	те́щ**і**
Soft 1	**-і**	бабу́ся	бабус-	бабу́с**і**
Soft 2	**-ї**	ле́кція	лекці-	ле́кці**ї**

Practise Oral Exercise 17.1

C.2 Masculine Nouns

1. Animate Nouns

For all masculine *animate* nouns, the genitive singular endings are the same as the accusative singular endings: [=aAsg]. (See Lesson 15, C.2.)

Hard, Mixed, Soft 1, and Soft 2 Declensions: [=aAsg]

Masculine Animate Nouns: Genitive Singular Endings				
Declension	***Endings***	***Nominative Singular***	***Stem***	***Genitive Singular***
Hard	**-а**	брат	брат-	бра́**та**
Mixed	**-а**	ро́дич	родич-	ро́дич**а**
Soft 1	**-я**	продаве́ць	продавц-	продавц**я́**
Soft 2	**-я**	поліца́й	поліца-	поліца́**я**

Practise Oral Exercise 17.2

2. Inanimate Nouns

There are two sets of endings for masculine **inanimate** nouns in the genitive case and there are rules to help you determine which set to use. You will find, however, that these rules do not always apply because of subtle differences in meaning that are associated with the endings, and because there are differences in usage among speakers and writers of Ukrainian.

Hard and Mixed Declensions: **-а, -у**

Soft 1 and Soft 2 Declensions: **-я, -ю**

1. The **-а/-я** endings are used for nouns that refer to:
   1) concrete objects (pencil, notebook)
   2) names of days, months (Monday, January)
   3) some measurements (acre, pound)
   4) money (cent, dollar)
2. The **-у/-ю** endings are used for nouns that refer to:
   1) collective units
      – groupings of people (choir, crowd)
      – substances (sugar, honey)
   2) physical features
      – natural phenomena (rain, snow)
      – massive natural configurations (world, steppe)
      – large man-made structures (stadium, palace)
   3) words borrowed from other languages (garage, museum)
      – except: machines and scientific instruments
   4) abstract concepts and feelings (time, anger)

Masculine Inanimate Nouns: Genitive Singular Endings				
Declension	*Endings*	*Nominative Singular*	*Stem*	*Genitive Singular*
Hard	**-а**	словни́к	словник-	словника́
	-у	стадіо́н	стадіон-	стадіо́н**у**
Mixed	**-а**	ніж	ніж-	нож**а́**
	-у	ґара́ж	ґараж-	ґара́ж**у**
Soft 1	**-я**	сі́чень	січн-	сі́чн**я**
	-ю	готе́ль	готел-	готе́л**ю**
Soft 2	**-ю**	музе́й	музе-	музе́**ю**

Practise Oral Exercise 17.3

C.3 Neuter Nouns

For almost all neuter nouns, the genitive singular endings are the same as the nominative plural endings: [=Npl]. (See Lesson 12, F.)

Hard, Mixed, Soft 1, and Soft 2 Declensions: [=Npl]

It may also be helpful for you to remember that the genitive singular endings are the same for **neuter nouns**, for all **masculine animate nouns**, and for **the first group of masculine inanimate nouns**.

While the genitive singular and the nominative plural forms of neuter nouns look identical, in some neuter nouns the stress is different in these two cases.

Neuter Nouns: Genitive Singular Endings				
Declension	*Endings*	*Nominative Singular*	*Stem*	*Genitive Singular*
Hard	**-а**	а́вто	авт-	а́вт**а**
Mixed	**-а**	прі́звище	прізвищ-	прі́звищ**а**
Soft 1	**-я**	мі́сце	місц-	мі́сц**я**
Soft 2	**-я**	завда́ння	завданн-	завда́нн**я**

Practise Oral Exercise 17.4

C.4 Summary Chart: Genitive Singular Endings

Summary: Genitive Singular Endings				
	Hard	*Mixed*	*Soft 1*	*Soft 2*
Feminine	**-и** [=Npl]	**-і** [=Npl]	**-і** [=Npl]	**-ї** [=Npl]
Masculine				
– Animate	**-а** [=*a*Asg]	**-а** [=*a*Asg]	**-я** [=*a*Asg]	**-я** [=*a*Asg]
– Inanimate	**-а** [=*a*Asg]	**-а** [=*a*Asg]	**-я** [=*a*Asg]	**-я** [=*a*Asg]
	-у	**-у**	**-ю**	**-ю**
Neuter	**-а** [=Npl]	**-а** [=Npl]	**-я** [=Npl]	**-я** [=Npl]

Practise Oral Exercises 17.5, 17.6, 17.7

Do Written Exercises 17.1, 17.2, 17.3

D. GENITIVE PLURAL ENDINGS

D.1 Feminine Nouns

For both animate and inanimate feminine nouns, the genitive plural is formed in the same way as the accusative plural for *animate* nouns: [=*a*Apl]. (See Lesson 15, D.)

Hard Declension: **stem [=*a*Apl]**
- stems ending in a **consonant** and **к**, insert **о** before **к**
- stems ending in a **consonant** and **н**, **р**, or **л**, insert **е** before **н**, **р**, **л**

Mixed Declension: **stem [=*a*Apl]**

Soft 1 Declension: **-ь [=*a*Apl]**

Soft 2 Declension: **-й [=*a*Apl]**

Feminine Nouns: Genitive Plural Endings				
Declension	*Endings*	*Nominative Singular*	*Stem*	*Genitive Plural*
Hard	**stem**	ля́мпа	лямп-	лямп
	stem	посудоми́йка	посудомийк-	посудоми́йок
	stem	сестра́	сестр-	сесте́р
Mixed	**stem**	афі́ша	афіш-	афі́ш
Soft 1	**-ь**	продавни́ця	продавниц-	продавни́ць
Soft 2	**-й**	ле́кція	лекці-	ле́кцій

Learn the genitive plural forms of the following feminine nouns.

Nominative Singular	*Genitive Plural*	*Nominative Singular*	*Genitive Plural*
ку́хня	ку́хонь	шко́ла	шкіл
ліка́рня	ліка́рень	доро́га	догі́г
книга́рня	книга́рень		
віта́льня	віта́лень		
ї́да́льня	ї́да́лень		
		Exceptions	
		підло́га	підло́г
		комо́ра	комо́р

A few feminine nouns use masculine genitive plural endings.

Nominative Singular	*Genitive Plural*	*Nominative Singular*	*Genitive Plural*
ба́ба	баб**і́в**	сім'я́	сім**е́й** і сі́м'**ї́в**
ма́ма	мам**і́в**	ха́та	хат і хат**і́в**
па́нна	панн**і́в**		

Practise Oral Exercise 17.8

D.2 Masculine Nouns

For both animate and inanimate nouns, the genitive plural endings are the same as the accusative plural endings for *animate* nouns: [=aApl]. (See Lesson 15, D.)

Hard, Mixed, and Soft 1 Declensions: **-ів [=aApl]**

Soft 2 Declension: **-їв [=aApl]**

Masculine Nouns: Genitive Plural Endings				
Declension	***Endings***	***Nominative Singular***	***Stem***	***Genitive Plural***
Hard	**-ів**	брат	брат-	брат**і́в**
Mixed	**-ів**	това́риш	товариш-	товариш**і́в**
Soft 1	**-ів**	олів́ець	олівц-	олівц**і́в**
Soft 2	**-їв**	поліца́й	поліца-	поліца́**їв**

Practise Oral Exercise 17.9

D.3 Neuter Nouns

Hard, Mixed, and Soft 1 Declension neuter nouns form their genitive plurals like feminine nouns. This means that you must pay special attention to the stems of neuter nouns that end in either **a consonant and -к**, or a **consonant and -л** or **-н**.

Hard Declension: **stem**
- stems ending in a **consonsant** and **к**, insert **о** before **к**
- stems ending in a **consonant** and **л**, or **н**, insert **е** before **л**, **н**

Mixed Declension: **stem**

Soft 1 Declension: **-ь**

Soft 2 Declension: **-ь**, **-ів**
- stems ending in a doubled consonant: delete one consonant and add **-ь**
- stems ending in two different consonants: add **-ів**

Neuter Nouns: Genitive Plural Endings

Declension	*Endings*	*Nominative Singular*	*Stem*	*Genitive Plural*
Hard	**stem**	мі́сто	міст-	міст
	stem	лі́жко	ліжк-	лі́жок
	stem	шатро́ (tent)	шатр-	ша́тер
Mixed	**stem**	прі́звище	прізвищ-	прі́звищ
Soft 1	**-ь**	мі́сце	місц-	місць
Soft 2	**-ь**	завда́ння	завданн-	завда́нь
	-ів	перехре́стя	перехрест-	перехре́стів

Learn the genitive plural forms of the following neuter nouns:

Nominative Plural	*Stem*	*Genitive Plural*
село́	сел-	сіл
вікно́	вікн-	ві́кон

D.4 Nouns That Are Always Plural

Learn the genitive endings of the nouns that you know that are always plural.

	Nominative Plural	*Genitive Plural*
Animate	батькú	батьк**íв**
	дíти	діт**éй**
	лю́ди	люд**éй**
	дівчáта	дівчáт
Inanimate	мéблі	мéбл**ів**
	схóди	схóд**ів**
	цимбáли	цимбáл**ів**
	шáхи	шáх**ів**
	двéрі	двер**éй**
	грóші	грóш**ей**
	шá**шки**	шá**шок**
	нóжиці	нóжиц**ь**

D.5 Summary Chart: Genitive Plural Endings

Summary: Genitive Plural Endings				
	Hard	*Mixed*	*Soft 1*	*Soft 2*
Feminine	**stem** [=*a*Apl]	**stem** [=*a*Apl]	**-ь** [=*a*Apl]	**-й** [=*a*Apl]
Masculine	**-ів** [=*a*Apl]	**-ів** [=*a*Apl]	**-ів** [=*a*Apl]	**-їв** [=*a*Apl]
Neuter	**stem**	**stem**	**-ь**	**-ь, -ів**

Practise Oral Exercises 17.10 17.11

Do Written Exercises 17.4, 17.5

LESSON 18

A. VOCABULARY

Nouns

address	адре́са
airplane	літа́к
bicycle, bike	велосипе́д
bus	авто́бус
bus stop	зупи́нка
camera	фотоапара́т
cash	готі́вка *[sg]*
cent, penny	цент
change *[money]*	зда́ча *[sg]*
church	це́рква
dollar	до́ляр *[h]*, до́лар *[h]*
envelope	конве́рта, конве́рт
eyeglasses	окуля́ри *[pl]*, окуля́рів
flashlight	ліхта́рик
gift, present	подару́нок (подарунк-)
key	ключ
letter	лист
motorcycle	мотоци́кл
package, carton	па́чка
parcel	паку́нок (пакунк-)
passport	па́спорт
photograph, photo	фотогра́фія, фо́то *[n, indecl.]*
postcard	листі́вка
post office	по́шта
purse	торби́нка, пуля́ре́с, *су́мка*
souvenir	сувені́р *[h]*
stamp, postage stamp	ма́рка
suitcase, valise	валі́зка, *чемода́н*
traffic light	світлофо́р *[h]*
train	пої́зд, по́тяг
umbrella, parasol	парасо́ля, *парасо́ль, зо́нтик*
visa	ві́за
wallet	гамане́ць (гаманц-)

Verbs

to come out of, to exit	вихóдити: вихóджу, вихóд-иш
to look for, to search	шукáти: шукá-ю, -єш

Prepositions

after	пícля
by, beside	бíля, кóло
for	для
from	від
from out of	з
toward	до
without	без

B. GENITIVE CASE: DECLENSION OF PRONOUNS

Pronouns, like nouns, may serve as direct objects of negated vertbs. They are also used with prepositions that govern the genitive case.

B.1 Interrogative Pronouns

In English, **who** changes to **whom** when it is used as the direct object of an affirmative verb, and of a negated one. The pronoun **what** does not change.

	Affirmative Verb	*Negated Verb*
who	**Whom** do you see?	**Whom** don't you see?
what	**What** do you see?	**What** don't you see?

In Ukrainian, **хто** changes when it serves as the direct object of **an affirmative verb**, but **що** does not change.

хто	**Когó** ти бáчиш?	**Whom** do you *[s]* see?
що	**Що** ти бáчиш?	**What** do you *[s]* see

Both **хто** and **що** change when they serve as the direct object of **a negated verb**.

хто	**Когó** ти не бáчиш?	**Whom** don't you *[s]* see?
що	**Чогó** ти не бáчиш?	**What** don't you *[s]* see?

B.2 Personal Pronouns

In English, the **five** personal pronouns that change when they are used as the direct objects of an affirmative verb, also change when they are used as the direct object of a negated verb. (See Lesson 16, B.2.)

In Ukrainian, **all** the personal pronouns change when they are used as the direct object either of an affirmative verb, or of a negated one.

	Affirmative Verb (Accusative Case)	*Negated Verb (Genitive Case)*
я	Хто ба́чить **мене́**?	Хто не ба́чить **мене́**?
ти	Хто ба́чить **тебе́**?	Хто не ба́чить **тебе́**?
вона́	Хто ба́чить **її́**?	Хто не ба́чить **її́**?
він	Хто ба́чить **його́**?	Хто не ба́чить **його́**?
воно́	Хто ба́чить **його́**?	Хто не ба́чить **його́**?
ми	Хто ба́чить **нас**?	Хто не ба́чить **нас**?
ви	Хто ба́чить **вас**?	Хто не ба́чить **вас**?
вони́	Хто ба́чить **їх**?	Хто не ба́чить **їх**?

Practise Oral Exercises 18.1, 18.2

Do Written Exercise 18.1

C. PREPOSITIONS

The following **nine** prepositions govern (are followed by) nouns and pronouns in the genitive case: **без**, **бі́ля**, **від**, **для**, **до**, **з**, **ко́ло**, **пі́сля**, and **у**.

Remember that when third person pronouns appear after prepositions, the consonant **н-** is prefixed to them. **The prefixed н- forms of these pronouns are the same for the accusative and genitive cases.**

It is also important to remember that the stress in a two-syllable preposition shifts to the first syllable after a preposition: **без ко́го, без ме́не, без те́бе, без нього, без не́ї.**

	Accusative Case	*Genitive Case*
вона́	Хто гово́рить **про не́ї**?	Хто йде́ **без не́ї**?
він	Хто гово́рить **про нього**?	Хто йде́ **без нього**?
воно́	Хто гово́рить **про нього**?	Хто йде́ **без нього**?
вони́	Хто гово́рить **про них**?	Хто йде́ **без них**?

C.1 без

Nouns and pronouns that follow the preposition **без** are always in the genitive case.

Чи ти мóжеш читáти **без окуля́рів**?
Can you *[s]* read **without eyeglasses**?

Чи ти мóжеш читáти **без <u>н</u>их**?
Can you *[s]* read **without them**?

Він ї́де на пóшту **без дітéй**.
He's going to the post office **without** (his) **children**.

Practise Oral Exercise 18.3

C.2 бíля, кóло

The prepositions **бíля** and **кóло** are identical in meaning and may be used interchangeably.

Хто стої́ть **бíля (кóло) поліцáя**?
Who is standing **by the police officer**?

Хто стої́ть **бíля (кóло) <u>н</u>ьóго**.
Who is standing **by him**?

Вони́ сидя́ть **бíля (кóло) дверéй**.
They are sitting **by the door**.

Practise Oral Exercise 18.4

C.3 від

The preposition **від** indicates movement away from a person, or away from being beside (but not in) something or someplace.

Це подарýнок **від товáришки**.
This is a gift **from a friend**.

Це подарýнок **від <u>н</u>éї**.
This is a gift **from her**.

Зáраз він ідé додóму **від зупи́нки**.
Right now he's walking home **from the bus stop**.

Practise Oral Exercise 18.5

C.4 для

The preposition **для** always governs the genitive case.

Я купу́ю кни́жку **для діте́й**.
I'm buying a book **for the children**.

Я купу́ю кни́жку **для них**.
I'm buying a book **for them**.

Practise Oral Exercise 18.6

C.5 до

The preposition **до** is used to indicate movement directed towards a person or towards or into a place.

Вона́ пи́ше **до това́ришки**.
She is writing **to a friend**.

Вона́ пи́ше **до не́ї**.
She is writing **to her**.

Ді́ти біжа́ть **до зупи́нки**.
The children are running **to the bus stop**.

Він щоти́жня хо́дить **до це́ркви**.
He goes **to church** every week.

Practise Oral Exercise 18.7

C.6 з

When the preposition з governs the genitive case it indicates movement from out of a place, or from an event.

Студе́нти вихо́дять з **поме́шкання**.
The students are coming **out of the apartment**.

Студе́нти вихо́дять з **ньо́го**.
The students are coming **out of it**.

Дівча́та йду́ть додо́му з **конце́рту**.
The girls are going home **from the concert**.

Practise Oral Exercise 18.8

C.7 після

The preposition **після** always governs the genitive case.

Ýчні вхóдять у шкóлу **після вчителів.**
The pupils enter the school **after the teachers**.

Ýчні вхóдять у шкóлу **після них**.
The pupils enter the school **after them**.

Куди́ ви йдетé **після футбóлу**?
Where are you *[p]* going **after the football game**?

Practise Oral Exercise 18.9

C.8 у

1. **Animate** nouns and the pronouns that replace them are placed in the **genitive case** after the preposition **у** to indicate that someone or something is at someone's place (home).

у + genitive case of an *animate* noun

У кóго Софíя живé?
At whose place does Sophia live?

Софíя живé **у дя́дька.** Sophia lives at (her) uncle's (place/home).	Вонá живé **в ньóго.** She lives **at his place**.

У кóго відео?
At whose place is the VCR?

Вíдео в Софíї. The VCR is **at Sophia's** (place/home).	**Вíдео в нéї.** The VCR is **at her place**.

у + locative case of an *inanimate* noun

Remember that with **inanimate** nouns and the pronouns that replace them, the preposition **у** is followed by the **locative case** to indicate the location of someone or something in a physical place.

Де Дани́ло?
Where is Danylo?

Дани́ло **в áвті.** Danylo is **in the car**.	Дани́ло **у ньóму.** Danylo is **in it**.

Practise Oral Exercise 18.10

2. **Animate** nouns and the pronouns that replace them may also be used in the **genitive case** after the preposition **у** to state that someone **has** something.

   In Ukrainian, there are two ways of saying that someone "has" something.

   1) You already know how to use the verb **мáти** (to have).

      In the two sentences given below, **Ларúса** and **вонá** are the subjects in the nominative case; **хáту** is the direct object in the accusative case.

      Ларúса мáє хáту.
      Larysa has a house.

      Вонá мáє хáту.
      She has a house.

   2) The same statements can be made by using the preposition **у + an animate noun in the genitive case**.

      In the two sentences given below, the verb **є** is used. The subject is **хáта** in the nominative case; **Ларúси** and **нéї** are in the **genitive case** after the preposition **у**.

      У Ларúси є хáта.
      Larysa has a house.

      У нéї є хáта.
      She has a house

      There is no difference in meaning between these two different ways of expressing the idea of **having** something in Ukrainian.

      Let's look at a few more examples.

Турúст мáє парасóлю. The tourist *[m]* has an umbrella.	**Він мáє** парасóлю. He has an umbrella.
У турúста є парасóля. The tourist *[m]* has an umbrella.	**У ньóго є** парасóля. He has an umbrella.
Чи **покупцí мáють** готíвку? Do the customers have cash?	Чи **вонú мáють** готíвку? Do they have cash?
Чи **в покупцíв є** готíвка? Do the customers have cash?	Чи **в них є** готíвка? Do they have cash?

Practise Oral Exercises 18.11, 18.12

Do Written Exercises 18.2, 18.3, 18.4

D. VERBS

Some ideas are expressed in Ukrainian by using a verb with a noun in the genitive case, or a verb and a preposition with a noun in the genitive case.

D.1 боя́тися

The verb **боя́тися** is always followed by a direct object in the **genitive case**.

боя́тися + the genitive case

Когó дíти боя́ться? Дíти боя́ться **злодíїв**.	**Whom** do the children fear? The children fear **the thieves**.
Чи дíти боя́ться **злодíїв**? Так, вони́ боя́ться **їх**.	Are the chidren afraid of **thieves**? Yes, they're afraid of **them**.
Чогó дíти боя́ться? Дíти боя́ться **літакá.**	**What** do the children fear? The children fear **the airplane**.
Чи дíти боя́ться **літакá**? Так, вони́ боя́ться **йогó**.	Are the children afraid of **the airplane**? Yes, they are afraid of **it**.

Practise Oral Exercise 18.13

D.2 сміЯтися

When **смія́тися** means "to laugh at someone or something", it is followed by з **and the genitive case.**

смія́тися з + the genitive case

З кóго він смíється? Він смíється з **дітéй**.	**At whom** is he laughing? He's laughing **at the children**.
Чи він смíється з **дітéй**? Так, він смíється з **них**.	Is he laughing **at the children**? Yes, he's laughing **at them**.
З чóго вонá смíється? Вонá смíється з **áвта**.	**At what** is she laughing? She's laughing **at the car**.
Чи він смíється з **áвта**? Ні, він не смíється з **ньóго**.	Is he laughing **at the car**? No, he's not laughing **at it**.

Practise Oral Exercise 18.14

D.3 питáти, шукáти, хотíти

The direct objects of **питáти**, **шукáти**, and **хотíти** are used in either the **accusative case** or the **genitive case**, depending upon whether or not they are specifically identified.

Accusative Case

The accusative case is usually used after these verbs if the direct object is preceded by the definite article **the** in English.

1. **питáти + the accusative case**

Когó школярí питáють?	**Whom** are the pupils asking?
Вони́ питáють **учи́тельку**.	They're asking **the teacher** *[f]*.
Школярí питáють **учи́тельку**?	Are the pupils asking **the teacher** *[f]*?
Так, вони́ її́ питáють.	Yes, they're asking **her**.

2. **шукáти + the accusative case**

Когó він шукáє?	For **whom** is he looking?
Він шукáє **офіція́нтку**.	He's looking for **the waitress**.
Чи він шукáє **офіція́нтку**?	Is he looking for **the waitress**?
Так, він її́ шукáє.	Yes, he's looking for **her**.
Що вонá шукáє?	For **what** is she looking?
Вонá шукáє **парасóлю**.	She's looking for **the umbrella**.
Чи вонá шукáє **парасóлю**?	Is she looking for **the umbrella**?
Так, вонá її́ шукáє.	Yes, she's looking for **it**.

3. **хотіти + the accusative case**

Що жінка хóче?	**What** does the woman want?
Жінка хóче **вáзу**.	The woman wants **the vase**.
Чи жінка хóче **вáзу**?	Does the woman want **the vase**?
Так, вонá її́ хóче.	Yes, she wants **it**.

Genitive Case

If the direct object in English is preceded by the indefinite article **a** or **an**, the genitive case is usually used in Ukrainian.

1. **питати + the genitive case**

Когó школярí питáють?	**Whom** are the pupils asking?
Вони́ питáють бібліотéкарки.	They're asking **a librarian** *[f]*.
Когó тури́сти питáють?	**Whom** are the tourists asking?
Вони́ питáють **офіція́нтки**.	They're asking **a waitress**.

2. хоті́ти + the genitive case

Чого́ жі́нка хо́че?	**What** does the woman want?
Жі́нка хо́че **ва́зи**.	The woman wants **a vase**.
Чого́ ді́ти хо́чуть?	**What** do the children want?
Вони́ хо́чуть **ножа́**.	They want **a knife**.

3. шука́ти + the genitive case

Кого́ він шука́є?	**For whom** is he looking?
Він шука́є **бібліоте́карки**.	He's looking for **a librarian** *[f]*.
Чого́ вона́ шука́є?	**For what** is she looking?
Вона́ шука́є **холоди́льника**.	She's looking for **a refrigerator**.

The direct object of **пита́ти** may also be expressed in Ukrainian by using the preposition **у/в** with the genitive case; in English, such a direct object is usually preceded by the definite article **the**.

пита́ти у + the genitive case

У ко́го вони́ пита́ють?	**Whom** do the pupils ask?
Вони́ пита́ють **в учи́тельки**.	They're asking **the teacher** *[f]*.

Practise Oral Exercises 18.15, 18.16

Do Written Exercise 18.5

LESSON 19

A. VOCABULARY

Nouns

bacon	соloни́на, *бекóн*
borshch	борщ
bread	хліб
bun	бýлочка
butter	мáсло
cabbage roll	голубéць (голубц-)
cake	торт
cheese	сир *[h]*
cookie	тíстечко
cream *[sweet]*	вершки́ *[pl]*, вершкíв
cream *[sour]*	сметáна
crepe, nalysnyk	нали́сник
dessert	десéрт
dumpling, varenyk, perogy	варéник, пирíг (пирог-)
egg	яйцé, *g.pl.* яєць
fish	ри́ба
ham	ши́нка
honey	мед
ice cream	морóзиво
jam	пови́дло, *джем*
kilogram	кілогрáм
lemon	цитри́на, *лимóн*
lettuce, salad	салáта, *салат*
margarine	марґари́на, *маргари́н*
marmalade	мармеля́да, *мармелáд*
meat	м'я́со
mushroom	гриб
nut	горíх, *l.sg.* … горíсі
porridge	кáша
pudding	пýдинґ, *пýдинг*
sandwich	сáндвіч
sausage	ковбасá
soup	ю́шка, зýпа, *суп*
sugar	цýкор *[h]* (цукр-)

Adverbs

enough	до́сить
not much, a little bit	тро́хи
some, several, a few	кі́лька
so much, so many	сті́льки
there is no, there are no	нема́/нема́є

Vocabulary Notes

In English, the plurals of nouns like **varenyk**, **nalysnyk**, and **holubets** usually correspond to their Ukrainian nominative plural form: **varenyky**, **nalysnyky**, **holubtsi**.

B. ADVERBS OF QUANTITY

In Ukrainian, nouns are always in the **genitive case** when they are used with adverbs that indicate a quantity of something. You already know the following adverbs of quantity: **бага́то**, **бі́льше**, **до́сить**, **кі́лька**, **ма́ло**, **ме́нше**, **небага́то**, **скі́льки**, **сті́льки**, and **тро́хи**.

B.1 Singular and Plural Nouns

In Ukrainian, nouns that refer to **things that may be counted** are in the **genitive plural** after adverbs of quantity.

Скі́льки помара́нч ти купу́єш?	**How many oranges** are you *[s]* buying?
Я купу́ю **кі́лька помара́нч**.	I'm buying **a few oranges**.
Скі́льки олівці́в він ма́є?	**How many pencils** does he have?
Він ма́є **бага́то олівці́в**.	He has **a lot of pencils**.

Nouns that refer to **substances that may not be counted** are in the **genitive singular** after adverbs of quantity.

Скі́льки ка́ви ви ма́єте?	**How much coffee** do you *[p]* have?
Ми ма́ємо лише́ **тро́хи ка́ви**.	We have only **a little bit of coffee**.
Скі́льки молока́ вони́ ма́ють?	**How much milk** do they have?
Вони́ ма́ють **бага́то молока**.	They have **a lot of milk**.

Practise Oral Exercises 19.1, 19.2

Do Written Exercise 19.1

B.2 Subject of a Sentence

In English, plural verbs are used in sentences that contain words like **how many**, **many**, **a lot of**, and **a few**.

How many people **are dining** here?
A lot of people **are dining** here.

In Ukrainian, when an adverb of quantity is the **subject** of the sentence, it is treated as a **neuter singular noun** and the **third person singular verb form** is used with it.

In the following examples, the **subjects** of the sentences are **скíльки**, **багáто**, and **мáло** (**not** the plural nouns **людéй** and **горíхів**), and therefore the **singular third person verb forms** are used as predicates.

Present Tense

Скíльки людéй тут **обíдає**?	How many people are dining here?
Тут **багáто** людéй **обíдає**.	A lot of people are dining here.
Скíльки горíхів **є** в тóрті?	How many nuts are there in the cake?
У тóрті **є багáто** горíхів.	There are many nuts in the cake.

Past Tense

Скíльки людéй там **булó**?	How many people were there there?
Там **булó дóсить** людéй.	There were enough people there.
Скíльки горíхів **булó** в тóрті?	How many nuts were there in the cake?
У тóрті **булó дóсить** горíхів.	There were enough nuts in the cake.

Future Tense

Скíльки людéй тут **бýде**?	How many people will there be here?
Тут **бýде небагáто** людéй.	There won't be many people here.
Скíльки горíхів **бýде** в тóрті?	How many nuts will there be in the cake?
У тóрті **бýде небагáто** горíхів.	There won't be many nuts in the cake.

Practise Oral Exercises 19.3. 19.4

Do Written Exercise 19.2

C. PARTITIVE GENITIVE

In some sentences an adverb of quantity may be implied even if it is not stated. When this happens, the direct object is known as the **partitive genitive**.

The partitive genitive is used to indicate either an indefinite amount of a substance, or a measured amount of it.

Nouns that refer to substances that may not be counted are in the **genitive singular**. Nouns that refer to things that may be counted are in the **genitive plural**.

C.1 Partitive Genitive: An Indefinite Amount

In English, the words **some** or **any** are used to indicate an unspecified amount of a substance.

Singular Nouns	***Plural Nouns***
Who wants **some** meat?	Who wants **some** eggs?
Does he want **any** meat?	Does he want **any** eggs?

In Ukrainian, the words **some** and **any** are **not** used; instead, **the partitive genitive is used as the direct object**.

Singular Nouns	***Plural Nouns***
Who wants **some meat**?	Who wants **some eggs**?
Хто хóче **м'я́са**?	Хто хóче **яє́ць**?
Does he want **any meat**?	Does he want **any eggs**?
Чи він хóче **м'я́са**?	Чи він хóче **яє́ць**?

Practise Oral Exercises 19.5, 19.6

C.2 Partitive Genitive: A Measured Amount

In English, when a measured quantity of a substance is referred to, it is preceded by the preposition **of**.

Here's a glass **of milk**!
Here's a kilogram **of coffee**!

In Ukrainian, the partitive genitive is used without a preposition.

Here's a glass **of milk**!
Ось склянка **молока́**!

Here's a kilogram **of coffee**!
Ось кілогрáм **ка́ви**!

Practise Oral Exercises 19.7, 19.8

Do Written Exercise 19.3

D. EXPRESSING THE ABSENCE OF SOMEONE/SOMETHING

In English, we do not make any changes to a subject when we say that someone/something is not present or does not exist.

Present Tense

The child ***is*** at home.
The child ***isn't*** at home.

Future Tense

They ***will be*** at school.
They ***won't be*** at school.

Past Tense

There ***was*** **a girl** here.
There ***wasn't*** **a girl** here.

In Ukrainian, the subject of a sentence is placed in the **genitive case** to indicate its absence or non-existence.

The negated predicate is different in all three tenses.

D.1 Present Tense: нема́ (нема́є) + genitive

When the absence or non-existence of **either a singular or a plural subject** is referred to in the present tense, the predicate is always **нема́** (also written as **нема́є**).

Affirmative	*Negative*
The child is at home. **Дити́на** (є) вдо́ма.	The child isn't at home **Дити́ни нема́ (нема́є)** вдо́ма.
The children are at home. **Ді́ти** (є) вдо́ма.	The children aren't at home. **Діте́й нема́ (нема́є)** вдо́ма.
They are at home. **Вони́** (є) вдо́ма.	They aren't at home. **Їх нема́ (нема́є)** вдо́ма.

Remember, that the verb **є** may be omitted in most affirmative sentences in the present tense. In negative statements, however, the word **нема́ (нема́є)** must be used.

Do not confuse **немáє** (is not) with the negated verb **не мáє** (does not have).

> На столí **немáє** ля́мпи, бо він **не мáє** ля́мпи.
> There **is no** lamp on the table, because he **doesn't have** a lamp.
>
> Чому́ в гаманці́ **немáє** грóшей? Бо він **не мáє** грóшей!
> Why **isn't** there money in the wallet? Because he **has no** money!

Practise Oral Exercise 19.9

D.2 Future Tense: не бу́де + genitive

When the absence or non-existence of **either a singular or a plural subject** is referred to in the future tense, the predicate is **не бу́де**.

Affirmative	*Negative*
The girl will be in school. **Дівчина бу́де** в шкóлі.	The girl won't be in school. **Дівчини не бу́де** в шкóлі.
The boys will be at school. **Хлóпці бу́дуть** у шкóлі.	The boys won't be in school. **Хлóпців не бу́де** в шкóлі.
We will be at home. **Ми бу́демо** вдóма.	We won't be at home. **Нас не бу́де** вдóма.

Practise Oral Exercise 19.10

D.3 Past Tense: не булó + genitive

When the absence or non-existence of **either a singular or plural subject** is referred to in the past tense, the predicate is **не булó**.

Affirmative	*Negative*
There was a girl here. Тут **булá дівчина**.	There wasn't a girl here. Тут **не булó дівчини**.
There were boys here. Тут **були́ хлóпці**.	There weren't any boys here. Тут **не булó хлóпців**.
We were at home. **Ми були́** вдóма.	We weren't at home. **Нас не булó** вдóма.

Practise Oral Exercises 19.11, 19.12

Do Written Exercise 19.4

E. CARDINAL NUMBERS

Study the following chart carefully; pay close attention to the use of the soft sign (**ь**).

0	зе́ро, нуль						
1	оди́н	11	одина́дцять				
2	два	12	двана́дцять	20	два́дцять	200	дві́сті
3	три	13	трина́дцять	30	три́дцять	300	три́ста
4	чоти́ри	14	чотирна́дцять	40	со́рок	400	чоти́риста
5	п'ять	15	п'ятна́дцять	50	п'ятдеся́т	500	п'ятсо́т
6	шість	16	шістна́дцять	60	шістдеся́т	600	шістсо́т
7	сім	17	сімна́дцять	70	сімдеся́т	700	сімсо́т
8	ві́сім	18	вісімна́дцять	80	вісімдеся́т	800	вісімсо́т
9	де́в'ять	19	дев'ятна́дцять	90	дев'ятдеся́т, *дев'яно́сто*	900	дев'ятсо́т
10	де́сять			100	сто	1000	ти́сяча

The preferred way of saying 90 in Ukraine is **дев'яно́сто**.

E.1 Using Cardinal Numbers

In English, cardinal numbers are not declined. In other words, regardless of how they are used in a sentence, they are always written the same way.

Subject (Nominative Case)
There's **one stamp** on the table.

Direct Object (Accusative Case)
He has **one stamp**.

In Ukrainian, cardinal numbers are declined.

Subject (Nominative Case)
There's **one stamp** on the table.
На столі́ **одна́ ма́рка**.

Direct Object (Accusative Case)
He has **one stamp**.
Він ма́є **одну́ ма́рку**.

In this lesson you will learn how to use cardinal numbers only with **inanimate nouns** in the **nominative** and **accusative** cases. This will enable you to talk about such things as money, age, telephone numbers, and weight in Ukrainian.

You will learn how to use cardinal numbers in other cases later in the text.

E.2 One and Numbers Ending in One

In Ukrainian, because the number **one** must agree in **gender** and in **case** with the noun that it accompanies, there are three ways of writing it: **одна́, оди́н, одне́**.

Let's look at the number **one** when it is used with **inanimate nouns that are either the subject of a sentence, or the direct object of an affirmative verb**.

In the examples that follow, only **одна** changes to **одну** in the accusative case; **один** and **одне** remain the same in both the nominative and accusative cases.

Nominative Case	Accusative Case
Feminine Noun	***Feminine Noun***
У кімна́ті **одна́ ля́мпа**. There's one lamp in the room.	Я ба́чу **одну́ ля́мпу** в кімна́ті. I see one lamp in the room.
Masculine Noun	***Masculine Noun***
У кімна́ті **оди́н стіл**. There's one table in the room.	Я ба́чу **оди́н стіл** у кімна́ті. I see one table in the room
Neuter Noun	***Neuter Noun***
У кімна́ті **одне́ крі́сло**. There's one chair in the room.	Я ба́чу **одне́ крі́сло** в кімна́ті. I see one chair in the room.

In numbers like **twenty-one**, **thirty-one**, **forty-one**, **fifty-one**, **sixty-one**, **seventy-one**, **eighty-one**, **ninety-one**, and **one hundred and one**, **one thousand and one**, only the last digit, **one**, changes.

Let's look at a few more examples.

Nominative Case	Accusative Case
Feminine Noun	***Feminine Noun***
Ось два́дцять **одна́ ма́рка**. Here are twenty-one stamps.	Я ма́ю два́дцять **одну́ ма́рку**. I have twenty-one satmps.
Masculine Noun	***Masculine Noun***
Ось со́рок **оди́н до́ляр**. Here are forty-one dollars.	Вона́ ма́є со́рок **оди́н до́ляр**. She has forty-one dollars.
Neuter Noun	***Neuter Noun***
Ось сто **одне́ перо́**. Here are a hundred and one pens.	Він ма́є сто **одне́ перо́**. He has a hundred and one pens.

Practise Oral Exercise 19.13

E.3 Two, Three, Four and Numbers Ending in 2, 3, and 4

In Ukrainian, the number **two** is written as **дві** with **feminine** nouns, and as **два** with **masculine and neuter nouns**.

The numbers **три** and **чоти́ри** do not change.

When **inanimate nouns** are used as **subjects or direct objects** after the numbers **два/дві**, **три** and **чоти́ри**, they are in the **nominative/accusative plural form**.

Although inanimate nouns are in the nominative/accusative plural form after the numerals two, three, and four, **the stress is like that of the genitive singular form**.

Stress in Nom. Sing.	*Stress in Gen. Sing.*	*Stress in Nom. Plural*	*Stress with Numeral*
вікно́	вікна́	ві́кна	два вікна́

1. **Nominative Case**

   Feminine Inanimate Noun

   У кімна́ті **дві** (**три**, **чоти́ри**) ля́мпи.
   There are two (three four) lamps in the room.

   Masculine/Neuter Inanimate Nouns

   У кімна́ті **два** (**три**, **чоти́ри**) **столи́/крі́сла**.
   There are two (three, four) tables/chairs in the room.

2. **Accusative Case**

   Feminine Inanimate Noun

   Я ба́чу **дві** (**три**, **чоти́ри**) **ля́мпи** в кімна́ті.
   I see two (three, four) lamps in the room.

   Masculine/Neuter Inanimate Nouns

   Я ба́чу **два** (**три**, **чоти́ри**) **столи́/крі́сла** в кімна́ті.
   I see two (three, four) tables/chairs in the room.

In numbers like **twenty-two**, **thirty-two**, and f**orty-two**, only the last digit, **two**, changes.

У конве́рті три́дцять **дві ма́рки**.
There are **thirty-two** stamps in the envelope.

У гаманці́ші́стдеся́т **два до́ляри**.
There are **sixty-two** dollars in the wallet.

Practise Oral Exercise 19.14

E.4 5-20; 30, 40, 50, 60, 70, 80, 90; 100, 200, 300, 400, 500, 600, 700, 800, 900, 1000; and Numbers Ending in 5, 6, 7, 8, and 9

All the numbers from **five through twenty are followed by nouns in the genitive plural case**.

In addition, **thirty, forty, fifty, sixty, seventy, eighty, ninety, the hundreds, one thousand,** and **numbers that end in five, six, seven, eight, and nine, are followed by nouns in the genitive plural case.**

When these cardinal numbers are the subject of a sentence they are treated like neuter singular nouns and they are used with third person singular verbs. In this respect, they are like adverbs of quantity. (See B.2 in this lesson.)

Nominative Case	*Accusative Case*
У па́чці є **п'ять ґу́мок**. There are five erasers in the package.	Він купу́є **п'ять ґу́мок**. He is buying five erasers.
У па́чці **було́ шість олівці́в**. There were six pencils in the package.	Він купу́є **шість олівці́в**. He is buying six pencils.
У па́чці **бу́де twelveдвана́дцять пер**. There will be twelve pens in the package.	Він купу́є **двана́дцять пер**. He is buying twelve pens.
Чи тут є **два́дцять до́ларів**? Are there twenty dollars here?	Вона ма́є **два́дцять до́ларів**. She has twenty dollars.
Чи тут **було́ со́рок ві́сім до́ларів**? Were there forty-eight dollars here?	Вона́ ма́є **со́рок ві́сім до́ларів**. She has forty-eight dollars.
Чи тут **бу́де сімдеся́т сім до́ларів**? Will there be seventy-seven dollars here?	Вона́ ма́є **сімдеся́т сім до́ларів**. She has seventy-seven dollars.
Ось **дві́сті це́нтів**! Here are two hundred pennies!	Хто ма́є **дві́сті це́нтів**? Who has two hundred pennies?
Ось **п'ятсо́т це́нтів**! Here are five hundred pennies!	Хто ма́є **п'ятсо́т це́нтів**? Who has five hundred pennies?

In the accusative case, **ти́сяча** changes to **ти́сячу**.

Ось **ти́сяча до́ларів**! Here's one thousand dollars!	Хто ма́є **ти́сячу до́ларів**? Who has a thousand dollars?

Practise Oral Exercises 19.15, 19.16, 19.17, 19.18

Do Written Exercise 19.5

LESSON 20

A. VOCABULARY

Nouns

bathing suit	купáльник
belt	пасóк (паск-), рéмінь (ремен-)
blouse	блюзка, *блýзка*
boot	чóбіт (чобот-) *g.pl.* чобíт
cap, baseball cap	шáпка, *кéпка*
clothing, clothes	óдяг *[sg]*
coat, overcoat *[winter]*	пальтó
coat *[spring, fall]*	плащ
dress	сукóнка, сукéнка, *плáття [n]*
fur coat	хýтро, кожýх, *шýба*
glove	рукави́чка
hat	капелюх
jacket	жакет, куртка
jeans	джíнси *[pl]*, джíнсів, *джи́нси*
kerchief	хýстка
mitt, mitten	рукави́ця
necktie, tie	кравáтка, *гáлстук*
pants, slacks	штани́ *[pl]*, штанíв
parka	пáрка
pullover	пулóвер *[h]*
pyjamas	піжáма *[sg]*
raincoat	дощови́к
running shoe, gym shoe	тенісíвка, *кед*
sandal	босоні́жка, сандáля
scarf	шáлик
shirt	сорóчка
shoe	череви́к, *тýфля*
shorts	шóрти *[pl]*, шóртів
skirt	спідни́ця
slipper	кáпець (капц-)
sock	шкарпéтка
stocking	панчóха
suit	костюм
sweater, cardigan	свéтер *[h]* (светр-), *светр [h]*
T-shirt	тéніска, футбóлка

Verbs

to give	дава́ти: да-ю́, -є́ш
to help, to assist	помага́ти: помага́-ю, -є́ш
to lend, to borrow	позича́ти: позича́-ю, -єш
to send	посила́ти: посила́-ю, -єш
to thank	дя́кувати: дя́ку-ю, -єш

Vocabulary Notes

When **позича́ти** means **to lend**, it is used with the **dative case**; when **позича́ти** means **to borrow**, it is used with **у + the genitive case**. (See section H in this lesson.)

B. DATIVE CASE

In Ukrainian, nouns are used in the dative case to express the **indirect object** in a sentence.

The indirect object indicates **for whom (for what)**, or **to whom (to what)** something is being done.

Although both animate and inanimate nouns may be used as indirect objects, in most instances the indirect object is an animate noun.

B.1 Indirect Object

In English, there are two ways of constructing sentences in which an indirect object is used. Let's examine the following two sentences.

1. **The woman is buying the child a cap.**

Subject:	(Who is buying?)	**The woman**.
Predicate:	(What is she doing?)	She **is buying**.
Direct Object:	(What is she buying?	**A cap**.
Indirect Object:	(For whom is she buying it?)	**For the child**.

2. **The man is sending the boy a present.**

Subject:	(Who is sending?)	**The man**.
Predicate:	(What is he doing?)	He **is sending**.
Direct Object:	(What is he sending?)	**A present**.
Indirect Object:	(To whom is he sending it?)	**To the boy**.

As you can see from the questions asked in the analysis of the two sentences, the indirect object in both sentences may be replaced by a prepositional phrase.

In the first sentence, the prepositional phrase that replaces the indirect object begins with **for**, and in the second one, with **to**.

1. The woman is buying **the child** a cap.
   or
   The woman is buying a cap **for the child**.

2. The man is sending **the boy** a present.
   or
   The man is sending a present **to the boy**.

Usually the indirect object precedes the direct object, while the prepositional phrase comes after it.

In these sentences, the nouns **child** and **boy** remain the same when they are used as an indirect object, and when they form part of a prepositional phrase.

The interrogative pronoun **who** changes to **whom**.

In Ukrainian, the indirect object is expressed in the same way as in English, but the endings of the nouns change.

The interrogative pronouns also change; **хто** becomes **комý**, and **що** becomes **чомý**.

Let's examine the Ukrainian translations of these two sentences.

1. **Жíнка купýє дити́ні шáпку.**

Subject:	(Хто купýє?)	**Жíнка**.
Predicate:	(Що жíнка рóбить?)	Вонá **купýє**.
Direct Object:	(Що вона купýє?)	**Шáпку**.
Indirect Object:	(Комý вонá купýє шáпку?)	**Дити́ні**.

2. **Чоловíк посилáє хлóпцеві подарýнок.**

Subject:	(Хто посилáє?)	**Чоловíк**.
Predicate:	(Що чоловíк рóбить?)	Він **посилáє**.
Direct Object:	(Що він посилáє?)	**Подарýнок**.
Indirect Object:	(Комý він посилáє подарýнок?)	**Хлóпцеві**.

As with the English sentences, the indirect objects in both of these Ukrainian sentences may be replaced by prepositional phrases beginning with **для** or **до**; unlike English, however, these two prepositions determine that the endings of the nouns in the prepositional phrases must be in the **genitive case**.

1. Жíнка купýє **дити́ні** шáпку.
   or
   Жíнка купýє шáпку **для дити́ни**.

2. Чоловíк **хлóпцеві** посилáє подарýнок.
   or
   Чоловíк посилáє подарýнок **до хлóпця**.

C. DATIVE PLURAL ENDINGS

The dative plural endings are the same for nouns of all genders.

C.1 All Genders

Hard and Mixed Declensions: **-ам**

Soft 1 and Soft 2 Declensions: **-ям**

Feminine Nouns: Dative Plural Endings				
Declension	***Endings***	***Nominative Singular***	***Stem***	***Dative Plural***
Hard	**-ам**	сестрá	сестр-	сéстр**ам**
Mixed	**-ам**	тéща	тещ-	тéщ**ам**
Soft 1	**-ям**	учени́ця	учениц-	учени́ц**ям**
Soft 2	**-ям**	Марíя	Марі-	Марí**ям**

Masculine Nouns: Dative Plural Endings				
Declension	***Endings***	***Nominative Singular***	***Stem***	***Dative Plural***
Hard	**-ам**	брат	брат-	брат**áм**
Mixed	**-ам**	товáриш	товариш-	товариш**áм**
Soft 1	**-ям**	ýчень	учн-	ýчн**ям**
Soft 2	**-ям**	злóдій	злоді-	злодí**ям**

Neuter Nouns: Dative Plural Endings				
Declension	***Endings***	***Nominative Singular***	***Stem***	***Dative Plural***
Hard	**-ам**	лíжко	ліжк-	лíжк**ам**
Mixed	**-ам**	прíзвище	прізвищ-	прíзвищ**ам**
Soft 1	**-ям**	мíсце	місц-	місц**я́м**
Soft 2	**-ям**	завдáння	завданн-	завдáнн**ям**

C.2 Nouns That Are Always Plural

Learn the dative endings of the nouns that are always plural. (It is highly unlikely that you will ever have the occasion to use the inanimate nouns in the dative case.)

	Nominative Plural	*Dative Plural*
Animate	батькй́	батька́**м**
	дівча́та	дівча́та**м**
	ді́ти	ді́т**ям**
	лю́ди	лю́д**ям**
Inanimate	схо́ди	схо́д**ам**
	цимба́ли	цимба́л**ам**
	ша́хи	ша́х**ам**
	гро́ші	гро́ш**ам**
	ша́шки	ша́шк**ам**
	но́жиці	но́жиц**ям**
	ме́блі	ме́бл**ям**
	две́рі	две́р**ям**

C.3 Summary Chart: Dative Plural Endings

Summary: Dative Plural Endings				
	Hard	*Mixed*	*Soft 1*	*Soft 2*
Feminine	**-ам**	**-ам**	**-ям**	**-ям**
Masculine	**-ам**	**-ам**	**-ям**	**-ям**
Neuter	**-ам**	**-ам**	**-ям**	**-ям**

Practise Oral Exercises 20.1, 20.2

Do Written Exercises 20.1, 20.2

D. DATIVE SINGULAR ENDINGS

For feminine and masculine nouns, the dative singular endings are very similar to the **locative** singular endings.

D.1 Feminine Nouns

For feminine nouns, the endings for the dative singular case are the same as for the locative singular: [=Lsg]. (See Lesson 14, D.1.)

The stems of Hard Declension nouns ending in **-г, -к, -х** are changed before the dative singular ending is added: stems ending in **г**: **г** → **з**; stems ending in **к**: **к** → **ц**; stems ending in **х**: **х** → **с**.

Hard, Mixed, and Soft 1 Declensions: **-і** [=Lsg]

Soft 2 Declension: **-ї** [=Lsg]

Feminine Nouns: Dative Singular Endings				
Declension	***Endings***	***Nominative Singular***	***Stem***	***Dative Singular***
Hard	-і	сестрá	сестр-	сестрí
	-і	Óльга	Ольг-	Óльзі
	-і	дочкá	дочк-	дочцí
	-і	свекрýха	свекрух-	свекрýсі
Mixed	-і	тéща	тещ-	тéщі
Soft 1	-і	ученúця	учениц-	ученúці
Soft 2	-ї	Марíя	Марі-	Марíї

Practise Oral Exercise 20.3

D.2 Masculine Nouns

For both masculine animate and inanimate nouns, the endings for the dative singular case are the same as for the locative singular of masculine *animate* nouns. (See Lesson 14, D.2.)

Hard Declension: **-ові** [=aLsg]

Mixed and Soft 1 Declensions: **-еві** [=aLsg]

Soft 2 Declension: **-єві** [=aLsg]

Masculine Animate Nouns: Dative Singular Endings				
Declension	*Endings*	*Nominative Singular*	*Stem*	*Dative Singular*
Hard	**-ові**	офіція́нт	офіціянт-	офіція́нт**ові**
Mixed	**-еві**	това́риш	товариш-	това́риш**еві**
Soft 1	**-еві**	продаве́ць	продавц-	продавц**е́ві**
Soft 2	**-єві**	ге́ній	гені-	ге́ні**єві**

Masculine Inanimate Nouns: Dative Singular Endings				
Declension	*Endings*	*Nominative Singular*	*Stem*	*Dative Singular*
Hard	**-ові**	по́їзд	поїзд-	по́їзд**ові**
Mixed	**-еві**	ґара́ж	ґараж-	ґара́ж**еві**
Soft 1	**-еві**	готе́ль	готел-	готе́л**еві**
Soft 2	**-єві**	музе́й	музе-	музе́**єві**

There is an alternate set of endings that is used sometimes for both masculine animate and inanimate nouns in the dative case.

It is helpful to be able to recognize these endings if you should happen to come across them; however, at this point in your study of Ukrainian you are not expected to use them.

Alternate Masculine Dative Singular Endings

Hard and Mixed Declensions: **-у**

Soft 1 and Soft 2 Declensions: **-ю**

Masculine Animate Nouns: Alternate Dative Singular Endings				
Declension	*Endings*	*Nominative Singular*	*Stem*	*Dative Singular*
Hard	**-у**	офіція́нт	офіціянт-	офіція́нт**у**
Mixed	**-у**	това́риш	товариш-	това́риш**у**
Soft 1	**-ю**	у́чень	учн-	у́чн**ю**
Soft 2	**-ю**	ге́ній	гені-	ге́ні**ю**

Masculine Inanimate Nouns: Alternate Dative Singular Endings				
Declension	*Endings*	*Nominative Singular*	*Stem*	*Dative Singular*
Hard	**-у**	пóїзд	пóїзд-	пóїзд**у**
Mixed	**-у**	ґарáж	ґараж-	ґарáж**у**
Soft 1	**-ю**	готéль	готел-	готéл**ю**
Soft 2	**-ю**	музéй	музе-	музé**ю**

Practise Oral Exercise 20.4

D.3 Neuter Nouns

In these early stages of learning Ukrainian, you will rarely, if ever, need to use a neuter noun in the dative case; however, a brief summary of the endings is being given now so that you will be able to refer to them if you should ever need them.

The dative singular endings for neuter nouns are like the alternate endings for masculine nouns.

Hard and Mixed Declensions: **-у**

Soft 1 and Soft 2 Declensions: **-ю**

Neuter Nouns: Dative Singular Endings				
Declension	*Endings*	*Nominative Singular*	*Stem*	*Dative Singular*
Hard	**-у**	крíсло	крісл-	крíсл**у**
Mixed	**-у**	прíзвище	прізвищ-	прíзвищ**у**
Soft 1	**-ю**	мíсце	місц-	мíсц**ю**
Soft 2	**-ю**	помéшкання	помешканн-	помéшканн**ю**

Some neuter nouns may also have, as alternate endings, the primary masculine endings **-ові** or-**еві**. You should be able to recognize such nouns, but, at this point in your studies, it is not likely that you will have occasion to use them.

D.4 Summary Chart: Dative Singular Endings

Summary: Dative Singular Endings				
	Hard	*Mixed*	*Soft 1*	*Soft 2*
Feminine	**-i** [=Lsg]	**-i** [=Lsg]	**-i** [=Lsg]	**-ї** [=Lsg]
Masculine	**-ові** [=*a*Lsg] **-y**	**-еві** [=*a*Lsg] **-y**	**-еві** [=*a*Lsg] **-ю**	**-єві** [=*a*Lsg] **-ю**
Neuter	**-y** **-ові**	**-y** **-еві**	**-ю** **-еві**	**-ю** **-еві**

Practise Oral Exercises 20.5, 20.6

Do Written Exercises 20.3, 20.4

E. DATIVE CASE: DECLENSION OF PRONOUNS

Pronouns, like nouns, serve as indirect objects in sentences.

E.1 Interrogative Pronouns

In English, as stated in B.1, only **who** changes to **whom** in the dative case: **what** does not change.

In Ukrainian, both interrogative pronouns change in the dative case: **хто** becomes **комý**; **що** becomes **чомý**.

E.2 Personal Pronouns

In English, **it**, **you***[s]* and **you***[p]* do not change; the five remaining personal pronouns do change.

Singular Pronouns		Plural Pronouns	
Subject	*Indirect Object*	*Subject*	*Indirect Object*
I	**me**	**we**	**us**
he	**him**	**they**	**them**
she	**her**		

In Ukrainian, all the personal pronouns change when they are used as indirect objects.

Singular Pronouns		**Plural Pronouns**	
Nominative Case	*Dative Case*	*Nominative Case*	*Dative Case*
я	**мені́**	**ми**	**нам**
ти	**тобі́**	**ви**	**вам**
вона́	**їй**	**вони́**	**їм**
він	**йому́**		
воно́	**йому́**		

F. VERBS AND THE DATIVE CASE

At this point in your studies, you will not be learning any prepositions that are used with the dative case; however, you should pay close attention to the use of the dative case with a number of Ukrainian verbs.

F.1 позича́ти

First of all, let's look at the verb **позича́ти.**

When **позича́ти** means **to lend**, the person **to whom** something is being lent is referred to in the **dative case**.

As you can see in the example that follows, there is nothing unusual about this construction; the noun **books**, as the direct object of an affirmative verb, is in the accusative case; the noun **friend**, as the indirect object, is in the dative case.

Кому́ ти позича́єш книжки́**?**	**To whom** do you *[s]* lend books**?**
Я позича́ю книжки́ **това́ришеві.**	I lend books **to a friend**.

When **позича́ти** means **to borrow**, the person from whom something is being borrowed is referred to by using the preposition **у/в + the genitive case**.

У ко́го ти позича́єш книжки́?	**From whom** do you *[s]* borrow books?
Я позича́ю книжки́ **в това́риша**.	I borrow books **from a friend**.

F.2 Other Verbs

Some Ukrainian verbs require an indirect object in the dative case even when the direct object is only implied, but is not actually present.

Let's look at the verb **помага́ти**. As you can see in the example that follows, the direct object **help** is not actually present, but it is implied; therefore, the person who is receiving this help is in the dative case as the indirect object.

Кому́ він помага́є?	**Whom** is he helping? (**To whom** is he giving help?)
Він помага́є **учи́телеві**.	He is helping **the teacher**, (He is giving help **to the teacher**.)

Of the verbs that you know, the following are among those falling into this category.

дя́кувати	писа́ти	телефонува́ти
каза́ти	помага́ти	чита́ти
плати́ти	ска́ржитися	шепта́ти

 **Practise Oral Exercises 20.7, 20.8**

Do Written Exercise 20.5

G. AGE

In English, we ask people how old they are when we want to know their age.

Ivan, how old are you?

The person who answers uses the verb **to be** and states his/her age in years.

I **am** twenty (years old).

In Ukrainian, you will hear two ways of talking about age.

The structure that puts **the subject into the dative case** is considered to be the proper way of speaking about age, and you will be using it in this course.

Іва́не, скі́льки **тобі́** ро́ків?	Ivan, how old are you?
Мені́ два́дцять ро́ків.	I'm twenty years old.

You should be prepared, however, to understand speakers of Ukrainian who use the verb **ма́ти**, as in the following example.

Іва́не, скі́льки ро́ків **ти ма́єш**?	Ivan, how old are you?
Я ма́ю два́дцять ро́ків.	I'm twenty years old.

For babies who are under a year old, one talks about months, not years.

Скільки місяців **дити́ні**? — How many months old is the child?
Дити́ні де́сять мі́сяців. — The child is ten months old.

Скільки місяців **дити́на ма́є**? — How many months old is the child?
Дити́на ма́є де́сять мі́сяців. — The child is ten months old.

Practise Oral Exercises 20.9, 20.10

Do Written Exercise 20.6

H. ТРЕ́БА, ПОТРІ́БНО

The most common way of saying that you need something in Ukrainian is to use either **тре́ба** or **потрі́бно**.

When either **тре́ба** or **потрі́бно** is used, the person who needs something is in the **dative case**, while the thing that he/she is in need of is in the **genitive case**.

Їй тре́ба **дощовика́**.
She needs a raincoat.

Їй потрі́бно **дощовика́**.
She needs a raincoat.

Йому́ тре́ба **па́рки**.
He needs a parka.

Йому́ потрі́бно **па́рки**.
He needs a parka.

Notice that the words **тре́ба** and **потрі́бно** stay the same regardless of who is in need or what is needed.

When the words **тре́ба** or **потрі́бно** are used with verbs (see Lesson 9), the one who needs to do something is in the **dative case**.

Їй тре́ба вчи́тися.
She needs to study.

Їй потрі́бно вчи́тися.
She needs to study.

Йому́ тре́ба спа́ти.
He needs to sleep.

Йому́ потрі́бно спа́ти.
He needs to sleep.

Practise Oral Exercises 20.11, 20.12

Do Written Exercise 20.7

LESSON 21

A. VOCABULARY

Nouns

barn	ста́йня, стодо́ла
beach	пляж
bee	бджола́
bench	ла́ва, ла́вка
bird	птах, пта́шка
boat	чо́вен (човн-)
bridge	міст (мост-)
bush	кущ
butterfly	мете́лик
cat	кіт (кот-)
cow	коро́ва
dog	пес (пс-)
fence	парка́н
field	по́ле
flower	кві́тка
fly	му́ха
forest	ліс
grass	трава́
horse	кінь (кон-); *g.pl.* ко́ней
lake	о́зеро
monument	па́м'ятник
mosquito	кома́р *[h]*
mountain	гора́
park	парк
path	сте́жка
picnic	пікні́к
river	ріка́
sea	мо́ре
shore, bank *[of a river]*	бе́рег
snake *[garter snake]*	вуж
tree	де́рево
weed	бур'я́н
yard	дві́р *[h]* (двор-)

Verbs

to cut, to slice	кра́яти: кра́-ю, -єш
to fix, repair	ла́годити: ла́го**дж**у, ла́год-иш
to photograph	фотографува́ти: фотографу́-ю,-єш
to stir, to mix, to shuffle	міша́ти: міша́-ю, -єш
to take care of, look after	догляда́ти: догляда́-ю, -єш

Prepositions

before, in front of	пе́ред
behind, beyond	за
beneath, under	під
between, among	між
overhead, above	над
with, along with	з

Vocabulary Notes

1. As you already know, the suffix **-ка** is often added to a masculine noun to create a feminine noun: **школя́р – школя́рка**. In addition, **-ка** can have a diminutive meaning: thus, **ла́ва** is a bigger bench, while **ла́вка** is a smaller bench; **птах** is a bigger bird, while **пта́шка** is a smaller bird.

2. The word **кома́р** belongs to the masculine hard declension; however, the nominative plural form is **комарі́**.

3. The locative singular form of **бе́рег** is **... бе́резі or ... бе́регові**.

4. As you will learn later on, there are many words for **cat** and **dog** in Ukrainian, but **кіт** and **пес** will be understood by all speakers of Ukrainian.

5. Learn the following expressions regarding travel.

to go to the mountains	ї́хати в го́ри
to go to the fields	ї́хати в по́ле
to go to the forest	ї́хати в ліс/до лі́су
to go to the park	ї́хати в парк/до па́рку
to go to the lake	ї́хати до о́зера/на о́зеро
to go to the sea	ї́хати до мо́ря/на мо́ре
to go to the river	ї́хати до ріки́/на ріку́
to go to the shore	ї́хати до бе́рега/на бе́рег
to go to the beach	ї́хати на пляж

B. INSTRUMENTAL CASE

In Ukrainian, the instrumental case performs several functions.

1. It indicates the agent or instrument by means of which an action is performed.
2. It expresses a temporary state or condition.
3. It is used with some verbs.
4. It forms prepositional phrases with some prepositions.

B.1 Instrument of Means

In English, prepositional phrases beginning with either **by** or **with** are used to express the instrument by which an action is performed.

1. **The professor is going by car.**

Subject:	(Who is going?)	**The professor**.
Predicate:	(What is he doing?)	He **is going**.
Instrument:	(By what means is he going?)	**By car**.

2. **The waiter is writing with a pen.**

Subject:	(Who is writing?)	**The waiter**.
Predicate:	(What is he doing?)	He **is writing**.
Instrument:	(With what is he writing?)	**With a pen**.

In these sentences, the nouns **car** and **pen** did not change; however they did have to be used with the **prepositions by** and **with** to indicate that they were **the instrument or the means by which something was being done.**

In Ukrainian, prepositional phrases are not used; however, the endings of the nouns **áвто** and **перó** must change.

In asking the questions "by means of whom'' or "by means of what", the interrogative pronouns **хто** and **що** are changed to **ким** and **чим** respectively.

1. **Профéсор ї́де áвтом.**

Subject:	(Хто ї́де?)	**Профéсор** ї́де.
Predicate:	(Що він рóбить?)	Він **ї́де**.
Instrument:	(Чим він ї́де?)	**Áвтом**.

2. **Офіція́нт пи́ше перóм.**

Subject:	(Хто пи́ше?)	**Офіція́нт** пи́ше.
Predicate:	(Що він рóбить?)	Він **пи́ше**.
Instrument:	(Чим він пи́ше?)	**Перóм**.

B.2 Temporary State or Condition

In Lesson 12 you learned that a noun, used as a complement of **бу́ти**, is placed in the nominative case.

Петро́ Коза́к (є) **учи́тель.**

Now you are ready to learn that a noun complement is in the nominative case only if the state or condition that is being referred to is looked upon as being permanent, or as existing at the present time.

Петро́ Коза́к (є) **учи́тель.**
Petro Kozak is a teacher (and this isn't changing).

If the state or condition that is being expressed is temporary, or one that is likely to change, then the noun complement is placed in the **instrumental case**.

Петро́ Коза́к **був учи́телем**.
Petro Kozak was a teacher (but no longer is one).

Петро́ Коза́к **бу́де вчи́телем**.
Petro Kozak will be a teacher (but isn't one as yet).

C. INSTRUMENTAL PLURAL ENDINGS

The instrumental plural endings are the same for all three genders of Ukrainian nouns.

C.1 All Genders

Hard and Mixed Declensions: **-ами**

Soft 1 and Soft 2 Declensions: **-ями**

Feminine Nouns: Instrumental Plural Endings				
Declension	*Endings*	*Nominative Singular*	*Stem*	*Instrumental Plural*
Hard	**-ами**	банду́ра	бандур-	банду́р**ами**
Mixed	**-ами**	афі́ша	афіш-	афі́ш**ами**
Soft 1	**-ями**	ву́лиця	вулиц-	ву́лиц**ями**
Soft 2	**-ями**	ле́кція	лекці-	ле́кці**ями**

Masculine Nouns: Instrumental Plural Endings				
Declension	*Endings*	*Nominative Singular*	*Stem*	*Instrumental Plural*
Hard	**-ами**	літáк	літак-	літак**áми**
Mixed	**-ами**	ніж	нож-	нож**áми**
Soft 1	**-ями**	олівéць	олівц-	олівц**ями́**
Soft 2	**-ями**	злóдій	злоді-	злоді**ями**

Neuter Nouns: Instrumental Plural Endings				
Declension	*Endings*	*Nominative Singular*	*Stem*	*Instrumental Plural*
Hard	**-ами**	перó	пер-	пéр**ами**
Mixed	**-ами**	прíзвище	прізвищ-	прíзвищ**ами**
Soft 1	**-ями**	мíсце	місц-	місц**я́ми**
Soft 2	**-ями**	завдáння	завданн-	завдáнн**ями**

C.2 Nouns That Are Always Plural

Learn the instrumental endings of the following nouns that are always plural in Ukrainian.

Nominative Plural	*Instrumental Plural*
дíти	ді**тьми**
лю́ди	лю**дьми́**
батьки́	батьк**áми**
дівчáта	дівчáт**ами**
схóди	схóд**ами**
цимбáли	цимбáл**ами**
шáхи	шáх**ами**
шáшки	шáшк**ами**
нóжиці	нóжиц**ями**
мéблі	мéбл**ями**
двéрі	**дверми́** or **двери́ма**
грóші	**грíшми** or **гроши́ма**

C.3 Summary Chart: Instrumental Plural Endings

Summary: Instrumental Plural Endings				
	Hard	*Mixed*	*Soft 1*	*Soft 2*
Feminine	**-ами**	**-ами**	**-ями**	**-ями**
Masculine	**-ами**	**-ами**	**-ями**	**-ями**
Neuter	**-ами**	**-ами**	**-ями**	**-ями**

Practise Oral Exercises 21.1, 21.2

D. INSTRUMENTAL SINGULAR ENDINGS

D.1 Feminine Nouns

The instrumental singular endings of feminine nouns do not resemble any other endings.

Hard Declension: **-ою**

Mixed and Soft 1 Declensions: **-ею**

Soft 2 Declension: **-єю**

Feminine Nouns: Instrumental Singular Endings				
Declension	*Endings*	*Nominative Singular*	*Stem*	*Instrumental Singular*
Hard	**-ою**	банду́ра	бандур-	банду́**рою**
Mixed	**-ею**	афі́ша	афіш-	афі́ш**ею**
Soft 1	**-ею**	ву́лиця	вулиц-	ву́лиц**ею**
Soft 2	**-єю**	ле́кція	лекці-	ле́кці**єю**

D.2 Masculine Nouns

The instrumental singular endings are the same for masculine animate and inanimate nouns.

Hard Declension: **-ом**

Mixed and Soft 1 Declensions: **-ем**

Soft 2 Declension: **-єм**

Masculine Nouns: Instrumental Singular Endings				
Declension	*Endings*	*Nominative Singular*	*Stem*	*Instrumental Singular*
Hard	**-ом**	літáк	літак-	літак**óм**
Mixed	**-ем**	ніж	нож-	нож**éм**
Soft 1	**-ем**	олівéць	олівц-	олівц**éм**
Soft 2	**-єм**	злóдій	злоді-	злóді**єм**

D.3 Neuter Nouns

Except for the Soft 2 Declension ending, the neuter instrumental singular endings are the same as the masculine instrumental singular endings.

Hard Declension: **-ом**

Mixed and Soft 1 Declensions: **-ем**

Soft 2 Declension: **-ям**

Neuter Nouns: Instrumental Singular Endings				
Declension	*Endings*	*Nominative Singular*	*Stem*	*Instrumental Singular*
Hard	**-ом**	перó	пер-	пер**óм**
Mixed	**-ем**	прíзвище	прізвищ-	прíзвищ**ем**
Soft 1	**-ем**	мíсце	місц-	мíсц**ем**
Soft 2	**-ям**	завдáння	завданн-	завдáнн**ям**

D.4 Summary Chart: Instrumental Singular Endings

Summary: Instrumental Singular Endings				
	Hard	*Mixed*	*Soft 1*	*Soft 2*
Feminine	**-ою**	**-ею**	**-ею**	**-єю**
Masculine	**-ом**	**-ем**	**-ем**	**-єм**
Neuter	**-ом**	**-ем**	**-ем**	**-ям**

Practise Oral Exercises 21.3, 21.4, 21.5

Do Written Exercises 21.1, 21.2, 21.3

E. PREPOSITIONS

At this time you will learn how to use the instrumental case with prepositions that indicate location and with the preposition з.

E.1 Location

The following five prepositions are used with the instrumental case to indicate **location**: **за**, **між**, **над**, **пéред**, and **під**.

1. **за** — Касúр стоїть **за кáсою.**
   The cashier is standing **behind the cash register**.

   Бабýся живé **за лíсом**.
   Grandmother lives **beyond the forest**.

2. **між** — Зóшит лежúть **між книжкáми**.
   The notebook is lying **among the books**.

   Хто сидúть **між мáмою і тáтом**?
   Who's sitting **between mom and dad**?

3. **над** — Пташкú літáють **над дерéвами**.
   The birds are flying around **above the trees**.

4. **пéред** — Хто стоїть **пéред вітрúною**?
   Who's standing **in front of the showcase**?

5. **під** — Діти сидять **під дерéвами**.
   The children are sitting **beneath the trees**.

E.2 з

The preposition з is used with the instrumental case to indicate that someone is doing something **with** someone else, or that something is being used along **with** something else.

Remember that the instrumental case is used **without a preposition** if the English preposition **with** implies "by means of".

З ким вонú розмовляють? **With whom** are they are talking?	**З учúтелем.** **With the teacher.**
З чим ти п'єш чай? **With what** do you *[s]* drink (your) tea?	**З цýкром.** **With sugar.**

The preposition з has three alternate forms: **із**, **зі**, and **зо**.

– **із** is used between **a consonant** and **the consonant blends** ст-, сп-, сл-, **стр-**:

– **зі** or **зо** is used between **a vowel** and **the consonant blends** мн-, сн-, ст-, **стр-**:

Вони́ розмовля́**ють із сту**де́нтами

Вона́ розмовля́**є зі** (зо) **сту**де́нтом.

Practise Oral Exercise 21.6, 21.7, 21.8

Do Written Exercises 21.4, 21.5

F. VERBS

Some verbs govern the instrumental case themselves, whereas others are used with prepositions that govern this case.

1. тішитися

The verb **тішитися** is always followed by nouns or pronouns in the instrumental case.

Дочка́ тішиться **о́дягом**.
The daughter is happy **with the clothing**.

Батьки́ тішаться **дітьми**.
The parents are happy **with** (their) **children**.

2. іти́/ходи́ти

Verbs of motion like **іти́/ходи́ти** are often followed by nouns in the instrumental case to indicate the physical space or area through which the movement takes place.

Дівча́та йду́ть **ву́лицею**.
The girls are walking **along the street**.

Хло́пці біжа́ть **доро́гою**.
The boys are running **down the road**.

3. одру́жуватися з

The verb **одру́жуватися** is used with the preposition з and nouns or pronouns in the instrumetal case,

З ким вона́ одру́жується?
Whom is she marrying?

Вона́ одру́жується з **фа́рмером**.
She is marrying **a farmer**.

G. INSTRUMENTAL CASE: DECLENSION OF PRONOUNS

Pronouns are used like nouns in the instrumental case.

G.1 Interrogative Pronouns

In English, the interrogative pronoun **who** changes to **whom** after prepositions; **what** does not change.

In Ukrainian, both interrogative pronouns change in the instrumental case: **хто** becomes **ким**; **що** becomes **чим**.

G.2 Personal Pronouns

In English, only five personal pronouns change after prepositions. (See Lessons 14, 15, 17.)

In Ukrainian, all the personal pronouns change when they are used in the instrumental case.

Singular Pronouns		**Plural Pronouns**	
Nominative Case	*Instrumental Case*	*Nominative Case*	*Instrumental Case*
я	**мнóю**	**ми**	**нáми**
ти	**тобóю**	**ви**	**вáми**
вонá	**нéю**	**вони́**	**ни́ми**
він	**ним**		
вонó	**ним**		

When **з** comes before **мною**, it changes to **зі** or **зо**.

Він ідé **зі** мнóю. Він ідé **зо** мнóю.

Practise Oral Exercises 21.9, 21.10, 21.11

Do Written Exercise 21.6

LESSON 22

A. Vocabulary

Nouns

assistant	асисте́нт; асисте́нтка
banquet	бенке́т
bouquet	буке́т
broom	мітла́, ві́ник
button	ґу́дзик
calculator	калькуля́тор *[h]*
calorie	кальо́рія, *кало́рія*
diet	діє́та
flower bed	квітни́к
hedge	живопло́т
laboratory	ляборато́рія, *лаборато́рія*
lawn	травни́к
lawn mower	коса́рка
menu	меню́ *[indecl.]*
pillow	по́душка
pocket	кише́ня
quilt	ко́вдра
serviette	серве́тка
stain, spot	пля́ма
stone	ка́мінь (камен-)
tablecloth	обру́с, скатерти́на

Pronoun

oneself	себе́

Prepositions

across from, against	про́ти
across, through, because of	че́рез
among, in the middle of	се́ред
besides, except for	крім
for	по
instead of, in place of	за́мість
near, close to	бли́зько
not far from	недале́ко

Verbs

to clean	чи́стити: чи́**щ**у, чи́**ст**-иш
to fall	па́дати: па́да-ю, -єш
to find	знахо́дити: знахо́**дж**у, знахо́д-иш
to forget	забува́ти: забува́-ю, -єш
to leave	лиша́ти: лиша́-ю, -єш
to lose	губи́ти: губ-**л**ю́, -иш
to receive	оде́ржувати: оде́ржу-ю, -єш
to rest	відпочива́ти: відпочива́-ю, -єш

B. PRONOUNS

In addition to consolidating your knowledge of personal and interrogative pronouns, you will learn one new pronoun in this lesson, the reflexive pronoun **себе́**. You will also learn how to decline **indefinite pronouns**.

B.1 Personal Pronouns: Consolidation

Remember that the genitive and accusative **н-** forms given in parentheses for the **third person pronouns** are used only after prepositions.

Singular Personal Pronouns

N.	я	ти	вона́	він/воно́
G.	мене́	тебе́	її (не́ї)	його́ (ньо́го)
A.	[=G]	[=G]	[=G]	[=G]
I.	мно́ю	тобо́ю	не́ю	ним
D.	мені́	тобі́	їй	йому́
L.	... ме́ні	... то́бі	... ній	... ньо́му

Plural Personal Pronouns

N.	ми	ви	вони́
G.	нас	вас	їх (них)
A.	[=G]	[=G]	[=G]
I.	на́ми	ва́ми	ни́ми
D.	нам	вам	їм
L.	... нас	... вас	... них

B.2 Reflexive Pronoun себé

In both English and Ukrainian, a reflexive pronoun refers back to the **subject** of the sentence, or the clause.

Let's examine a few sentences that have reflexive pronouns in them.

He sees **himself** in the mirror.
Він бáчить **себé** в дзéркалі.

In this first sentence, the reflexive pronoun **himself** refers back to **he, the subject of the sentence**.

Do you *[s]* know if **she** can see **herself** in the mirror?
Чи ти знáєш, чи **вонá** мóже бáчити **себé** в дзéркалі?

In this sentence, the reflexive pronoun **herself** refers back to **she, the subject of the subordinate clause**.

No, but I know that **I** can't see **myself** in the mirror.
Ні, алé я знáю, що **я** не мóжу бáчити **себé** в дзéркалі.

In this sentence, the reflexive pronoun **myself** refers back to **I, the subject of the subordinate clause**.

From the examples given above, you can see that a different reflexive pronoun is used in the three English sentences: **himself**, **herself**, and **myself**.

At the same time, you will have noticed that the same reflexive pronoun, **себé**, is used in all three Ukrainian sentences. This draws attention to one of the basic differences between English and Ukrainian reflexive pronouns.

In English, there are **eight** reflexive pronouns.

In Ukrainian, the reflexive pronoun **себé is the same for all persons, genders, and number**.

I see **myself**.	Я бáчу **себé**.
You *[s]* see **yourself**.	Ти бáчиш **себé**.
He sees **himself.**	Він бáчить **себé**.
She sees **herself.**	Вонá бáчить **себé**.
It sees **itself**.	Вонó бáчить **себé**.
We see **ourselves**.	Ми бáчимо **себé**.
You *[p]* see **yourselves**.	Ви бáчите **себé**.
They see **themselves**.	Вонú бáчать **себé**.

There is still another important difference between **себé** and the English reflexive pronouns.

In English, the reflexive pronoun never changes.

In Ukrainian, the reflexive pronoun **себé** is declined; its case depends upon its use in a sentence or clause.

In the following example, **himself** is the **indirect object**, and **себé** is in the **dative case**: **собí.**

He is buying **himself** a computer.
Він купýє **собí** комп'ютер.

In the next example, **himself** is the **direct object of an affirmative verb**, and **себé** is in the **accusative case**: **себé**.

He sees **himself** in the mirror.
Він бáчить **себé** у дзéркалі.

The reflexive pronoun **себé** is declined similarly to the personal pronouns **я** and **ти.**

Ukrainian Reflexive Pronoun себé	
N.	—
G.	себé
A.	[=G]
I.	собóю
D.	собí
L.	... сóбі

Practise Oral Exercises 22.1, 22.2, 22.3

B.3 Interrogative Pronouns

The complete declensions of the interrogative pronouns **хто** and **що** are presented below for review purposes.

Interrogative Pronouns		
N.	хто	що
G.	когó	чогó
A.	[=G]	[=N]
I.	ким	чим
D.	комý	чомý
L.	... кóму	... чóму

B.4 Indefinite Pronouns

Knowing how to decline **хто** and **що** makes it easy to decline indefinite pronouns that have **хто** or **що** as one of their component parts.

1. Declension of Indefinite Pronouns

If you look carefully at the following declensions of these pronouns, you will see that it is only the **хто** or **що** component of these pronouns that is declined.

N.	**хтось**	**щось**	**хто**не́будь	**що**не́будь
G.	**кого́сь**	**чого́сь**	**кого**не́будь	**чого**не́будь
A.	[=G]	[=N]	[=G]	[=N]
I.	**кимсь**	**чимсь**	**ким**не́будь	**чим**не́будь
D.	**кому́сь**	**чому́сь**	**кому**не́будь	**чому**не́будь
L.	... **ко́мусь**	... **чо́мусь**	... **ко́му**небудь	... **чо́му**небудь

N.	де́**хто**	де́**що**	ні**хто́**	ні**що́**
G.	де́**кого**	де́**чого**	ні**ко́го**	ні**чо́го**
A.	[=G]	[=N]	[=G]	[=N]
I.	де́**ким**	де́**чим**	ні**ки́м**	ні**чи́м**
D.	де́**кому**	де́**чому**	ні**ко́му**	ні**чо́му**
L.	... де́**кому**	... де́**чому**	ні ... **ко́му**	ні ... **чо́му**

2. Use of Prepositions with ніхто́, ніщо́, де́хто, де́що

When prepositions are used with **ніхто́** and **ніщо́**, they must be placed between the two component parts of the pronoun: **ні ... хто**; **ні ... що**.

When prepositions are used with **де́хто** and **де́що**, they may be placed either between the two component parts of the pronoun, or before it.

N.	ніхто́	ніщо́	де́хто	де́що
G.	ні **до** ко́го	ні **до** чо́го	де **до** ко́го **до** де́кого	де **до** чо́го **до** де́чого
A.	ні **про** ко́го	ні **про** що	де **про** ко́го **про** де́кого	де **про** що **про** де́що
I.	ні **з** ким	ні **з** чим	де **з** ким **з** де́ким	де **з** чим **з** де́чим
L.	ні **на** ко́му	ні **на** чо́му	де **на** ко́му **на** де́кому	де **на** чо́му **на** де́чому

B.5 Using ніхто́ in Negative Constructions

In English, there may be only one negative word in a sentence; therefore, in the following two sentences, it is correct to say either **there is no one**, or **there is not anyone**.

There's no one here.
There isn't anyone here.

It is **not** correct, however, to say **there is not no one**.

In Ukrainian, both the sentences given above are translated in the same way, using both **ніко́го** and **нема́ (нема́є)**.

There's no one here.
Тут **ніко́го нема́ (нема́є)**.

There isn't anyone here.
Тут **ніко́го нема́ (нема́є)**.

Similarly:

There **never is anyone** here.
Тут **ніко́ли ніко́го нема́ (нема́є)**.

I never talk about anyone.
Я ніко́ли ні про ко́го не говорю́.

I never go anywhere with anyone.
Я ніко́ли ніку́ди ні з ким не йду́.

Practise Oral Exercises 22.4, 22.5

Do Written Exercise 22.1

C. PREPOSITIONS

In this lesson you will learn how to use eight more prepositions: six with the genitive case; and two with the accusative case.

C.1 Prepositions Governing the Genitive Case

1. бли́зько

The preposition **бли́зько** is used with the genitive case to mean **near**, or **close to**.

We work **near** (our) **home**.
Ми працю́ємо **бли́зько до́му**.

We live **close to the school**.
Ми живемо́ **бли́зько шко́ли**.

2. за́мість

The preposition **за́мість** governs the genitive case. It means **instead of**, or **in place of**.

We're going to the store **instead of mother**.
Ми йдемо́ до крамни́ці **за́мість ма́ми**.

They have a flowerbed **in place of a lawn**.
У них квітни́к **за́мість травника́**.

3. крім

The genitive case is used with the preposition **крім**; it means **besides**, or **except for**.

Who was at the party **besides** (your) **friends**?
Хто був на вечі́рці **крім товаришів**?

Except for us, there was no one there.
Крім нас там ніко́го не було́.

4. недале́ко

The preposition **недале́ко** governs the genitive case. It means **not far from**.

The farm isn't **far from the city**.
Фа́рма **недале́ко мі́ста**.

We don't live **far from the stores**.
Ми живемо́ **недале́ко крамни́ць**.

5. про́ти

The genitive case is used with the preposition **про́ти** to mean to be **across from someone or something in a physical sense**, or to **oppose (to be against) someone or something**.

Who sits **across from you** in class?
Хто сиди́ть **про́ти те́бе** в кля́сі?

What do you have **against me**?
Що ти ма́єш **про́ти ме́не**?

6. се́ред

The preposition **се́ред** governs the gentitive case. It means **among**, or **in the middle of.**

Why is the police officer standing **among the children**?
Чому́ поліца́й стої́ть **се́ред діте́й**?

The tree is growing **in the middle of the field**.
Де́рево росте́ **се́ред по́ля**.

C.2 Prepositions Governing the Accusative Case

1. по

The preposition **по** is used with the accusative to mean **to go for someone or something**, or **to get (fetch) someone or something**.

Where is she going *[on foot]*? Куди́ вона́ йде́?	She's going **for milk**. Вона́ йде **по молоко́**.
Where is he going *[by vehicle]*? Куди́ він ї́де?	He's going **for (his) assistant**. Він ї́де **по асисте́нта**.

2. че́рез

The preposition **че́рез** governs the accusative case. It means **across**, **through**, or **on account of (because of)**.

The cat is running **across the road**.
Кіт біжи́ть **че́рез доро́гу**.

We like to walk to school **through the park**.
Ми любимо ходи́ти до шко́ли **че́рез парк**.

I can't sleep **because of the music**.
Я не мо́жу спа́ти **че́рез му́зику**.

Practise Oral Exercise 22.6

Do Written Exercises 22.2, 22.3, 22.4, 22.5, 22.6

LESSON 23

A. ASPECTS OF UKRAINIAN VERBS

As stated in Lesson 4, the Ukrainian verb system differs in an important way from the English verb system: for most English infinitives, there are two Ukrainian infinitives.

English Infinitive	*Ukrainian Infinitives*
to read	читáти, прочитáти

In English, the various present, past, and future tenses are formed from a single infinitive: **to read**.

In Ukrainian, some tenses are formed from the ***imperfective infinitive:*** **читáти**; other tenses are formed from the ***perfective infinitive:*** **прочитáти**.

The Ukrainian imperfective and perfective infinitives are referred to as two aspects (or two views) of the same verb, and they usually come in closely related aspectual pairs.

Imperfective Aspect	*Perfective Aspect*
читáти	прочитáти

A.1 Imperfective Aspect

The tenses that are formed from the imperfective infinitive express an ongoing, repeated, habitual, or generalized action, without any indication as to the completion or termination of such an action.

An incompleted action may be seen as occurring in the present, in the past, or in the future; therefore, three tenses are formed from the imperfective infinitive.

1. Present Tense
2. Past Imperfective Tense
3. Future Imperfective Tense

A.2 Perfective Aspect

The tenses that are formed from the perfective infinitive express an action that has already been completed or terminated, or one that is going to be undertaken and completed or terminated in the future.

A completed action, therefore, may be seen as one that has occurred in the past or as one that will occur (and will be finished) in the future.

Because an action that is seen as being completed or terminated either in the past or in the future can never be happening in the present, only two tenses can be formed from the perfective infinitive.

1. Past Perfective Tense
2. Future Perfective Tense

There are some imperfective verbs that have no perfective aspect. Thus far, you have learned five such verbs.

	Imperfective Aspect	*Perfective Aspect*
to be	бу́ти	—
to be frightened	боя́тися	—
to cost	коштува́ти	—
to have	ма́ти	—
to know	зна́ти	—

B. FORMATION OF PERFECTIVE INFINITIVES

All the verbs that you learned in Lessons 4-22 were **imperfective infinitives**. Most **perfective infinitives** are formed in one of three ways.

1. A prefix is added to the imperfective infinitive.

For some verbs, several prefixes may be added to their imperfective infinitives to form perfective infinitives, but you need to know only the ones presented here.

A perfective infinitive that is formed by adding a prefix to the imperfective infinitive belongs to the same conjugation and group as the imperfective infinitive.

	Imperfective Aspect		*Perfective Aspect*	
to read	чита́ти	[I,vs.1]	**про**чита́ти	[I,vs.1]
to dance	танцюва́ти	[I,vs.2]	**по**танцюва́ти	[I,vs.2]
to grow	рости́	[I,cs.1]	**ви́**рости	[I,cs.1]
to write	писа́ти	[I,cs.2]	**на**писа́ти	[I,cs.2]
to fight	боро́тися	[I,mixed]	**по**боро́тися	[I,mixed]
to talk	говори́ти	[II,лнр]	**по**говори́ти	[II,лнр]
to be silent	мовча́ти	[II,жчшщ]	**за**мовча́ти	[II,жчшщ]
to do	роби́ти	[II,бвмпф]	**з**роби́ти	[II,бвмпф]
to pay	плати́ти	[II,дзст]	**за**плати́ти	[II,дзст]
to stand	стоя́ти	[II,vs]	**по**сто́яти	[II,vs]
to eat	ї́сти	[III]	**з'**ї́сти	[III]

2. The suffix of the imperfective infinitive is changed.

A perfective infinitive that is formed by changing the suffix of the imperfective infinitive may belong to the same conjugation and group as the imperfective infinitive; usually, however, the perfective infinitive belongs to a different conjugation and/or group.

	Imperfective Aspect	*Perfective Aspect*
to choose	ви**бир**а́ти [I,vs.1]	ви́брати [I,cs.2]
to buy	куп**ува́**ти [I,vs.2]	куп**и́**ти [II,бвмпф]

3. A completely different word is used.

For the imperfective infinitive **бра́ти**, the perfective infinitive is **взя́ти**.

	Imperfective Aspect	*Perfective Aspect*
to take	бра́ти [I,cs.2]	узя́ти/взя́ти [I,cs.2]

B.1 The Prefix по-

Most frequently, perfective infinitives are formed by adding the prefix **по-** to imperfective infinitives.

In Lessons 4-22, you learned 105 imperfective infinitives. The perfective infinitives of about a third of them are formed with the prefix **по-**. **In every instance, both of the infinitives belong to the same conjugation and group.**

	Imperfective Aspect [I,vs.1]	*Perfective Aspect [I,vs.1]*
to converse	розмовля́ти	**по**розмовля́ти
to have breakfast	сні́дати	**по**сні́дати
to have dinner	обі́дати	**по**обі́дати
to have supper	вече́ряти	**по**вече́ряти
to hear	чу́ти	**по**чу́ти
to listen	слу́хати	**по**слу́хати
to look for	шука́ти	**по**шука́ти
to play	гра́ти	**по**гра́ти
to stir, mix	міша́ти	**по**міша́ти
to think	ду́мати	**по**ду́мати
to wait	чека́ти	**по**чека́ти

	Imperfective Aspect [I,vs.2]	*Perfective Aspect [I,vs.2]*
to cut	кра́яти	**по**кра́яти
to dance	танцюва́ти	**по**танцюва́ти
to joke	жартува́ти	**по**жартува́ти
to telephone	телефонува́ти	**по**телефонува́ти
to thank	дя́кувати	**по**дя́кувати
to work	працюва́ти	**по**працюва́ти

	Imperfective Aspect [I,cs.1]	*Perfective Aspect [I,cs.1]*
to live	жи́ти	**по**жи́ти
to put	кла́сти	**по**кла́сти

	Imperfective Aspect [I,mixed]	*Perfective Aspect [I,mixed]*
to fight	боро́тися	**по**боро́тися

	Imperfective Aspect [II,лнр]	*Perfective Aspect [II,лнр]*
to shave oneself	голи́тися	**по**голи́тися
to smoke	кури́ти	**по**кури́ти
to talk	говори́ти	**по**говори́ти
to worry	жури́тися	**по**жури́тися

	Imperfective Aspect [II,жчшщ]	*Perfective Aspect [II,жчшщ]*
to be lying down	лежа́ти	**по**ле́жати
to complain	ска́ржитися	**по**ска́ржитися
to hurry	спіши́ти	**по**спіши́ти
to see	ба́чити	**по**ба́чити

	Imperfective Aspect [II,бвмпф]	*Perfective Aspect [II,бвмпф]*
to look at	диви́тися	**по**диви́тися
to love, like	люби́ти	**по**люби́ти
to sleep	спа́ти	**по**спа́ти

	Imperfective Aspect [II,дзст]	*Perfective Aspect [II,дзст]*
to clean	чи́стити	**почи́стити**
to be sitting	сиді́ти	**поси́діти**
to request	проси́ти	**попроси́ти**
to wear	носи́ти	**поноси́ти**

	Imperfective Aspect [II,vs]	*Perfective Aspect [II,vs]*
to be standing	стоя́ти	**посто́яти**

Practise Oral Exercise 23.1

B.2 The Prefix по- and Verbs of Motion

For six of the verbs of motion, the perfective aspect of both the durative and the iterative imperfective infinitives is formed by adding the prefix **по-** to the durative imperfective infinitive.

To form the perfective aspect for **іти́** and **ходи́ти**, the prefix **п-** is added to **іти́**, the durative imperfective infinite.

	Imperfective Aspect			*Perfective Aspect*	
	Iterative	*Durative*			
to carry	носи́ти	нести́	[I,cs.1]	**понести́**	[I,cs.1]
to fly	літа́ти	леті́ти	[II,дзст]	**полеті́ти**	[II,дзст]
to go, come	ходи́ти	іти́	[I,cs.1]	**піти́**	[I,cs.1]
to go, come	ї́здити	ї́хати	[I,cs.2]	**пої́хати**	[I,cs.2]
to haul	вози́ти	везти́	[I,cs.1]	**повезти́**	[I,cs.1]
to run	бі́гати	бі́гти	[II,жчшщ]	**побі́гти**	[II,жчшщ]
to swim	пла́вати	плисти́	[I,cs.1]	**поплисти́**	[I,cs.1]

Practise Oral Exercise 23.2

B.3 Other Prefixes

Of the verbs that you know, almost a third form their perfective aspect by adding one of the following prefixes: **ви-**, з-, **за-**, **на-**, **про-**, **с-** and **у-/в-**.

In every instance, both of the infinitives belong to the same conjugation and group.

1. The prefix ви-

	Imperfective Aspect	*Perfective Aspect*	
to drink	пи́ти	**ви́**пити	[I,vs.2]
to grow	рости́	**ви́**рости	[I,cs.1]

2. The prefix з-

	Imperfective Aspect	*Perfective Aspect*	
to be able	могти́	**з**могти́	[I,cs.1]
to do	роби́ти	**з**роби́ти	[II,бвмпф]
to eat	ї́сти	**з**'ї́сти	[III,їсти]
to fix, to repair	ла́годити	**з**ла́годити	[II,дзст]
to have to	му́сити	**з**му́сити	[II,дзст]
to know how	умі́ти	**з**умі́ти	[I,vs.1]
to plough	ора́ти	**з**ора́ти	[I,mixed]
to prepare	готува́ти	**з**готува́ти	[I,vs.2]
to understand	розумі́ти	**з**розумі́ти	[I,vs.1]
to weigh	ва́жити	**з**ва́жити	[II,жчшщ]

3. The prefix за-

	Imperfective Aspect	*Perfective Aspect*	
to be silent	мовча́ти	**за**мовча́ти	[II,жчшщ]
to cry	пла́кати	**за**пла́кати	[I,cs.2]
to groan	стогна́ти	**за**стогна́ти	[I,cs.2]
to laugh	смія́тися	**за**смія́тися	[I,vs.2]
to lose	губи́ти	**за**губи́ти	[II,бвмпф]
to pay	плати́ти	**за**плати́ти	[II,дзст]
to remember	пам'ята́ти	**за**пам'ята́ти	[I,vs.1]
to sing	співа́ти	**за**співа́ти	[I,vs.1]

4. The prefix на-

	Imperfective Aspect	Perfective Aspect	
to learn, study	учи́тися	**на**вчи́тися	[II,жчшщ]
to write	писа́ти	**на**писа́ти	[I,cs.2]

5. The prefix про-

	Imperfective Aspect	Perfective Aspect	
to read	чита́ти	**про**чита́ти	[I,vs.1]

6. The prefix с-

	Imperfective Aspect	Perfective Aspect	
to ask, inquire	пита́ти	**с**пита́ти	[I,vs.1]
to bathe oneself	купа́тися	**с**купа́тися	[I,vs.1]
to photograph	фотографува́ти	**с**фотографува́ти	[I,vs.2]
to say	каза́ти	**с**каза́ти	[I,cs.2]
to want	хоті́ти	**с**хоті́ти/**за**хоті́ти	[I,cs.2]

7. The prefix у-/в-

	Imperfective Aspect	Perfective Aspect	
to be glad	ті́шитися	**у**ті́шитися/ **в**ті́шитися	[II,жчшщ]
to steal	кра́сти	**у**кра́сти/ **в**кра́сти	[I,cs.1]

Practise Oral Exercise 23.3

Do Written Exercise 23.1

B.4 Changes in the Suffix

As stated in section B of this lesson, if the perfective aspect is formed by changing the suffix of the imperfective infinitive, the imperfective and perfective infinitives usually belong to different groups and/or conjugations.

	Imperfective Aspect [I,vs.1]	*Perfective Aspect*	
to send	пос**и**ла́ти	посла́ти	[I,mixed]
to fall	па́**д**ати	**у**па́**с**ти	[I,cs.1]
to forget	забу**ва́**ти	забу́ти	[I,cs.1]
to help	пома**га́**ти	по**м**о**г**ти́	[I,cs.1]
to lie down	ляг**а́**ти	лягти́	[I,cs.1]
to rest	відпочи**ва́**ти	відпочи́ти	[I,cs.1]
to sit down	сі**да́**ти	сі́**с**ти	[I,cs.1]
to choose	виб**и**ра́ти	ви́брати	[I,cs.2]
to dress oneself	одяга́тися	одяг**ну́**тися	[I,cs.2]
to look after	доглядá́ти	догля́**ну**ти	[I,cs.2]
to leave	лиша́ти	лиши́ти	[II,жчшщ]
to lend	позича́ти	пози́**чи**ти	[II,жчшщ]
to order	замов**ля́**ти	замо́**ви**ти	[II,бвмп]

	Imperfective Aspect [I,vs.2]	*Perfective Aspect*	
to get up	уста**ва́**ти	уста́ти	[I,cs.1]
to buy	куп**ува́**ти	куп**и́**ти	[II,бвмп]
to marry	одру́**жу**ватися	одру**жи́**тися	[II,жчшщ]
to receive	оде́ржу**ва**ти	оде́ржати	[II,жчшщ]
to give	да**ва́**ти	да́ти	[III,да́ти]
to sell	прода**ва́**ти	прода́ти	[III,да́ти]

	Imperfective Aspect [I,cs.2]	*Perfective Aspect*	
to tell a lie	брехá́ти	брех**ну́**ти	[I,cs.2]
to whisper	шеп**та́**ти	шеп**ну́**ти	[I,cs.2]

	Imperfective Aspect *[II,жчшщ]*	*Perfective Aspect*
to shout, scream	крича́ти	кри́кнути [I,cs.2]

	Imperfective Aspect *[II,дзст]*	*Perfective Aspect*	
to enter	вхо́дити	увійти́	[I,cs.1]
to exit	вихо́дити	ви́йти	[I,cs.1]
to find	знахо́дити	знайти́	[I,cs.1]

B.5 Different Words

You know only one verb in which the imperfective and perfective infinitives are different words.

	Imperfective Aspect *[I,cs.2]*	*Perfective Aspect*
to take	бра́ти	узя́ти/взя́ти [I,cs.2]

Practise Oral Exercise 23.4

Do Written Exercises 23.2, 23.3, 23.4, 23.5

C. ADDITIONAL INFORMATION

Although there is usually only one prefix that is used to form the "basic" perfective infinitive, other prefixes may be used to form additional perfective infinitives that differ in meaning from the original imperfective infinitive.

These additional perfective infinitives may then be altered to form new imperfective infinitives, some of which may give rise to other perfective infinitives – a kind of chain reaction!

Let's look at some of the verbs that it is possible to form by adding prefixes to the imperfective infinitive **писáти**.

"Basic" Perfective Infinitive	*Meaning*	
написáти	to write	
Other Perfective Infinitives	***New Meaning Infinitives***	***New Imperfective***
ви́писати	to strike from a list to order something to write at great length	випи́сувати
відписáти	to reply in writing to copy from someone	відпи́сувати
дописáти	to finish writing to write for a newspaper	допи́сувати
записáти	to write down, to enroll	запи́сувати
надписáти	to inscribe	надпи́сувати
описáти	to describe	опи́сувати
переписáти	to rewrite, to recopy	перепи́сувати
підписáти	to sign	підпи́сувати
пописáти	to write all over	попи́сувати
приписáти	to prescribe, to ascribe	припи́сувати
списáти	to make a list	спи́сувати
уписáти/вписáти	to register	упи́сувати

At this point in your studies, you need to know only the perfective infinitives that are presented in this text.

A perfective verb with the prefix **по-** usually means to do something for a while.

посмія́тися — to laugh for while

A perfective verb with the prefix **за-** usually implies the beginning of an action.

засмія́тися — to begin to laugh

LESSON 24

A. VOCABULARY

Nouns

accountant	бухга́льтер *[h]*, *бухга́лтер [h]*
actor	акто́р *[h]*
actress	акто́рка, *актри́са*
architect	архіте́кт, архіте́ктор *[h]*
artist	худо́жник; худо́жниця
baker	пе́кар *[s]*; пе́карка
builder, construction worker	будівни́к, будіве́льник
client	кліє́нт; клієнтка
chef, cook	ку́хар *[s]*; куха́рка
dancer	танцюри́ст; танцюри́стка
dentist	денти́ст, *данти́ст*; денти́стка, *данти́стка*
editor	реда́ктор *[h]*; реда́кторка
electrician	еле́ктрик
engineer	інжене́р *[h]*
hair stylist, hairdresser	перука́р *[s]*; перука́рка
janitor	сто́рож
journalist	журналі́ст; журналі́стка
lawyer	адвока́т, юри́ст
musician	музика́нт; музика́нтка
oculist, optometrist	окулі́ст
painter	маля́р *[mx]*; маля́рка
pharmacist, druggist	апте́кар *[s]*; апте́карка
photographer	фото́граф
pilot	піло́т
plumber	санте́хнік
priest	свяще́ник
psychiatrist	психія́тр *[h]*, *психіа́тр [h]*
psychologist	психо́лог
scientist	науко́вець (науковц-)
singer	співа́к; співа́чка
surgeon	хіру́рг
telephone operator	телефоні́ст; телефоні́стка

B. FUTURE TENSES

There are two future tenses in Ukrainian.

1. The Future Imperfective Tense
2. The Future Perfective Tense

You already know all the endings that are used in forming these two tenses; however, you will have to think carefully about which tense should be used when you want to express an action that is to take place in the future.

C. FUTURE IMPERFECTIVE TENSE

There are two ways of forming the future tense of an imperfective verb.

The **imperfective infinitive** is used in both of these forms of the future imperfective tense.

1. The future tense of the verb **бу́ти** is used as an auxiliary verb with the **imperfective infinitive**.

2. The endings **-му, -меш, -ме, -мемо, -мете, -муть** are added to the **imperfective infinitive**. Except for the consonant **м**, these endings are identical to the present tense endings of the two consonant groups of the First Conjugation.

   These two forms of the future imperfective tense are identical in meaning and they may be used interchangeably.

C.1 Conjugation of Verbs

1. Future Imperfective Tense

Infinitive: чита́ти				
	Singular		***Plural***	
First Person	я	**бу́ду** чита́ти	ми	**бу́демо** чита́ти
Second Person	ти	**бу́деш** чита́ти	ви	**бу́дете** чита́ти
Third Person	він	**бу́де** чита́ти	вони́	**бу́дуть** чита́ти
	вона́	**бу́де** чита́ти		
	воно́	**бу́де** чита́ти		

2. Future Imperfective Tense

Infinitive: **чита́ти**				
		Singular		*Plural*
First Person	я	чита́ти**му**	ми	чита́ти**мемо**
Second Person	ти	чита́ти**меш**	ви	чита́ти**мете**
Third Person	він	чита́ти**ме**	вони́	чита́ти**муть**
	вона́	чита́ти**ме**		
	воно́	чита́ти**ме**		

C.2 Conjugation of Reflexive Verbs

Reflexive imperfective verbs form their future tense in the same way as verbs that are not reflexive. When the **-м** endings are used in conjugating a reflexive verb, **ть** is inserted between the personal ending **-ме** and the reflexive particle **-ся**.

1. Future Imperfective Tense

Infinitive: **одяга́тися**				
		Singular		*Plural*
First Person	я	**бу́ду** одяга́тися	ми	**бу́демо** одяга́тися
Second Person	ти	**бу́деш** одяга́тися	ви	**бу́дете** одяга́тися
Third Person	він	**бу́де** одяга́тися	вони́	**бу́дуть** одяга́тися
	вона́	**бу́де** одяга́тися		
	воно́	**бу́де** одяга́тися		

2. Future Imperfective Tense

Infinitive: **одяга́тися**				
		Singular		*Plural*
First Person	я	одяга́ти**му**ся	ми	одяга́ти**мемо**ся
Second Person	ти	одяга́ти**меш**ся	ви	одяга́ти**мете**ся
Third Person	він	одяга́ти**меть**ся	вони	одяга́ти**муть**ся
	вона́	одяга́ти**меть**ся		
	воно́	одяга́ти**меть**ся		

C.3 Using the Future Imperfective Tense

The future tense that is formed from the imperfective infinitive expresses 1) an ongoing, 2) a repeated/habitual, or 3) a generalized action that will be occurring in the future, without any indication as to the completion or termination of such an action.

1. **An ongoing action**

He **will be reading** the newspaper this morning.
Він **бу́де чита́ти** газе́ту сього́дні вра́нці.
Він **чита́тиме** газе́ту сього́дні вра́нці.

I **will be playing** chess this evening.
Я **бу́ду гра́ти** в ша́хи сього́дні вве́чорі.
Я **гра́тиму** в ша́хи сього́дні вве́чорі.

2. **A repeated/habitual action**

He **will read** the newspaper every day.
Він **бу́де чита́ти** газе́ту щодня́.
Він **чита́тиме** газе́ту щодня́.

She **will phone** us every week.
Вона́ нам **бу́де телефонува́ти** щоти́жня.
Вона́ нам **телефонува́тиме** щоти́жня.

3. **A generalized action**

Will he **be reading** slowly?
Чи він **бу́де чита́ти** пові́льно?
Чи він **чита́тиме** пові́льно?

They **will be studying** in the library.
Вони́ **бу́дуть учи́тися** в бібліоте́ці.
Вони́ **вчи́тимуться** в бібліоте́ці.

Practise Oral Exercises 24.1, 24.2

Do Written Exercises 24.1, 24.2, 24.3

D. FUTURE PERFECTIVE TENSE

There is only one way to form the future tense of a perfective verb: **the personal endings that are used as the present tense endings of imperfective verbs are added to the future tense stem of the perfective verb**.

Because the same personal endings are used for both the present tense of an imperfective verb and the future tense of a perfective verb, they are sometimes referred to as the **present/future** personal endings.

D.1 Future Perfective Stems

The future tense stem of a perfective infinitive is formed in exactly the same way as the present tense stem of an imperfective infinitive.

The following chart contains examples of how present and future tense stems are formed for verbs belonging to all of the conjugations and groups that you have studied.

	Imperfective Verb		*Perfective Verb*	
	Infinitive	***Stem***	***Infinitive***	***Stem***
[I,vs.1]	пита́ти	пит**а**-	спита́ти	спит**а**-
[I,vs.2]	кра́яти	кр**а**-	покра́яти	покр**а**-
[I,cs.1]	нести́	не**с**-	понести́	поне**с**-
[I,cs.1]	кра́сти	кра**д**-	укра́сти	укра**д**-
[I,cs.2]	писа́ти	пи**ш**-	написа́ти	напи**ш**-
[I,mixed]	ора́ти	о**р**-	зора́ти	зо**р**-
[II,лнр]	говори́ти	гово**р**-	поговори́ти	погово**р**-
[II,жчшщ]	лежа́ти	ле**ж**-	полéжати	поле**ж**-
[II,бпвм]	роби́ти	ро**б**-	зроби́ти	зро**б**-
[II,дзст]	плати́ти	пла**т**- (я плачу́)	заплати́ти	запла**т**- (я заплачу́)
[II,vs]	стоя́ти	ст**о**-	посто́яти	пост**о**-
[III,їсти]	ї́сти	**ї**-	з'ї́сти	з'**ї**-

The future tense stems of some verbs are formed irregularly. Learn the future tense stems of the following perfective verbs.

	Perfective Verb		*Future Perfect Stem*
[I,mixed]	посла́ти	(посл-ати)	по**шл**-
[I,cs.2]	ви́брати	(ви**бр**-ати)	ви**бер**-
[I,cs.1]	лягти́	(ляг-ти)	ля**ж**-
[I,cs.1]	помогти́	(помог-ти)	помо**ж**-
[I,cs.1]	уста́ти	(уста-ти)	уста**н**-
[I,cs.1]	відпочи́ти	(відпочи-ти)	відпочи**н**-
[I,cs.1]	сі́сти	(сі-сти)	**ся**д-
[I,cs.1]	упа́сти	(упа-сти)	упад-
[I,cs.1]	забу́ти	(забу-ти)	забу**д**-
[I,cs.1]	увійти́	(увій-ти)	увій**д**-
[I,cs.1]	ви́йти	(вий-ти)	вий**д**-
[I,cs.1]	знайти́	(знай-ти)	знай**д**-
[I,cs.1]	взя́ти	(взя-ти)	**вiзьм**-

D.2 Conjugation of Verbs

You must remember that there is only one way to form the future perfective tense: **the present/future personal endings are added to the stem of a perfective infinitive**.

Future Perfective Tense		
Infinitive: прочита́ти		**Stem: прочита-**
	Singular	*Plural*
First Person	я прочита́**ю**	ми прочита́**ємо**
Second Person	ти прочита́**єш**	ви прочита́**єте**
Third Person	він прочита́**є** вона́ прочита́**є** воно́ прочита́**є**	вони́ прочита́**ють**

D.3 Conjugation of Reflexive Verbs

Reflexive perfective verbs form their future tense in the same way as perfective verbs that are not reflexive.

Remember that in the third person singular forms of a First Conjugation reflexive verb, **ть** is inserted between the personal ending (**-є** or **-е**) and the reflexive particle **-ся**.

Future Perfective Tense		
	Infinitive: одягну́тися	**Stem: одягн-**
	Singular	*Plural*
First Person	я одягну́ся	ми одя́гнемося
Second Person	ти одя́гнешся	ви одя́гнетеся
Third Person	він одя́гнеться вона́ одя́гнеться воно́ одя́гнеться	вони́ одя́гнуться

D.4 Third Conjugation Verbs

There are two groups in the third conjugation of verbs: **ї́сти** [III,**ї́сти**] and **да́ти** [III,**да́ти**].

In Lesson 10 you learned how to conjugate the imperfective verb **ї́сти** in the present tense. Let's see how the perfective verbs **з'ї́сти** and **да́ти** are conjugated in the future tense.

Future Perfective Tense		
	Infinitive: з'їсти	**Stem: з'ї-**
	Singular	*Plural*
First Person	я з'ї**м**	ми з'ї**мо́**
Second Person	ти з'ї**си́**	ви з'ї**сте́**
Third Person	він з'ї**сть** вона́ з'ї**сть** воно́ з'ї**сть**	вони́ з'ї**дя́ть**

Future Perfective Tense				
	Infinitive: дати		**Stem: да-**	
	Singular		***Plural***	
First Person	я	**дам**	ми	**дамó**
Second Person	ти	**даси́**	ви	**дастé**
Third Person	він	**дасть**	вони́	**даду́ть**
	вонá	**дасть**		
	вонó	**дасть**		

As you can see, the only difference between the conjugation of these two perfective verbs is found in the third person plural form: вони́ **їдя́ть**, вони́ **даду́ть**.

You have had only one other perfective verb that belongs to the third conjugation. The perfective verb **продáти** belongs to the **дáти** group [III,дáти].

D.5 Using the Future Perfective Tense

The future tense that is formed from the perfective infinitive expresses an action that is going to be undertaken and **completed or terminated in the future**.

Study the following examples carefully.

He **will have read** the newspaper before breakfast.
Він **прочитáє** газéту до снідáнку.

Who **will tell** them about the picnic?
Хто їм **скáже** про пíкнік?

When **will** they **buy** a house?
Коли́ вони́ **ку́плять** хáту?

Will you *[p]* **lend** me the book?
Чи ви **пози́чите** менí кни́жку?

He **will prepare** supper for us tonight.
Він **зготу́є** нам вечéрю сьогóдні ввéчорі.

We **shall bathe** in the lake after breakfast.
Ми **скупáємося** в óзері пíсля снідáнку.

Will you *[p]* **help** me **repair** the car?
Чи ви **помóжете** менí **злáгодити** áвто?

When **will** the professor **enter** the classroom?
Коли́ профéсор **увійдé** в кля́су?

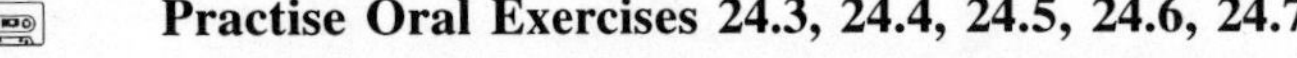

Practise Oral Exercises 24.3, 24.4, 24.5, 24.6, 24.7

Do Written Exercises 24.4, 24.5, 24.6

LESSON 25

A. VOCABULARY

Nouns

animal *[in general]*	твари́на
animal *[wild]*	звір *[h]*
baby sitter, nanny	ня́ня, ня́нька
bag	торби́нка, міше́чок (мішечк-)
baggage	бага́ж
ball *[games, sports]*	м'яч
basket	ко́шик
bonfire	ва́тра, *g.pl.* ва́тер
box	коро́бка
cassette	касе́та
cottage	ко́тедж, *да́ча*
excursion, outing	екску́рсія
fountain	водогра́й, фонта́н
guest	гість (гост-); го́стя
neighbour	сусі́д; сусі́дка
plant *[in general]*	росли́на
playground	майда́нчик
record *[music]*	платі́вка, *пласти́нка*
sailboat	вітри́льник
sand	пісо́к (піск-)
school holidays	кані́кули *[pl]*, кані́кул
slide	спуска́лка
summer camp	та́бір *[h]* (табор-), осе́ля
swimming pool	басе́йн
swing	го́йдалка
tent	шатро́, *g.pl.* ша́тер
toy	за́бавка, *і́грашка*
tractor	тра́ктор *[h]*
trunk *[of a car]*	бага́жник
vacation	вака́ції *[pl]*, вака́цій
walk	прогу́лянка, прохі́д (проход-)
zoo	зоопа́рк

B. PAST TENSES

In this lesson you will learn two past tenses in Ukrainian.

1. The Past Imperfective Tense
2. The Past Perfective Tense

You will find it very easy to form these two tenses because you already know how to use **бу́ти** in the past tense; however you will have to think carefully about which one of them you should use when you want to express an action that took place in the past.

C. PAST TENSE STEMS

The past tense stem for most imperfective and perfective verbs is formed by dropping the suffix **-ти** from the infinitive.

	Imperfective Infinitive	*Past Tense Stem*	*Perfective Infinitive*	*Past Tense Stem*
[I,vs.1]	чита́ти	чита-	прочита́ти	прочита-
[I,vs.2]	кра́яти	кра**я**-	покра́яти	покра**я**-
[I,cs.1]	нести́	нес-	понести́	понес-
[I,cs.2]	писа́ти	писа-	написа́ти	написа-
[I,mixed]	ора́ти	ора-	зора́ти	зора-
[II,лнр]	говори́ти	говор**и**-	поговори́ти	поговор**и**-
[II,жчшщ]	мовча́ти	мовча-	замовча́ти	замовча-
[II,бвмп]	роби́ти	роб**и**-	зроби́ти	зроб**и**-
[II,дзст]	сиді́ти	сиді-	поси́діти	посиді-
[II,vs]	стоя́ти	сто**я**-	посто́яти	посто́**я**-
[III,да́ти]			прода́ти	прода-

For infinitives that end in **-сти**, drop this suffix in forming their past tense stem.

	Imperfective Infinitive	*Past Tense Stem*	*Perfective Infinitive*	*Past Tense Stem*
[I,cs.1]	кра́сти	кра-	укра́сти	укра-
[I,cs.1]	кла́сти	кла-	покла́сти	покла-
[I,cs.1]			сі́сти	сі-
[I,cs.1]			упа́сти	упа-
[I,cs.1]	плисти́	пл**и**-	поплисти́	попл**и**-
[III,ї́сти]	ї́сти	ї-	з'ї́сти	з'ї-

C.1 Irregular Past Tense Stems

Learn the past tense stems of the following imperfective and perfective verbs.

	Imperfective Infinitive	*Past Tense Stem*	*Perfective Infinitive*	*Past Tense Stem*
[I,cs.1]	іти́	**іш-**	піти́	пі**ш-**
[I,cs.1]			увійти́	увій**ш-**
[I,cs.1]			ви́йти	вий**ш-**
[I,cs.1]			знайти́	знай**ш-**

D. PAST TENSE CONJUGATION

You'll find it very easy to conjugate imperfective and perfective verbs in the past tense because you already know how to conjugate **бу́ти** in the past tense. (See Lesson 16.)

D.1 Past Tense Endings

The past tense **singular endings** are marked by **gender**.

Masculine Ending: **-в**

Feminine Ending: **-ла**

Neuter Ending: **-ло**

The past tense **plural ending** for all persons is **-ли**.

Plural Ending: **-ли**

D.2 Imperfective Verbs

Imperfective Infinitive: чита́ти				**Stem: чита-**
		Singular		*Plural*
Person	***Masculine***	***Feminine***	***Neuter***	***All Genders***
First	я чита́**в**	я чита́**ла**	я чита́**ло**	ми чита́**ли**
Second	ти чита́**в**	ти чита́**ла**	ти чита́**ло**	ви чита́**ли**
Third	він чита́**в**	вона́ чита́**ла**	воно́ чита́**ло**	вони́ чита́**ли**

D.3 Perfective Verbs

Perfective Infinitive: з'ї́сти			**Stem: з'ї-**	
	Singular			*Plural*
Person	***Masculine***	***Feminine***	***Neuter***	***All Genders***
First	я з'їв	я з'ї́ла	я з'ї́ло	ми з'ї́ли
Second	ти з'їв	ти з'ї́ла	ти з'ї́ло	ви з'ї́ли
Third	він з'їв	вона́ з'ї́ла	воно́ з'ї́ло	вони́ з'ї́ли

D.4 Reflexive Verbs

Imperfective and perfective reflexive verbs form their past tenses in the same way as verbs that are not reflexive.

Imperfective Infinitive: боя́тися			**Stem: боя-ся**	
	Singular			*Plural*
Person	***Masculine***	***Feminine***	***Neuter***	***All Genders***
First	я боя́вся	я боя́лася	я боя́лося	ми боя́лися
Second	ти боя́вся	ти боя́лася	ти боя́лося	ви боя́лися
Third	він боя́вся	вона́ боя́лася	воно́ боя́лося	вони́ боя́лися

Perfective Infinitive: уми́тися			**Stem: уми-ся**	
	Singular			*Plural*
Person	***Masculine***	***Feminine***	***Neuter***	***All Genders***
First	я вми́вся	я вми́лася	я вми́лося	ми вми́лися
Second	ти вми́вся	ти вми́лася	ти вми́лося	ви вми́лися
Third	він уми́вся	вона́ вми́лася	воно́ вми́лося	вони́ вми́лися

Practise Oral Exercises 25.1, 25.2

Do Written Exercises 25.1, 25.2, 25.3

D.5 Verbs with Irregular Past Tense Stems

In C.1 of this lesson you learned the irregular past tense stems of five verbs: **іти́, піти́, увійти́, ви́йти, знайти́.**

In all five of these verbs, the vowel **o** is inserted between the past tense stem and the personal ending of the masculine singular past tense verb form: він **ішо́в**, він **пішо́в**, він увій**шо́в**, він **ви́йшов, він** знай**шо́в**.

Let's look at the following two examples.

Imperfective Infinitive: іти́			**Stem: іш-**	
		Singular		***Plural***
Person	***Masculine***	***Feminine***	***Neuter***	***All Genders***
First	я йш**о́в**	я йш**ла́**	я йш**ло́**	ми йш**ли́**
Second	ти йш**о́в**	ти йш**ла́**	ти йш**ло́**	ви йш**ли́**
Third	він іш**о́в**	вона́ йш**ла́**	воно́ йш**ло́**	вони́ йш**ли́**

Perfective Infinitive: піти́			**Stem: пiш-**	
		Singular		***Plural***
Person	***Masculine***	***Feminine***	***Neuter***	***All Genders***
First	я пiш**о́в**	я пiш**ла́**	я пiш**ло́**	ми пiш**ли́**
Second	ти пiш**о́в**	ти пiш**ла́**	ти пiш**ло́**	ви пiш**ли́**
Third	він пiш**о́в**	вона́ пiш**ла́**	воно́ пiш**ло́**	вони́ пiш**ли́**

D.6 Past Tense Stems: Closed Syllables

In a few verbs there is a vowel change in the past tense stem of the verb forms for **masculine singular***[m,s]* persons. This change occurs because the past tense stem becomes a closed syllable after the suffix **-ти** is dropped from the infinitive. (See Lesson 12, E.2)

The ending **-в** is not added to the masculine singular verb form of these verbs.

There is no vowel change in the past tense stem for the feminine, neuter, or plural verb forms.

	Imperfective Infinitive	*Past Tense Stem*	*Perfective Infinitive*	*Past Tense Stem*
[I,cs.1]	нести́	нес- (ніс *[m,s]*)	понести́	понес- (поні́с *[m,s]*)
[I,cs.1]	везти́	вез- (віз *[m,s]*)	повезти́	повез- (пові́з *[m,s]*)
[I,cs.1]			лягти́	ляг- (ліг *[m,s]*)
[I,cs.1]	могти́	мог- (міг *[m,s]*)	змогти́	змог- (зміг *[m,s]*)
[I,cs.1]			помогти́	помог- (помі́г *[m,s]*)
[I,cs.1]	рости́	рос- (ріс *[m,s]*)	ви́рости	вирос- (ви́ріс *[m,s]*)

Let's look at the following two examples.

Imperfective Infinitive: нести́		**Stem: нес-**		
		Singular		*Plural*
Person	*Masculine*	*Feminine*	*Neuter*	*All Genders*
First	я ніс	я несла́	я несло́	ми несли́
Second	ти ніс	ти несла́	ти несло́	ви несли́
Third	він ніс	вона́ несла́	воно́ несло́	вони́ несли́

Perfective Infinitive: лягти́		**Stem: ляг-**		
		Singular		*Plural*
Person	*Masculine*	*Feminine*	*Neuter*	*All Genders*
First	я ліг	я лягла́	я лягло́	ми лягли́
Second	ти ліг	ти лягла́	ти лягло́	ви лягли́
Third	він ліг	вона́ лягла́	воно́ лягло́	вони́ лягли́

Practise Oral Exercises 25.3, 25.4, 25.5, 25.6

Do Written Exercise 25.4

E. USING THE PAST TENSES

As stated earlier, you must think carefully about which of the past tenses you should use when you want to express an action that occured in the past.

E.1 Past Imperfective Tense

The past tense that is formed from the imperfective infinitive expresses 1) an ongoing action, 2) a repeated/habitual action, or 3) a generalized action that was occurring in the past without any indication as to the completion or termination of such an action.

1. An ongoing action

She **looked after** (her) parents for a long time.
Вона́ до́вго **догляда́ла** батькі́в.

Where **were** they **smoking** when you *[m,s]* **saw** them?
Де вони́ **кури́ли**, коли ти їх **бачив**?

I think they **were playing** cards last night.
Я ду́маю, що вони́ **гра́ли** в ка́рти учо́ра вве́чорі.

2. A repeated/habitual action

He **read** the newspaper every day.
Він **чита́в** газе́ту щодня́.

They **phoned** me every week.
Вони́ мені́ **телефонува́ли** щоти́жня.

They always **talked** and **laughed** in class.
Вони́ завжди́ **говори́ли** і **смія́лися** в кля́сі.

3. A generalized action

He **read** slowly when he **was** a child.
Він **чита́в** пові́льно, коли́ він **був** дити́ною.

They say she **still used to sing** beautifully then!
Ка́жуть, що вона́ тоді́ ще прекра́сно **співа́ла**.

She **liked to joke,** and he **liked to complain**.
Вона́ **люби́ла жартува́ти**, а він **люби́в ска́ржитися**.

✍ **Do Written Exercise 25.5**

E.2 Past Perfective Tense

The past tense that is formed from the perfective inifinitive expresses **an action that was undertaken and was completed or terminated in the past.**

Study the following examples carefully.

He **read** the newspaper before breakfast.
Він **прочита́в** газе́ту до сніда́нку.

She **chose** the tie for (her) husband.
Вона́ **ви́брала** крава́тку для чолові́ка.

They **got up**, **washed**, and **had breakfast**.
Вони́ **вста́ли**, **уми́лися**, і **посні́дали**.

Have they already **ordered** dinner in the restaurant?
Чи вони́ вже **замо́вили** обі́д у рестора́ні?

When **did** you *[p]* **sell** (your) house?
Коли́ ви **прода́ли** ха́ту?

Did they **get married** in June or July?
Чи вони́ **одружи́лися** в че́рвні, чи в ли́пні?

Who **photographed** the children at the picnic?
Хто **сфотографува́в** діте́й на пі́кніку?

Last night he **repaired** the dishwasher.
Учо́ра вве́чорі він **зла́годив** посудоми́йку.

What **did** she **tell** you *[p]* about (her) vacation?
Що вона́ вам **сказа́ла** про вака́ції?

Practise Oral Exercises 25.7, 25.8, 25.9, 25.10

Do Written Exercise 25.6

LESSON 26

A. VOCABULARY

Adjectives

bad	пога́ний
beautiful	прекра́сний, *краси́вий*
big, great	вели́кий
capable, bright *[mentally]*	зді́бний
cheap, inexpensive	деше́вий, недороги́й
clean	чи́стий
dirty	брудни́й
expensive, costly	дороги́й
foolish, stupid	дурни́й
fortunate, lucky	щасли́вий
good	до́брий
happy	весе́лий
healthy	здоро́вий
hungry	голо́дний
intelligent	розу́мний
little, small	мали́й, мале́нький
long	до́вгий
new	нови́й
nice, pretty	га́рний, *хоро́ший*
old	стари́й
pleasant	прие́мний
poor	бі́дний
rich	бага́тий
sad	сумни́й
short, brief	коро́ткий
sick, ill	хво́рий
strong	си́льний
tall, high	висо́кий
unfortunate, unlucky	нещасли́вий
unhappy, miserable	нещасний
unpleasant	неприє́мний
wise, smart	му́дрий
young	молоди́й

Adjectives (Colours)

black	чóрний
blue	си́ній *[s]*
brown	кори́чневий
green	зелéний
grey	сíрий, си́вий *[of hair]*
orange	помарáнчовий, *орáнжевий*
pink	рожéвий
purple	пурпурóвий, *пурпýрний*
red	червóний
white	бíлий
yellow	жóвтий

Pronouns

which	котри́й
what (kind)	яки́й

Verbs

to iron	прасувáти: прасý-ю, -єш *pf.* ви́прасувати: ви́прасу-ю, -єш
to launder	прáти: пер-ý, -éш *pf* ви́прати: ви́пер-у, -еш
to sew	ши́ти: ши́-ю, -єш *pf* поши́ти: поши́-ю, -єш

Vocabulary Notes

1. The abbreviation *[s]* after **си́ній** *[s]* indicates that this adjective belongs to the Soft Declension of adjectives. (See C.3.)

2. Beginning with this lesson, both the imperfective and perfective infinitives of Ukrainian verbs are given. The verb forms for the first two singular persons (**я** and **ти**) are also provided; this enables you can identify the conjugation and group to which the verbs belong.

   The **perfective** infinitive is preceded by the abbreviation *pf.*

3. ***In Ukrainian***, the word for **bridegroom** is **моло́ди́й**; for **bride**, it is **молодá**. In forming these two words, the adjective **моло́ди́й** is used as a substantive. (See section E in this lesson.)

B. ADJECTIVES

In both English and Ukrainian, adjectives are used to describe or modify a noun.

This is a **new** car. Це **нове́** а́вто.

An attributive adjective precedes the noun that it modifies.

This is a **new** car. Це **нове́** а́вто.

A predicate adjective modifies the subject, but it stands alone after the verb in a sentence.

This car is **new**. Це а́вто (є) **нове́.**

C. DECLENSION OF ADJECTIVES

In Ukrainian, adjectives agree with nouns in **gender**, **number**, and **case**.

C.1 Agreement of Adjectives and Nouns

1. Gender and Number

In English, an adjective does not change, regardless of the gender or the number of the noun that it modifies.

In Ukrainian, an adjective must change so that it agrees both in **gender** and in **number** with the noun that it modifies.

The **new** waiter is **nice**.	**Нови́й** офіція́нт **га́рний**.
The **new** waitress is **nice**.	**Нова́** офіція́нтка **га́рна**.
The **new** car is **nice**.	**Нове́** а́вто **га́рне**.
The **new** waiters are **nice**.	**Нові́** офіція́нти **га́рні**.

2. Case

In English, an adjective never changes, regardless of the function of the noun that it modifies.

This is a **new car**.
I don't have a **new car**.

In Ukrainian, an adjective must change so that it is in the same **case** as the noun that it modifies.

This is a **new car.**	Це **нове́ а́вто**.
I don't have a **new car**.	Я не ма́ю **ново́го а́вта**.

C.2 Two Declensions of Ukrainian Adjectives

In Ukrainian, adjectives belong to one of two declensions: **hard** or **soft**.

Adjectives are identified as being **hard** or **soft** by their endings in their nominative singular forms.

In dictionaries, adjectives are always entered under their **masculine** nominative singular form. Usually, the endings for the feminine and neuter adjectival forms are also given.

1. Hard Declension Adjectives

Hard Declension adjectives are identified by a specific set of endings in their nominative singular forms.

Masculine Ending: **-ий**

Feminine Ending: **-а**

Neuter Ending: **-е**

Most adjectives belong to the hard declension.

2. Soft Declension Adjectives

Soft Declension adjectives are also identified by a specific set of endings in their nominative singular forms.

Masculine Ending: **-ій**

Feminine Ending: **-я**

Neuter Ending: **-є**

The few adjectives that belong to the **soft** declension are marked *[s]* in the Vocabularies.

C.3 Formation of Adjectival Stems

The **stem** of an adjective is formed by dropping either the singular or plural endings from the **nominative** forms.

Hard Declension Adjectives		
Nominative Forms		***Adjectival Stem***
нови́й	(нов-ий)	**нов-**
нова́	(нов-а)	**нов-**
нове́	(нов-е)	**нов-**
нові́	(нов-і)	**нов-**

Soft Declension Adjectives		
Nominative Forms		*Adjectival Stem*
си́ній	(син-ій)	син-
си́ня	(син-я)	син-
си́нє	(син-є)	син-
си́ні	(син-і)	син-

C.4 Declension of Adjectives

The singular and plural endings for both Hard and Soft Declension adjectives are presented below in chart form.

The masculine and neuter adjectival forms are the same in the genitive, instrumental, dative, and locative cases.

Hard Declension Adjectives				
	Feminine Singular	*Masculine Singular*	*Neuter Singular*	*All Genders Plural*
N.	зеле́**на**	зеле́**ний**	зеле́**не**	зеле́**ні**
G.	зеле́**ної**	зеле́**ного**		зеле́**них**
A.	зеле́**ну**	[=G or N]	[=N]	[=G or N]
V.	[=N]	[=N]	[=N]	[=N]
I.	зеле́**ною**	зеле́**ним**		зеле́**ними**
D.	зеле́**ній**	зеле́**ному**		зеле́**ним**
L.	... зеле́**ній**	... зеле́**ному** (... зеле́**нім**)		... зеле́**них**

Soft Declension Adjectives				
	Feminine Singular	*Masculine Singular*	*Neuter Singular*	*All Genders Plural*
N.	си́**ня**	си́**ній**	си́**нє**	си́**ні**
G.	си́**ньої**	си́**нього**		си́**ніх**
A.	си́н-**ю**	[=G or N]	[=N]	[=G or N]
V.	[=N]	[=N]	[=N]	[=N]
I.	си́**ньою**	си́**нім**		си́**німи**
D.	си́**ній**	си́**ньому**		си́**нім**
L.	... си́**ній**	... си́**ньому** (... си́**нім**)		... си́**ніх**

Practise Oral Exercises 26.1, 26.2

Do Written Exercise 26.1

D. INTERROGATIVE PRONOUNS

The interrogative pronouns **яки́й** and **котри́й** must agree in **gender**, **number,** and **case** with the person or object about which they are asking a question.

They are declined like Hard Declension adjectives.

D.1 яки́й

The interrogative pronoun **яки́й** is used in a question that asks about an **attribute** of a person or object.

Яки́й костю́м вона́ ма́є? **What kind of suit** does she have?	Вона́ ма́є **роже́вий костю́м.** She has a **pink suit.**
Яку́ ха́ту вона́ ма́є? **What kind of house** does she have?	Вона́ ма́є **вели́ку ха́ту.** She has a **big house.**
Яке́ а́вто вона́ ма́є? **What kind of car** does she have?	Вона́ ма́є **си́нє а́вто.** She has a **blue car.**
Які́ череви́ки вона́ ма́є? **What kind of shoes** does she have?	Вона́ ма́є **дорогі́ череви́ки.** She has **expensive shoes.**

D.2 котри́й

The interrogative pronoun **котри́й** is used in a question that **asks about one item out of a group of two or more items.**

Котри́й костю́м вона́ купу́є, роже́вий чи бі́лий?
Which suit is she buying, the pink one or the white one?

Котру́ ху́стку вона́ но́сить, жо́вту чи зеле́ну?
Which kerchief is she wearing, the yellow or the green?

Котре́ перо́ вона́ купу́є, си́нє, черво́не, чи чо́рне?
Which pen is she buying, the blue one, the red one, or the black one?

Котрі́ череви́ки вона́ но́сить, бі́лі, кори́чневі, чи чо́рні?
Which shoes is she wearing, the white, the brown, or the black?

D.3 Declension: який

	Feminine Singular	*Masculine Singular*	*Neuter Singular*	*All Genders Plural*
N.	**яка́**	**яки́й**	**яке́**	**які́**
G.	**яко́ї**	**яко́го**		**яки́х**
A.	**яку́**	[=G or N]	[=N]	[=G or N]
V.	—	—	—	—
I.	**яко́ю**	**яки́м**		**яки́ми**
D.	**які́й**	**яко́му**		**яки́м**
L.	... **які́й**	... **яко́му** (... **які́м**)		... **яки́х**

D.4 Declension: котрий

	Feminine Singular	*Masculine Singular*	*Neuter Singular*	*All Genders Plural*
N.	**котра́**	**котри́й**	**котре́**	**котрі́**
G.	**котро́ї**	**котро́го**		**котри́х**
A.	**котру́**	[=G or N]	[=N]	[=G or N]
V.	—	—	—	—
I.	**котро́ю**	**котри́м**		**котри́ми**
D.	**котрі́й**	**котро́му**		**котри́м**
L.	... **котрі́й**	... **котро́му** (... **котрі́м**)		... **котри́х**

Practise Oral Exercises 26.3, 26.4, 26.5

Do Written Exercise 26.2

E. SUBSTANTIVES

A **substantive** is a noun or any word or phrase that acts like a noun in a sentence.

In English, adjectives (mostly plural ones) are sometimes used as substantives.

The **healthy** do not understand the **sick**.

In this sentence it is clear that the omitted noun is **people**: **healthy people** and **sick people**.

In Ukrainian, adjectives are also used as substantives.

In a Ukrainian sentence the endings of the adjectives tell you which word is the subject and which is the direct object.

Здоро́ві хво́рих не розумі́ють.

In English, there is a problem using singular adjectives as substantives because they do not show the gender of the noun that is omitted.

A healthy (?) doesn't understand **a sick** (?).

If the statement is to make sense, it has to include more information.

A healthy man doesn't understand **a sick one**.
A healthy woman doesn't understand **a sick one**.
A healthy man doesn't understand **a sick woman**.

In Ukrainian, singular adjectives may be used much more readily as substantives because they do show the gender and the case of the omitted noun.

Здоро́вий хво́рого не розумі́є.
Здоро́ва хво́рої не розумі́є.
Здоро́вий хво́рої не розумі́є.

In the Vocabulary Notes in this lesson, your attention was drawn to the Ukrainian words for **bridegroom** and **bride**: **молодий** and **молода́**. In Ukrainian, there are many words like this that have become independent of the adjective from which they were originally formed.

Practise Oral Exercise 26.6

✍ **Do Written Exercise 26.3**

LESSON 27

A. VOCABULARY

Nouns

anniversary	ювілéй
birthday	день нарóдження*[n]* урóди́ни *[pl]*, урóдин
calendar	календáр *[s]*
century	сторíччя*[n]*, столíття*[n]*
christening, baptism	христи́ни *[pl]*, христи́н
conference, convention	з'їзд
date *[calendar]*	дáта, числó
earth, ground	земля́
funeral	пóхорон
heaven, sky	нéбо
hell	пéкло
holiday, feast day	свя́то
meeting	збóри *[pl]*, збóрів; засíдання*[n]*
numeral	числíвник
page	сторíнка
paradise	рай
wedding ceremony, marriage	вíнчáння *[n]*, шлюб
wedding reception	весíлля*[n]*
word	слóво
world	світ

Verbs

to arrive *[by vehicle]*	приїжджáти: приїжджá-ю. -єш *pf.* приї́хати: приї́д-у, -еш
to be born	нарóджуватися: нарóджу-юся, -єшся *pf.* народи́тися: народжýся, нарóд-ишся
to celebrate	святкувáти: святкý-ю, -єш *pf.* відсвяткувáти: відсвяткý-ю, -єш
to depart *[by vehicle]*	від'їжджáти: від'їжджá-ю, -єш *pf.* від'ї́хати: від'ї́д-у, -еш
to die	умирáти: умирá-ю, -єш *pf.* у/по/мéрти: у/по/мр-ý, -éш
to hide, to conceal; to bury	ховáти: ховá-ю, -єш *pf.* (hide) сховáти: сховá-ю, -єш *pf.* (bury) поховáти:908поховá-ю,-єш
to take place, to happen	відбувáтися: відбувá-юся, -єшся *pf.* відбýтися: відбýд-уся, -ешся

Demonstrative Adjectives/Pronouns

that	той, та, те, ті
this	цей, ця, це, ці

Ordinal Numerals

first	пе́рший
second	дру́гий
third	тре́тій *[s]*
fourth	четве́ртий
fifth	п'я́тий
sixth	шо́стий
seventh	сьо́мий
eighth	во́сьмий
ninth	дев'я́тий
tenth	деся́тий
eleventh	одина́дцятий
twelfth	двана́дцятий
thirteenth	трина́дцятий
fourteenth	чотирна́дцятий
fifteenth	п'ятна́дцятий
sixteenth	шістна́дцятий
seventeenth	сімна́дцятий
eighteenth	вісімна́дцятий
nineteenth	дев'ятна́дцятий
twentieth	двадця́тий
thirtieth	тридця́тий
fortieth	сороко́вий
fiftieth	п'ятдеся́тий
sixtieth	шістдеся́тий
seventieth	сімдеся́тий
eightieth	вісімдеся́тий
ninetieth	дев'ятдеся́тий, *дев'яно́стий*
hundredth	со́тий

Vocabulary Notes

1. There are many words for **meeting** in Ukrainian. Of the two that are presented here, **засі́дання** usually refers to an executive meeting, or a meeting with only a few people present; the word **збо́ри** usually refers to a general or open meeting attended by a larger number of people.

2. In the phrase **день наро́дження**, the word **наро́дження** is always in the genitive singular case.

   Сього́дні день **наро́дження** Іва́на.
   Today is Ivan's birthday.

   Я забу́ла про день **наро́дження** Іва́на.
   I forgot about Ivan's birthday.

3. Learn the following expressions:

   Віта́ю Вас (Тебе́) з днем наро́дження!
   Happy birthday! (I salute you on your birthday!)

   Віта́ю Вас (Тебе́) з ювіле́єм!
   Happy anniversary! (I salute you on your anniversary!)

4. The verb **відбува́тися/відбу́тися** is most commonly used in the **third person singular or plural**.

Засі́дання **відбу́деться** за́втра.	The meeting will take place tomorrow.
Збо́ри **відбули́ся** вчо́ра.	The meeting took place yesterday.

5. The verb **наро́джувати/народи́ти** (without the reflexive particle **-ся**) means **to give birth**.

   Вона́ **народи́ла** дочку́.
   She **gave birth** to a daughter.

6. When the reflexive particle **-ся** is added to the verb **хова́ти/схова́ти**, the new verb, **хова́тися/схова́тися,** means **to hide or conceal oneself**.

   Дити́на лю́бить **хова́тися** в комо́рі.
   The child likes **to hide** in the pantry.

   Ді́ти **схова́лися** в ста́йні.
   The children **hid** (themselves) in the barn.

B. ORDINAL NUMERALS

In English, ordinal numerals are not declined.

In Ukrainian, ordinal numerals are declined like adjectives.
They agree with the noun that they modify in **number**, **gender**, and **case**.

B.1 Declension of Ordinal Numerals

All the numerals, except **третій**, are declined like Hard Declension adjectives.
The numeral **третій** is declined like a Soft Declension adjective.

Hard Declension Numerals

	Feminine Singular	*Masculine Singular*	*Neuter Singular*	*All Genders Plural*
N.	пе́рша	пе́рший	пе́рше	пе́рші
G.	пе́ршої	пе́ршого		пе́рших
A.	пе́ршу	[=G or N]	[=N]	[=G or N]
V.	[=N]	[=N]	[=N]	[=N]
I.	пе́ршою	пе́ршим		пе́ршими
D.	пе́ршій	пе́ршому		пе́ршим
L.	... пе́ршій	... пе́ршому (... пе́ршім)		... пе́рших

Soft Declension Numeral: третій

	Feminine Singular	*Masculine Singular*	*Neuter Singular*	*All Genders Plural*
N.	тре́тя	тре́тій	тре́тє	тре́ті
G.	тре́тьої	тре́тього		тре́тіх
A.	тре́тю	[=G or N]	[=N]	[=G or N]
V.	[=N]	[=N]	[=N]	[=N]
I.	тре́тьою	тре́тім		тре́тіми
D.	тре́тій	тре́тьому		тре́тім
L.	... тре́тій	... тре́тьому (... тре́тім)		... тре́тіх

Practise Oral Exercise 27.1

Do Written Exercise 27.1

C. DATES OF THE MONTH

In both English and Ukrainian, ordinal numerals are used to state the date.

C.1 The Date

In English, we usually give the date in one of two ways.

What's the date today?	It's the **first** of September. It's September **first**.

Sometimes you will hear still another way of talking about the date.

What's the date today?	It's September **one**.

In Ukrainian, we can ask about the date in one of two ways, and the answer comes back in one of two ways.

What's the date today? **Котрóго** сьогóдні?	It's the **first** of September. Сьогóдні **пéршого** вéресня.
What's the date today? **Котрé** сьогóдні **числó**?	It's the first of September. Сьогóдні **пéрше** вéресня.

Practise Oral Exercise 27.2

C.2 On Which Date?

In English, we do not always use the preposition **on** when we talk about a specific date.

(On) **what day** was he born? (When was he born?)	(On) the **eleventh** of May.

In Ukrainian, the **genitive case** is used, both for the numeral and for the month, to state the specific date of an occurence.

(On) **what day** was he born? **Котрóго дня** він народи́вся? (Коли́ він народи́вся?)	(On) the **eleventh** of May. **Одинáдцятого** трáвня.

Practise Oral Exercise 27.3

C.3 From ... To ...

In English, we use the prepositions **from** and **to** when we want to indicate a specific period of time.

They were here **from** June tenth **to** July twentieth.

In Ukrainian, the prepositions **від** and **до** are used with the **genitive case** of the numerals. The month is also in the genitive case.

They were here f**rom** June tenth **to** July twentieth.
Вони́ були́ тут **від деся́того** че́рвня **до двадця́того** ли́пня.

There is an alternate way in Ukrainian of expressing **to** a certain date: by using the preposition **по** and the accusative case of the numeral.

They were here f**rom** June tenth **to** July twentieth.
Вони́ були́ тут **від деся́того** че́рвня **по двадця́те** ли́пня.

Practise Oral Exercise 27.4

Do Written Exercise 27.2

D. YEARS

D.1 The Year

In English, we use the same pattern for stating a year in the present century or in another century.

[1994]	What year is it?	It's nineteen ninety-four.
[1845]	What year was it?	It was eighteen forty-five.

In Ukrainian, if reference is being made to a year that's in the present century, only the year has to be stated.

[1994]	What year is it?	It's nineteen ninety-four.
	Котри́й це рік?	Це дев'ятдеся́т четве́ртий рік.

If the year that is being referred to is in another century, all the information has to be stated.

[1845]	What year was it?	It was eighteen forty-five.
	Котри́й це був рік?	Це був ти́сяча вісімсо́т со́рок **п'я́тий** рік.

You will notice from these examples that it is only the last numeral **(четве́ртий**, **п'я́тий)** that has to agree in **gender**, **number**, and **case** with the noun **рік** that it modifies.

D.2 In Which Year?

In ***English***, we state the year in which something happened (or will happen) by using the preposition **in.**

[1841] When did she die?
She died **in** eighteen forty-one.

In Ukrainian, there are two ways of stating the year in which something happened (or will happen). In both instances, **only the last numeral is declined.**

1. The preposition **у/в** is used with the **locative case.**

[1841] Колú воná вмéрла?
Воná вмéрла **у** тúсяча вісімсóт сóрок пéрш**ому** рóці.

2. The **genitive case** is used **without a preposition.**

[1841] Колú воná вмéрла?
Воná вмéрла тúсяча вісімсóт сóрок пéрш**ого** рóку.

Practise Oral Exercise 27.5

D.3 From ... To ...

In English, the prepositions **from** and **to** are used to indicate a period of time during which something happened.

[1672-1735] He lived here **from** sixteen seventy-two **to** seventeen thirty-five.

In Ukrainian, the prepositions **від** and **до** are used and the **last numeral is declined to agree with the noun рік in the genitive case (рóку).**

[1672-1735] Він жив тут **від** тúсяча шістсóт сімдесят дрýг**ого рóку**
до тúсяча сімсóт трúдцять п'ят**ого рóку.**

[1983-1994] Вонú жилú тут **від** вісімдесят трéтього рóку
до дев'ятдесят четвéртого рóку.

Practise Oral Exercise 27.6

E. Centuries

In both English and Ukrainian, ordinal numerals are used in speaking about the centuries.

E.1 The Century

In both English and Ukrainian, the same pattern is used in referring to the centuries.

It's the twentieth century now.
За́раз двадця́те сторі́ччя (столі́ття).

E.2 In Which Century?

In both English and Ukrainian, we speak about something happening **in** a specific century.

In English, a prepositional phrase beginning with **in** is used.

We live **in** the twentieth century.

In Ukrainian, the prepositional phrase begins with **у/в** and, in this phrase, the preposition **у/в** governs the **locative case**.

We live **in** the twentieth century.
Ми живемо́ **в** двадця́**тому сторі́ччі** (столі́тті).

They lived **in** the sixteenth century.
Вони́ жили́ **в** шістна́дцят**ому сторі́ччі** (столі́тті).

E.3 From ... To ...

In English, the prepositions **from** and **to** are used to indicate the centuries during which something happened.

In Ukrainian, the prepositions **від** and **до** are used and **the numeral is declined** to agree with the noun **сторі́ччя (столі́ття)** in the **genitive case**.

Notice that the word **сторі́ччя (столі́ття)** follows the **second** numeral.

It stood there **from** the first century **to** the sixth one.
Воно́ стоя́ло там **від** пе́рш**ого** **до** шо́ст**ого** **сторі́ччя**.

Practise Oral Exercises 27.7, 27.8, 27.9

Do Written Exercises 27.3, 27.4, 27.5

F. DEMONSTRATIVE PRONOUNS

The demonstrative pronouns **цей** and **той** may be used either as **modifiers** or as **pronouns.**

F.1 Modifiers

When **цей** and **той** are used as modifiers, they must agree with the nouns that they modify in **gender**, **number**, and **case**.

Modifier

Хто зна́є **цього́ чолові́ка**?
Who knows **this man**?

Ніхто́ не зна́є **цього́ чолові́ка**.
No one knows **this man**.

Хто зна́є **ту дівчину?**
Who knows **that girl?**

Ніхто́ не зна́є **тіє́ї дівчини**.
No one knows **that girl**.

F.2 Pronouns

When **цей** and **той** are used as pronouns, they take the place of the noun that they are understood to modify.

Modifier

Чи ти зна́єш **цих чолові́ків**?
Do you *[s]* know **those men**?

Хто зна́є **цих дівча́т**?
Who knows **those girls**?

Pronoun

Я зна́ю **цього́**, але́ не **того́**.
I know **this one**, but not **that one**.

Ми зна́ємо і **цю,** і **ту**.
We know both **this one**, and **that one**.

F.3 Declension: цей

	Feminine Singular	*Masculine Singular*	*Neuter Singular*	*All Genders Plural*
N.	ця	цей	це	ці
G.	ціє́ї	цього́	цього́	цих
A.	цю	[=G or N]	[=N]	[=G or N]
V.	—	—	—	—
I.	ціє́ю	цим	цим	ци́ми
D.	цій	цьому́	цьому́	цим
L.	.... цій	... цьо́му (... цім)	... цьо́му (... цім)	... цих

F.4 Declension: той

	Feminine Singular	*Masculine Singular*	*Neuter Singular*	*All Genders Plural*
N.	**та**	**той**	**те**	**ті**
G.	**тіє́ї**	**того́**		**тих**
A.	**ту**	[=G or N]	[=N]	[=G or N]
V.	—	—	—	—
I.	**тіє́ю**	**тим**		**ти́ми**
D.	**тій**	**тому́**		**тим**
L.	**... тій**	**... то́му** (... **тім**)		**... тих**

Practise Oral Exercise 27.10

Do Written Exercise 27.6

LESSON 28

A. VOCABULARY

Nouns

advertisement	оголо́шення *[n]*, рекля́ма, *рекла́ма*
bathtub	ва́нна
bracelet	брасле́т
brush	щі́тка
comb	гре́бінь (гребен-)
coral beads	кора́лі *[pl]*, кора́лів
deodorant	дезодора́нт
drycleaning shop	хемчи́стка, *хімчи́стка*
ear	ву́хо
earring	ку́льчик, сере́жка
finger	па́лець (пальц-)
hair	воло́сся *[n]*
hairdo	за́чіска
hand, arm	рука́
hand lotion	крем для рук
lip	губа́; уста́/вуста́ *[pl]*, уст/вуст
lipstick	губна́ пома́да
neck	ши́я
necklace	нами́сто
perfume	па́хощі *[pl]*, па́хощів духи́ *[pl]*, духі́в
pharmacy, drugstore	апте́ка
razor, shaver	бри́тва, електробри́тва
ring	пе́рстінь (перстен-), кільце́
shampoo	шампу́нь
shower	душ
soap	ми́ло
tooth	зуб
toothbrush	зубна́ щі́тка
toothpaste	зубна́ па́ста
towel	рушни́к

Possessives

her, hers	її́ *[indecl.]*
his	його́ *[indecl.]*
its	його́ *[indecl.]*
my, mine	мій, моя́, моє́, мої́
our, ours	наш, на́ша, на́ше, на́ші
their, theirs	і́хній, і́хня, і́хнє, і́хні; їх *[indecl.]*
your *[p]*, yours *[p]*	ваш, ва́ша, ва́ше, ва́ші
your *[s]*, yours *[s]*	твій, твоя́, твоє́, твоєї́

Reflexive Possessive

one's own	свій, своя́, своє́, свої́

Interrogative Possessive

whose	чий, чия́, чиє́, чиї́

Verbs

to accept, to welcome	прийма́ти: прийма́-ю, -єш *pf.* прийн**я́**ти:(future) прий**м**-у́, -е́ш, (past) прий**ня́**-в, -ла́, -ло́, -ли́
to comb oneself	зачі́суватися: зачі́су-юся, -єшся *pf.* заче**са́**тися: заче**ш**-у́ся, -ешся
to dry oneself	витира́тися: витира́-юся, -єшся *pf.* ви́т**е**ртися: ви́тр-уся, ешся
to use	ужива́ти: ужива́ю, -єш *pf.* ужи́ти: ужи**в**-у́, -еш
to wash oneself	умива́тися: умива́-юся, -єшся *pf.* уми́тися: уми́-юся, -єшся

Vocabulary Notes

1. Learn the expression **прийма́ти душ – to take a shower**.

2. In Ukrainian dictionaries, the possessives that are declined are always listed under their masculine singular form; the feminine and neuter forms, if they are given, are placed after the masculine singular form.

3. The Ukrainian possessive **і́хній** has an alternate form: **їх**. This alternate form is indeclinable, like **його́** and **її́**. (See C.1)

B. REFLEXIVE VERBS

Some Ukrainian verbs, like **смія́тися** and **диви́тися**, are always conjugated with the reflexive particle **-ся**.

There are other Ukrainian verbs, however, that have one meaning when they are conjugated **with** the reflexive particle **-ся**, and a slightly different meaning when they are conjugated **without** the reflexive particle **-ся.**

Let's look at the verb **одяга́тися**. This verb is **intransitive,** that is, **a direct object is not required to complete its meaning.**

The **transitive** counterpart to this verb is written without the reflexive particle **-ся**: **одяга́ти**. The verb **одяга́ти does require a direct object to complete its meaning.**

Intransitive Verb

одяга́ти**ся**

Ма́ма **одяга́ється**.

Mother is dressing (herself).

Transitive Verb

одяга́ти

Ма́ма **одяга́є себе́.**
Mother **is dressing herself**.

Ма́ма **одяга́є дити́ну.**
Mother **is dressing the child**.

Several verbs that you know fall into this category.

Intransitive Verb	*Transitive Verb*
витира́тися/ви́тертися	витира́ти/витерти
голи́тися/поголи́тися	голи́ти/поголи́ти
зачі́суватися/зачеса́тися	зачі́сувати/зачеса́ти
ті́шитися/уті́шитися	ті́шити/уті́шити
умива́тися/уми́тися	умива́ти/уми́ти

As reflexive verbs like this are introduced in the Vocabularies, they will be drawn to your attention in the Vocabulary Notes.

It is interesting to note that some of the transitive verbs that you have already learned may be turned into reflexive verbs by adding the particle **-ся**.

You should be able to recognize verbs that are changed in this way; however, do not try to create your own reflexive verbs until you know the language much better!

Ма́ма **пере́** блю́зку.
Mom **is washing** the blouse.

Ця блю́зка до́бре **пере́ться**.
This blouse **washes** well.

C. POSSESSIVES

In both English and Ukrainian, possessives may be used either as **modifiers** or as **pronouns**.

C.1 Possessives: Modifiers

When possessives are used as modifiers, they indicate that something belongs to someone.

This is **my** key.	Це **мій** ключ.

In English, all the possessives remain the same, regardless of the gender, number or case of the noun with which they are used.

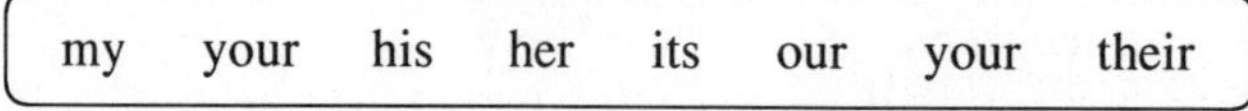
my your his her its our your their

As an example, let's look at how the English possessive **my** is used as a modifier. Notice that **my** does not change, regardless of the gender or number of the noun that it modifies.

This is **my daughter**.	These are **my daughters**.
This is **my son**.	These are **my sons**.
This is **my car**.	These are **my cars**.

In Ukrainian, **four** of the possessives do not agree in gender, number and case with the noun that they modify.

її́ його́ його́ їх

Let's look at how **her** and **his** are used both in Ukrainian and in English.

Її́ дочка́ вдо́ма.	**Her daughter** is at home.
Її́ син удо́ма.	**Her son** is at home.
Її́ а́вто вдо́ма.	**Her car** is at home.
Її́ ді́ти вдо́ма.	**Her children** are at home.
Його́ дочка́ вдо́ма.	**His daughter** is at home.
Його́ син удо́ма.	**His son** is at home.
Його́ а́вто вдо́ма.	**His car** is at home.
Його́ ді́ти вдо́ма.	**His children** are at home.

Five of the Ukrainian possessives must agree in **gender**, **number**, and **case** with the noun that they modify.

мій твій наш ваш ї́хній

Let's look at how the Ukrainian possessive **мій** changes. Notice that there is no change in the English possessive **my**.

Моя́ дочка́ вдо́ма.	**My daughter** is at home.
Чи ви зна́єте **мою́ дочку́**?	Do you know **my daughter**?
Мій син удо́ма.	**My son** is at home.
Чи ви зна́єте **мого́ си́на**?	Do you know my **son**?
Моє́ а́вто вдо́ма.	**My car** is at home.
Чому́ кіт у **моє́му а́вті**?	Why is the cat in **my car**?
Мої́ ді́ти вдо́ма.	**My children** are at home.
Чи ви зна́єте **мої́х діте́й**?	Do you know **my children**?

C.2 Declension: мій, твій

The declension of the Ukrainian possessives **мій** and **твій** resembles the soft declension of adjectives.

Except for the masculine nominative singular form, the stems of **мій** and **твій** are **мо-** and **тво-**.

The possessive **мій** is declined below for you; **твій** is declined exactly like **мій**.

Declension of the Possessive мій

	Feminine Singular	*Masculine Singular*	*Neuter Singular*	*All Genders Plural*
N.	моя́	мі̲й	моє́	мої́
G.	моє́ї	мого́	мого́	мої́х
A.	мою́	[=G or N]	[=N]	[=G or N]
V.	[=N]	[=N]	[=N]	[=N]
I.	моє́ю	мої́м	мої́м	мої́ми
D.	мої́й	моє́му	моє́му	мої́м
L.	... мої́й	... моє́му (... мої́м)	... моє́му (... мої́м)	... мої́х

Practise Oral Exercise 28.1

C.3 Declension: наш, ваш

The Ukrainian possessive pronouns **наш** and **ваш** are declined like **Hard Declension** adjectives.

The stem for **наш** is **наш-**; for **ваш**, it is **ваш-**.

Remember that **the stem is used as the masculine singular nominative form.**

Declension of the Possessive наш

	Feminine Singular	*Masculine Singular*	*Neuter Singular*	*All Genders Plural*
N.	на́ша	наш	на́ше	на́ші
G.	на́шої	на́шого		на́ших
A.	на́шу	[=G or N]	[=N]	[=G or N]
V.	[=N]	[=N]	[=N]	[=N]
I.	на́шою	на́шим		на́шими
D.	на́шій	на́шому		на́шим
L.	... на́шій	... на́шому (... на́шім)		... на́ших

C.4 Declension: ї́хній

The Ukrainian possessive **ї́хній** is declined like a **Soft Declension** adjective.

Declension of the Possessive ї́хній

	Feminine Singular	*Masculine Singular*	*Neuter Singular*	*All Genders Plural*
N.	ї́хня	ї́хній	ї́хнє	ї́хні
G.	ї́хньої	ї́хнього		ї́хніх
A.	ї́хню	[=G or N]	[=N]	[=G or N]
V.	—	—	—	—
I.	ї́хньою	ї́хнім		ї́хніми
D.	ї́хній	ї́хньому		ї́хнім
L.	... ї́хній	... ї́хньому (... ї́хнім)		... ї́хніх

Practise Oral Exercises 28.2, 28.3

Do Written Exercise 28.1

C.5 Possessives As Pronouns

In addition to modifying or expressing possession of nouns, the possessives may stand alone as pronouns.

Modifier	*Pronoun*
Це **мій** олівéць.	Він **мій**.
This is **my** pencil.	It's **mine**.
Це **нáша** хáта.	Вонá **нáша**.
This is **our** house.	It's **ours**.
Це **ї́хнє** áвто.	Воно́ **ї́хнє**.
This is **their** car.	It's **theirs**.

In English, except for **his** and **its**, all the possessives change when they stand alone as pronouns.

In Ukrainian, all the possessives remain the same, whether they are used as modifiers, or as pronouns.

Modifier	*Pronoun*	*Modifier*	*Pronoun*
This is **my** key.	It's **mine**.	Це **мій** ключ.	Це **мій**.
This is **your** key.	It's **yours**.	Це **твій** ключ.	Це **твій**.
This is **her** key.	It's **hers**.	Це **ї́ї** ключ.	Це **ї́ї**.
This is **his** key.	It's **his**.	Це **його́** ключ.	Це **його́**.
This is **its** key.	It's **its**.	Це **його́** ключ.	Це **його́**.
This is **our** key.	It's **ours**.	Це **наш** ключ.	Це **наш**.
This is **your** key.	It's **yours**.	Це **ваш** ключ.	Це **ваш**.
This is **their** key.	It's **theirs**.	Це **ї́хній** ключ.	Це **ї́хній**.
		Це **їх** ключ.	Це **їх**.

From the above examples you can see that possessives serve as pronouns in the same way that descriptive adjectives serve as substantives/nouns. (See Lesson 26, C.)

Practise Oral Exercise 28.4

Do Written Exercise 28.2

D. REFLEXIVE POSSESSIVE: СВІЙ

In English, if we want to leave no doubt that a possessive refers back to the subject of the sentence or clause in which it is found, we use the word **own** with the possessive.

In Ukrainian, when a possessive refers back to the **subject** of a sentence or of a clause, the possessive **свій** is used.

D.1 Reflexive Possessive Modifier

Examine the possessives in the following sentences. In Ukrainian, the possessive **свій** always agrees in **gender**, **number**, and **case with the noun that it modifies**, and <u>**not**</u> **with the subject to which it refers.**

Reflexive Possessive:* свій** ***(Refers Back to the Subject)	***Possessives*** ***(Do Not Refer Back to the Subject)***
I have **my own** pen. **Я** мáю **своє́** перó.	**I** have **your** *[p]* pen. **Я** мáю **вáше** перó.
The boy has **his own** cap. **Він** мáє **свою́** шáпку.	**The boy** has **his** (another boy's) cap. **Він** мáє **йогó** шáпку.
The girl has **her own** key. **Дíвчина** мáє **свій** ключ.	**The girl** has **her** (another girl's) key. **Дíвчина** мáє **її́** ключ.
We have **our own** car. **Ми** мáємо **своє́** áвто.	**We** have **their** car. **Ми** мáємо **ї́хнє** áвто.
You have **your own** box. **Ви** мáєте **свою́** корóбку.	**You** have **my** box. **Ви** мáєте **мою́** корóбку.
They have **their own** bags. **Вони́** мáють **свої́** торби́нки.	**They** have **their** (<u>not</u> their own) bags. **Вони́** мáють **ї́хні** торби́нки.

D.2 Reflexive Possessive Pronoun

In addition to being used as a modifier, the possessive **свій**, like other possessives, may also be used as a **pronoun**.

Modifier	***Pronoun***
Чи вонá мáє **своє́ перó**? Does she have **her own pen**?	Так, вонá мáє **своє́**. Yes, she has **her own**.
Чи він мáє **свої́ грóші**? Does he have **his own money**?	Так, він мáє **свої́**. Yes, he has **his own**.

D.3 Declension: свій

The reflexive possessive **свій** is declined like the possessives **мій** and **твій**.

Declension of the Reflexive Possessive свій				
	Feminine Singular	*Masculine Singular*	*Neuter Singular*	*All Genders Plural*
N.	своя́	сві́й	своє́	свої́
G.	своє́ї	сво́го́		свої́х
A.	свою́	[=G or N]	[=N]	[=G or N]
V.	—	—	—	—
I.	своє́ю	свої́м		свої́ми
D.	свої́й	своє́му		свої́м
L.	.... свої́й	... своє́му (... свої́м)		... свої́х

Practise Oral Exercise 28.5

Do Written Exercise 28.3

E. INTERROGATIVE POSSESSIVE: ЧИЙ

The interrogative possessive **чий** functions either as a **modifier** or as a **pronoun**.

E.1 Interogative Possessive Modifier

In English, **whose** does not change regardless of the gender, number or case of the noun that it modifies.

In Ukrainian, the interrogative possessive **чий** must agree with the noun that it modifies in **gender**, **number**, and **case**.

Whose son is this?	**Чий** це **син**?
Whose son do you know?	**Чийо́го си́на** ти зна́єш?
Whose daughter is this?	**Чия́** це **дочка́**?
Whose daughter do you like?	**Чию́ дочку́** ти лю́биш?
Whose car is this?	**Чиє́** це **а́вто**?
With **whose car** did you go?	**Чиї́м а́втом** ти поїхав?
Whose children are these?	**Чиї́** це **ді́ти**?
Whose children did you see?	**Чиї́х діте́й** ти ба́чив?

E.2 Interrogative Possessive Pronoun

In addition to being used as a modifier, the interrogative possessive **чий** may stand alone as a pronoun.

Modifier	***Pronoun***
Чиїх дітéй він бáчив?	**Чиїх** він бáчив?
Whose children did he see?	**Whose** did he see?
Чиїм батькáм він помагáє?	**Чиїм** він помагáє?
Whose parents is he helping?	**Whose** is he helping?

E.3 Declension: чий

Except for the masculine and neuter **genitive**, **dative**, and **locative** singular cases, **чий** is declined like the possessive **мій**.

Declension of the Interrogative Possessive чий				
	Feminine Singular	*Masculine Singular*	*Neuter Singular*	*All Genders Plural*
N.	**чия́**	**чий**	**чиє́**	**чиї́**
G.	**чиє́ї**	**чийо́го**		**чиї́х**
A.	**чию́**	[=N or G]	[=N]	[=N or G]
V.	—	—	—	—
I.	**чиє́ю**	**чиї́м**		**чиї́ми**
D.	**чиї́й**	**чийо́му**		**чиї́м**
L.	**... чиї́й**	**... чийо́му (... чиї́м)**		**... чиї́х**

Practise Oral Exercises 28.6, 28.7, 28.8

Do Written Exercises 28.4, 28.5, 28.6

LESSON 29

A. VOCABULARY

Nouns

accident	ава́рія, ви́падок (випадк-)
alarm clock	буди́льник
appointment, date	поба́чення *[n]*
beginning	поча́ток (початк-)
end	кіне́ць (кінц-)
evening	ве́чір *[h]* (вечор-)
exam	і́спит, екза́мен
hall	за́ля, *зал*
hour	годи́на
itinerary	маршру́т
minute	хвили́на, міну́та
morning	ра́нок (ранк-)
news item	новина́, нови́нка
night	ніч *[f]* (ноч-)
quarter, one-fourth	чверть *[f]*
radio program	радіопереда́ча
second *[time]*	секу́нда
station *[train]*	ста́нція
streetcar	трамва́й
subway	підзе́мка, метро́ *[n, indecl.]*
television program	телепереда́ча
time	час
trolley bus	троле́йбус
twenty-four hour period	доба́
work	пра́ця, робо́та

Adverbs

at midnight	опі́вночі
at noon	опі́вдні
for a short time	ненадо́вго
half	пів
half an hour	півгоди́ни
soon, in a short time	незаба́ром
too early	завча́сно
too late	запі́зно

Indefinite Pronoun

all	увéсь, усі́, усé, усí

Prepositions

at *[in time expressions]*	о/об
in *[in time expressions]*	за, чéрез

Verbs

to arrive *[on foot]*	прихóдити: прихóд**ж**у, прихóд-иш *pf.* прийти́: прийд-ý, -éш
to begin	починáти: починá-ю, -єш *pf.* по**ч**áти: поч**н**-ý, -éш
to close	зачиня́ти: зачиня́-ю, -єш *pf.* зачини́ти: зачи́н-ю, -иш
to depart *[on foot]*	відхóдити: відхóд**ж**у, відхóд-иш *pf.* відійти́: відійд-ý, -éш
to finish, end	кінчáти: кінчá-ю, -єш *pf.* скінчи́ти: скінч-ý, -и́ш
to open	відчиня́ти: відчиня́-ю, -єш *pf.* відчини́ти: відчи́н-ю, -иш
to praise	хвали́ти: хвал-ю́, -иш *pf.* похвали́ти: похвал-ю́, -иш
to return, to give back	повертáти: повертá-ю, -єш *pf.* повернýти: поверн-ý, -еш

Vocabulary Notes

1. The word **авáрія** refers to an accident resulting from the collision of moving vehicles; **ви́падок** refers to an accidental or unexpected occurence or event.

2. The Ukrainian word **добá** means either a twenty-four hour period, or a whole day and night. There is no equivalent word for it in English.

3. The declension of the feminine nouns **чверть** and **ніч** will be given later in this text. Learn the forms that are presented in this lesson: **чверть** (nominative and accusative); **ніч** (nominative and accusative); and **нóчі** (genitive).

4. Learn the following time expressions in Ukrainian:

   Годи́нник спіши́ть на п'ять хвили́н.
   The clock is five minutes fast.

   Годи́нник відстає́ на п'ять хвили́н.
   The clock is five minutes slow.

5. In Ukraine, the preposition **че́рез** is favoured in speaking about a period of time. In Canada, the preposition **за** is used more frequently.

Я там бу́ду **че́рез** півгоди́ни.	I'll be there in half an hour.
Я там бу́ду **за** півгоди́ни.	I'll be there in half an hour.

6. The verbs **ї́здити/ї́хати/пої́хати**, **приїжджа́ти/приї́хати** and **від'їжджа́ти/від'ї́хати** are used to talk about people going, arriving, and departing by vehicle.

   Куди́ гість **ї́де**?
   Where is the guest going *[by vehicle]*?

   Коли́ гість **приїжджа́є**?
   When will the guest be arriving *[by vehicle]*?

   Ходи́ти/іти́/піти́, **прихо́дити/прийти́**, and **відхо́дити/відійти́** are used to talk not only about people coming and going on foot, but also **about vehicles going**, **coming, arriving**, and **departing**.

Куди́ гість **іде́**? Where **is** the guest **going** *[on foot]*?	Куди́ по́їзд **іде́**? Where does the train **go**?
Коли́ гість **прихо́дить**? When is the guest coming *[on foot]*?	Коли́ по́їзд **прихо́дить**? When does the train **come in**?
Коли́ гість **відхо́дить**? When is the guest leaving *[on foot]*?	Коли́ по́їзд **відхо́дить**? When does the train **leave**?

7. To indicate travel by taxi or on the subway, the indeclinable nouns **метро́** and **таксі́** are used in the phrases **на метро́** and **на таксі́**.

   Ми звича́йно ї́здимо туди́ **на таксі́/на метро́.**
   We usually go there **by taxi/by subway**.

8. A number of the **transitive verbs** in the Vocabulary may be changed into **intransitive verbs** by adding the reflexive particle **-ся** to them.

Transitive Verb	***Intransitive Verb***
відчиня́ти/відчини́ти	відчиня́тися/відчини́тися
зачиня́ти/зачини́ти	зачиня́тися/зачини́тися
кінча́ти/скінчи́ти	кінча́тися/скінчи́тися
поверта́ти/поверну́ти	поверта́тися/поверну́тися
почина́ти/поча́ти	почина́тися/поча́тися
хвали́ти/похвали́ти	хвали́тися/похвали́тися

B. INDEFINITE PRONOUN: УВЕ́СЬ

The indefinite pronoun **уве́сь** may be used either as a modifier, or as a pronoun.

B.1 Indefinite Modifier

In English, **all** does not change, regardless of the gender, number, or case of the noun that it modifies.

In Ukrainian, **уве́сь** must agree with the noun that it modifies in **gender**, **number**, and **case**.

Він працюва́в **уве́сь день**.	He worked **all day**.
Він ви́пив **усю́ ка́ву**.	He drank **all the coffee**.
Він з'їв **усе́ моро́зиво**.	He ate **all the ice cream**.
Він загуби́в **усі́ гро́ші**.	He lost **all the money**.

B.2 Indefinite Pronoun

In addition to modifying or possessing nouns, **уве́сь** may stand alone as a pronoun.

Modifier	***Pronoun***
Він з'їв **усе́ моро́зиво**.	Він з'їв **усе́**.

B.3 Declension: уве́сь

Notice that the instrumental plural ending is **-іма**.

Declension of the Indefinite Pronoun **увесь**				
	Feminine Singular	***Masculine Singular***	***Neuter Singular***	***All Genders Plural***
N.	уся́ (вся)	уве́сь (ввесь)	усе́ (все)	усі́ (всі)
G.	усіє́ї	усього́		усі́х
A.	усю́	[=G or N]	[=N]	[=G or N]
V.	—	—	—	—
I.	усіє́ю	усі́м		усіма́
D.	усі́й	усьому́		усі́м
L.	.... усі́й	... усьо́му (... усі́м)		... усі́х

Practise Oral Exercise 29.1

Do Written Exercise 29.1

C. TIME EXPRESSIONS

In Ukrainian, ordinal numerals are used to tell time.

C.1 Telling the Time

In English, we ask about the **time**, and a **cardinal number** is used in the response.

What **time** is it?	It's **one o'clock**.

In Ukrainian, to find out about the time we ask about the **hour**, and an **ordinal numeral** is used in the response.

Котрá годúна? (**Which** hour is it?)	**Пéрша** годúна. (It's the **first** hour.)

This difference, that is, talking about **time** in English and **the hour** in Ukrainian, is seen in all the expressions relating to the time of day.

Let's look at some examples.

In Canada, **по + the locative** and **до + the genitive** are more widely used than the other forms.

In Ukraine, **на + the accusative**, **the genitive**, and **за + the accusative** are preferred. There is still another way of speaking about time **to** the hour, but you will not be able to use it until you have learned how to decline cardinal numbers later in this text.

	по + locative	*на + accusative*
7:05	П'ять по сьóмій.	П'ять на вóсьму.
7:15	Чверть по сьóмій.	Чверть на вóсьму.
7:20	Двáдцять по сьóмій.	Двáдцять на вóсьму.
7:30	Пів по сьóмій.	Пів на вóсьму.

	до + genitive	*за + accusative*
7:30	Пів до вóсьмої.	За пів вóсьма.
7:40	Двáдцять до вóсьмої.	За двáдцять вóсьма.
7:45	Чверть до вóсьмої.	За чверть вóсьма.
7:50	Дéсять до вóсьмої.	За дéсять вóсьма.

Practise Oral Exercise 29.2

C.2 At What Time?

In English, we do not always use the preposition **at** when we ask at what time something is happening.

(**At**) **what time** do you *[s]* get up?

In Ukrainian, when we ask at what time something happens, we use the preposition **o** and the **locative case**.

О котрі́й годи́ні ти встає́ш? (**At which hour** do you get up?)	**At what time** do you *[s]* get up?

If we answer the question by giving the exact hour, we use **o** and the **locative** case. If we state a time that is before or after the hour, the use of **o** is optional.

(At) eight (o'clock).	О во́сьмій (годи́ні).
Quarter past seven.	Чверть по сьо́мій. Чверть на во́сьму.
Seven thirty.	Пів по сьо́мій. Пів до во́сьмої. Пів на во́сьму. За пів во́сьма. Пів во́сьмої.
Ten to eight.	Де́сять до во́сьмої. За де́сять во́сьма.

Before a word that begins in a vowel, **o** becomes **об**.

О<u>б</u> <u>о</u>дина́дцятій годи́ні.

For setting a time for a formal occasion, like a meeting, still another way of telling time may be used.

7:30	Сьо́ма три́дцять. О сьо́мій три́дцять. Сім три́дцять.
7:15	Сьо́ма п'ятна́дцять. О сьо́мій п'ятна́дцять. Сім п'ятна́дцять.
7:45	Сьо́ма со́рок п'ять. О сьо́мій со́рок п'ять. Сім со́рок п'ять.

 **Practise Oral Exercise 29.3**

 **Do Written Exercise 29.2**

C.3 From ... To ...

In English, we indicate the length of a time period by using the prepositions **from** and **to**.

In Ukrainian, the prepositions **від** and **до** are used with the **genitive** case.

An alternate way of saying **to** the hour is to use the prepostion **по** and the accusative case.

We sleep **from** ten **to** six.
Ми спимó **від деся́тої** (годи́ни) **до шóстої** (годи́ни)/**по шóсту** (годи́ну).

We sleep **from** half past ten **to** half past five.
Ми спимó **від** пів (до) **одина́дцятої** до пів (до) **шóстої**.

Practise Oral Exercise 29.4

Do Written Exercise 29.3

C.4 A.M. and P.M.

In both English and Ukrainian, the 24-hour period is divided into four smaller periods.

English	*Ukrainian*	*Approximate Time Periods*
morning	ра́нок	6:00 a.m. – 12:00 noon
day	день	12:00 noon – 6:00 p.m.
evening	ве́чір	6:00 p.m. – 12:00 midnight
night	ніч	12:00 midnight – 6:00 a.m.

In English, the abbreviations **a.m.** and **p.m.** are used to distinguish between the two halves of a 24-hour period.

midnight to noon	–	a.m.
noon to midnight	–	p.m.

In Ukrainian, the four periods of the day are used in the **genitive singular** case.

English	*Ukrainian*
At 7:00 a.m.	О сьóмій годи́ні **ра́нку**.
At 2:00 p.m.	О дру́гій годи́ні **дня**.
At 7:00 p.m.	О сьóмій годи́ні **ве́чора**.
At 2:00 a.m.	О дру́гій годи́ні **нóчі**.

C.5 The 24-Hour Clock

In both English and Ukrainian, the international 24-hour clock is used for official timetables such as travel schedules at bus depots, train stations, airports, etc.

The bus arrives at 0230.	(2:30 a.m.)
Автóбус прихóдить о 02.30.	(2:30 нóчі)
The bus departs at 0815.	(8:15 a.m.)
Автóбус відхóдить о 08.15.	(8:15 ráнку)
The train arrives at 1400.	(2:00 p.m.)
Пóїзд прихóдить о 14.00.	(2:00 дня)
The train departs at 1905.	(7:05 p.m.)
Пóїзд відхóдить о 19.05.	(7:05 вéчора)

Practise Oral Exercises 29.5, 29.6, 29.7

Do Written Exercises 29.4, 29.5, 29.6

LESSON 30

A. VOCABULARY

Nouns

apricot	абрикóса
baked goods, pastry	пéчиво *[sg]*
beans	квасóля *[sg]*, фасóля *[sg]*
beet	бурáк
berry	я́года
bottle	пля́шка
cabbage	капýста *[sg]*
can, tin	бляшáнка, *бáнка*
candy, sweets	цукéрка, цукéрок (цукерк-)
carrots	мóрква *[sg]*
celery	селéра *[sg]*
chocolate bar	шоколя́дка, *шоколáдка*
corn	кукурýдза *[sg]*
cucumber	огірóк (огірк-)
doughnut	пампýшка
dozen	дю́жина
fruit	садовинá *[sg]*, óвоч, *фрукт*
garden	горóд
garlic	часни́к *[sg]*
grapes	виногрáд *[sg]*
jar	слóїк, *бáнка*
litre	літр *[h]*
loaf of bread	хліби́на
onions	цибýля *[sg]*
orchard	сад
peach	пéрсик
pear	грýша, грýшка
peas	горóх *[sg]*
plum	сли́ва, сли́вка
potatoes	картóпля *[sg]*
pound	фунт
purchase, purchased item	покýпка
strawberry	суни́ця, полуни́ця
tomato	помідóр *[h]*
vegetables	горóдина *[sg]*, яринá *[sg]*, *óвочі*

Adjectives

easy, light	легки́й
fast	швидки́й
heavy	тяжки́й
narrow	вузьки́й
sweet	соло́дкий
talented	талanoви́тий
tasty	смачни́й
wide	широ́кий

Conjunctions

as, like, than	як
than	ніж

Vocabulary Notes

In the Vocabulary in this lesson, about half of the nouns that refer to fruits and vegetables may be used in both singular and plural forms, that is, you can talk about a single **apricot** or **beet**, or about many **apricots** or **beets**.

The nouns that refer to the other half of the fruits and vegetables, however, are used only in the singular, but their meaning is plural. In other words, although **карто́пля** is a singular noun, it means **potatoes**.

The following fruits and vegetables presented in this lesson, belong to this second group: **квасо́ля**, **капу́ста**, **мо́рква**, **селе́ра, кукуру́дза**, **часни́к**, **виногра́д**, **цибу́ля**, **горо́х**, and **карто́пля**. The terms **горо́дина**, **ярина́**, and **садовина́** are also used only as singular nouns.

For some of the fruits and vegetables in this second group, there are ways in which to designate a single unit. For example, a single potato is a **картопли́на**; a head of cabbage is referred to as a **голо́вка капу́сти**; and a cob of corn is called a **кача́н кукуру́дзи**. At this point in your study of Ukrainian, however, all you need to know are the terms given to you in the Vocabulary.

When you are talking about these fruits and vegetables, be careful to remember that the terms used for them are singular:

> I like to eat **peas** and **carrots**.
> Я люблю́ ї́сти **горо́х** і **мо́ркву**.
>
> Where does she buy **vegetables**?
> Де вона́ купу́є **горо́дину**?

B. COMPARISON OF ADJECTIVES

In English, many adjectives may be changed or "compared" to indicate that the person or thing that is being modified is either superior or inferior in some way or degree to other persons or things.

Let's look at how the adjectives **rich** and **poor** are compared in English.

I have **rich** parents.	I have **poor** parents.
He has **richer** parents.	He has **poorer** parents.
She has the **richest** parents.	She has the **poorest** parents.

In English, these three levels of comparison are known as degrees, and each degree has its own name.

Positive Degree	*Comparative Degree*	*Superlative Degree*
rich	rich**er**	rich**est**
poor	poor**er**	poor**est**

In Ukrainian, many adjectives may also be "compared" according to the same three levels.

Let's look at the English examples used above and their Ukrainian equivalents.

I have **rich** parents.	У ме́не **бага́ті** батьки́.
He has **richer** parents.	У ньо́го **бага́тші** батьки́.
She has the **richest** parents.	У не́ї **найбага́тші** батьки́.
I have **poor** parents.	У ме́не **бі́дні** батьки́.
He has **poorer** parents.	У ньо́го **бідні́ші** батьки́.
She has the **poorest** parents.	У не́ї **найбідні́ші** батьки́.

B.1 Formation of the Comparative and Superlative Degrees

In both English and Ukrainian, the comparative and superlative degrees of adjectives are formed in one of three ways.

1. ***In English***, some adjectives form their comparative and superlative degrees in an irregular manner.

Positive Degree	*Comparative Degree*	*Superlative Degree*
good	better	best
bad	worse	worst

In Ukrainian, the comparative degree of a few adjectives is also formed irregularly.

The superlative degree is formed by adding the prefix **най-** to the comparative form.

Positive Degree	*Comparative Degree*	*Superlative Degree*
вели́кий	бі́льший	**най**бі́льший
мали́й	ме́нший	**най**ме́нший
до́брий	кра́щий/лі́пший	**най**кра́щий/**най**лі́пший
пога́ний	гі́рший	**най**гі́рший

2. ***In English***, longer adjectives are compared by using more and most, or less and least, along with the positive form.

Positive Degree	*Comparative Degree*	*Superlative Degree*
miserable	**more** miserable	**most** miserable
talented	**less** talented	**least** talented

In Ukrainian, the words **більш** or **менш** are used with the positive degree of some adjectives to form the comparative degree.

The superlative degree is formed by adding the prefix **най-** to either **більш** or **менш**.

Positive Degree	*Comparative Degree*	*Superlative Degree*
нещá сний	**більш** нещáсний	**най**бі́льш нещáсний
талановúтий	**менш** талановúтий	**най**ме́нш талановúтий

3. ***In English***, most shorter adjectives have the suffix **-er** added to the positive degree to form the comparative degree, and the suffix **-est** to form the superlative degree.

Positive Degree	*Comparative Degree*	*Superlative Degree*
rich	rich**er**	rich**est**
poor	poor**er**	poor**est**

In Ukrainian, the comparative degree of some adjectives may be formed by adding either the suffix **-ш** or **-іш** to the adjectival stem of the positive form.

The superlative degree is always formed by adding the prefix **най-** to the comparative degree.

1) **-ш** The suffix **-ш** is added to most adjectival stems that end in **one consonant**.

Positive Degree	*Adjectival Stem*	*Comparative Degree*	*Superlative Degree*
бага́тий	бага**т**-	бага́**тш**ий	**най**бага́тший
деше́вий	деше**в**-	деше́**вш**ий	**най**деше́вший
здоро́вий	здоро**в**-	здоро́**вш**ий	**най**здоро́вший
молоди́й	моло**д**-	моло́**дш**ий	**най**моло́дший
стари́й	ста**р**-	ста́**рш**ий	**най**ста́рший

2) **-іш** The suffix **-іш** is added to most adjectival stems that end in **two consonants**.

Positive Degree	*Adjectival Stem*	*Comparative Degree*	*Superlative Degree*
бі́дний	бі**дн**-	бідн**іш**ий	**най**бідніший
бру́дни́й	бру**дн**-	брудн**іш**ий	**най**брудніший
га́рний	га**рн**-	гарн**іш**ий	**най**гарніший
голо́дний	голо**дн**-	голодн**іш**ий	**най**голодніший
дурни́й	ду**рн**-	дурн**іш**ий	**най**дурніший
здíбний	зді**бн**-	здібн**іш**ий	**най**здібніший
му́дрий	му**др**-	мудр**іш**ий	**най**мудріший
приє́мний	приє**мн**-	приємн**іш**ий	**най**приємніший
розу́мний	розу**мн**-	розумн**іш**ий	**най**розумніший
сильни́й	си**льн**-	сильн**іш**ий	**най**сильніший
смачни́й	сма**чн**-	смачн**іш**ий	**най**смачніший
сумни́й	су**мн**-	сумн**іш**ий	**най**сумніший
чи́стий	чи**ст**-	чист**іш**ий	**най**чистіший

The suffix **-іш** is also added to some adjectival stems that end in one consonant. Learn these as exceptions.

Positive Degree	*Adjectival Stem*	*Comparative Degree*	*Superlative Degree*
весе́лий	весел-	весел**і́ш**ий	**най**веселі́ший
нови́й	нов-	нов**і́ш**ий	**най**нові́ший
хво́рий	хвор-	хвор**і́ш**ий	**най**хворі́ший
щасли́вий	щаслив-	щаслив**і́ш**ий	**най**щасливі́ший

A few of the colours may be compared. For all of them the suffix **-іш** is added to the adjectival stem to form the comparative degree.

Positive Degree	*Adjectival Stem*	*Comparative Degree*	*Superlative Degree*
бі́лий	біл-	біл**і́ш**ий	**най**білі́ший
жо́втий	жовт-	жовт**і́ш**ий	**най**жовті́ший
зеле́ний	зелен-	зелен**і́ш**ий	**най**зелені́ший
си́ній	син-	син**і́ш**ий	**най**сині́ший
си́вий	сив-	сив**і́ш**ий	**най**сиві́ший
сі́рий	сір-	сір**і́ш**ий	**най**сірі́ший
черво́ний	червон-	червон**і́ш**ий	**най**червоні́ший
чо́рний	чорн-	чорн**і́ш**ий	**най**чорні́ший

3) **-ш** The suffix **-ш** usually replaces **-к** or **-ок** at the end of an adjectival stem.

Positive Degree	*Adjectival Stem*	*Comparative Degree*	*Superlative Degree*
коро́ткий	корот**к**-	коро́т**ш**ий	**най**коро́тший
легки́й	лег**к**-	ле́г**ш**ий	**най**ле́гший
соло́дкий	солод**к**-	соло́д**ш**ий	**най**соло́дший
швидки́й	швид**к**-	шви́д**ш**ий	**най**шви́дший
широ́кий	шир**ок**-	ши́р**ш**ий	**най**ши́рший
Exception:			
високий	вис**ок**-	ви́**щ**ий	**най**ви́щий

4) **-жч** The suffix **-жч** usually replaces **-зьк, -зк, -жк, -ж, -г** at the end of an adjectival stem.

Positive Degree	*Adjectival Stem*	*Comparative Degree*	*Superlative Degree*
вузьки́й	вуз**ьк**-	ву́**жч**ий	**най**ву́жчий
дороги́й	доро**г**-	доро́**жч**ий	**най**доро́жчий
тяжки́й	тя**жк**-	тя́**жч**ий	**най**тя́жчий
Exception			
до́вгий	дов**г**-	до́**вш**ий	**най**до́вший

B.2 Using the Comparative Degree

In English, comparisons involving the comparative degree are made by using the conjunction **than**.

Halyna is **younger than** Oksana.
This cucumber is **longer than** that one.

In Ukrainian, the same comparison may be made in a number of different ways. At this time, the four most common ones are being presented: two with conjunctions, and two with prepositions.

1. The conjunctions **ніж** and **як** may be used.

ніж + nominative	Гали́на **моло́дша, ніж** Окса́на. Цей огіро́к **до́вший, ніж** той.
як + nominative	Гали́на **моло́дша, як** Окса́на. Цей огіро́к **до́вший, як** той.

2. The prepositions **від** and **за** may be used.

від + genitive	Гали́на **моло́дша від** Окса́ни. Цей огіро́к **до́вший від** то́го.
за + accusative	Гали́на **моло́дша за** Окса́ну. Цей огіро́к **до́вший за** той.

Practise Oral Exercise 30.1

Do Written Exercise 30.1

B.3 Using the Superlative Degree

In English, the superlative degree is used to make a comparison among three or more persons or things.

Darusia is **the youngest** of our children.
This orchard is **the biggest** of all the orchards.

In Ukrainian, a comparison involving the superlative degree may be made by using a number of different prepositions.

At this time, the **three prepositions** that are most commonly used are being presented.

1. **з + genitive**	Дару́ся **наймоло́дша** з на́ших діте́й. Цей сад **найбі́льший** з усі́х саді́в.
2. **се́ред + genitive**	Дару́ся **наймоло́дша се́ред** на́ших діте́й. Цей сад **найбі́льший се́ред** усі́х саді́в.
3. **між + instrumental**	Дару́ся **наймоло́дша між** на́шими ді́тьми. Цей сад **найбі́льший між** усіма́ сада́ми.

B.4 The Intensified Superlative

At this point in your study of Ukrainian, you should be able to recognize the intensified superlative, but you are not expected to know how to use it.

In English, it is possible to create a higher degree of the superlative for some adjectives by using the words **the very** with the superlative degree of an adjective, or the words **most**, or **all**, or the prefix **al-** with the positive degree.

In Ukrainian, this intensified superlative is expressed by adding either the prefix **що** or **як-** to the superlative degree, or the prefix **все-** or **пре-** to the positive degree of some adjectives.

They are the very best parents.
Вони́ **як**найкра́щі батьки́.

She bought the most expensive car.
Вона́ купи́ла **що**найдоро́жче а́вто.

I must thank my most benevolent grandfather for all of this.
Я дя́кую своє́му **пре**до́брому діду́севі за все це.

My all-wise granny told me this.
Моя́ **пре**му́дра бабу́ся мені́ це сказа́ла.

Only Almighty God can help me now.
Лише́ **Все**си́льний Бог мо́же тепе́р мені́ помогти́.

Practise Oral Exercises 30.2, 30.3, 30.4

Do Written Exercises 30.2, 30.3, 30.4

LESSON 31

A. VOCABULARY

Nouns

abdomen	живíт (живот-), чéрево
ankle	кíсточка
back *[lower]*	кри́жі *[pl],* кри́жів
back *[upper]*	спи́на
bandage	бандáж
beard	бородá
body	тíло
bone	кíстка
cheek	щокá
chest, breast	грýди *[pl],* грудéй
chin	підборíддя *[n]*
elbow	лíкоть (лікт-)
eye	óко, *l.sg.* ... óці, *pl.* óчі, очéй
eyebrow	бровá
eyelash	вíя
face	лицé, обли́ччя *[n]*
fingernail, toenail	нíготь (нігт-)
fist	кулáк
foot	ногá
head	головá
heart	сéрце, *g.pl.* сердéць
heel	п'ятá
knee	колíно
medicine	лíки *[pl],* лíків
mouth	рот
muscle	мýскул, м'яз
mustache	вус, *pl.* вýса і вýси, *g.pl.* вус
nose	ніс (нос-)
pain, ache	біль (бол-)
pill	таблéтка, піґýлка, *пілю́ля*
shoulder	рамéно, плечé, *pl.* плéчі, плечéй
skeleton	скелéт, кістя́к
skin	шкíра

spine	хребе́т (хребт-)
stomach	шлу́нок (шлунк-)
tear	сльоза́, *g.pl.* сліз
throat	го́рло, *g.pl.* го́рел і го́рлів
toe	па́лець на нозі́ (пальц-)
tongue	язи́к
wrist	зап'я́сток (зап'ястк-)

Verbs

to ache, to hurt	болі́ти: боли́ть, боля́ть *pf.* заболі́ти: заболи́ть, заболя́ть
to break	ломи́ти: лом-лю́, -иш *pf.* зломи́ти: злом-лю́, -иш
to knock	сту́кати: сту́ка-ю, -єш *pf.* сту́кнути: сту́кн-у, -еш
to ring	дзвони́ти: дзвон-ю́, -иш *pf.* подзвони́ти: подзвон-ю́, -иш
to show	пока́зувати: пока́зу-ю, -єш *pf.* показа́ти: покаж-у́ -еш
to smile	усміха́тися: усміха́-юся, -єшся *pf.* усміхну́тися: усміхн-у́ся, -е́шся
to sprain	звиха́ти: звиха́-ю, -єш *pf.* звихну́ти: звихн-у́, -е́ш
to swallow	ковта́ти: ковта́-ю, -єш *pf.* ковтну́ти: ковтн-у́, -е́ш
to whistle	свистати: свищ-у́, -еш *pf.* засвистати: засвищ-у́, -еш

B. EXPRESSING PAIN

In English, we express pain by saying that something hurts.

My head hurts.	Danylo's teeth hurt.

In Ukrainian, the preferred way of expressing pain is to use the **nominative case** for the part of the body that hurts, and the preposition **у** and the **gentive** case for the person who is experiencing the pain.

Що **у вас** боли́ть? What hurts you?	**У ме́не** боли́ть голова́. My head hurts.
Що боли́ть **у Дани́ла**? What hurts Danylo?	**У Дани́ла** боля́ть зу́би. Danylo's teeth hurt.

C. ADVERBS

In both English and Ukrainian, adverbs are used in four ways.

1. To modify a verb.

   She works **quickly**. — Вона́ **шви́дко** працю́є.

2. To modify an adjective.

   She is a **very** good worker. — Вона́ **ду́же** до́бра праці́вни́ця.

3. To modify another adverb.

   She works **very quickly**. — Вона́ **ду́же шви́дко** працю́є.

4. To link a subordinate clause to a principal clause.

   I know **where** she works. — Я зна́ю, **де** вона́ працю́є.

C.1 Formation of Adverbs from Adjectives

In English, many adverbs are formed by adding the ending **-ly** to the positive degree of an adjective.

In Ukrainian, many adverbs are formed by adding the ending **-o** (occasionally **-e**) to the stem of an adjective. Usually, the adverb and the adjective from which it was formed are identical, or very close, in meaning.

Let's look at how adverbs are formed from the adjectives that you know.

Adjective	***Adjectival Stem***	***Adverb***	***Meaning***
бага́тий	багат-	бага́то	much, richly
весе́лий	весел-	ве́село	happily, merrily
га́рний	гарн-	га́рно	nicely, admirably
до́брий	добр-	до́бре	well, fine
до́вгий	довг-	до́вго	for a long time
мали́й	мал-	ма́ло	little, not much
пога́ний	поган-	пога́но	badly
прие́мний	приємн-	прие́мно	pleasantly
смачни́й	смачн-	сма́чно	tastily
соло́дкий	солодк-	со́лодко	sweetly
сумни́й	сумн-	су́мно	sadly
швидки́й	швидк-	шви́дко	quickly

D. COMPARISON OF ADVERBS

In English, some adverbs may be compared in the same three degrees as adjectives: **positive**, **comparative**, and **superlative**. Let's look at the following examples.

We get up **late**.
He gets up **later**.
She gets up **the latest**.

Positive Degree	*Comparative Degree*	*Superlative Degree*
late	later	latest

In Ukrainian, some adverbs may also be compared.

Let's look at the English examples used above and their Ukrainian equivalents.

We get up **late**.	Ми **пізно** встаємó.
He gets up **later**.	Він **пізніше** встаé.
She gets up **the latest**.	Вонá **найпізніше** встаé.

In Ukrainian, most of the adverbs that may be compared are derived from adjectives.

D.1 Formation of the Comparative and Superlative Degrees

In both English and Ukrainian, adverbs, like adjectives, form their comparative and superlative degrees in one of three ways.

1. ***In English***, some adverbs form their comparative and superlative degrees irregularly.

Positive Degree	*Comparative Degree*	*Superlative Degree*
badly	worse	worst
well	better	best

In Ukrainian, the comparative degree of a few advebs is also formed irregularly. The superlative degree is formed by adding the prefix **най-** to the comparative form.

Positive Degree	*Comparative Degree*	*Superlative Degree*
багáто	бíльше	найбíльше
дóбре	крáще/лíпше	найкрáще/найлíпше
мáло	мéнше	наймéнше
погáно	гíрше	найгíрше

2. ***In English***, some adverbs are compared by using **more** and **most**, or **less** and **least** with the positive form.

Positive Degree	*Comparative Degree*	*Superlative Degree*
quickly	**more** quickly	**most** quickly
capably	**less** capably	**least** capably

In Ukrainian, the words **більш** or **менш** are used with the positive degree of some adverbs to form the comparative degree. The superlative degree is formed by adding the prefix **най-** to either **більш** or **менш**.

Positive Degree	*Comparative Degree*	*Superlative Degree*
щасли́во	**більш** щасли́во	**най**бíльш щасли́во
талановúто	**менш** талановúто	**най**мéнш талановúто

3. ***In English***, some adverbs have the suffix **-er** added to the positive degree to form the comparative degree, and **-est** to form the superlative degree.

Positive Degree	*Comparative Degree*	*Superlative Degree*
early	earl**ier**	earl**iest**

In Ukrainian, the comparative degree of many adverbs is formed by adding either the suffix **-ш** or **-іш** to the positive degree. The superlative degree is formed by adding the prefix **най-** to the comparative degree.

1) **-ш** The suffix **-ш** is added to most adverbial stems that end in **a single consonant**.

Positive Degree	*Adjectival Stem*	*Comparative Degree*	*Superlative Degree*
бага́то	бага**т**-	бага́т**ше**	**най**бага́тше
де́шево	деше**в**-	деше́в**ше**	**най**деше́вше
здо́рово	здоро**в**-	здоро́в**ше**	**най**здоро́вше
мо́лодо	моло**д**-	моло́д**ше**	**най**моло́дше
ти́хо	ти**х**-	ти́х**ше**	**най**ти́хше

2) **-іш** The suffix **-іш** is added to most adverbial stems that end in **two consonants**.

Positive Degree	***Adjectival Stem***	***Comparative Degree***	***Superlative Degree***
бі́дно	бід**н**-	бідн**іше**	**най**бідніше
бру́дно	бру**дн**-	брудн**іше**	**най**брудніше
га́рно	га**рн**-	гарн**іше**	**най**гарніше
го́лодно	голо**дн**-	голодн**іше**	**най**голодніше
го́лосно	голо**сн**-	голосн**іше**	**най**голосніше
ду́рно	ду**рн**-	дурн**іше**	**най**дурніше
зді́бно	зді**бн**-	здібн**іше**	**най**здібніше
му́дро	му**др**-	мудр**іше**	**най**мудріше
пі́зно	пі**зн**-	пізн**іше**	**най**пізніше
пові́льно	пові**льн**-	повільн**іше**	**най**повільніше
прие́мно	прие**мн**-	приємн**іше**	**най**приємніше
розу́мно	розу**мн**-	розумн**іше**	**най**розумніше
си́льно	си**льн**-	сильн**іше**	**най**сильніше
сма́чно	сма**чн**-	смачн**іше**	**най**смачніше
су́мно	су**мн**-	сумн**іше**	**най**сумніше
ча́сто	ча**ст**-	част**іше**	**най**частіше
чи́сто	чи**ст**-	чист**іше**	**най**чистіше

The suffix **-іш** is also added to some adverbs that have a stem ending in one consonant. **Learn these adverbs as exceptions to the rule given above.**

Positive Degree	***Adjectival Stem***	***Comparative Degree***	***Superlative Degree***
ве́село	весел-	весел**іше**	**най**веселіше
звича́йно	звичайн-	звичайн**іше**	**най**звичайніше
ра́но	ран-	ран**іше**	**най**раніше
щасли́во	щаслив-	щаслив**іше**	**най**щасливіше

For adverbs that are derived from adjectives denoting colours, the suffix **-іш** is added to the stem to form the comparative degree.

Positive Degree	*Adjectival Stem*	*Comparative Degree*	*Superlative Degree*
біло	біл-	біл**іш**е	**най**біліше
жо́вто	жовт-	жовт**і́ш**е	**най**жовтіше
зе́лено	зелен-	зелен**і́ш**е	**най**зеленіше
си́ньо	син-	син**і́ш**е	**най**синіше
сі́ро	сір-	сір**і́ш**е	**най**сіріше
черво́но	червон-	червон**і́ш**е	**най**червоніше
чо́рно	чорн-	чорн**і́ш**е	**най**чорніше

3) **-ш** The suffix **-ш** usually replaces the **-к** or **-ок** that appears at the end of an adverbial stem.

Positive Degree	*Adjectival Stem*	*Comparative Degree*	*Superlative Degree*
ко́ротко	корот**к-**	коро́т**ш**е	**най**коро́тше
ле́гко	лег**к-**	ле́г**ш**е	**най**ле́гше
рі́дко	рід**к-**	рі́д**ш**е	**най**рі́дше
со́лодко	солод**к-**	соло́д**ш**е	**най**соло́дше
шви́дко	швид**к-**	шви́д**ш**е	**най**шви́дше
ши́роко	шир**ок-**	ши́р**ш**е	**най**ши́рше
Exception:			
ви́соко	вис**ок-**	ви́**щ**е	**най**ви́ще

4) **-жч** The suffix **-жч** usually replaces the **-зьк**, **-зк**, **-жк**, **-ж**, **-г** at the end of an adverbial stem.

Positive Degree	*Adjectival Stem*	*Comparative Degree*	*Superlative Degree*
ву́зько	ву**зьк-**	ву́**жч**е	**най**ву́жче
до́рого	доро**г-**	доро́**жч**е	**най**доро́жче
Exception:			
до́вго	дов**г-**	до́в**ш**е	**най**до́вше

D.2 Using the Comparative Degree

In English, comparisons involving the comparative degree are made between **two persons or things** by using the conjunction **than**.

He sings **more** loudly **than** I do.

In Ukrainian, the same comparison may be made in a number of different ways. At this time, the most common ways are being presented.

1. The conjunctions **ніж** and **як** may be used.

ніж + nominative	Він співáє голоснíше, **ніж я**.
як + nominative	Він співáє голоснíше, **як я**.

2. The prepositions **від** and **за** may be used.

від + genitive	Він співáє голоснíше **від мéне**.
за + accusative	Він співáє голоснíше **за мéне**.

Practise Oral Exercise 31.1

Do Written Exercise 31.1

D.3 Using the Superlative Degree

In English, the superlative degree and a prepositional phrase are used to make a comparison among **three or more persons or things**.

He sings the **most** loudly **of all of our children**.

In Ukrainian, a comparison involving the superlative degree may be made by using a number of different prepositions.

At this time, the three prepositions that are used most frequently are being presented.

1.	**з + genitive**	Він співáє **найголоснíше з усíх нáших дітéй**.
2.	**сéред + genitive**	Він співáє **найголоснíше сéред усíх нáших дітéй**.
3.	**між + instrumental**	Він співáє **найголоснíше між усімá нáшими дíтьми**.

Practise Oral Exercises 31.2, 31.3, 31.4

Do Written Exercises 31.2, 31.3, 31.4, 31.5

LESSON 32

A. VOCABULARY

Nouns

artifact	експона́т
battery	батаре́йка
block *[child's toy]*	ку́бик
candle	сві́чка
candlestick	свічни́к
carving, carved artifact	різьба́
colour	ко́лір *[h]* (кольор-)
competition	ко́нкурс
cross	хрест
dance	тане́ць (танц-)
doll	ля́лька
dough *[for bread, etc.]*	ті́сто
embroidered article	ви́шивка
exhibition, public display	ви́ставка
fabric	ткани́на
film	фільм
game	гра, *pl.* і́гри, і́гор
glass	скло
hobby	улю́блене заня́ття *[n]*
icon	іко́на
kindergarten	садо́чок (садочк-) *дитсадо́к (дитсадк-)*
lottery	льотерія, *лотере́я*
metal	мета́ль, мета́л
music	му́зика
optimist	оптимі́ст; оптимі́стка
paint	фа́рба
paper	папі́р *[h]* (папер-)
pessimist	песимі́ст; песимі́стка
pysanka, Easter egg	пи́санка
raffle	розі́гравка
song	пі́сня, *g.pl.* пісе́нь
straw	соло́ма
teddy bear	ведме́дик
trunk, chest	скри́ня
wood	де́рево *[sg]*

Adjectives

boring	нудни́й
difficult	трудни́й
embroidered	ви́шитий
favorite	улю́блений
important	важли́вий
interesting	ціка́вий
mischievous	збито́чний
obedient, polite	че́мний
slow	пові́льний

Verbs

to bake	пекти́: печ-у́, -е́ш *pf.* спекти́: спеч-у́, -е́ш
to believe	ві́рити: ві́р-ю, -иш *pf.* пові́рити: пові́р-ю, -иш
to build	будува́ти: буду́-ю, -єш *pf.* збудува́ти: збуду́-ю, -єш
to embroider	вишива́ти: вишива́-ю, -єш *pf.* ви́шити: ви́ши-ю, -єш
to hope	наді́ятися: наді́-юся, -єшся
to kiss	цілува́ти: цілу́-ю, -єш *pf.* поцілува́ти: поцілу́-ю, -єш
to lose *[opp. of to win]*	програва́ти: програ-ю́, -є́ш *pf.* програ́ти: програ́-ю, -єш
to paint	малюва́ти: малю́-ю, -єш *pf.* (a picture) намалюва́ти *pf.* (a building) помалюва́ти
to recall, to remind	прига́дувати: прига́ду-ю, -єш *pf.* пригада́ти: пригада́-ю, -єш
to win	вигрaва́ти: вигра-ю́, -є́ш) *pf.* ви́грати: ви́гра-ю, -єш

Vocabulary Note

In Ukrainian, the verb **писа́ти** is used in reference to icons and Easter eggs.

Вона́ **пи́ше** іко́ни.	She **paints** icons.
Вона́ **пи́ше** писанки́.	She **decorates** Easter eggs.

B. POSSESSIVE ADJECTIVES

In Lesson 16 you learned how to indicate possession by using a noun in the genitive case. In translating these Ukrainian sentences into English, you used either an apostrophe to indicate possession, or a prepositional phrase.

> Це банду́ра **дя́дька**.
>
> This is **uncle's** bandura.
> This is the bandura **of uncle**.

In this lesson, you will learn how to indicate possession in Ukrainian **by transforming animate nouns into possessive adjectives**.

In theory, possessive adjectives may be formed from any Ukrainian animate noun. In practice, however, they usually are formed only from personal names and from terms that designate kinship or other close personal ties.

Possessive adjectives formed from animate nouns other than personal names and terms of kinship may sometimes be used in casual conversation and in literary writings. In business dealings, official documents, scholarly and scientific writings, the genitive case of nouns is used to indicate possession rather than possessive adjectives.

To form a possessive adjective, **a suffix is added to the stem of an animate noun**. Possessive adjectives agree in **gender**, **number**, and **case** with the noun that they modify (possess). They are declined like **Hard Declension adjectives**.

B.1 The Formation of Possessive Adjectives from Feminine Nouns

The suffix **-ин** is added to the stems of Hard, Mixed, and Soft 1 Declension nouns. The suffix **-їн** is added to the stems of Soft 2 Declension nouns.

Noun stems ending in **-к**, **-г**, and **-х** change, respectively, to **-ч**, **-ж**, and **-ш** before the suffix **-ин** is added.

Men's names ending in **-а** are treated like feminine Hard Declension nouns.

Possessive Adjectives Formed from Feminine Nouns

Declension	*Nominative*	*Noun Stem*	*Adjectival Stem*
Hard	дружи́на	дружин-	дружин-**ин**-
к → ч	дочка́	доч**к**-	доч**ч**-**ин**-
г → ж	О́льга	Оль**г**-	Оль**ж**-**ин**-
х → ш	свекру́ха	свекру**х**-	свекру**ш**-**ин**-
Мико́ла	Мико́ла	Микол-	Микол-**ин**-
Mixed	те́ща	тещ-	тещ-**ин**-
Soft 1	бабу́ся	бабус-	бабус-**ин**-
Soft 2	Марі́я	Марі-	Марі-**їн**-

B.2 Declension of Possessive Adjectives Formed from Feminine Nouns

Possessive Adjectives Formed from Hard, Mixed, Soft 1 Declension Feminine Nouns				
	Feminine Singular	*Masculine Singular*	*Neuter Singular*	*All Genders Plural*
N.	ма́м-ин-**а**	ма́м-ин	ма́м-ин-е	ма́м-ин-**і**
G.	ма́м-ин-**ої**	ма́м-ин-**ого**		ма́м-ин-**их**
A.	ма́м-ин-**у**	[=G or N]	[=N]	[=G or N]
V.	[=N]	[=N]	[=N]	[=N]
I.	ма́м-ин-**ою**	ма́м-ин-**им**		ма́м-ин-**ими**
D.	ма́м-ин-**ій**	ма́м-ин-**ому**		ма́м-ин-**им**
L.	... ма́м-ин-**ій**	... ма́м-ин-**ому** (... ма́м-ин-**ім**)		... ма́м-ин-**их**

Possessive Adjectives Formed from Soft 2 Declension Feminine Nouns				
	Feminine Singular	*Masculine Singular*	*Neuter Singular*	*All Genders Plural*
N.	Марі́-їн-**а**	Марі́-їн	Марі́-їн-**е**	Марі́-їн-**і**
G.	Марі́-їн-**ої**	Марі́-їн-**ого**		Марі́-їн-**их**
A.	Марі́-їн-**у**	[=G or N]	[=N]	[=G or N]
V.	[=N]	[=N]	[=N]	[=N]
I.	Марі́-їн-**ою**	Марі́-їн-**им**		Марі́-їн-**ими**
D.	Марі́-їн-**ій**	Марі́-їн-**ому**		Марі́-їн-**им**
L.	... Марі́-їн-**ій**	... Марі́-їн-**ому** (... Марі́-їн-**ім**)		... Марі́-їн-**их**

B.3 Using Possessive Adjectives Formed from Feminine Nouns

In using possessive adjectives, it is important to remember that they agree in **gender**, **number**, and **case** with the noun that they modify (possess). Notice that the masculine nominative singular form **does not have the ending -ий**.

Це Марі**їн** хрест.	This is **Maria's** cross.
Це ма́м**ина** ви́шивка.	This is **mother's** embroidery.
Це Марі́**їне** улю́блене заня́ття.	This is **Maria's** hobby.
Це ма́м**ині** писанки́.	These are **mother's** pysanky.

Practise Oral Exercise 32.1

Do Written Exercise 32.1

B.4 The Formation of Possessive Adjectives from Masculine Nouns

The suffix **-ів** is added to the stems of Hard, Mixed, and Soft 1 Declension nouns. The suffix **-їв** is added to the stems of Soft 2 Declension Nouns.

Possessive Adjectives Formed from Masculine Nouns			
Declension	***Nominative***	***Noun Stem***	***Adjectival Stem***
Hard	брат	брат-	брат-**ів**-
Mixed	ро́дич	родич-	родич-**ів**-
Soft 1	діду́сь	дідус-	дідус-**ів**-
Soft 2	Ю́рій	Юрі-	Юрі-**їв**-

B.5 Declension of Possessive Adjectives Formed from Masculine Nouns

In declining possessive adjectives formed from masculine animate nouns, it is important to remember that **the vowel in the adjectival suffix changes when the closed syllable becomes an open syllable.**

1. The **і** in the closed syllable **-ів** of a Hard Declension masculine possessive adjective changes to **-о**.
2. The **і** in the closed syllable **-ів** of Mixed and Soft 1 Declension masculine posssessive adjectives changes to **-е**.
3. The **ї** in the closed syllable **-їв** of a Soft 2 Declension masculine possessive adjective changes to **-є**.

Possessive Adjectives Formed from Hard Declension Masculine Nouns				
	Feminine Singular	***Masculine Singular***	***Neuter Singular***	***All Genders Plural***
N.	бра́т-ов-**а**	бра́т-ів	бра́т-ов-**е**	бра́т-ов-**і**
G.	бра́т-ов-**ої**	бра́т-ов-**ого**		бра́т-ов-**их**
A.	бра́т-ов-**у**	[=G or N]	[=N]	[=G or N]
V.	[=N]	[=N]	[=N]	[=N]
I.	бра́т-ов-**ою**	бра́т-ов-**им**		бра́т-ов-**ими**
D.	бра́т-ов-**ій**	бра́т-ов-**ому**		бра́т-ов-**им**
L.	... бра́т-ов-**ій**	... бра́т-ов-**ому** (... бра́т-ов-**ім**)		... бра́т-ов-**их**

Possessive Adjectives Formed from Mixed, Soft 1 Declension Masculine Nouns				
	Feminine Singular	*Masculine Singular*	*Neuter Singular*	*All Genders Plural*
N.	зя́т-ев-**а**	зя́т-**ів**	зя́т-ев-**е**	зя́т-ев-**і**
G.	зя́т-ев-**ої**	зя́т-ев-**ого**		зя́т-ев-**их**
A.	зя́т-ев-**у**	[=G or N]	[=N]	[=G or N]
V.	[=N]	[=N]	[=N]	[=N]
I.	зя́т-ев-**ою**	зя́т-ев-**им**		зя́т-ев-**ими**
D.	зя́т-ев-**ій**	зя́т-ев-**ому**		зя́т-ев-**им**
L.	... зя́т-ев-**ій**	... зя́т-ев-**ому** (... зя́т-ев-**ім**)		... зя́т-ев-**их**

Possessive Adjectives Formed from Soft 2 Declension Masculine Nouns				
	Feminine Singular	*Masculine Singular*	*Neuter Singular*	*All Genders Plural*
N.	Ю́рі-єв-**а**	Ю́рі-**їв**	Ю́рі-єв-**е**	Ю́рі-єв-**і**
G.	Ю́рі-єв-**ої**	Ю́рі-єв-**ого**		Ю́рі-єв-**их**
A.	Ю́рі-єв-**у**	[=G or N]	[=N]	[=G or N]
V.	[=N]	[=N]	[=N]	[=N]
I.	Ю́рі-єв-**ою**	Ю́рі-єв-**им**		Ю́рі-єв-**ими**
D.	Ю́рі-єв-**ій**	Ю́рі-єв-**ому**		Ю́рі-єв-**им**
L.	... Ю́рі-єв-**ій**	... Ю́рі-єв-**ому** (... Ю́рі-єв-**ім**)		... Ю́рі-єв-**их**

B.6 Using Possessive Adjectives Formed from Masculine Nouns

Remember that the masculine nominative singular form **does not have the ending -ий**; instead, it ends in a **closed syllable**.

Це бра́**тів** експона́т.	This is the (my) brother's artifact.
Це бра́**това** скри́ня.	This is (my) brother's trunk.
Це бра́**тові** ку́бики.	These are (my) brother's blocks.
Це зя́**тів** мета́ль.	This is (our) son-in-law's metal.
Це зя́**тева** різьба́.	This is (our) son-in-law's carving.
Це зя́**теві** фа́рби.	These are (our) son-in-law's paints.
Це Ю́рі**їв** хрест.	This is Yuriy's cross.
Це Ю́рі**єве** де́рево.	This is Yuriy's wood.
Це Ю́рі**єві** батаре́йки.	These are Yuriy's batteries.

Practise Oral Exercises 32.2, 32.3

Do Written Exercises 32.2, 32.3

C. MASCULINE SHORT ADJECTIVES

In Ukrainian, there are a few adjectives that have an alternate short form in the masculine nominative and vocative singular cases. There is no change in any of the other forms of these adjectives.

C.1 пови́нний/пови́нен

The adjective **пови́нен/пови́нний** means **ought** or **should**. It is one of the adjectives that appears more frequently in its short form, **пови́нен** in the masculine nominative singular case, than in its long form, **пови́нний**.

Він **пови́нен** (повинний) купи́ти квито́к на розі́гравку.
He ought to buy a ticket for the raffle.

Хто **пови́нен** (пови́нний) спекти́ ті́стечка на пере́куску?
Who should bake the cookies for the lunch?

Вона́ **пови́нна** ви́шити блю́зку для ону́ки.
She ought to embroider a blouse for her granddaughter.

Вони́ **пови́нні** помалюва́ти свою́ ха́ту.
They ought to paint their house.

Ді́ти, ви **пови́нні** лягти́ спа́ти о дев'я́тій годи́ні.
Children, you should go to bed at nine o'clock.

C.2 ви́нний/ви́нен

The adjective **ви́нен/ви́нний** has two different meanings: **to be owing something to someone**; or **to be guilty**, **to be at fault**, or **to be blamable for something**. The short form **ви́нен** is used more frequently for the masculine nominative singular case than the long form, **ви́нний**.

Ю́рію, скі́льки гро́шей ти **ви́нен** своє́му бра́тові?
Yuriy, how much money do you owe your brother?

Вона́ мені́ **ви́нна** за квитки́ на конце́рт.
She owes me for the tickets to the concert.

Вони́ всі **ви́нні**, що він злом́ив но́гу.
They are all to blame that he broke his leg.

Хто тут **ви́нен**? Ми всі **ви́нні**!
Who is guilty? We're all guilty!

Я ду́маю, що ніхто́ не **ви́нен**.
I think that no one is at fault.

C.3 пéвний/пéвен

The adjective **пéвний/пéвен** means **sure** or **certain**. The long form, **пéвний**, is used more commonly for the masculine nominative singular case than the short form, **пéвен**.

Він **пéвний** (пéвен), що він поїде на екскýрсію.
He's sure that he'll go on the excursion.

Хто **пéвний** (пéвен), що гóсті зáвтра приїдуть?
Who is certain that the guests will arrive tomorrow?

Вонá **пéвна**, що її мáма найкрáща.
She is sure that her mother is the prettiest.

Ми **пéвні**, що ми вúграємо багáто грóшей.
We are certain that we'll win a lot of money.

C.4 кóжний/кóжен

The adjective **кóжний/кóжен** means **every** when it is used as a modifier, and either **everyone** or **anyone** when it is used as a substantive.

Modifier

Бабýся печé торт **кóжен** (кóжний) день.
Granny bakes a cake every day.

Ýчні вже знáють **кóжну** пíсню.
The pupils know every song already.

Substantive

Кáжуть, що **кóжен** (кóжний) мóже вúграти льотерíю.
They say that anyone can win a lottery.

Кóжний (Кóжен) мóже бýти абó оптимíстом, абó песимíстом!
Everyone can be either an optimist or a pessimist!

Practise Oral Exercise 32.4

Do Written Exercise 32.4

LESSON 33

A. VOCABULARY

Nouns

bad weather	неróда
breeze	вітерéць (вітерц-)
climate	клíмат
cloud	хмáра
fog	тумáн
frost	морóз
hail	град
heatwave	спéка
hurricane	гураґáн, *ураґáн*
lightning	бли́скавка
rain	дощ
rainbow	весéлка
rainy weather	сльотá
snow	сніг
snowstorm	завір'ю́ха
star	зíрка
storm	бýря
sun	сóнце
temperature	температýра
thermometer	термóметр
thunder	грім (гром-)
tornado	торнáдо
weather	погóда
weather forecast	прогнóз погóди
wind	вíтер *[h]* (вітр-)

Adjectives

cold	холóдний
dark	тéмний
early	рáнній *[s]*
fall	осíнній *[s]*
former	бýвший
last	остáнній *[s]*
late	пíзній *[s]*
next, following	настýпний

past	мину́лий
spring	весня́ний
summer	лі́тній *[s]*
warm	те́плий
winter	зимо́вий

Verbs

to appeal	подо́батися: подо́ба-юся, -єшся *pf.* сподо́батися: сподо́ба-юся, -єшся
to blow	ві́яти: ві́-ю, -єш *pf.* пові́яти: пові́-ю, -єш
to change oneself	змі́нюватися: змі́ню-юся, -єшся *pf.* зміни́тися: змін-ю́ся, -ишся
to seem	здава́тися: зда-ю́ся, -є́шся *pf.* зда́тися: зда́-мся, -си́ся
to shine	світи́ти: свічу́, сві́т-иш *pf.* посвіти́ти: посвічу́, посві́т-иш
to warm	пригріва́ти: пригріва́-ю, -єш *pf.* пригрі́ти: пригрі́-ю, -єш

B. WEATHER EXPRESSIONS

In both English and Ukrainian, there are two ways of talking about the weather: impersonal expressions and ordinary sentences.

B.1 Impersonal Weather Expressions with Verbs

In both English and Ukrainian, there are some sentences in which the subject is a nebulous **they** or **it** instead of being an actual person or object.

In English, as you saw in the expression **they say** (see Lesson 9), the pronouns **they** or **it** usually appear in impersonal constructions. In such instances, these pronouns are known as the **grammatical subject**.

It is thundering. (**It** is the **grammatical subject**.)

In Ukrainian, the grammatical subject, **they** or **it**, is understood, but does not appear in impersonal constructions; instead, only the verb form is used.

Гримйть. (The grammatical subject **it** is understood.)

When **it** is the grammatical subject of a sentence in Ukrainian, the **neuter third person singular verb form** is used.

Let's see how sentences with the grammatical subect **it** are formed in the present, future, and past tenses for the verb **гримі́ти – to thunder**.

Present Tense

It is thundering.
Гримить.

Future Imperfective Tense	***Future Perfective Tense***
It will be thundering.	It will have thundered.
Бу́де гримі́ти.	Загримить.

Past Imperfective Tense	***Past Perfective Tense***
It was thundering.	It thundered.
Гримі́ло.	Загримі́ло.

Learn the third person forms of the verbs listed below that are used like **гримі́ти** in impersonal expressions about the weather.

to become cloudy, overcast	хма́ритися: хма́риться; хма́рилося *pf.* захма́ритися: захма́риться; захма́рилося
to flash lightning, to lighten	бли́скати: бли́скає; бли́скало *pf.* забли́скати: забли́скає: забли́скало
to freeze	моро́зити: моро́зить; моро́зило *pf.* заморо́зити: заморо́зить; заморо́зило
to thaw, to melt	та́нути: та́не; та́нуло *pf.* розта́нути: розта́не; розта́нуло

B.2 Impersonal Weather Expressions with Adverbs

In English, the grammatical subject **it** is often used with an adjective in impersonal weather expressions.

In Ukrainian, an **adverb** is used without the grammatical subject **it**.

How's the weather?	Як пого́да?
It's clear.	Я́сно.
It's cloudy.	Хма́рно.
It's cold.	Хо́лодно.
It's foggy.	Тума́нно.
It's hot.	Ду́шно.
What was it like outside?	Як було́ надво́рі?
It was sultry.	Було́ па́рно
It was sunny.	Було́ со́нячно.
It was warm.	Було́ те́пло.
It was windy.	Було́ ві́тряно.

In talking about the temperature, the adverbs **ви́ще** and **ни́жче** are used.

What's the temperature today?	Яка́ температу́ра сього́дні?
It's 10 degrees above zero.	Де́сять ви́ще ну́ля. (Плюс де́сять.)
It's 10 degrees below zero.	Де́сять ни́жче ну́ля. (Мі́нус де́сять.)

B.3 Idiomatic Weather Expressions

In English, we talk about rain, snow, and hail f**alling** or **coming down**; we can also use an impersonal construction.

In Ukrainian, the verbs **іти́/піти́** are usually used instead of **па́дати/упа́сти**, although you will hear the latter verbs used as well.

The rain is falling. It's raining.	Дощ іде́ (па́дає).
The snow is falling. It's snowing.	Сніг іде́ (па́дає).
The hail is coming down. It's hailing.	Град іде́ (па́дає).

For **rain** and **snow** there are also impersonal verbs that are used colloquially.

To rain: it's raining.	Дощи́ти: дощи́ть.
To snow: it's snowing.	Сніжи́ти: сніжи́ть.

B.4 Other Weather Expressions

What's the weather forecast?	Яки́й прогно́з пого́ди?
It will be a miserable day.	Бу́де пога́ний день.
It will be a nice day.	Бу́де га́рний день.
It will be clear and sunny.	Бу́де я́сно й со́нячно.
It will be cloudy and cold.	Бу́де хма́рно й хо́лодно.
It will be very windy.	Бу́де си́льний ві́тер.
There will be a storm.	Бу́де бу́ря.

What's the weather like today?	Яка́ пого́да сього́дні?
The sun is shining.	Со́нце сві́тить.
The sun is shining warmly.	Со́нце пригріва́є.
The weather is changing.	Пого́да змі́нюється.
The wind is blowing.	Ві́тер віє.

Practise Oral Exercise 33.1

Do Written Exercise 33.1

C. IMPERSONAL SENTENCES

In both English and Ukrainian, impersonal constructions are quite widely used.

C.1 здава́тися/зда́тися

In both English and Ukrainian, when something **seems** or **appears to be** to someone, this uncertainty may be stated in two different ways:

1. **I think** that she's a singer.
   Я ду́маю, що вона́ співа́чка.
2. **It seems to me** that she's a singer.
   Мені́ здає́ться, що вона́ співа́чка.

Let's look at the second sentence, the one that contains an impersonal expression.

In both English and Ukrainian, there are two clauses in this sentence:

1) a principal clause: It seems to me/Мені́ здає́ться
2) a subordinate clause: that she's a singer/що вона́ співа́чка

In both English and Ukrainian, the grammatical subject in the principal clause is the impersonal **it** (**it seems/здає́ться**), while the person who is doing the thinking, that is, "to whom something seems" is the indirect object.

In Ukrainian, this indirect object is expressed by the **dative case**.

Мені́ здає́ться, що вона́ співа́чка.
It seems **to me** that she's a singer.

Кому́ здає́ться, що сього́дні холодно?
To whom does it seem cold today?

Студе́нтці здава́лося, що вона́ все́ зна́ла.
It seemed **to the student***[f]* that she knew everything.

Профе́сорові здава́лося, що надво́рі було́ те́пло.
It seemed **to the professor** that it was warm outside.

C.2 подо́батися/сподо́батися

In both English and Ukrainian, the following two sentences are close in meaning; however, in both languages, the first sentence expresses the feelings of a person who has had more time to gain a fuller appreciation of the flowers.

1. **He likes** these flowers.
   Він лю́бить ці квітки́.
2. These flowers **appeal to him**.
   Йому́ подо́баються ці квітки́.

In both English and Ukrainian, both sentences are constructed in the same way.

1. He likes these flowers.
   Він лю́бить ці квітки́.

Subject:	(Who likes these flowers?)	**He./Він.**
Predicate:	(What does he do?)	He **likes.**/Він **лю́бить.**
Direct Object:	(What does he like?)	**These flowers./Ці квітки́.**

2. These flowers appeal to him.
   Йому́ подо́баються ці квітки́.

Subject:	(What appeals?)	**These flowers./Квітки́.**
Predicate:	(What do these flowers do?)	They **appeal./Подо́баються.**
Indirect Object:	(To whom do they appeal?)	**To him./Йому́.**

Let's look at a few more examples.

Дити́ні подо́бається ведме́дик.
The teddy bear appeals to the child. (The child likes the teddy bear.)

Жі́нці сподо́бається ця ткани́на.
This fabric will appeal to the woman. (The woman will like this fabric.)

Чолові́кові подо́баються свічники́.
The candlesticks appeal to the man. (The man likes the candlesticks.)

Котра́ іко́на **вам** сподо́балася?
Which icon appealed to you *[p]*? (Which icon did you *[p]* like?)

Practise Oral Exercise 33.2

Do Written Exercise 33.2

C.3 хоті́тися/схоті́тися

In English, we say that we **feel** like doing something.

In Ukrainian, the third person singular form of **хоті́тися/схоті́тися** is used impersonally to express the fact that we feel like doing something. The person who experiences the feeling is referred to in **the dative case**.

Мені́ хо́четься піти́ в кіно́ сьо́годні вве́чорі.
I feel like going to the movies this evening.

Паціє́нтові за́раз схо́четься спа́ти.
The patient *[m]* will feel like sleeping right away.

Де́кому хоті́лося гра́ти в ка́рти, а **де́кому** не хоті́лося.
Some felt like playing cards, and some didn't feel like it.

C.4 сни́тися/присни́тися

In English, we say that we **dream** about something.

In Ukrainian, the verb **сни́тися/присни́тися** means **to appear in a dream to someone**. The person to whom something appears in a dream is referred to in the **dative case**.

Ти **мені́** ча́сто сни́шся.
I often dream about you *[s]*.

Та́тові ніко́ли ніщо́ не сни́ться.
Dad never dreams about anything.

Ма́мі присни́лося, що вона́ ви́грала льотері́ю.
Mom dreamed that she won the lottery.

C.5 дивува́ти/здивува́ти

In both English and Ukrainian, we say that we are astonished, amazed, or surprised at something, or that something astonishes, amazes, or surprises us.

In Ukrainian, the verb **дивува́ти/здивува́ти** is used in both these instances, and the person who is experiencing the astonishment, amazement, or surprise is referred to in the **accusative case**.

Мене́ диву́є, що ніхто́ не прийшо́в на конце́рт.
I'm surprised that no one came to the concert.

Журналі́стку здивува́ло, що було́ сті́льки писано́к на ви́ставці.
The journalist *[f]* was amazed that there were so many pysanky in the display.

Її́ ви́шивки здивува́ли **бабу́сю**.
Her embroideries amazed grandmother.

C.6 ціка́вити/заціка́вити

In both English and Ukrainian, we say that something interests us.

In Ukrainian, the verb **ціка́вити/заціка́вити** is used to indicate that **something is of interest to someone**. The person who is interested is referred to in the **accusative case**.

Ці експона́ти **мене́** ціка́влять.
I'm interested in these artifacts. (These artifacts interest me.)

Ця пі́сня заціка́вила **тури́стів**.
The tourists became interested in this song. (This song interested the tourists.)

Чи **акто́рку** ціка́вить цей фільм?
Is the actress interested in this film? (Does this film interest the actress?)

C.7 Impersonal Expressions with Adverbs

In English, **predicate adjectives** are often used to indicate how someone is feeling.

In Ukrainian, **impersonal expressions with adverbs are used to express how someone feels**; the person who is experiencing the feeling is looked upon as being the indirect object (the receiver of the feeling) and, therefore, is in the **dative case**.

I am **bored**.	**Мені́** ну́дно.
He feels **sad**.	**Йому́** су́мно.
She feels **happy**.	**Їй** ве́село.

The adverb **ціка́во** is used in impersonal constructions to indicate the interest that someone has in something or someone. The **person who evinces this interest is referred to in the dative case.**

Кому́ ціка́во прочита́ти цю кни́жку?
Who's interested in reading this book?

Ону́ці ціка́во говори́ти з діду́сем.
The granddaughter finds it interesting to talk with her grandfather.

C.8 To Need – потрі́бний

In Ukrainian, the idea of needing something may be expressed either by using **тре́ба** or **потрі́бно** (see Lesson 20, H), or by using the adjective **потрі́бний.**

The adjective **потрі́бний** is declined like a Hard Declension adjective, and it must agree in **gender**, **number**, and **case with the thing that is needed**.

In an impersonal sentence that uses the adjective **потрі́бний**, **the thing that is needed is in the nominative case**, while **the person who is in need of it is in the dative case**.

Мені́ потрі́бн**а** сві́чк**а**.	I need a candle.
Йому́ потрі́бн**ий** велосипе́д.	He needs a bicycle.
Їй потрі́бн**е** ві́де**о**.	She needs a VCR.
Нам потрі́бн**і** журна́л**и**.	We need magazines.

The adjective **потрі́бний** also has a short form **потрі́бен** for the masculine nominative and vocative singular cases. The two forms are interchangeable.

Мені́ **потрі́бний** (потрі́бен) буди́льник.
I need an alarm clock.

Кому́ **потрі́бен** (потрі́бний) цей словни́к?
Who needs this dictionary?

Practise Oral Exercise 33.3

Do Written Exercises 33.3, 33.4

LESSON 34

A. Vocabulary

Nouns

contest	змага́ння *[n]*
fan *[enthusiatic supporter]*	болі́льник
frizbee	фри́збі *[indecl.]*
hill	горб
horseback rider	ве́ршник; ве́ршниця
ice	лі́д (льод-)
jungle gym	ла́занка
kilometer	кіломе́тр *[h]*
ladder	драби́на
medal	меда́ля, *меда́ль [f]*
merry-go-round	карусе́ля, *карусе́ль [f]*
mile	ми́ля
prize	нагоро́да, *приз*
roller skate	ро́лик
skate	ковза́н
skateboard	скейт
skater	ковзаня́р *[h]*; ковзаня́рка
skating rink	ко́взанка
ski	ли́жа
skier	ли́жник; ли́жниця
skipping rope	скака́лка
sled	са́нки́ *[pl]*, са́но́к
snowball	сні́жка
snowman	снігова́ ба́ба, снігови́й дід
snowmobile	мотоса́ни *[pl]*, мотосане́й автоса́ни *[pl]*, автосане́й
sport	спорт
success	у́спіх
surprise	несподі́ванка, *сюрпри́з*
team	кома́нда
toboggan	тобо́ґан
trampoline	трамплі́н
tricycle	триколі́сник
trophy	трофе́й
wagon	візо́к (візк-)
water skis	водяні́ ли́жі
wave *[of water]*	хви́ля

Adverbs

on foot	пішки
on horseback	ве́рхи
on tiptoe	навшпи́ньки

Preposition

all over, about	по

Verbs

to catch	лови́ти: лов-лю́, -иш *pf.* злови́ти: злов-лю́, -иш
to climb, to crawl	ла́зити *[it.]*: ла́жу, ла́з-иш лі́зти *[dur.]*: лі́з-у, -еш *pf.* полі́зти: полі́з-у, -еш
to engage in a leisure activity that involves movement on something	ката́тися: ката́-юся, -єшся *pf.* players ката́тися: ката́-юся, -єшся
to jump, to leap	скака́ти: скач-у́, -еш *pf.* ско́чити: ско́ч-у, -иш
to play	ба́витися: ба́в-люся, -ишся *pf.* поба́витися: поба́в-люся, -ишся
to skate	ко́взатися: ко́вза-юся, -єшся *pf.* поко́взатися: поко́вза-юся, -єшся
to swing, to rock	го́йдатися: го́йда-юся, -єшся *pf.* пого́йдатися: пого́йда-юся, -єшся
to throw	кида́ти: кида́-ю, -єш *pf.* ки́нути: ки́н-у, -еш

Vocabulary Notes

1. Several verbs that you know are used to express involvement in a sport.

to go biking	ката́тися на велосипе́ді
to go boating	ката́тися на човні́
to bounce a ball	гра́ти в м'яч
to go sledding	ї́здити/ката́тися на санка́х
to go snowmobiling	ї́здити/ката́тися на мотоса́нях
to go tobogganing	ї́здити/ката́тися на тобо́ґані
to have a game of frizbee	гра́ти в фри́збі
to have a snowball fight	гра́ти в сні́жки
to ride horseback	ї́здити ве́рхи

to ride on a skateboard	ката́тися на ске́йті
to roller-skate	ко́взатися/ката́тися на ро́ликах
to skate	ко́взатися/ката́тися на ковзана́х
to ski *[cross-country]*	ходи́ти (бі́гати) на ли́жах
to ski *[down-hill]*	ї́здити/ката́тися на ли́жах
to water-ski	ї́здити/ката́тися на водяни́х ли́жах

2. You will learn how to decline feminine nouns like ***карусе́ль*** and ***меда́ль*** in Lesson 36.

3. The words **мотоса́ни** and **автоса́ни** both contain the word **са́ни** which means **sleigh**.

B. MOOD

In most languages, it is possible to express oneself in one of three ways or **moods**.

B.1 Indicative Mood

In both English and Ukrainian, we express ourselves most frequently by making factual (declarative) statements, or by posing factual questions.

David is buying a car.
Is David buying a car?

In both English and Ukrainian, when we make a declarative statement or pose a factual question, we are expressing ourselves in the **indicative mood**.

In Ukrainian, there are five tenses in the indicative mood. You now know all five of these tenses.

1. The Present Tense
2. The Past Imperfective Tense
3. The Past Perfective Tense
4. The Future Imperfective Tense
5. The Future Perfective Tense

Up to now in this text, only factual or declarative statements have been made, and, except for a few expressions in the mini-conversations in *Oral Exercises,* only factual questions have been posed.

B.2 Conditional Mood

In both English and Ukrainian, it is possible to make statements or to pose questions that express wishful thinking, an imagined condition, something unrealizable, or an improbable situation.

If David had enough money, he would buy a car.
If David had enough money, would he buy a car?

In Ukrainian, when we express such subjective statements and questions, we are using the **conditional mood**.

You will learn how to use the conditional mood in Ukrainian in the next lesson.

B.3 Imperative Mood

In both English and Ukrainian, it is also possible to give a command, or to make a request.

David, buy a car!

When we give commands, we are using the **imperative mood**.

It is the imperative mood that is the focus of this lesson.

C. IMPERATIVE MOOD

In both English and Ukrainian, the imperative mood is used to give commands and to make requests.

In English, the same imperative form is used in speaking either to one person or to a group of people.

Child, run home! Children, run home!

If the speaker includes himself/herself in the command, then the words **let us** (**let's**) are used along with the imperative form of the verb.

Let us run home! Let's run home!

In Ukrainian, **three** imperative forms are used.

1. The **second person singular imperative form** is used when a command or a request is made to someone who is referred to as **ти**.

   Дити́но, біжи́ додо́му!
   Child, run home!

2. The **second person plural imperative form** is used when a command or a request is made either to a group of people, or to one person who is being addressed politely as **ви**.

   Діти, біжíть додóму!
   Children, run home!

   Пáне Козáк, біжíть додóму!
   Mr. Kozak, run home!

3. The **first person plural imperative form** is used if the speaker includes himself/herself in the command.

   Біжíмо додóму!
   Let's run home!

C.1 Forming the Imperative

In English, the imperative form for all verbs is identical to the stem of the infinitive.

Infinitive	*Infinitive Stem*
to run	run
to read	read
to write	write

In Ukrainian**, imperative endings are added to the stem of a verb to form the imperative mood.**

To form the imperative mood of an **imperfective verb**, the imperative endings are added to the **present tense stem.**

To form the imperative mood of a **perfective verb**, the imperative endings are added to the **future perfective tense stem.**

C.2 Verb Stems Ending in a Vowel

If either the present tense stem or the future perfective tense stem ends in a **vowel**, the following endings are added to form the imperative mood:

2nd Person Singular: **-й**
1st Person Plural: **-ймо**
2nd Person Plural: **-йте**

Imperfective Infinitive	*Present Stem*	*2nd Person Singular*	*1st Person Plural*	*2nd Person Plural*
чита́ти	чита-	чита́й	чита́ймо	чита́йте
смія́тися	смі-ся	смі́йся	смі́ймося	смі́йтеся

Perfective Infinitive	*Future Stem*	*2nd Person Singular*	*1st Person Plural*	*2nd Person Plural*
прочита́ти	прочита-	прочита́й	прочита́ймо	прочита́йте
засмія́тися	засмі-ся	засмі́йся	засмі́ймося	засмі́йтеся

If the verb stem ends in the vowel **о**, this **о** usually changes to **і**.

Infinitive	*Stem*	*2nd Person Singular*	*1st Person Plural*	*2nd Person Plural*
боя́тися	бо-ся	бі́йся	бі́ймося	бі́йтеся
стоя́ти	сто-	стій	сті́ймо	сті́йте
посто́яти	посто-	пості́й	пості́ймо	пості́йте

If the suffix **-ава** is found in an infinitive, it is retained in the imperative mood.

Infinitive	*Stem*	*2nd Person Singular*	*1st Person Plural*	*2nd Person Plural*
дава́ти	**дава**-	**дава́**й	**дава́**ймо	**дава́**йте
прод**ава́**ти	прод**ава**-	прод**ава́**й	прод**ава́**ймо	прод**ава́**йте
уст**ава́**ти	уст**ава**-	уст**ава́**й	уст**ава́**ймо	уст**ава́**йте

In forming the imperative mood for **пи́ти**, the endings are added to the stem **пи-**.

Infinitive	*Stem*	*2nd Person Singular*	*1st Person Plural*	*2nd Person Plural*
пи́ти	**пи-**	**пи**й	**пи́**ймо	**пи́**йте

Practise Oral Exercise 34.1

Do Written Exercise 34.1

C.3 Verb Stems Ending in a Consonant

If the stem of a verb ends in a **consonant**, the position of **the stress in the first person singular** must be taken into consideration when the imperative mood is being formed.

1. If **the stress is on the final syllable of the verb form for я**, the following imperative endings are added and stressed:

   2nd Person Singular: **-и**

   1st Person Plural: **-ім(о)** (о is optional)

   2nd Person Plural: **-іть**

Imperfective Infinitive	***Present Stem***	***2nd Person Singular***	***1st Person Plural***	***2nd Person Plural***
нести́	нес- (я несу́)	неси́	несі́мо	несі́ть
ора́ти	ор- (я орю́)	ори́	орі́мо	орі́ть
говори́ти	говор- (я говорю́)	говори́	говорі́мо	говорі́ть
жи́ти	жив- (я живу́)	живи́	живі́мо	живі́ть
сиді́ти	сид- (я сиджу́)	сиди́	сиді́мо	сиді́ть

Perfective Infinitive	***Future Stem***	***2nd Person Singular***	***1st Person Plural***	***2nd Person Plural***
поча́ти	почн- (я почну́)	почни́	почні́мо	почні́ть
написа́ти	напиш- (я напишу́)	напиши́	напиші́мо	напиші́ть
ужи́ти	ужив- (я уживу́)	уживи́	уживі́мо	уживі́ть
прийня́ти	прийм- (я прийму́)	прийми́	приймі́мо	приймі́ть
зроби́ти	зроб- (я зроблю́)	зроби́	зробі́мо	зробі́ть

Practise Oral Exercise 34.2

Do Written Exercise 34.2

2. If **the stress is <u>not</u> on the final syllable of the verb form for я,** and if the verb stem ends in **ж,ч,ш,щ**, or **б,в,м,п,ф**, or **р**, the following unstressed imperative endings are added:

   2nd Person Singular: (no ending)

   1st Person Plural: **-мо**

   2nd Person Plural: **-те**

Imperfective Infinitive	***Present Stem***	***2nd Person Singular***	***1st Person Plural***	***2nd Person Plural***
пла́кати	пла**ч**- (я пла́чу)	пла**ч**	пла́**ч**мо	пла́**ч**те
ска́ржитися	скар**ж**-ся (я ска́ржуся)	ска́р**ж**ся	ска́р**ж**мося	ска́р**ж**теся
ба́витися	ба**в**-ся (я ба́влюся)	ба́**в**ся	ба́**в**мося	ба́**в**теся

Perfective Infinitive	***Future Stem***	***2nd Person Singular***	***1st Person Plural***	***2nd Person Plural***
ско́чити	ско**ч**- (я ско́чу)	ско**ч**	ско́**ч**мо	ско́**ч**те
замо́вити	замо**в**- (я замо́влю)	замо́**в**	замо́**в**мо	замо́**в**те
уті́шитися	уті**ш**-ся (я вті́шуся)	уті́**ш**ся	уті́**ш**мося	уті́**ш**теся

Third conjugation verbs that are conjugated like the verb **ї́сти** also take this set of imperative endings. To form their imperative mood, **-ж** is attached to the stem before the imperative endings are added.

Infinitive	***Stem***	***2nd Person Singular***	***1st Person Plural***	***2nd Person Plural***
ї́сти	ї**ж**-	ї**ж**	ї́**ж**мо	ї́**ж**те
з'ї́сти	з'ї**ж**-	з'ї**ж**	з'ї́**ж**мо	з'ї́**ж**те

Practise Oral Exercise 34.3

Do Written Exercise 34.3

3. If **the stress is <u>not</u> on the final syllable of the verb form for я** and if the verb stem ends in **д,з,с,т**, or **ц**, or **н,л**, the following unstressed imperative endings are added:

2nd Person Singular: **-ь**
1st Person Plural: **-ьмо**
2nd Person Plural: **-ьте**

Imperfective Infinitive	*Present Stem*	*2nd Person Singular*	*1st Person Plural*	*2nd Person Plural*
ї́хати	їд- (я ї́ду)	їдь	ї́дьмо	ї́дьте
знахо́дити	знаход- (я знахо́джу)	знахо́дь	знахо́дьмо	знахо́дьте

Perfective Infinitive	*Future Stem*	*2nd Person Singular*	*1st Person Plural*	*2nd Person Plural*
поси́діти	посид- (я поси́джу)	поси́дь	поси́дьмо	поси́дьте
уста́ти	уста**н**- (я вста́ну)	уста́**нь**	уста́**нь**мо	уста́**нь**те
догля́нути	догля**н**- (я догля́ну)	догля́**нь**	догля́**нь**мо	догля́**нь**те

Practise Oral Exercise 34.4

Do Written Exercise 34.4

4. Learn the imperative forms for the following verbs.

Perfective Infinitive	*Future Stem*	*2nd Person Singular*	*1st Person Plural*	*2nd Person Plural*
ви́прати	випер- (я ви́перу)	ви́пери	ви́перім	ви́періть
ви́тертися	витр-ся (я ви́труся)	ви́трися	ви́трімся	ви́тріться
кри́кнути	крикн- (я кри́кну)	кри́кни	кри́кнім	кри́кніть
сту́кнути	стукн- (я сту́кну)	сту́кни	сту́кнім	сту́кніть

D. INDIRECT COMMANDS AND REQUESTS

In English, other imperatives are formed by using the words **let me, let him**, **let her**, **let it**, or **let them** along with the imperative form of the verb.

In Ukrainian, comparable imperatives are formed by using **хай** or **нехáй** along with **the present tense** or **the future perfective tense**. (You may also hear some people use the colloquial **най** instead of **хай** or **нехай**.)

Let me run home!	**Хай/Нехáй** я біжý додóму!
Let him run home!	**Хай/Нехáй** він біжи́ть додóму!
Let her run home!	**Хай/Нехáй** вонá біжи́ть додóму!
Let it run home!	**Хай/Нехáй** вонó біжи́ть додóму!
Let them run home!	**Хай/Нехáй** вони́ біжáть додóму!

E. USING IMPERFECTIVE AND PERFECTIVE IMPERATIVES

Imperfective and perfective imperatives may be used interchangeably in many instances; however, the perfective imperative usually implies a more forceful command.

E.1 Imperfective Imperative

The **imperfective** imperative is used to tell someone to do something 1) in general, 2) repeatedly, or 3) on an ongoing basis. It is also usually used in **negative commands**.

1.	**Пий** багáто молокá.	Drink a lot of milk.
2.	**Пий** молокó щодня́.	Drink milk every day.
3.	**Пий** молокó і слýхай.	Drink (your) milk and listen.
4.	**Не пий** кáви!	Don't drink coffee!
	Не говорíть!	Don't talk!

E.2 Perfective Imperative

The **perfective** imperative is usually used to give a command that is to be obeyed immediately and without question. It is also used in a **negative command** if that command refers to an immediate, single action,

1.	**Ви́пий** молокó!	Drink the milk!
2.	**Не покажи́** їй котá!	Don't show her the cat!
	Не скажíть йомý!	Don't tell him!

Practise Oral Exercises 34.5, 34.6, 34.7

Do Written Exercises 34.5, 34.6, 34.7, 34.8, 34.9

LESSON 35

A. VOCABULARY

Nouns

airport	летóвище, *аеродрóм, аеропóрт*
ambulance	швидкá допомóга
auditorium	авдитóрія, *аудитóрія*
bakery	пекáрня
block *[city block]*	квартáл
city hall	рáтуша
crosswalk	перехíд (переход-)
driveway	заїзд
elevator *[in a building)]*	ліфт
entrance	вхід (вход-)
exit	ви́хід (виход-)
factory	фáбрика, *завóд*
fire fighter	пожéжник
fire truck	пожéжна маши́на
gallery	ґалерíя, *галерéя*
garbage can	смітни́к
gasoline	бензи́на, *бензи́н*
gas station	запрáвка
hair salon	перукáрня
helicopter	вертолíт (вертольот-)
highway	шосé *[indecl.]*, автострáда
hydrant	гідрáнт
institute	інститýт
jail	тюрмá, в'язни́ця
jeep	джіп
kiosk	кióск
mailbox	поштóва скри́нька
map	кáрта, мáпа
market	базáр *[h]*, ри́нок (ринк-)
meat market	м'ясáрня
parking lot	автостáвка, *стоя́нка*
parking meter	лічи́льник
pay telephone	телефóн-автомáт
queue, line-up	чéргá
siren	сирéна

street light	ліхта́р *[s]*
telephone booth	телефо́нна бу́дка
traffic	рух (ву́личний рух)
truck	ванта́жка, *грузови́к*
tunnel	туне́ль

Verbs

to advise, to give advice	ра́дити: ра́**дж**у, ра́д-иш *pf.* пора́дити: пора́**дж**у, пора́д-иш
to answer, to reply	відповіда́ти: відповіда́-ю, -єш *pf.* відпові́сти: відпові́-м, -си́
to be late	спі́знюватися: спі́зню-юся, -єшся *pf.* спізни́тися: спізн-ю́ся, -ишся
to call, to summon	кли́**к**ати: кли́**ч**-у, -еш *pf.* покли́**к**ати: покли́**ч**-у, -еш
to explain	поя́снювати: поя́сню-ю, -єш *pf.* поясни́ти: поясн-ю́, -и́ш
to get	достава́ти: діста-ю́, -є́ш *pf.* діста́ти: дістá**н**-у, еш
to meet	зустріча́тися: зустріча́-юся, -єшся *pf.* зустрі́нутися <u>і</u> зустрі́тися: зустрі́ну-ся, -ишся
to repeat	повто́рювати: повто́рю-ю, -єш <u>і</u> повторя́ти: повторя́-ю, -єш *pf.* повтори́ти: повтор-ю́, -иш

B. CONDITIONAL MOOD

When we speak in the conditional mood, we are suggesting that what might happen is conditional upon something else happening.

B.1 Expressing the Conditional Mood

The following English sentence consists of two clauses.

If they got married, he would buy them a house.

1. The first clause outlines the condition.

   If they got married ...

2. The second clause states the result or consequence if the condition were met.

   ... he would buy them a house.

In Ukrainian, the clause that outlines the condition must begin with either **якби́**, or **якщо́ б**.

> If they got married ...
> **Якби́** (**Якщо́ б**) вони́ одружи́лися ...

The clause that states the result or consequence must contain the particle **би**.

> ... he would buy them a house.
> ... він купи́в **би** їм ха́ту.

When the particle **би** follows a word ending in a consonant, it is written as **би**; when it follows a word ending in a vowel, it is written as **б**.

> Якби́ вони́ одружи́лися, він **купи́в би** їм ха́ту.
> If they got married, he would buy them a house.

> Якби́ вони́ одружи́лися, вона́ **купи́ла б** їм ха́ту.
> If they got married, she would buy them a house.

The particle **би** (or **б**) usually follows either the predicate or the subject; however, it occasionally may appear elsewhere in the clause.

> Якби́ вони́ одружи́лися, він **купи́в би** їм ха́ту.
> Якби́ вони́ одружи́лися, він **би купи́в** їм ха́ту.
> If they got married, he would buy them a house.

B.2 Expressing Tense in the Conditional Mood

In Ukrainian, **the verbs in both clauses must be in the past tense** even if the general time frame that is being referred to is in the present tense or the future tense.

Let's look at the following examples. The first sentence gives the time frame and makes a factual statement. This second sentence states the condition and the consequences arising from it.

1. **Present tense time frame**

   It's too bad they aren't getting married.
   If they did get married, he would buy them a house.

   Шкода́, що вони́ не **одру́жуються**.
   Якби́ вони́ **одружи́лися**, він **купи́в** би їм ха́ту.

2. **Future tense time frame**

   It's too bad they won't be getting married.
   If they would get married, he would buy them a house.

   Шкода́, що вони́ не **бу́дуть одру́жуватися**.
   Якби́ вони́ **одружи́лися**, він **купи́в** би їм ха́ту.

3. Past tense time frame

If it is implied that the consequence stated in the result clause can no longer be fulfilled because the opportunity for doing so has passed, then **the past tense of the verb бу́ти** is used with the past tense of the verb in both clauses of the conditional sentence.

It's too bad they didn't get married.
If they had got married, he would have bought them a house.

Шкода́, що вони́ не **одружи́лися**.
Якби́ вони́ **були́ одружи́лися**, він би **був купи́в** їм ха́ту.

Practise Oral Exercise 35.1

Do Written Exercise 35.1

B.3 Aspect in the Conditional Mood

Up to now in this lesson, only the past perfective tense has been used in all the conditional sentences; however, depending on the context of what is being said, verbs in a conditional sentence may be in either the past imperfective tense or the past perfective tense.

1. Both verbs in the past imperfective tense

Якби́ він **мав** гро́ші, він ча́сто **купува́в** би квитки́.
If he had the money, he would (he'd) often buy tickets.

2. Both verbs in the past perfective tense

Якби́ він **купи́в** квито́к, він **пішо́в** би на конце́рт.
If he bought a ticket, he would (he'd) go to the concert.

3. Two verbs in different past tenses

1) imperfective past (**мав**), and perfective past (**купи́в**)

Якби́ він **мав** гро́ші, він **купи́в** би квитки́.
If he had the money, he would (he'd) buy the tickets.

2) perfective past (**купи́в**), and imperfective past (**ходи́в**)

Якби́ він **купи́в** квитки́, він **ходи́в** би на конце́рти.
If he bought the tickets, he would (he'd) go to the concerts.

Practise Oral Exercise 35.2

Do Written Exercise 35.2

B.4 The Use of Auxiliary Verbs

When an auxiliary verb is used in either clause of a conditional sentence, it is used in **the past tense together with the infinitive of the main verb.**

Якби́ ми **вмі́ли пла́вати**, ми б пла́вали.
If we **knew how to swim**, we'd be swimming.

Якби́ він **хоті́в ї́сти**, він зготува́в би пере́куску.
If he **wanted to eat**, he'd prepare a snack.

Якби́ вони́ жили́ тут, вони́ **му́сили** б **працюва́ти.**
If they lived here, they'd have **to work**.

Якби́ він **був хоті́в жи́ти** тут, він **му́сив** би **був працюва́ти**.
If he **had wanted** to live here, he **would have had** to work.

Practise Oral Exercise 35.3

Do Written Exercise 35.3

C. ЩОБ

The conjunction **щоб** is sometimes confused with the interrogative pronoun **що** when it is used with the particle **б** in a conditional sentence (**що б**).

C.1 The Difference between що б and щоб

Let's look at the difference between **що б** and **щоб**.

1. що б

Like other pronouns, the interrogative pronoun **що** may be used as either the subject or the direct object in a sentence. When it appears as the subject or direct object in the result/consequence clause of a conditional sentence, it is followed by the particle **б**.

1) **що** as the **subject** of the result/consequence clause

Якби́ фа́рмер зора́в по́ле, **що** б на ньо́му росло́?
If the farmer ploughed the field, **what** would grow on it?

2) **що** as the **direct object** in the result/consequence clause

Якби́ вона́ пішла́ до крамни́ці, **що** б вона́ купи́ла?
If she went to the store, **what** would she buy?

Practise Oral Exercise 35.4

2. щоб

The **conjunction щоб** is used in sentences in which either a statement of purpose or a request is made.

In the subordinate clauses that **щоб** introduces, the verb is always in **the past tense**.

The verb in the main clause in the sentence may be in the **present**, **past**, or **future** tense.

1. Statement of Purpose

1) principal clause: present tense verb

Я **говорю́** пові́льно, **щоб** студе́нти мене́ **розумі́ли**.
I **speak** slowly **so that** the students **will understand** me.

2) principal clause: past tense verb

Вони́ **крича́ли** го́лосно, щоб усі́ їх **могли́ чу́ти**.
They **shouted** loudly **so that** everyone **could hear** them.

3) principal clause: future tense verb

Ми **пої́демо** до о́зера, щоб ді́ти не **пла́кали**.
We **shall go** to the lake **so that** the children **won't cry**.

2. Request

1) principal clause: present tense verb

Вона́ **про́сить**, щоб студе́нти слу́хали.
She **is asking** the students to listen.
(She's requesting that the students listen.)

2) principal clause: past tense verb

Чи вони́ **проси́ли**, щоб ми співа́ли?
Did they **ask** us to sing?
(Did they request that we sing?)

3) principal clause: future tense verb

Ми **попро́симо**, щоб у́чні пішли́ надві́р.
We **shall ask** the pupils to go outdoors.
(We'll request that the pupils go outdoors.)

Practise Oral Exercises 35.5, 35.6, 35.7

Do Written Exercises 35.4, 35.5, 35.6, 35.7, 35.8

LESSON 36

A. VOCABULARY

Nouns

adventure	приго́да
answer, reply	ві́дповідь *[f]*
assistance, help	по́міч *[f]* (помоч-), допомо́га
ballet	бале́т
blood	кров *[f]*
death	смерть *[f]*
description	о́пис
detective	детекти́в
fable, tale	ба́йка
fairy tale	ка́зка
fiancé	нарече́ний *[substantive]*
fiancée	нарече́на *[substantive]*
flood	по́вінь *[f]* (повен-)
hero	геро́й
heroine	герої́ня
honeymoon	медо́вий мі́сяць
life	життя́ *[n]*
love	любо́в *[f]*
mother	ма́ти *[f]*
name *[of book, object]*	на́зва
novel	рома́н
novelette	по́вість *[f]*
oven	піч *[f]*, (печ-)
play	п'є́са
poem *[short]*	вірш
poem *[long]*	пое́ма
poet	пое́т; поете́са
poetry	пое́зія
prose	про́за
quality	я́кість *[f]*, (якост-)
quantity	кі́лькість *[f]*, (кількост-)
question	пита́ння *[n]*
salt	сіль *[f]* (сол-)
short story	оповіда́ння *[n]*
speech	до́повідь *[f]*

thing	річ *[f]* (реч-)
translation	пере́клад
translator	перекладáч; перекладáчка
trip	пóдорож *[f]*
writer	письмéнник; письмéнниця

Adjectives

adventureful	пригóдницький
detective	детекти́вний
funny	смішни́й
historical	істори́чний
other, another	íнший
ready, prepared	готóвий
serious	серйóзний
similar	поді́бний

Verbs

to acquaint	знайóмити: знайóм-лю, -иш *pf.* познайóмити: познайóм-лю, -иш
to become acquainted	знайóмитися: знайóм-люся, -ишся *pf.* познайóмитися: познайóм-люся, -ишся
to become engaged	зарýчуватися: зарýчу-юся, -єшся *pf.* заручи́тися: заруч-ýся, -ишся
to dare	смíти: смí-ю, -єш *pf.* посмíти: посмí-ю, -єш
to invite	запрóшувати: запрóшу-ю, -єш *pf.* запроси́ти: запрошý, запрóс-иш
to love, to cherish	кохáти: кохá-ю, -єш *pf.* покохáти: покохá-ю, -єш
to translate	перекладáти: перекладá-ю, -єш *pf.* переклáсти: переклад-ý, -еш

Vocabulary Notes

1. The nouns **óсінь** and **пíвніч** in Lesson 16, **ніч** and **чверть** in Lesson 29, and ***карусéль*** and ***медáль*** in Lesson 34, also belong to the consonant declension of feminine nouns.

2. The words **наречéний** and **наречéна** are substantives that are declined like adjectives.

B. FEMININE NOUNS: CONSONANT DECLENSION

All the feminine nouns that you have learned to decline thus far have ended in either the vowel **а** or **я** in the nominative singular case, whereas the masculine nouns have ended in a consonant, including **ь** and **й**.

You will now learn how to decline feminine nouns that end in consonants in the nominative singular case. In the Vocabularies, these nouns are identified as follows: *[f]*.

B.1 Grouping Feminine Nouns in the Consonant Declension

Feminine nouns belonging to the consonant declension may be assigned to one of two broad groups according to their stems.

1. Group 1 – Nouns with stems ending in two consonants: смерт-
2. Group 2 – Nouns with stems ending in a single consonant: доповід-

B.2 Singular Declension: Groups 1 and 2

The singular endings for nouns in Groups 1 and 2 **differ in the genitive and instumental cases.**

1. Genitive Case

In materials printed in Ukraine, all nouns in Groups 1 and 2 have the ending **-і** in the genitive singular case.

In most materials printed outside of Ukraine, **-и** is used as the genitive singular ending for all nouns in Group 1, and for the following nouns in Group 2: **кров – кро́ви**; **любо́в – любо́ви**; **о́сінь – о́сени**; and **сіль – со́ли**.

2. Instrumental Case

Group 1: the ending **ю** is added to the stem.

Group 2: for nouns with stems ending in one of **б**, **в**, **м**, **п**, or **р**, an **apostrophe** is inserted between the stem and the ending **ю**. For all other nouns, **the consonant is doubled** before the ending **ю** is added.

	Group 1	*Group 2 [б,в,м,п,р,ф]*	*Group 2*	*Group 2 [ж,ч,ш,щ]*
N.	смерт-ь	любо́в	до́повід-ь	ніч
G.	сме́рт-и	любо́в-и	до́повід-і	но́ч-і
A.	[=N]	[=N]	[=N]	[=N]
V.	сме́рт-е	любо́в-е	до́повід-е	но́ч-е
I.	сме́рт-ю	любо́в'-ю	до́повідд-ю	ні́чч-ю
D.	сме́рт-і	любо́в-і	до́повід-і	но́ч-і
L.	сме́рт-і	любо́в-і	до́повід-і	но́ч-і

B.3 Plural Declension: Groups 1 and 2

Most nouns in Group 2 with stems ending in one of **б**, **в**, **м**, **п**, or **р** are used only in the singular.

Nouns in Group 2 with stems ending in one of **ж**, **ч**, **ш**, or **щ** have the endings **-ами**, **-ам**, **-ах** in the instrumental, dative, and locative cases; all other nouns have the endings **-ями**, **-ям**, **-ях** in these cases.

	Group 1	*Group 2*	*Group 2 [ж,ч,ш,щ]*
N.	сме́рт-і	відповід-і	но́ч-і
G.	сме́рт-ей	відповід-ей	ноч-е́й
A.	[=N]	[=N]	[=N]
V.	[=N]	[=N]	[=N]
I.	сме́рт-ями	відповід-ями	ноч-а́ми
D.	сме́рт-ям	відповід-ям	ноч-а́м
L.	сме́рт-ях	відповід-ях	ноч-а́х

B.4 Declension: ма́ти

You will now learn how to decline **ма́ти**, the formal word for **mother**.

In the singular genitive, dative, and locative cases, and in all the plural cases, the noun **ма́ти** has the suffix **-ер** added to its stem. This suffix changes to **-ір** in the singular accusative and instrumental cases.

	Singular	*Plural*
N.	ма́т-и	мат-ер-і́
G.	ма́т-ер-і	мат-ер-і́в
A.	ма́т-ір	[=G]
V.	[=N]	[=N]
I.	ма́т-ір'-ю	мат-ер-я́ми
D.	ма́т-ер-і	мат-ер-я́м
L.	ма́т-ер-і	мат-ер-я́х

Practise Oral Exercises 36.1, 36.2, 36.3

Do Written Exercises 36.1, 36.2

C. DECLENSION OF CARDINAL NUMBERS

In English, cardinal numbers do not change regardless of how they are used in a sentence.

In Ukrainian, all cardinal numbers are declined. You were introduced to this idea in Lesson 19, when you learned how to use cardinal numbers with inanimate nouns in both the nominative and accusative cases. In this lesson you will learn how to decline the cardinal numbers in all the cases with both animate and inanimate nouns.

C.1 Declension: оди́н

Один is declined like the demonstrative pronoun **той**.

	Feminine Singular	*Masculine Singular*	*Neuter Singular*	*All Genders Plural*
N.	одна́	оди́н	одне́	одні́
G.	одніє́ї	одного́		одни́х
A.	одну́	[=G or N]	[=N]	[=G or N]
V.	—	—	—	—
I.	одніє́ю	одни́м		одни́ми
D.	одні́й	одному́		одни́м
L.	... одні́й	... одно́му (... одні́м)		... одни́х

C.2 Using оди́н

Оди́н may be used either as a **modifier** or as a **substantive**.

1. Modifier

When **оди́н** is used as a modifier, it always agrees with the noun that it modifies in gender, number, and case.

As a modifier, **оди́н** can have two different meanings:
1) a specific numerical quantity, **one**, or 2) a non-specific **a** (**a certain**).

1) Specific Numerical Quantity

У ме́не **оди́н** син, **одна́** дочка́, **одне́** а́вто, й **одні́** но́жиці.
I have **one** son, **one** daughter, **one** car, and **one** (pair of) scissors.

2) Non-Specific Modifier

Сього́дні в па́рку ми розмовля́ли з **одни́м** тури́стом.
Today we talked with **a certain** tourist *[m]* in the park.

Сього́дні в па́рку ми зустрі́нулися з **одніє́ю** тури́сткою.
Today we met **a certain** tourist *[f]* in the park.

2. Substantive

When **оди́н** is used as a substantive, it assumes the gender, number, and case of the noun that it replaces.

As a substantive, it takes on the meaning of 1) one, other, or 2) one another, each other.

1) one, other

Одна́ смія́лася, а **одна́** пла́кала.
One (female) was laughing, and **one** was crying.

Оди́н чита́в, а **оди́н** спав.
One (male) was reading, and **one** was sleeping.

Одне́ було́ тут, а **одне́** було́ там.
One (thing) was here, and **one** was there.

Одні́ розмовля́ли, а **одні́** танцюва́ли.
Some (people) were conversing, and **some** were dancing.

2) one another, each other

Whenever the construction **one another** or **each other** is used, the first word (**одна́**, **оди́н**, **одне́**, **одні́**) is in the nominative case, while the second word is in the case required by the verb or the preposition. In the second word of the construction **one another**, **each other**, the stress shifts to the first syllable: **одна́ о́дну**, **одна́ про о́дну**, **оди́н о́дного**.

About two females

Вони́ зна́ють **одна́ о́дну**.	They know **one another**.
Вони́ ду́мають **одна́** про **о́дну**.	They think about **each other**.

About two males

Вони́ розумі́ють **оди́н о́дного**.	They understand **one another**.
Вони́ чека́ють **оди́н** на **о́дного**.	They wait for **each other**.

About a male and a female

Вони́ хва́лять **одне́ о́дного**.	They praise **each other**.
Вони́ помага́ють **одне́ о́дному**.	They help **one another**.

About two groups of people

Вони́ ба́чать **одні́ о́дних**.	They see **one another**.
Вони́ дя́кують **одні́ о́дним**.	They thank **one another**.

Practise Oral Exercise 36.4

Do Written Exercise 36.3

C.3 Declension of два/дві, три, чотири

Except for the nominative and accusative cases, **два/дві** is declined in the same way for all three genders. The numbers **три** and **чоти́ри** are declined in the same way for all three genders.

	Feminine	*Masculine and Neuter*	*All Genders*	*All Genders*
N.	дві	два	три	чоти́ри
G.	двох		трьох	чотирьо́х
A.	[= G or N]	[= G or N]	[= G or N]	[= G or N]
V.	—	—	—	—
I.	двома́		трьома́	чотирма́
D.	двом		трьом	чотирьо́м
L.	... двох		... трьох	... чотирьо́х

C.4 Using два/дві, три, чоти́ри

The nominative form of these numbers is used with the nominative plural forms of both animate and inanimate nouns to form the subject of a sentence. Remember that **дві** is used with feminine nouns, and **два** is used with masculine and neuter nouns.

Animate Nouns: Nominative Case

У кімна́ті **дві жі́нки** і **два чолові́ки.**

There are **two women** and **two men** in the room.

Inanimate Nouns: Nominative Case

У кімна́ті **дві ля́мпи, три столи́**, і **чоти́ри крі́сла.**

There are **two lamps, three tables, and four chairs** in the room.

When one of these numbers and **an animate noun** are used as a direct object, both the number and the noun are declined in the accusative [= G] case.

Animate Nouns: Accusative Case

Я ба́чу **двох жіно́к** і **трьох чолові́ків** у кімна́ті.

I see **two women** and **three men** in the room.

When one of these numbers and **an inanimate noun** are used as a direct object, both the number and the inanimate noun are declined in the accusative [=N] case.

Inanimate Nouns: Accusative Case

Я ба́чу **дві ля́мпи, три столи́**, і **чоти́ри крі́сла** в кімна́ті.

I see **two lamps**, **three tables**, and **four chairs** in the room.

No distinction is made between animate and inanimate nouns in the remaining cases. In every instance, the number is declined to agree with the noun.

Genitive Case:

Я не зна́ю тих **двох письме́нників.**
I don't know those **two writers** *[m]*.

Я печу́ то́рти **для двох сусі́док.**
I'm baking cakes **for the two neighbours** *[f]*.

У цій кни́жці нема́є тих **трьох пое́мів.**
Those **three poems** aren't in this book.

Instrumental Case:

Він розмовля́є з **трьома́ товариша́ми.**
He is conversing **with three friends** *[m]*.

Між двома́ буди́нками є за́їзд.
There's a driveway between the **two buildings.**

Dative Case:

Вона́ пи́ше **чотирьо́м товаришка́м.**
She is writing **to four friends** *[f]*.

Locative Case:

Я ба́чила цей рома́н **у трьо́х книга́рнях.**
I saw this novel **in three bookstores.**

Ді́ти ката́лися **на двох тобо́ґанах.**
The children were tobogganing **on two toboggans,**

Practise Oral Exercise 36.5

Do Written Exercise 36.4

C.5 Declension of 7 and 8

The declension of 7 and 8 is like that of **two**. Both these numbers are declined in the same way for all genders.

	All Genders	*All Genders*
N.	сім	ві́сім
G.	сімо́х (семи́)	вісьмо́х (восьми́)
A.	[= G or N]	[= G or N]
V.	—	—
I.	сьома́ (сімома́)	вісьма́ (вісьмома́)
D.	сімо́м (семи́)	вісьмо́м (восьми́)
L.	... сімо́х (семи́)	... вісьмо́х (восьми́)

C.6 Declension of 5, 6, 9, 10-20, 30, 50, 60, 70, 80, 90

The numbers five, six, nine, ten to twenty, 30, 50, 60, 70, 80, and 90 (when it's written as **дев'ятдеся́т**) are declined in the same way for all genders. Examples of the declension of four such numbers are presented below.

	All Genders	*All Genders*
N.	п'ять	трина́дцять
G.	п'ятьо́х (п'яти́)	тринадцятьо́х (тринадцяти́)
A.	[= G or N]	[= G or N]
V.	—	—
I.	п'ятьма́ (п'ятьома́)	тринадцятьма́ (тринадцятьома́)
D.	п'ятьо́м (п'яти́)	тринадцятьо́м (тринадцяти́)
L.	... п'ятьо́х (п'яти́)	... тринадцятьо́х (тринадцяти́)

	All Genders	*All Genders*
N.	два́дцять	сімдеся́т
G.	двадцятьо́х (двадцяти́)	сімдесятьо́х (сімдесяти́)
A.	[= G or N]	[= G or N]
V.	—	—
I.	двадцятьма́ (двадцятьома́)	сімдесятьма́ (сімдесятьома́)
D.	двадцятьо́м (двадцяти́)	сімдесятьо́м (сімдесяти́)
L.	... двадцятьо́х (двадцяти́)	... сімдесятьо́х (сімдесяти́)

C.7 Declension of 40, 90 (дев'яно́сто), сто

	All Genders	*All Genders*	*All Genders*
N.	со́рок	дев'яно́сто	сто
G.	сорока́	дев'яно́ста	ста
A.	[= G or N]	[= G or N]	[= G or N]
V.	—	—	—
I.	сорока́ (сорокма́)	дев'яно́ста (дев'яностома́)	ста (стома́)
D.	сорока́	дев'яно́ста	ста
L.	... сорока́	... дев'яно́ста	... ста

C.8 Using Numbers 5-20, 30, 40, 50, 60, 70, 80, 90, 100

When one of these numbers and either an animate or an inanimate noun are used as the subject of the sentence, the number, in the nominative case, is followed by the noun in the genitive plural case.

Animate Nouns: Nominative Case	*Inanimate Nouns: Nominative Case*
У кімнаті було́ **п'ять дівча́т**. There were **five girls** in the room.	У па́чці було́ **шість ґу́мок**. There were six **erasers** in the package.
У кімна́ті було́ **де́сять хло́пців**. There were **ten boys** in the room.	Там було́ **двана́дцять олівці́в/пер**. There were **twelve pencils/pens** there.

When one of these numbers and **an animate noun** are the direct object, the accusative [= G] form of the number is used along with the accusative [= G] plural form of the animate noun.

Animate Nouns: Accusative Case

Я ба́чу **п'ятьо́х дівча́т** у кімна́ті. I see **five girls** in the room.	Я ба́чу **шістьо́х хло́пців** у кімна́ті. I see **six boys** in the room.

When one of these numbers and **an inanimate noun** are the direct object, the accusative [= N] form of the number is used with the genitive plural form of the inanimate noun.

Inanimate Nouns: Accusative Case

Він купу́є **п'ять ґу́мок**. He is buying **five erasers**.	Він купу́є **п'ять олівці́в/пер.** He is buying **five pencils/pens.**

There are no distinctions between animate and inanimate nouns in the remaining cases.

Genitive Case:	Ми купу́ємо сувені́ри **для двадцятьо́х ро́дичів**. We are buying souvenirs **for twenty relatives**.
	Ми не ма́ємо **ста ма́рок**. We don't have **a hundred stamps**.
Instrumental Case:	Він розмовля́є з **вісьма́ товариша́ми**. He is conversing **with eight friends** *[m]*.
Dative Case:	Вона́ пи́ше **десятьо́м товаришка́м**. She is writing **to ten friends** *[f]*.
Locative Case:	Я ба́чила цей рома́н **у п'ятьо́х книга́рнях**. I saw this novel **in five bookstores**.

Practise Oral Exercise 36.6

Do Written Exercises 36.5, 36.6

LESSON 37

A. VOCABULARY

Nouns

angel	áнгел
baby, infant *[human]*	дитя́ *[n]*, немовля́ *[n]*
best man *[groom's attendant]*	дрýжба *[m]*
bridesmaid	дрýжка
calf *[cow's offspring]*	теля́ *[n]*
carpenter	тéсля *[m]*
colt	лошá *[n]*
council	рáда
coward	боягýз
cowboy	ковбóй
cripple	калíка *[m,f]*
debt	борг
devil	дíдько, дия́вол, чорт, біс
director	дирéктор *[h]*; дирéкторка
drunkard	п'яни́ця *[m,f]*
fairy	фéя
God	Бог
grandchild	онучá, внучá
hypocrite	лицемíр *[h]*
interview	íнтерв'ю *[indecl.]*
judge	суддя́ *[m]*
lazybones, idler	нерóба *[m,f]*
letter carrier	листонóша *[m,f]*
loan	пóзичка
match-maker, starosta	стáроста *[m]*
mayor	мер *[h]*
mermaid	русáлка
miser	скупáр *[s]*
name, personal name	ім'я́ *[n]*, *pl.* іменá
nuisance *[of a person]*	причéпа *[m,f]*
orphan	сиротá *[m,f]*
salary, wages	платня́
slob	нечепýра *[m,f]*
soul	душá
witch	вíдьма, *g.pl.* **вíдьом**

Adjectives

dishonest, dishonourable	нече́сний
honest, honourable	че́сний
impatient	нетерпели́вий
married	одру́жений
patient	терпели́вий
tired, exhausted	сто́млений, зму́чений
unmarried	неодру́жений
worried	зажу́рений

Vocabulary Notes

1. The noun **ста́роста** was formerly used for the male go-between who asked for a young girl's hand in marriage on behalf of the would-be groom; it is still used for the master of ceremonies at a wedding reception.

2. It should be noted that some of the **neuter nouns denoting young offspring** have another neuter form that includes either the suffix **-ат** or **-ят**. These forms would probably be easier for you to use as they end in the familiar ending **-о** and are declined like neuter hard declension nouns: **дитя́ – дитя́тко, немовля́ – немовля́тко, внуча́ – внуча́тко, теля́ – теля́тко, лоша́ – лоша́тко.**

B. MASCULINE NOUNS: -А/-Я

You already know the Hard, Mixed, Soft 1, and Soft 2 Declensions of masculine nouns. You also know that masculine personal names like **Мико́ла** are declined like feminine nouns.

There are a number of other masculine nouns that end in either **-а** or **-я** in the nominative singular case. Some of them refer almost exclusively to males; others may be used in reference to either males or females.

B.1 Nouns Referring to Both Males and Females

Some masculine nouns ending in either **-а** or **-я** in the nominative singular case, like **сирота́**, have traditionally been applied to either male or female beings,

Він **сирота́**.	Вона́ теж **сирота́**.
He's an orphan.	She's also an orphan.

When nouns like **сирота́** are modified, the modifiers have masculine endings if they refer to a male being, and feminine endings if they refer to a female being.

Він **нещá<u>сний</u> сирота́**.	Вона́ **нещá<u>сна</u> сирота́**.
He's an ill-fated orphan.	She's an ill-fated orphan.

In the Vocabularies in this text, these nouns are designated as *[m,f]*.

B.2 Declension: Masculine Nouns, -а/-я *[m,f]*

Masculine nouns ending in **-а** that refer to both males and females are declined exactly like feminine nouns ending in **-а**. To help you remember this fact, the declension of the ***feminine noun* кузи́на** and the ***masculine noun* сирота́** is presented below.

	Singular		Plural	
	Feminine Noun	*Masculine Noun*	*Feminine Noun*	*Masculine Noun*
N.	кузи́н-а	сирот-а́	кузи́н-и	си́рот-и
G.	кузи́н-и	сирот-и́	кузи́н	си́ріт
A.	кузи́н-у	сирот-у́	[=G]	[=G]
V.	кузи́н-о	сирот-о́	[=N]	[=N]
I.	кузи́н-ою	сирот-о́ю	кузи́н-ами	си́рот-ами
D.	кузи́н-і	сирот-і́	кузи́н-ам	си́рот-ам
L.	... кузи́н-і	... сирот-і́	... кузи́н-ах	... си́рот-ах

B.3 Nouns Referring Almost Exclusively to Males

A few of the masculine nouns ending in either **-а** or **-я** in the nominative singular case are either inherently masculine, or refer to what used to be traditionally male roles in society.

The word **дру́жба** (a bridegroom's attendant or best man) is a good example of a noun that is inherently masculine. The words **суддя́** (judge), **те́сля** (carpenter), and **ста́роста** (match-maker) are examples of nouns that refer to what were once traditionally male occupations.

The declension of nouns like **суддя́** differs from the feminine hard declension in only the **genitive plural case**. For **суддя́** and nouns like it, the genitive plural ending is the masculine ending **-ів**.

Nouns like **суддя́** are modified by adjectives that have masculine endings even when reference is being made to a woman.

Він **до́брий суддя́**.	Вона́ **до́брий суддя́**.
He's a good judge.	She's a good judge.

In the Vocabularies in this text, these nouns are designated as *[m]*.

B.4 Declension: Masculine Nouns, -а/-я *[m]*

To help you see that there is only one difference between the declension of ***feminine nouns*** that end in **-а** or **-я**, and ***masculine nouns*** (that refer almost exclusively to males) that end in **-а** or **-я,** their declensions are juxtaposed below.

1. Hard Declension Nouns

	Singular		Plural	
	Feminine Noun	***Masculine Noun***	***Feminine Noun***	***Masculine Noun***
N.	кузи́н-а	дру́жб-а	кузи́н-и	дру́жб-и
G.	кузи́н-и	дру́жб-и	кузи́н	дру́жб-**ів**
A.	кузи́н-у	дру́жб-у	[=G]	[=G]
V.	кузи́н-о	дру́жб-о	[=N]	[=N]
I.	кузи́н-ою	дру́жб-ою	кузи́н-ами	дру́жб-ами
D.	кузи́н-і	дру́жб-і	кузи́н-ам	дру́жб-ам
L.	.... кузи́н-і	... дру́жб-і	кузи́н-ах	дру́жб-ах

2. Soft Declension Nouns

	Singular		Plural	
	Feminine Noun	***Masculine Noun***	***Feminine Noun***	***Masculine Noun***
N.	учени́ц-я	судд-я́	учени́ц-і	су́дд-і
G.	учени́ц-і	судді́	учени́ц-ь	су́дд-**ів**
A.	учени́ц-ю	судд-ю́	[=G]	[=G]
V.	учени́ц-е	судд-е́	[=N]	[=N]
I.	учени́ц-ею	суд-е́ю	учени́ц-ями	су́дд-ями
D.	учени́ц-і	судд-і́	учени́ц-ям	су́дд-ям
L.	... учени́ц-і	... судд-і́	... учени́ц-ях	... су́дд-ях

Practise Oral Exercises 37.1, 37.2

Do Written Exercise 37.1

C. NEUTER NOUNS: -А/-Я

You already know the Hard, Mixed, Soft 1, and Soft 2 Declensions of neuter nouns. In this lesson you will learn the declension of neuter nouns that end in either **-а** or **-я** in the nominative singular case. Most of these nouns refer to the young offspring of humans and animals.

C.1 Using Neuter Nouns Ending in -а/-я

Although neuter nouns ending in **-а** or **-я** in the nominative singular case refer to animate beings, the adjectives that are used to modify them have neuter endings.

Де **гáрне немовля́**?
Where's **the nice infant**?

When a pronoun is substituted for these animate neuter nouns, it is **the neuter pronoun** that is used.

Де **немовля́**? — **Вонó** тут.
Where is **the infant**? — **It** is here.

C.2 Declension: Neuter Nouns: -а/-я

When neuter nouns ending in either **-а** or **-я** in the nominative singular case are declined, a **suffix** is added to the stem in several of the cases.

The suffix **-ат** is added to nouns ending in **-а,** and **-ят** is added to nouns ending in **-я**.

	Singular		Plural	
	Nouns in -а	*Nouns in -я*	*Nouns in -а*	*Nouns in -я*
N.	лош-á	тел-я́	лош-**áт**-а	тел-**я́т**-а
G.	лош-**áт**-и	тел-**я́т**-и	лош-**áт**	тел-**я́т**
A.	[=N]	[=N]	[=N]	[=N]
V.	[=N]	[=N]	[=N]	[=N]
I.	лош-áм	тел-я́м	лош-**áт**-ами	тел-**я́т**-ами
D.	лош-**áт**-і	тел-**я́т**-і	лош-**áт**-ам	тел-**я́т**-ам
L.	... лош-**áт**-і	... тел-**я́т**-і	... лош-**áт**-ах	... тел-**я́т**-ах

C.3 Declension: ім'я́, небеса́

There are two inanimate nouns in the neuter **-а**, **-я** declension that you will learn at this time. The suffix **-ен** is added to **ім'я́** in both its singular and plural forms; the suffix **-ес** is added to **не́бо** in its **plural** declensional forms.

	Singular ім'я	*Plural* ім'я	*Plural* небо
N.	ім'-я́	ім-**ен**-а́	неб-**ес**-а́
G.	і́м-**ен**-и	ім-**е́н**	неб-**е́с**
A.	[=N]	[=N]	[=N]
V.	[=N]	[=N]	[=N]
I.	і́м-**ен**-ем (ім'-я́м)	ім-**ен**-а́ми	неб-**ес**-а́ми
D.	і́м-**ен**-і	ім-**ен**-а́м	неб-**ес**-а́м
L.	... і́м-**ен**-і	... ім-**ен**-а́х	... неб-**ес**-а́х

Practise Oral Exercise 37.3

Do Written Exercise 37.2

D. COLLECTIVE NUMERALS

Collective numerals are used with nouns that are always plural, with groups of people, and with pronouns.

The collective numerals that are commonly used are listed for you now.

		11	одина́дцятеро
2	дво́є	12	двана́дцятеро
3	тро́є	13	трина́дцятеро
4	че́тверо	14	чотирна́дцятеро
5	п'я́теро	15	п'ятна́дцятеро
6	ше́стеро	16	шістна́дцятеро
7	се́меро	17	сімна́дцятеро
8	во́сьмеро	18	вісімна́дцятеро
9	де́в'ятеро	19	дев'ятна́дцятеро
10	де́сятеро	20	два́дцятеро
		30	три́дцятеро

The collective numerals from 1-9 may also be used with cardinal numbers from 40-100 (e.g. **со́рок тро́є**).

D.1 Declension of Collective Numerals

Except for their nominative forms, the collective numerals are declined like their respective cardinal numbers. A few examples (without the alternate forms that were given in Lesson 36 for numbers like 5 and 7) are presented below.

N.	двóє	трóє	п'я́теро	сéмеро
G.	двох	трьох	п'ятьóх	сімóх
A.	[= G or N]	[= G or N]	[= G or N]	[= G or N]
V.	—	—	—	—
I.	двомá	трьомá	п'ятьмá	сімомá
D.	двом	трьом	п'ятьóм	сімóм
L.	... двох	... трьох	п'ятьóх	сімóх

D.2 Using Collective Numerals

Collective numerals agree with the noun that they modify in number and case with only two exceptions.

1. When collective numerals are used in the nominative case, they are followed by the genitive plural form of a noun or pronoun.

    Nominative Case

    У кімнáті булó **трóє жінóк.**
    There were **three women** in the room.

    У кімнáті булó **трóє чоловíків.**
    There were **three men** in the room.

    У кімнáті булó **трóє дверéй.**
    There were **three doors** in the room.

    У кімнáті **нас** булó **трóє.**
    There were **three of us** in the room.

2. When collective numerals are used with inanimate nouns in the accusative case, the numeral is in the nominative form, while the inanimate noun that follows it is in the genitive plural form.

    Accusative Case

    У кімнáті ми бáчили **трóє дверéй.**
    We saw **three doors** in the room.

E. обидва, обидві, обоє

In English, no distinction is made in the use of the word **both** when we speak about males or females.

In Ukrainian, we use **обидва** in the nominative case to speak about two masculine nouns, **обидві** to speak about two feminine nouns, and the collective numeral **обоє** to speak about masculine and feminine nouns together.

E.1. Declension: обидва, обидві, обоє

The words **обиива, обидві, обоє** are declined like **два**.

	Feminine	*Mixed Genders*	*Masculine and Neuter*
N.	обидві	обоє	обидва
G.		обох	
A.	[= G or N]	[= G or N]	[= G or N]
V.	—	—	—
I.	обома́	обома́	обома́
D.	обо́м	обо́м	обо́м
L.	... обо́х	... обо́х	... обо́х

E.2 Using обидва, обидві, обоє

With **animate** nouns, the forms **обидва** and **обидві** are used only in the nominative case. In the accusative case, **обо́х** is used.

Nominative Case	*Accusative Case*
Оби́два студе́нти вча́ться. **Both students** *[m]* are studying.	Ми ба́чили **обо́х студе́нтів**. We saw **both students** *[m]*.
Оби́дві студе́нтки вча́ться. **Both students** *[f]* are studying.	Ми ба́чили **обо́х студе́нток**. We saw **both students** *[f]*.

With **inanimate** nouns **обидва** and **обидві** are used in both the nominative and accusative cases.

Nominative Case	*Accusative Case*
Оби́два зо́шити на столі́. **Both notebooks** are on the table.	Він купи́в **оби́дві кни́жки**. He bought **both books**.
Оби́дві кни́жки на поли́ці. **Both books** are on the shelf.	Вона́ купи́ла **оби́два зо́шити**. She bought **both notebooks**.

In all the remaining cases, the forms of **обóє** are used with both animate and inanimate nouns.

Genitive Case:	Ми не мóжемо бáчити **обóх сестéр**. We can't see **both sisters**.
Instrumental Case:	Вонá пообíдала з **обомá братáми**. She had dinner **with both brothers**.
Dative Case:	Вони́ потелефонувáли **обóм зятя́м**. They telephoned **both sons-in-law**.
Locative Case:	Він читáв про авáрію **в обóх газéтах**. He read about the accident **in both newspapers**.

Practise Oral Exercises 37.4, 37.5

Do Written Exercise 37.3

F. ADVERBS OF QUANTITY

In English, adverbs, like **many** and **few**, do not change.

In Ukrainian, adverbs of quantity, like **кíлька** and **багáто**, are declined when they are used with ***plural nouns***.

F.1 Declension: Adverbs of Quantity

Most of the adverbs of quantity are declined like the numeral **два**. Let's look at the declensions of **два** and **кíлька**.

	два	**кíлька**
N.	два	кíлька
G.	двох	кількóх
A.	[= G or N]	[= G or N]
V.	—	—
I.	двомá	кількомá
D.	двом	кількóм
L.	двох	кількóх

Two of the adverbs of quantity that you know, **бага́то** and **небага́то** are declined like the numeral **три**, except for a slight difference in the instrumental case.

Let's look at the declension of **три** and **бага́то.**

	три	**бага́то**
N.	три	бага́то
G.	трьох	багатьо́х
A.	[= G or N]	[= G or N]
V.	—	—
I.	трьома́	багатьма́
D.	трьом	багатьо́м
L.	трьох	багатьо́х

F.2 Using Adverbs of Quantity

When adverbs of quantity are used as the subject of the sentence, they are followed by nouns in the genitive plural case. For inanimate nouns the nominative and accusative cases are formed identically.

1. **Nominative Case**

   Кі́лька чолові́ків вихо́дило з теа́тру.
   A few men were leaving the theatre.

   Кі́лька книжо́к лежа́ло на столі́.
   A few books were lying on the table.

2. **Accusative Case**

   Ми ба́чили **кілько́х чолові́ків** у теа́трі.
   We saw **a few men** in the theatre.

   Ми ба́чили **кі́лька книжо́к** на столі́.
   We saw **a few books** on the table.

In all the remaining cases, adverbs of quantity are declined along with the noun.

Practise Oral Exercise 37.6

Do Written Exercises 37.4, 37.5, 37.6

LESSON 38

A. VOCABULARY

Nouns

ambassador	посóл (посл-)
border *[of a country]*	грани́ця, кордóн
Christian	християни́н; христия́нка
citizen	громадя́нин; громадя́нка
country	край, краї́на, держáва
customs *[at a border crossing]*	ми́тниця
duty *[tax on imported goods]*	ми́то
embassy	посóльство, амбасáда
foreigner	чужи́нець (чужинц-); чужи́нка інозéмець (інозéмц-); інозéмка
goods, merchandise	товáр *[h]*
government	ýряд
language	мóва
nation	нáція, нарóд
peasant	селяни́н; селя́нка
percent	процéнт, відсóток (відсотк-)
population	насéлення *[n]*
president	президéнт
property, wealth	майнó *[sg]*
province	провíнція
Slav	слов'яни́н; слов'я́нка
tax	подáток (податк-)
United Nations (UN)	Організáція Об'є́днаних Нáцій (ООН)

Adjectives

foreign	чужи́й, інозéмний
native	рíдний

Pronoun

alone, oneself	сам/сами́й

Countries

Country		*Adjective*	*Male Inhabitant*	*Female Inhabitant*
America	**Амéрика**	американський	американець	американка
Australia	**Австрáлія**	австралíйський	австралíєць	австралíйка
Canada	**Канáда**	канáдський канадíйський	канáдець канадíєць	канáдка канадíйка
China	**Китáй**	китáйський	китáєць	китáйка
England	**Áнглія**	англíйський	англíєць	англíйка
Europe	**Еврóпа**	европéйський	европéєць	европéйка
France	**Фрáнція**	францýзький	францýз	францýженка
Germany	**Німéччина**	німéцький	нíмець	німкéня, нíмка
Greece	**Грéція**	грéцький	грек	грекíня
India	**Íндія**	індíйський	індíєць	індíйка
Ireland	**Ірля́ндія**	ірля́ндський	ірля́ндець	ірля́ндка
Italy	**Ітáлія**	італíйський	італíєць	італíйка
Japan	**Япóнія**	япóнський	япóнець	япóнка
Korea	**Корéя**	корéйський	корéєць	корéйка
Mexico	**Мéхіко**	мехікáнський	мехікáнець	мехікáнка
Poland	**Пóльща**	пóльський	поля́к	пóлька
Russia	**Росíя**	росíйський	росія́нин	росія́нка
Scotland	**Шотля́ндія**	шотля́ндський	шотля́ндець	шотля́ндка
Spain	**Еспáнія**	еспáнський	еспáнець	еспáнка
Ukraine	**Украї́на**	украї́нський	украї́нець	украї́нка

Vocabulary Notes

1. ***In both English and Ukrainian***, the names of countries are capitalized.

   In English, the adjectives derived from the name of the country are also capitalized, as are the terms used for the male and female inhabitants: e.g. Canadian.

   In Ukrainian, the adjective derived from the name of a country is not capitalized, nor are the terms used for the male and female inhabitants.

2. **Мéхіко** is an indeclineable noun.

3. Four of the countries included in the above chart have alternate spellings that are preferred in Ukraine.

Europe	**Є**вр**ó**па	**є**вроп**é**йський	**є**вроп**é**єць	**є**вроп**é**йка
Ireland	**Í**рл**á**ндія	ірл**á**ндський	ірл**á**ндець	ірл**á**ндка
Mexico	М**é**ксіка	м**е**ксік**á**нськйи	м**е**ксік**á**нець	м**е**ксік**á**нка
Scotland	Шотл**á**ндія	шотл**á**ндський	шотл**á**ндець	шотл**á**ндка

4. There are changes in the noun stems of most of the nouns that refer to the male inhabitants of the countries listed in the chart.

америк**á**н**е**ць (американц-)
есп**á**н**е**ць (еспанц-)
ірл**á**нд**е**ць (ірландц-)
ірл**я́**нд**е**ць (ірл**á**ндц-)
кан**á**д**е**ць (канадц-)
мексік**á**н**е**ць (мексіканц-)
мехік**á**н**е**ць (мехіканц-)
н**í**м**е**ць (німц-)
укра**ї́**н**е**ць (українц-)
шотл**á**нд**е**ць (шотландц-)
шотл**я́**нд**е**ць (шотляндц-)
яп**ó**н**е**ць (японц-)

австрал**í**єць (австралі**й**ц-)
англ**í**єць (англі**й**ц-)
европ**é**єць (европе**й**ц-)
європ**é**єць (європе**й**ц-)
інд**í**єць (інді**й**ц-)
італ**í**єць (італі**й**ц-)
канад**í**єць (канаді**й**ц-)
кит**á**єць (кита**й**ц-)
кор**é**єць (коре**й**ц-)

5. ***In Ukrainian***, the full name for the United States of America is **Сполу́чені Шта́ти Аме́рики**, abbreviated as **США** (USA); however, the country is usually referred to as **Аме́рика**.

B. NOUNS: MASCULINE NOUNS ENDING IN -ИН

There are a few masculine nouns that end in the suffix **-ин**.

The stems of these nouns differ in the singular and plural declensions.

The stem for their singular declension is the whole word; the stem for the plural declension is formed by dropping the suffix **-ин**.

	Singular Stem	*Plural Stem*
громадя́нин	громадя**нин-**	громадя**н-**
росія́нин	росія**нин-**	росія**н-**
селяни́н	селя**нин-**	селя**н-**
християни́н	христия ни**н-**	христия**н-**

Except for the **genitive plural case**, these nouns are declined exactly like masculine Hard Declension nouns.

To form the genitive plural case of these masculine nouns, you simply use the stem of the noun.

	Singular	*Plural*
N.	селяни́н	селя́н-и
G.	селяни́н-а	селя́н
A.	[=G]	[=G]
V.	[=N]	[=N]
I.	селяни́н-ом	селя́н-ами
D.	селяни́н-ові	селя́н-ам
L.	... селяни́н-ові	... селя́н-ах

Notice that the corresponding feminine forms of the words do not have the suffix **-ин**.

Masculine Noun	*Feminine Noun*
громадя́н-**ин**	громадя́н-ка
росія́н-**ин**	росія́н-ка
селян-**и́н**	селя́н-ка
християн-**и́н**	христия́н-ка

Practise Oral Exercise 38.1

Do Written Exercise 38.1

C. INTENSIVE (EMPHATIC) PRONOUNS

In both English and Ukrainian, **intensive** (emphatic) pronouns are used to emphasize the fact that something is being done by a particular person.

In English, the pronoun **oneself**, which is used as a reflexive pronoun (see Lesson 22), is also used as an intensive pronoun.

English Reflexive Pronoun

He bought **himself** a car.

English Intensive Pronoun

He **himself** said that he bought himself a car.

In Ukrainian, the reflexive pronoun is **себé** (see Lesson 22); the intensive pronoun is **сам/сами́й**.

Ukrainian Reflexive Pronoun

Він купи́в **собі́** áвто.
He bought **himself** a car.

Ukrainian Intensive Pronoun

Він **сам** сказáв, що він купи́в собі́ áвто.
He **himself** said that he bought himself a car.

C.1 Declension of сам/сами́й

The intensive pronoun **сам/сами́й** is declined like a Hard Declension Adjective. In the masculine nominative singular case, the intensive pronoun may have either the short adjectival form **сам**, or the long adjectival form **сами́й**.

сам/сами́й				
	Feminine Singular	***Masculine Singular***	***Neuter Singular***	***All Genders Plural***
N.	самá	сам/сами́й	самé	самí
G.	самóї	самóго		сами́х
A.	самý	[=G or N]	[=N]	[=G or N]
V.	[=N]	[=N]	[=N]	[=N]
I.	самóю	сами́м		сами́ми
D.	самíй	самóму		сами́м
L.	... самíй	... самóму (... самíм)		... сами́х

C.2 Using Intensive Pronouns

Let's look at a few examples of how the intensive pronoun **сам/самúй** is used. Remember that it must agree in gender, number, and case with the noun or pronoun that it modifies.

He himself can fix the car.
Він сам (**самúй**) мóже злáгодити áвто.

She herself saw the accident.
Вонá самá бáчила авáрію.

The children themselves told me about the thief *[m]*.
Дíти самí менí сказáли про злóдія.

In Ukrainian, the intensive pronoun **сам** is often used to give special emphasis to the reflexive pronoun **себé**. (***In English,*** the intensive pronoun is usually omitted in such cases.)

Дíти самí себé мóжуть доглядáти.
The children (themselves) can look after **themselves**.

Вонá самá собí пошúла цю блю́зку.
She (herself) sewed this blouse **for herself**.

Він сам з собóю лю́бить говорúти.
He likes to talk **to himself**.

C.3 An Additional Use of Intensive Pronouns

In both English and Ukrainian, the intensive pronouns are also used to convey the meaning **alone** or **by oneself**.

Дíти самí вдóма.
The children are home **alone** (by themselves).

Чомý **ти сам** ходúв у кінó?
Why did **you** *[m,s]* go to the movies **by yourself** (alone)?

Чи **вонá самá** написáла ромáн?
Did **she** write the novel **by herself**?

Practise Oral Exercise 38.2

Do Written Exercise 38.2

D. RELATIVE CLAUSES

In both English and Ukrainian, subordinate clauses are widely used. You already know how to form clauses that begin with adverbs (see Lesson 8). You will now learn how to form subordinate clauses that begin with pronouns.

In English, the pronoun that introduces a subordinate clause is known as a relative pronoun and it refers, or is related to, a word in the principal clause.

In Ukrainian, relative clauses are formed in the same way as they are in English. The interrogative pronouns that you already know are used as relative pronouns to introduce them: **котри́й, яки́й, чий, хто, що**.

Let's look at a few examples. In all the sentences presented below, the relative clause is bolded and the relative pronoun is underlined.

We all know the skaters **<u>who</u> won the trophies**.
Ми всі зна́ємо ковзанярів, **<u>котрі́</u> ви́грали трофе́ї**.

My father built the house **in which we are living**.
Мій ба́тько збудува́в ха́ту, **у <u>які́й</u> ми живемо́**.

The ambassador **with <u>whom</u> you** *[p]* **spoke** no longer works here.
Посо́л, **з <u>яки́м</u> ви говори́ли,** уже́ тут не працю́є.

The student *[f]*, **in <u>whose</u> car we came here,** won the lottery.
Студе́нтка, **<u>чиї́м</u> а́втом ми сюди́ приї́хали,** ви́грала льотері́ю.

They know **<u>who</u> is to blame**.
Вони́ зна́ють, **<u>хто</u> ви́нен**.

Do you *[s]* remember **<u>what</u> was in the wallet**?
Чи ти пам'ята́єш, **<u>що</u> було́ в гаманці́**?

Points to Remember

1. In Ukrainian, a relative clause is always set off with commas.

2. The interrogative pronouns **котри́й, яки́й, чий, хто,** and **що,** are used as relative pronouns to introduce a subordinate relative clause.

3. The relative pronouns **яки́й** and **котри́й** are the same in **gender** and **number** as the word (antecedent) in the principal clause to which they are related.

   The **case** of **яки́й** and **котри́й** is determined by the function that they serve in the subordinate clause in which they are found.

Let's take a closer look at the examples that were presented earlier.

a) Ми всі зна́ємо ковзанярі́в, **котрі́ ви́грали трофе́ї.**

Котрі́ is plural in form to agree with its antecedent, the plural noun **ковзанярі́в**.

Котрі́ is in the nominative case because it is the subject in the subordinate clause. Its antecedent, **ковзанярі́в**, is in the accusative case as it is the direct object of the affirmative verb **зна́ємо** in the principal clause.

b) Мій ба́тько збудува́в ха́ту, **у які́й ми живемо́.**

Які́й is feminine singular in form to agree with its antecedent, **ха́ту**.

Які́й is in the locative case to indicate location after the preposition **у** in the subordinate clause. Its antecedent, **ха́ту**, is in the accusative case as it is the direct object of the affirmative verb **збудува́в** in the principal clause.

c) Посо́л, **з яки́м ви говори́ли**, вже́ тут не працю́є.

Яки́м is masculine singular in form to agree with its antecedent, **посо́л**.

Яки́м is in the instrumental case after the preposition **з** in the subordinate clause. Its antecedent, **посо́л**, is in the nominative case as it is the subject of the principal clause.

4. The relative pronoun **чий** agrees in gender, number, and case with the noun that it modifies in the subordinate clause.

   Студе́нтка, **чиї́м а́втом ми сюди́ приї́хали**, ви́грала льотері́ю.

   Чиї́м is in the neuter singular instrumental form to agree with **а́вто**.

5. When **хто** and **що** are used as relative pronouns, the antecedent is often omitted, even though it is understood to be there.

   Вони́ зна́ють (того́), **хто ви́нен.**

   Чи ти пам'ята́єш (те), **що було́ в гаманці́?**

   The case of the relative pronouns **хто** and **що** in a subordinate clause is determined by the function that they serve in that clause.

6. The relative pronoun **що** is often used as the equivalent of the English relative pronouns **who** and **that** when they are the subject of the subordinate relative clause.

   Who saw the bird **that was singing in the orchard**?
   Хто ба́чив пта́шку, **що співа́ла в саду́**?

   Do foreigners **who live in Canada** pay taxes?
   Чи чужи́нці, **що живу́ть у Кана́ді**, пла́тять пода́тки?

Practise Oral Exercise 38.3

Do Written Exercises 38.3, 38.4

APPENDIX A: DECLENSION OF NOUNS

1. Singular Endings

Feminine

	Hard	Mixed	Soft 1	Soft 2
N.	дружи́н-**а**	афі́ш-**а**	учени́ц-**я**	ле́кці-**я**
G.	дружи́н-**и**	афі́ш-**і**	учени́ц-**і**	ле́кці-**ї**
A.	дружи́н-**у**	афі́ш-**у**	учени́ц-**ю**	ле́кці-**ю**
V.	дружи́н-**о**	афі́ш-**е**	учени́ц-**е**	ле́кці-**є**
I.	дружи́н-**ою**	афі́ш-**ею**	учени́ц-**ею**	ле́кці-**єю**
D.	дружи́н-**і**	афі́ш-**і**	учени́ц-**і**	ле́кці-**ї**
L.	... дружи́н-**і**	... афі́ш-**і**	... учени́ц-**і**	... ле́кці-**ї**

Masculine Animate

	Hard	Mixed	Soft 1	Soft 2
N.	брат	ро́дич	учи́тел-**ь**	зло́ді-**й**
G.	бра́т-**а**	ро́дич-**а**	учи́тел-**я**	зло́ді-**я**
A.	[=G]	[=G]	[=G]	[=G]
V.	бра́т-**е**	ро́дич-**у**	учи́тел-**ю**	зло́ді-**ю**
I.	бра́т-**ом**	ро́дич-**ем**	учи́тел-**ем**	зло́ді-**єм**
D.	бра́т-**ові**	ро́дич-**еві**	учи́тел-**еві**	зло́ді-**єві**
L.	... бра́т-**ові**	... ро́дич-**еві**	... учи́тел-**еві**	... зло́ді-**єві**

Masculine Inanimate

	Hard	Mixed	Soft 1	Soft 2
N.	зо́шит	ключ	мі́сяц-**ь**	музе́-**й**
G.	зо́шит-**а**	ключ-**а́**	мі́сяц-**я**	музе́-**ю**
A.	[=N]	[=N]	[=N]	[=N]
V.	зо́шит-**е**	клю́ч-**у**	мі́сяц-**ю**	музе́-**ю**
I.	зо́шит-**ом**	ключ-**е́м**	мі́сяц-**ем**	музе́-**єм**
D.	зо́шит-**ові**	ключ-**е́ві**	мі́сяц-**еві**	музе́-**єві**
L.	... зо́шит-**і**	... ключ-**і́**	... мі́сяц-**і**	... музе́-**ї**

Neuter

	Hard	Mixed	Soft 1	Soft 2
N.	мі́ст-**о**	прі́звищ-**е**	по́л-**е**	завда́нн-**я**
G.	мі́ст-**а**	прі́звищ-**а**	по́л-**я**	завда́нн-**я**
A.	[=N]	[=N]	[=N]	[=N]
V.	[=N]	[=N]	[=N]	[=N]
I.	мі́ст-**ом**	прі́звищ-**ем**	по́л-**ем**	завда́нн-**ям**
D.	мі́ст-**у**	прі́звищ-**у**	по́л-**ю**	завда́нн-**ю**
L.	... мі́ст-**і**	... прі́звищ-**і**	... по́л-**і**	... завда́нн-**і**

2. Plural Endings

Feminine

	Hard (animate)	Mixed (inanimate)	Soft 1 (animate)	Soft 2 (inanimate)
N.	дружи́н-**и**	афі́ш-**і**	учени́ц-**і**	ле́кці-**ї**
G.	дружи́н	афі́ш	учени́ц-**ь**	ле́кці-**й**
A.	[=G]	[=N]	[=G]	[=N]
V.	[=N]	[=N]	[=N]	[=N]
I.	дружи́н-**ами**	афі́ш-**ами**	учени́ц-**ями**	ле́кці-**ями**
D.	дружи́н-**ам**	афі́ш-**ам**	учени́ц-**ям**	ле́кці-**ям**
L.	... дружи́н-**ах**	... афі́ш-**ах**	... учени́ц-**ях**	... ле́кці-**ях**

Masculine Animate

	Hard	Mixed	Soft 1	Soft 2
N.	брат-**и́**	ро́дич-**і**	учител-**і́**	злоді́-**ї**
G.	брат-**і́в**	ро́дич-**ів**	учител-**і́в**	злоді́-**їв**
A.	[=G]	[=G]	[=G]	[=G]
V.	[=N]	[=N]	[=N]	[=N]
I.	брат-**а́ми**	ро́дич-**ами**	учител-**я́ми**	злоді́-**ями**
D.	брат-**а́м**	ро́дич-**ам**	учител-**я́м**	злоді́-**ям**
L.	... брат-**а́х**	... ро́дич-**ах**	... учител-**я́х**	... злоді́-**ях**

Masculine Inanimate

	Hard	Mixed	Soft 1	Soft 2
N.	зо́шит-**и**	ключ-**і́**	місяц-**і́**	музе́-**ї**
G.	зо́шит-**ів**	ключ-**і́в**	місяц-**і́в**	музе́-**їв**
A.	[=N]	[=N]	[=N]	[=N]
V.	[=N]	[=N]	[=N]	[=N]
I.	зо́шит-**ами**	ключ-**а́ми**	місяц-**я́ми**	музе́-**ями**
D.	зо́шит-**ам**	ключ-**а́м**	місяц-**я́м**	музе́-**ям**
L.	... зо́шит-**ах**	... ключ-**ах**	... місяц-**я́х**	... музе́-**ях**

Neuter

	Hard	Mixed	Soft 1	Soft 2
N.	міст-**а́**	прі́звищ-**а**	пол-**я́**	завда́нн-**я**
G.	міст	прі́звищ	піл-**ь**	завда́н-**ь**
A.	[=N]	[=N]	[=N]	[=N]
V.	[=N]	[=N]	[=N]	[=N]
I.	міст-**а́ми**	прі́звищ-**ами**	пол-**я́ми**	завда́нн-**ями**
D.	міст-**а́м**	прі́звищ-**ам**	пол-**я́м**	завда́нн-**ям**
L.	... міст-**а́х**	... прі́звищ-**ах**	... пол-**я́х**	... завда́нн-**ях**

3. Plural Only Nouns

Note: Nouns from Lessons 11-22 that are used only in the plural are declined below for review purposes. Check the Vocabularies at the end of the text for the declension of plural nouns that are introduced in later lessons.

Animate Nouns

N.	діт-**и**	лю́д-**и**	батьк-**и́**	дівча́т-**а**
G.	діт-**е́й**	люд-**е́й**	батьк-**ів**	дівча́т
A.	[=G]	[=G]	[=G]	[=G]
V.	[=N]	[=N]	[=N]	[=N]
I.	діт-**ьми**	люд-**ьми́**	батьк-**а́ми**	дівча́т-**ами**
D.	діт-**ям**	лю́д-**ям**	батьк-**а́м**	дівча́т-**ам**
L.	... діт-**ях**	... люд-**ях**	... батьк-**а́х**	... дівча́т-**ах**

Inanimate Nouns

N.	джінс-**и**	схо́д-**и**	ша́х-**и**	штан-**и́**	шо́рт-**и**
G.	джінс-**ів**	схо́д-**ів**	ша́х-**ів**	штан-**ів**	шо́рт-**ів**
A.	[=N]	[=N]	[=N]	[=N]	[=N]
V.	[=N]	[=N]	[=N]	[=N]	[=N]
I.	джінс-**ами**	схо́д-**ами**	ша́х-**ами**	штан-**а́ми**	шо́рт-**ами**
D.	джінс-**ам**	схо́д-**ам**	ша́х-**ам**	штан-**а́м**	шо́рт-**ам**
L.	... джінс-**ах**	... схо́д-**ах**	... ша́х-**ах**	... штан-**а́х**	... шо́рт-**ах**

N.	окуля́р-**и**	цимба́л-**и**	ме́бл-**і**	гро́ш-**і**	две́р-**і**
G.	окуля́р-**ів**	цимба́л-**ів**	ме́бл-**ів**	гро́ш-**ей**	двер-**е́й**
A.	[=N]	[=N]	[=N]	[=N]	[=N]
V.	[=N]	[=N]	[=N]	[=N]	[=N]
I.	окуля́р-**ами**	цимба́л-**ами**	ме́бл-**ями**	гріш-**ми** грош-**и́ма**	двер-**ми́** двер-**и́ма**
D.	окуля́р-**ам**	цимба́л-**ам**	ме́бл-**ям**	гро́ш-**ам**	две́р-**ям**
L.	... окуля́р-**ах**	... цимба́л-**ах**	... ме́бл-**ях**	... гро́ш-**ах**	... две́р-**ях**

N.	ка́рт-**и**	ша́шк-**и**	каніку л-**и**	вака́ці-**ї**	но́жиц-**і**
G.	ка́рт	ша́шок	канікул	вака́ці-**й**	но́жиц-**ь**
A.	[=N]	[=N]	[=N]	[=N]	[=N]
V.	[=N]	[=N]	[=N]	[=N]	[=N]
I.	ка́рт-**ами**	ша́шк-**ами**	канікул-**ами**	вака́ці-**ями**	но́жиц-**ями**
D.	ка́рт-**ам**	ша́шк-**ам**	канікул-**ам**	вака́ці-**ям**	но́жиц-**ям**
L.	... ка́рт-**ах**	... ша́шк-**ах**	... канікул-**ах**	... вака́ці-**ях**	... но́жиц-**ях**

APPENDIX B: PREPOSITIONS

1. Locative Case

на	На **чо́му**?	По́суд уже́ **на столі́**. Він гра́є **на скри́пці**.
о	О **котрі́й**?	О котрі́й годи́ні ти ляга́єш спа́ти? **О деся́тій годи́ні**.
у	У **чо́му**?	Студе́нти розмовля́ють **у коридо́рі**

2. Genitive Case

без	Без **ко́го**? Без **чо́го**?	Він ї́де **без діте́й**. Я п'ю чай **без цу́кру**.
біля	Біля **ко́го**? Біля **чо́го**?	Хто сиди́ть **біля студе́нта**? Я живу́ **біля крамни́ці**.
бли́зько	Бли́зько **ко́го**? Бли́зько **чо́го**?	Дити́на сиди́ть **бли́зько ма́ми**. Ми живемо́ **бли́зько па́рку**.
від	Від **ко́го**? Від **чо́го**?	Чи це лист **від діду́ся**? Він біжи́ть додо́му **від зупи́нки**. Вона́ тут **від четверга́**.
для	Для **ко́го**? Для **чо́го**?	Де подару́нок **для дити́ни**? Ось о́браз **для помéшкання**.
до	До **ко́го**? До **чо́го**?	Дити́на біжи́ть **до бабу́сі**. Студе́нт іде́ **до табли́ці**. Я працю́ю **до вівті́рка**.
з	З **ко́го**? З **чо́го**?	Хто сміє́ться з **ге́нія**? У́чні вже вихо́дять з **шко́ли**.
за́місць	За́місць **ко́го**? За́місць **чо́го**?	Дочка́ готу́є сніда́нок **за́місць ма́ми**. Він купу́є шампу́нь **за́місць ми́ла**.
ко́ло	Ко́ло **ко́го**? Ко́ло **чо́го**?	Ді́ти сидя́ть **ко́ло та́та**. Вона́ стої́ть **ко́ло вікна́**.
крім	Крім **ко́го**? Крім **чо́го**?	**Крім діте́й**, у па́рку ніко́го не було́. **Крім зо́шитів**, у шухля́ді не було́ нічо́го.

недале́ко	Недале́ко **ко́го**?	Я сиджу́ **недале́ко това́ришки** в шко́лі.
	Недале́ко **чо́го**?	Фа́рма **недале́ко ріки́**.
після	Після **ко́го**?	Хто співа́є **після студе́нтки**?
	Після **чо́го**?	Ми обі́даємо **після футбо́лу**.
про́ти	Про́ти **ко́го**?	Що ти ма́єш **про́ти профе́сора**?
		Хто сиди́ть **про́ти те́бе** в лябора́то́рії?
	Про́ти **чо́го**?	Ща́фа стоі́ть **про́ти двере́й**.
се́ред	Се́ред **ко́го**?	Чому́ у́чень сиди́ть **се́ред учи́телів**?
	Се́ред **чо́го**?	Пес лежи́ть **се́ред хідника́**.
у	У **ко́го**?	Ми живемо́ **у дя́дька**.
		У сестри́ ма́ло гро́шей.

3. Accusative Case

за	За **ко́го**?	Хто пла́тить **за у́чнів**?
	За **що**?	Сього́дні я плачу́ **за ка́ву**.
на	На **ко́го**?	Ми чека́ємо **на студе́нтку**.
		Сестра́ ди́виться **на бра́та**.
	На **що**?	Ми чека́ємо **на по́їзд**.
		Він ди́виться **на банду́ру**.
		Я кладу́ зо́шит **на стіл**.
		Вона́ готу́є ю́шку **на вече́рю**.
		Ми йдемо́ **на го́кей**.
по	По **ко́го**?	Вона́ ї́де **по діте́й** до шко́ли.
	По **що**?	Вона́ йде **по хліб** до крамни́ці.
про	Про **ко́го**?	Вони́ говоря́ть **про вчи́тельку**.
		Ба́тько жу́риться **про си́на**.
	Про **що**?	Вона́ ду́має **про ле́кцію**.
		Я журю́ся **про завда́ння**.
у	У **що**?	Вона́ вхо́дить **у кімна́ту**.
		Ми всі гра́ємо **в ґольф**.
		Вони́ гра́ють **у ка́рти**.
че́рез	Че́рез **ко́го**?	Батьки́ не мо́жуть спа́ти **че́рез дити́ну**.
	Че́рез **що**?	До бабу́сі тре́ба йти́ **че́рез ліс**.
		Ми не мо́жемо вчи́тися **че́рез му́зику**.

4. Instrumental Case

з	З **ким**?	Вона́ розмовля́є з **това́ришем**. Він одру́жується з **акто́ркою**.
	З **чим**?	Я п'ю ка́ву з **цу́кром**.
за	За **ким**?	Він сиди́ть **за студе́нткою**. Ми шука́ємо **за вчи́телем**.
	За **чим**?	Вони́ чека́ють **за двери́ма**. Вони́ шука́ють **за поме́шканням**.
між	Між **ким**?	Я ба́чу дочку́ **між студе́нтками**.
	Між **чим**?	Перо́ тут, **між олівця́ми**.
над	Над **чим**?	Птахи́ літа́ють **над о́зером**.
перед	Пе́ред **ким**?	Вона́ стої́ть **пе́ред та́том**.
	Пе́ред **чим**?	Він чека́є **пе́ред книга́рнею**.
під	Під **чим**?	Пес спить **під лі́жком**.

APPENDIX C: ADVERBS OF QUANTITY

багáто	Багáто **когó?**	У теáтрі **багáто людéй.**
	Багáто **чогó?**	У тéчці **багáто зóшитів.** На тарíлці **багáто м'ясa.**
більше	Більше **когó?**	У мéне **більше студéнтів.**
	Більше **чогó?**	У ньóго **більше грóшей.** На полиці **більше мúла.**
дóсить	Дóсить **когó?**	У нас **дóсить робітникíв.**
	Дóсить **чогó?**	У неї **дóсить блюзóк.** У мéне **дóсить кáви.**
кілька	Кілька **когó?**	Я бáчу **кілька хлóпців.**
	Кілька **чого?**	Він купýє **кілька цитрúн.**
мáло	Мáло **когó?**	На концéрті **мáло людéй.**
	Мáло **чогó?**	У помéшканні **мáло мéблів.** На столí **мáло молокá.**
мéнше	Мéнше **когó?**	Сьогóдні в пáрку **мéнше дітéй.**
	Мéнше **чогó?**	Сьогóдні в ґарáжі **мéнше авт.** Я дýмаю, що в мéне **мéнше борщý.**
небагáто	Небагáто **когó?**	Біля зупúнки **небагáто ýчнів.**
	Небагáто **чогó?**	На полúці **небагáто книжóк.** Тут **небагáто ковбасú.**
скільки	Скільки **когó?**	**Скільки дітéй** у кля́сі?
	Скільки **чогó?**	**Скільки крíсел** на балькóні? **Скільки морóзива** в морозúльнику?
стільки	Стільки **когó?**	Чомý тут **стільки комарíв?**
	Стільки **чогó?**	Чомý тут **стільки мух?** Чомý тут **стільки водú?**
трóхи	Трóхи **чогó?**	На кúлимі **трóхи піскý.**

Remember: When an adverb of quantity is the subject of a sentence, it is treated like a **neuter singular noun** and a **singular** third person verb is used with it.

Скільки людéй **вихóдить** з теáтру?
Скільки людéй **бýде** на вечíрці?
Скільки людéй **булó** на концéрті?

APPENDIX D: EXPRESSIONS USED IN *ORAL EXERCISES*

UKRAINIAN-ENGLISH

А ви? – And how are you *[p]*? 3
А в тéбе? – And how are things with you? 5
А ти? – And you *[s]*? 3
А що такé? – What's the matter? 13

Бувáй – So long! 5
Будь лáска. – Please. 7
Будь лáска. – You're welcome! 12

Ви́бач, ... – I'm sorry, ... 13
Ви́бачте, ... – I'm sorry,.. 13

Гарáзд! – Okay! That's good! 13

Дíйсно? – Really? 8
Дóбре, дя́кую! – Fine, thanks. 3
Добри́день! – Hello. (Good day!) 5
Дóбрий вéчір! – Good evening! 5
Дóбрий день! – Good day! 11
Дóброго рáнку! – Good morning! 3
До зáвтра! – See you tomorrow! 5
До побáчення! – Good bye! 3
Дя́кую! – Thanks! 3

Звичáйно. – Of course. 8
Знáчить ... – That means ... It means ... 29

На все дóбре! – All the best! 3
На добрáніч! – Good night! 5
Невжé ж! – You don't say! 8
Немá зá що! – Don't mention it! Not at all! No problem! 11
Не мóже бýти! – That can't be so! 8
Непогáно. – Not bad. 5
Нічóго. – That's okay. It's nothing! Never mind! 13
Ну ... – Well ... 5
Ну, звичáйно! – But of course! 5

О! – Oh! 12
Оберéжно! – Watch out! Be careful! 13
Очеви́дно. – Obviously. It goes without saying. 8

по-англíйському – in English, 13
по-украї́нському – in Ukrainian, 13
Почекáйте! – Wait up! 12
Привíт! – Hi! 5
Приє́мно! – It's a pleasure! 12
Пробáчте! – Excuse me! 12
Прóшу. – You're welcome. 11
Прóшу дýже. – You're very welcome. 13
Скажи́, будь лáска ... – (You *[s]*) tell me, please ... 8
Скажíть, будь лáска ... – (You *[p]*) tell me, please ... 8
Смачнóго – Bon appetit! Enjoy your meal! 23
Спаси́бі. – Thanks! 12
Спрáвді? – Really? 5

Так собí! – So-so. 5
Такóж дóбре, дя́кую. – Also fine, thanks. 3

У чóму спрáва? – What's the matter? 12

Ходíмо ... – Let's go ... 13

Це неправильно. – That's wrong. That's incorrect. 13
Це прáвильно. – That's right. That's correct. 13
Цим рáзом ти мáєш рáцію. – This time you're *[s]* right. 28

Час ... – It's time ... 13
Чудóво! – Great! Just great! That's great! 5

Шкодá! – That's too bad! 13

Щасли́во! – All the best! 5
Щи́ро дя́кую! – Many thanks! 12
Що ти?! – What are you *[s]* saying? What do you *[s]* mean? 29

Як нікóли! – Never better! 5
Як спрáви? – How are things going? 5
Як ся мáєте? – How are you *[p]*? 3
Як ся мáєш? – How are you *[s]*? 3
Я́сно! – I see! I understand! 13

ENGLISH-UKRAINIAN

All the best! – На все дóбре! 3
All the best! – Щасли́во! 5
Also fine, thanks. – Такóж дóбре, дя́кую. 3
And how are things with you? – А в тéбе? 5
And how are you *[p]*? – А ви? 3
And you *[s]*? – А ти? 3

Be careful! – Оберéжно! 13
Bon appetit! – Смачнóго. 23
But of course! – Ну, звичáйно! 5

Don't mention it! – Немá зá що! 11

Enjoy your meal! – Смачнóго! 23
Excuse me! – Пробáчте! 12

Fine, thanks. – Дóбре, дя́кую! 3

Good bye! – До побáчення! 3
Good day! – Дóбрий день! 11
Good day! – Добри́день! 5
Good evening! – Дóбрий вéчір! 5
Good morning! – Дóброго рáнку! 3
Good night! – На добрáніч! 5
Great! – Чудóво! 5

Hello. – Добри́день! 5
Hi! – Привíт! 5
How are things going? – Як спрáви? 5
How are you *[p]*? – Як ся мáєте? 3
How are you *[s]*? – Як ся мáєш? 3

I'm sorry, ... – Ви́бач, ... 13
I'm sorry, ... – Ви́бачте, ... 13
in English – по-англíйському, 13
in Ukrainian – по-украї́нському, 13
I see! I understand! – Я́сно! 13
It goes without saying. – Очеви́дно. 8
It means ... – Знáчить ... 29
It's a pleasure! – Приє́мно! 12
It's nothing! – Нічóго. 13
It's time ... – Час ... 13

Just great! – Чудóво! 5

Let's go ... – Ходíмо ... 3

Many thanks! – Щи́ро дя́кую! 12

Never better! – Як нікóли! 5
Never mind!, – Нічóго. 13
No problem! – Немá зá що! 11
Not at all! – Немá зá що! 11
Not bad. – Непогáно. 5
Obviously. – Очеви́дно. 8
Of course. – Звичáйно. 8
Oh! – О! 12
Okay! – Гарáзд! 13

Please. – Будь лáска. 7

Really? – Дíйсно? 8
Really? – Спрáвді? 5

See you tomorrow! – До зáвтра! 5
So long! – Бувáй! 5
So-so. – Так собí! 5

Thanks! – Дя́кую! 3
Thanks! – Спаси́бі. 12
That can't be so! – Не мóже бýти! 8
That means ... – Знáчить ... 29
That's correct. – Це прáвильно. 13
That's good! – Гарáзд! 13
That's great! – Чудóво! 5
That's incorrect. – Це непрáвильно. 13
That's okay. – Нічóго. 13
That's right. – Це прáвильно. 13
That's too bad! – Шкодá! 13
That's wrong. – Це непрáвильно. 13
This time you're *[s]* right.
  – Цим рáзом ти маєш рáцію. 28

Wait up! – Почекáйте! 12
Watch out! – Оберéжно! 13
Well ... – Ну ... 5
What are you *[s]* saying? – Що ти?! 29
What do you *[s]* mean? – Що ти?! 29
What's the matter, – А що такé? 13
What's the matter? – У чому справа? 12

You don't say! – Невжé ж! 8
You're very welcome. – Прóшу дýже. 13
You're welcome! – Будь лáска. 12
You're welcome. – Прóшу. 11
(You *[p]*) tell me, please ...
  – Скажíть, будь лáска ... 8
(You *[s]*) tell me, please ...
  – Скажи́, будь лáска ... 8

APPENDIX E: PERSONAL NAMES AND SURNAMES

This Appendix includes the personal names and surnames that have been used in the *Text, Oral Exercises* and *Written Exercises.*

The numbers that follow the names indicate the first time that these names are used.

13	Lesson 13 in the *Text*
13o	Lesson 13 in *Oral Exercises*
13w	Lesson 13 in *Written Exercises*

The English versions that have been given for the Ukrainian names represent only a few of the many different ways in which Ukrainian names have been translated into English in Canada.

UKRAINIAN-ENGLISH

MASCULINE PERSONAL NAMES

Ада́м – Adam, 13o
Андрі́й – Andriy, Andrew, 13

Богда́н – Bohdan, Robert, Bob, 13
Бори́с – Borys, Boris, 13o
Васи́ль – Vasyl, Wasyl, William, Bill, 13o
Ві́ктор – Victor, 13o
Віта́лій – Vitaliy, 13o
Володи́мир *[h]* – Volodymyr, Walter, 13o

Григо́рій – Hryhoriy, Gregory, 13o

Дави́д – David, Dave, 13o
Дани́ло – Danylo, Daniel, Dan, 13o
Дени́с – Dennis, 17o
Дмитро́ – Dmytro, Metro, 13o

Е́двард – Edward, 13

Іва́н – Ivan, John, 12o
Іва́сь – Ivas, Johnny, 13o
І́гор – Ihor, 12w

Лука́ш – Lukash, 13o
Любоми́р – Lubomyr, 17w

Макси́м – Maksym, Maxim, 13o
Маркія́н – Markian, 17o
Марко́ – Marko, Mark, 12
Марти́н – Martin, 13o
Мики́та – Mykyta, 20o
Мико́ла – Mykola, 13
Миро́н – Myron, 13o

Миха́йло – Mykhaylo, Michael, 13o
Миха́сь – Mykhas, Mike, 13o

Наза́р *[h]* – Nazar, 13o
Не́стор *[h]* – Nestor, 13w

Оле́г – Oleh, 17o
Оле́кса – Oleksa, Alex, 13o
Олекса́ндер *[h]* – Oleksander, Alexander, 13o
Олексі́й – Oleksiy, Alex, 13o
Оре́ст – Orest, 12w
Оста́п – Ostap, 17o

Павло́ – Pavlo, Paul, 13o
Пе́трик – Petryk, Patrick, 13o
Петро́ – Petro, Peter, 12
Пили́п – Philip, 13o

Рома́н – Roman, 13
Ро́мко – Romko, 17o

Сергі́й – Serhiy, Serge, 13o
Сла́вко – Slawko, Slavko, 13o
Степа́н – Stefan, Stephan, Steven, Steve 13o
Стефа́н – Stefan, Stephan, Steven, Steve 13w

Тара́с – Taras, Terry, 13o
Тимоте́й – Timothy, 13o

Христофо́р – Christopher, 20w

Ю́рій – Yuriy, George, 13o

Яросла́в – Yaroslaw, 13w
Ясо́н – Jason, 13o

FEMININE PERSONAL NAMES

Алíна – Alina, 17o

Варвáра – Barbara, 13o
Віра – Vira, Vera, 13o

Гали́на – Halyna, Helen, 13o

Дáрія – Daria, 13o
Дарýся – Darusia, 13o
Діяна – Diana, Diane, Deana, 13

Єва – Eve, 17o

Івáнна – Ivanna, Joanne, 130
Іри́на – Iryna, Irene, 18o

Кали́на – Kalyna, 13o
Кари́на – Karyna, Karen, 17o
Катери́на – Katherine, Catherine, Kathryn, 13o
Катрýся – Katrusia, Kathy, Cathy, 13o

Лáра – Lara, 13o
Лари́са – Larysa, Larissa, 13o
Лéся – Lesia, Lesya, 13o
Лю́ба – Lyuba, Luba, 18o

Марíя – Maria, Mary, Marie, 12
Мари́на – Maryna, 13
Марíйка – Mariyka, Marika, 13o
Мáрта – Martha, 13
Марýся – Marusia, 13o
Мелáнія – Melania, Melanie, 13o

Надíя – Nadia, Nadiya, 13o
Нáдя – Nadia, Nadya, 13o
Натáлія – Natalia, 13o
Натáлка – Natalka, 17o
Натáля – Natalie, 13o
Ніна – Nina, 12w

Одáрка – Odarka, Audrey, 13w
Оксáна – Oksana, 13o
Óльга – Olha, Olga, 17o
Олексáндра – Oleksandra, Alexandra, 13o
Олéна – Olena, Elaine, 13o
Óля – Olia, Olya, 13o

Павли́на – Pavlyna, Pauline, Paula, 17o

Раїса – Raissa, Raisa, 13o
Рóма – Roma, 13o

Світлáна – Svitlana, 13w
Сóня – Sonia, Sonya, 12o
Софíя – Sophia, Sophie, 13o
Стефáнія – Stefania, Stefanie, 13o
Сузáнна – Susanna, 13

Тамáра – Tamara, 12o
Тáня – Tania, Tanya, 13o
Терéза – Theresa, 21w

Христи́на – Christine, 20w

SURNAMES

Антонéнко – Antonenko, 12w

Бóднар – Bodnar, 13w
Бойчýк – Boychuk, 13o

Гончáр – Honchar, 13

Дершкó – Dershko, 13w
Дóрош – Dorosh, 13w
Дудáр – Dudar, 12w
Дýдик – Dudyk, Dudyck, 13o

Жук – Zhuk, Zuck, Zuk, Zook, 16o

Іванéнко – Ivanenko, 13o

Кіндрáчук – Kindrachuk, 13w
Климéнко – Klymenko, 13o
Ковалéнко – Kovalenko, Kowalenko, 31w
Козáк – Kozak, 12
Кравчýк – Krawchuk, Kravchuk, 13o

Лабáч – Labach, 31w

Макáренко – Makarenko, 13o

Панчýк – Panchuk, 12w
Петри́шин – Petryshyn, 13w

Рáвлик – Rawlyk, 12w

Савчýк – Sawchuk, 12
Сенчýк – Senchuk, 12w
Сич – Sych, 13o
Сіркó – Sirko, 12o

Ткачýк – Tkachuk, 13w
Трач – Trach, 13o

Фари́на – Faryna, 12w
Федýн – Fedun, 13w
Франкó – Franko, 13w

Шевчéнко – Shevchenko, 13o
Шевчýк – Shewchuk, Shevchuk, 12o

Чáйка – Chayka, 18w
Чубáк – Chubak, 12w

ENGLISH-UKRAINIAN

MASCULINE PERSONAL NAMES

Adam – Ада́м, 13о
Alex – Оле́кса, Олексі́й, 13о
Alexander – Олекса́ндер, 13о
Andrew – Андрі́й, 13
Andriy – Андрі́й, 13

Bill – Васи́ль, 13о
Bob – Богда́н, 13
Bohdan – Богда́н, 13
Boris – Бори́с, 13о
Borys – Бори́с, 13о

Christopher – Христофо́р, 20w

Dan – Дани́ло, 13о
Daniel – Дани́ло, 13о
Danylo – Дани́ло, 13о
Dave – Дави́д, 13о
David – Дави́д, 13о
Dennis – Дени́с, 17о
Dmytro – Дмитро́, 13о

Edward – Е́два́рд, 13

George – Ю́рій, 13о
Gregory – Григо́рій, 13о

Hryhoriy – Григо́рій, 13о

Ihor – І́гор, 12w
Ivan – Іва́н, 12о
Ivas – Іва́сь, 13о

Jason – Ясо́н, 13о
John – Іва́н, 12о
Johnny – Іва́сь, 13о

Lubomyr – Любоми́р, 17w
Lukash – Лука́ш, 13о

Maksym – Макси́м, 13о
Mark – Марко́, 12
Markian – Маркія́н, 17о
Marko – Марко́, 12
Martin – Марти́н, 13о
Maxim – Макси́м, 13о
Metro – Дмитро́, 13о
Michael – Миха́йло, 13о
Mike – Миха́сь, 13о
Mykhas – Миха́сь, 13о
Mykhaylo – Миха́йло, 13о
Mykola – Мико́ла, 13
Mykyta – Мики́та, 20о
Myron – Миро́н, 13о

Nestor – Не́стор, 13w

Oleh – Оле́г, 17о
Oleksa – Оле́кса, 13о
Oleksander – Олекса́ндер, 13о
Oleksiy – Олексі́й, 13о
Orest – Оре́ст, 12w
Ostap – Оста́п, 17о

Patrick – Пе́трик, 13о
Paul – Павло́, 13о
Pavlo – Павло́, 13о
Peter – Петро́, 12
Petro – Петро́, 12
Petryk – Пе́трик, 13о
Philip – Пили́п, 13о

Robert – Богда́н, 13
Roman – Рома́н, 13
Romko – Ро́мко, 17о

Serge – Сергі́й, 13о
Serhiy – Сергі́й, 13о
Slavko – Сла́вко, 13о
Slawko – Сла́вко, 13о
Stefan – Степа́н, Стефа́н, 13о
Stephan – Степа́н, Стефа́н, 13о
Steve – Степа́н, Стефа́н, 13о
Steven – Степа́н, Стефа́н, 13о

Taras – Тара́с, 13о
Terry – Тара́с, 13о
Timothy – Тимоте́й, 13о

Vasyl – Васи́ль, 13о
Victor – Ві́ктор, 13о
Vitaliy – Віта́лій, 13о
Volodymyr – Володи́мир, 13о

Walter – Володи́мир, 13о
Wasyl – Васи́ль, 13о
William – Васи́ль, 13о

Yaroslaw – Яросла́в, 13w
Yuriy – Ю́рій, 13о

FEMININE PERSONAL NAMES

Alexandra – Олекса́ндра, 13o
Alina – Алі́на, 17o
Audrey – Ода́рка, 22o

Barbara – Варва́ра, 13o

Catherine – Катери́на, 13o
Cathy – Катру́ся, 13o
Christine – Христи́на, 20w

Daria – Да́рія, 13o
Darusia – Дару́ся, 13o
Deana – Дія́на, 13
Diana – Дія́на, 13
Diane – Дія́на, 13

Elaine – Оле́на, 13o
Eve – Є́ва, 17o

Halyna – Гали́на, 13o
Helen – Гали́на, 13o

Irene – Іри́на, 18o
Iryna – Іри́на, 18o
Ivanna – Іва́нна, 13o

Joanne – Іва́нна, 13o

Kalyna – Кали́на, 13o
Karen – Кари́на, 17o
Karyna – Кари́на, 17o
Katherine – Катери́на, 13o
Kathy – Катру́ся, 13o
Kathryn – Катери́на, 13o
Katrusia – Катру́ся, 13o

Lara – Ла́ра, 13o
Larissa – Лари́са, 13o
Larysa – Лари́са, 13o
Lesia – Ле́ся, 13o
Lesya – Ле́ся, 13o
Luba – Лю́ба, 18o
Lyuba – Лю́ба, 18o

Marika – Марі́йка, 13o
Mariyka – Марі́йка, 13o
Maria – Марі́я, 12
Marie – Марі́я, 12
Martha – Ма́рта, 13
Marusia – Мару́ся, 13o
Maryna – Мари́на, 13
Mary – Марі́я, 12
Melania – Мела́нія, 13o
Melanie – Мела́нія, 13o

Nadia – Наді́я, На́дя, 13o
Nadya – Наді́я, На́дя, 13o
Natalia – Ната́лія, 13o
Natalie – Ната́ля, 13o
Natalka – Ната́лка, 17o
Nina – Ні́на, 12w

Odarka – Ода́рка, 22o
Oksana – Окса́на, 13o
Oleksandra – Олекса́ндра, 13o
Olena – Оле́на, 13o
Olga – О́льга, 17o
Olha – О́льга, 17o
Olia – О́ля, 13o
Olya – О́ля, 13o

Pauline – Павли́на, 17o
Paula – Па́вла, 17o
Pavlyna – Павли́на, 17o

Raisa – Раї́са, 13o
Raissa – Раї́са, 13o
Roma – Ро́ма, 13o

Sonia – Со́ня, 12o
Sonya – Со́ня, 12o
Sophia – Софі́я, 13o
Sophie – Софі́я, 13o
Stefania – Стефа́нія, 13o
Stefanie – Стефа́нія, 13o
Susanna – Суза́нна, 13
Svitlana – Світла́на, 13w

Tamara – Тама́ра, 12o
Tania – Та́ня, 13o
Tanya – Та́ня, 13o
Theresa – Тере́за, 21w

Vera – Ві́ра, 13o
Vira – Ві́ра, 13o

SURNAMES

Antonenko – Антоне́нко, 12w

Bodnar – Бо́днар, 13w
Boychuk – Бойчу́к, 13o

Chayka – Ча́йка, 18w
Chubak – Чуба́к, 12w

Dershko – Дершко́, 13w
Dorosh – До́рош, 13w
Dudyck – Ду́дик, 13o
Dudyk – Ду́дик, 13o
Dudar – Дуда́р, 12w

Faryna – Фари́на, 12w
Fedun – Феду́н, 13w
Franko – Франко́, 13w

Honchar – Гонча́р, 13

Ivanenko – Іване́нко, 13o

Kindrachuk – Кіндра́чук, 13w
Klymenko – Климе́нко, 13o
Kovalenko – Ковале́нко, 31w
Kowalenko – Ковале́нко, 31w
Kozak – Коза́к, 12

Kravchuk – Кравчу́к, 13o
Krawchuk – Кравчу́к, 13o

Labach – Лаба́ч, 31w

Makarenko – Мака́ренко, 13o

Panchuk – Панчу́к, 12w
Petryshyn – Петри́шин, 13w

Rawlyk – Ра́влик, 12w

Sawchuk – Савчу́к, 12
Senchuk – Сенчу́к, 12w
Shevchenko – Шевче́нко, 13o
Shevchuk – Шевчу́к, 12o
Shewchuk – Шевчу́к, 12o
Sirko – Сірко́, 12o
Sych – Сич, 13o

Tkachuk – Ткачу́к, 13w
Trach – Трач, 13o

Zhuk – Жук, 16o
Zook – Жук, 16o
Zuck – Жук, 16o
Zuk – Жук, 16o

VOCABULARY LEGEND

General Comments

1. Every word is followed by the number of the lesson in which it is introduced: apple, 15.
2. Words used more commonly in Ukraine than in Canada are printed in slanted letters: lamp - ля́мпа, *ла́мпа*; lemon - цитри́на, *лимо́н*.
3. Synonyms are separated by a semi-colon: íнколи; íноді.
4. Words like **удо́ма/вдо́ма** are defined under **у** (удо́ма – at home); they are also listed under **в** with the following notation: (see удо́ма).

Adjectives

1. Only the masculine nominative singular forms are given: га́рний.
2. Adjectives are listed only in the positive degree, except for the comparative forms that are introduced prior to and during the discussion of the comparison of adjectives in Lesson 30.
3. Adjectives that belong to the soft declension are identified with the abbreviation *[s]*: си́ній *[s]*
4. Adjectives that have a special meaning when they are used as substantives are identified by the abbreviation *[sub.]*.

   молоди́й – young   молоди́й *[sub.]* – bridegroom
   молода́ *[sub.]* – bride

Adverbs

Adverbs are listed only in the positive degree, except for the comparative forms that are introduced prior to and during the discussion of the comparison of adverbs in Lesson 31.

Nouns

1. The genitive singular form is given for all masculine inanimate nouns and for nouns belonging to the consonant declension of feminine nouns.
2. Changes in noun stems are indicated: буди́**нок**, буди́**нку**; с**і**к, с**о́**ку.
3. If the stress shifts in the declension of a noun, the genitive singular and/or the nominative plural forms are given: співа́к, співака́, *pl.* співаки́.
4. If the genitive plural case of a noun is irregular or difficult to form, it is given: то́рба, *pl.* торби́, торб**і́в**; спа́льня, *g.pl.* спа́л**е**нь.
5. The genitive and locative forms are given for all nouns that are always used in the plural: христи́ни *[pl]*, христи́н, ... христи́нах.
6. Irregularities that occur in individual cases are noted: та́то, *v.sg.* та́т**у**; бе́рег, ... бе́рег**ові** і ... бе́ре**зі**.
7. Nouns that depart in most of their cases from the declensional rules given in this text are declined fully: о́ко, ... о́ці; *pl.* о́чі, оче́й, очи́ма, оча́м, ... оча́х.
8. The following abbreviations are used for nouns:

English Nouns

[f] or *[m]* to mark English nouns that do not clearly indicate gender: teacher *[f]* – учи́телька; teacher *[m]* – учи́тель.

Ukrainian Nouns

[f] for feminine nouns ending in a consonant: ніч *[f]*

[h] for hard declension masculine nouns ending in **р**: до́ктор *[h]*

[m] for masculine nouns ending in -а/-я: дру́жба *[m]*

[m,f] for nouns ending in -а/-я that may be used to refer to either males or females: листоно́ша *[m,f]*

[mx] for mixed declension masculine nouns ending in **р**: маля́р *[mx]*

[n] for neuter nouns ending in the vowel **я**: оповіда́ння *[n]*

[pl] for nouns that are always plural in Ukrainian: две́рі *[pl]*

[s] for soft declension masculine nouns ending in **р**: лі́кар *[s]*

[sg] for nouns that are always singular in Ukrainian: горо́дина *[sg]*

Prepositions

The case or cases that a preposition governs are indicated.

до *[+G]*

у *[+L]* у *[+A]* у *[+G]*

Pronouns

Pronouns that are declined like adjectives are listed under their masculine singular nominative form, followed by the feminine and neuter singular forms, and the plural nominative form:

цей, ця, це, ці

Verbs

For **imperfective verbs**, the present tense stem is identified, and the present tense endings of the verb forms for **я** and **ти** are given. Changes that occur in the present tense stem are bolded.

Perfective infinitives are identified with the abbreviation ***pf.*** The future perfective stem is identified, and the future tense endings of the verb forms for **я** and **ти** are given. Changes that occur in the future perfective stems are bolded.

Imperfective Verbs	Perfective Verbs
чита́ти: чита́-ю, -єш	*pf.* прочита́ти: прочита́-ю, -єш
писа́ти: пи**ш**-у́, -еш	*pf.* написа́ти: напи**ш**-у́, -еш
сиді́ти: си**дж**у́, сид-и́ш	*pf.* поси́діти: поси́**дж**у, поси́д-иш

UKRAINIAN-ENGLISH VOCABULARY

А

а – and, 3
а – but, 3
або́ – or, 3
або́ ... або́ – either... or, 3
абрико́са – apricot, 30
ава́рія – accident, collision, 29
авдито́рія – auditorium, 35
австралі́єць, австралі́йця – Australian *[m]*, 38
австралі́йка – Australian *[f]*, 38
австралі́йський – Australian, 38
Австра́лія – Australia, 38
а́вто – car, automobile, 12
авто́бус, -а – bus, 18
автоса́ни, *pl.* автосане́й, автосаньми́, ... автоса́нях – snowmobile, 34
автоста́вка – parking lot, 35
автостра́да – highway, 35
адвока́т – lawyer, 24
адре́са – address, 18
***аеродро́м**, -у* – airport, 35
***аеропо́рт**, -у* – airport, 35
акордео́н, -а – accordion, 16
акордіо́н, -а – accordion, 16
акто́р *[h]* – actor, 24
акто́рка – actress, 24
актри́са – actress, 24
але́ – but, 3
амбаса́да – embassy, 38
Аме́рика (США) – America (USA), 38
америка́нець, америка́нця – American *[m]*, 38
америка́нка – American *[f]*, 38
америка́нський – American, 38
а́нгел – angel, 37
англі́єць, англі́йця – Englishman, 38
англі́йка – Englishwoman, 38
англі́йський – English, 38
А́нглія – England, 38
анса́мбль, анса́мбля – band *[musical]*, 16
***апельси́н**, -а* – orange, 15
апте́ка – drugstore, pharmacy, 28
апте́кар *[s]* – pharmacist *[m]*, druggist *[m]*, 24
апте́карка – pharmacist *[f]*, druggist *[f]*, 24
архіте́кт – architect, 24
архіте́ктор *[h]* – architect, 24
асисте́нт – assistant *[m]*, 22
асисте́нтка – assistant *[f]*, 22
аудито́рія – auditorium, 35
афі́ша – poster, 11

Б

ба́ба, *pl.* баби́, бабі́в – grandmother, 13
бабу́ся – grandmother, granny, 13
ба́витися: ба́в-люся, -ишся – to play, 34
бага́ж, багажу́ – baggage, 25
бага́жник, -а – trunk *[of a car]*, 25
база́р *[h]*, -у – market, 35
бага́тий – rich, 26
бага́то – much, a lot, 4
бага́тше – more richly, 31
бага́тший – richer, 30
ба́йка, *pl.* байки́, байо́к – fable, tale, 36
бале́т, -у – ballet, 36
балко́н, -а – balcony, 14
баль, ба́лю, *pl.* **балі́** – formal dance, ball, 15
балько́н, -а – balcony, 14
бана́н, -а – banana, 15
ба́нда – band *[musical]*, 16
банда́ж, бандажа́, *pl.* бандажі́ – bandage, 31
банду́ра – bandura, 16
банк, ба́нку – bank *[building]*, 13
ба́нка – jar, can, tin, 30
бараба́н, -а – drum, 16
басе́йн, -у – swimming pool, 25
баскетбо́л, -у – basketball *[game]*, 15
батаре́йка – battery, 32
батьки́ *[pl]*, батькі́в – parents, 13
ба́тько, *pl.* батьки́, батькі́в – father, 13
ба́чити: ба́ч-у, -иш – to see, 8
бджола́, *pl.* бджо́ли, бджіл – bee, 21
без *[+G]* – without, 18
бейсбо́л, -у – baseball *[game]*, 15
***беко́н**, -у* – bacon, 19
***бензи́н**, -у* – gasoline, 35
бензи́на – gasoline, 35

бенке́т, -у – banquet, 22
бе́рег, бе́рега, ... бе́регові і ... бе́резі, *pl.* берегі́ – bank *[of a river]*, shore, 21
бе́резень, бе́резня – March, 16
бібліоте́ка – library, 12
бібліоте́кар *[s]* – librarian *[m]*, 12
бібліоте́карка – librarian *[f]*, 12
бі́гати: бі́га-ю, -єш *[it.]* – to run, 10
бі́гти: біжу́, -и́ш *[dur.]* – to run, 8
бі́дний – poor, 26
бідні́ше – more poorly, 31
бідні́ший – poorer, 31
бі́дно – poorly, 31
бі́лий – white, 26
білі́ший – whiter, 30
бі́ля *[+G]* – beside, by, 18
біль, бо́лю – pain, ache, 31
бі́льше – more, 4
бі́льший – bigger, 30
біс, бі́са, *pl.* бісі́ – devil, 37
бли́скавка – lightning, 33
бли́скати: бли́скає – to lighten, to flash lightning, 33
бли́зько *[+G]* – near, close to, 22
блу́зка, *pl.* *блузки́, блузо́к* – blouse, 20
блю́зка, *pl.* блюзки́, блюзо́к – blouse, 20
бляша́нка – can, tin, 30
бо – because, 6
Бог, Бо́га, *v.sg.* Бо́же! *pl.* боги́ – God, 37
болі́льник – fan *[enthusiastic supporter]*, 34
болі́ти: боли́ть, боля́ть – to ache, to hurt, 31
борг, бо́ргу, ... боргу́, *pl.* борги́ – debt, 37
борода́, *pl.* бо́роди, борі́д, … бо́родах – beard, 31
боро́тися: бор-ю́ся, -ешся – to struggle, to fight, 7
борщ, борщу́, *pl.* борщі́ – borshch, 19
босоні́жка – sandal, 20
боягу́з – coward, 37
боя́тися: бо-ю́ся, -ї́шся – to fear, to be frightened, 9
брасле́т, -а – bracelet, 28
брат, бра́та, *pl.* брати́ – brother, 13
бра́ти: бер-у́, -е́ш – to take, 7
бреха́ти: бреш-у́, -еш – to tell a lie; to lie, 7
брехну́ти: брехн-у́, -е́ш *pf.* – to tell a lie; to lie, 23
бри́тва – razor, 28
брова́, *pl.* бро́ви, брів – eyebrow, 31
брудни́й – dirty, 26
брудні́ше – more dirtily, 31
брудні́ший – dirtier, 30
бру́дно – dirtily, 31
бу́вший – former, 33
буди́льник, -а – alarm clock, 29
буди́нок, буди́нка і буди́нку – building, 12
буди́нок, будни́ка і буди́нку – house, 12
будіве́льник – builder, construction worker, 24
будівни́к, будівника́, *pl.* будівники́ – builder, construction worker, 24
будува́ти: буду́-ю, -єш – to build, 32
буке́т, -а – bouquet, 22
бу́лочка – bun, 19
бу́ря – storm, 33
буря́к, -а – beet, 30
бур'я́н, бур'яну́, *pl.* бур'яни́ – weed, 21
бу́ти: я є, ти є – to be, 2
буха́лтер – accountant, 24
буха́льтер – accountant, 24

В

в – (see у)
важли́вий – important, 32
ва́жити: ва́ж-у, -иш – to weigh, 8
ва́за – vase, 17
вазо́нок, вазо́нка – house plant, plant *[potted]*, 17
вака́ції *[pl]*, вака́цій, ... вакація́х – vacation, 25
валі́зка – suitcase, valise, 18
ва́нна – bathtub, 28
ванта́жка – truck, 35
варе́ник, -а – dumpling, varenyk, perogy, 19
ва́тра, *g.pl.* ва́тер – bonfire, 25
ваш, ва́ша, ва́ше, ва́ші – your *[p]*, yours *[p]*, 28
ввечорі́/вве́чері – (see увечорі́/уве́чері)
вго́ру – (see уго́ру)
вдень – (see уде́нь)
вдоли́ну – (see удоли́ну)
вдо́ма – (see удо́ма)
ведме́дик, -а – teddy bear, 32
везти́: вез-у́, -е́ш *[dur.]* – to haul, to transport, 6
вели́кий – big, great, 26
велосипе́д, -а – bicycle, bike, 18
вера́нда – veranda, 14
ве́ресень, ве́ресня – September, 16
вертолі́т, вертольо́та – helicopter, 35

ве́рхи – on horseback, 34
вершки́, *[pl]*, вершкі́в, ... вершка́х – cream *[sweet]*, 19
ве́ршник – horseback rider, 34
ве́ршниця – horseback rider, 34
весе́лий – happy, 26
веселі́ше – more happily, more merrily, 31
веселі́ший – happier, 30
весе́лка – rainbow, 33
ве́село – happily, merrily, 31
весі́лля *[n]* – wedding reception, 27
весна́ – spring, 16
весня́ний – spring, 33
вече́ря – supper, evening meal, 15
вече́ряти: вече́ря-ю, -єш – to have supper, 4
ве́чір *[h]*, ве́чора, *pl.* вечори́ – evening, 29
вечі́рка – party, evening social, 15
вже – (see уже́)
вжива́ти – (see ужива́ти)
вжи́ти – (see ужи́ти)
взи́мку – (see узи́мку)
взя́ти: візьм-у́, -е́ш *pf.* – to take, 23
ви – you *[p]*, 2
вибира́ти: вибира́-ю, -єш – to choose, to select, 17
ви́брати: ви́бер-у, -еш *pf.* – to choose, to select, 23
виграва́ти: вигра-ю́, -є́ш – to win, 32
ви́грати: ви́гра-ю, -єш *pf.* – to win, 32
виде́лка – fork, 17
ви́йти; ви́йд-у, -еш *pf.* – to come out of, to exit, 23
ви́нен/ви́нний – to be owing something, to be at fault, guilty, blameable, 32
вино́ – wine, 15
виногра́д *[sg]*, -у – grapes, 30
ви́падок, ви́падку – accident, 29
ви́пити: ви́п'-ю, -єш *pf.* – to drink, 23
ви́прасувати: ви́прасу-ю, -єш *pf.* – to iron, 26
ви́прати: ви́пер-у, -еш *pf.* – to launder, 26
ви́рости: ви́рост-у, -еш *pf.* – to grow, 23
висо́кий – high, tall, 26
ви́со́ко – highly, 31
ви́ставка – exhibition, public display, 32
ви́терти: ви́тр-у, -еш *pf.* – to dry, 28
ви́тертися: ви́тр-уся, -ешся *pf.* – to dry oneself, 28
витира́ти: витира́-ю, -єш – to dry, 28
витира́тися: витира́-юся, -єшся – to dry oneself, 28
ви́хід, ви́ходу, *pl.* ви́ходи – exit, 35
вихо́дити: вихо́джу, вихо́д-иш – to come out of, to exit, 18
вишива́ти: вишива́-ю, -єш – to embroider, 32
ви́шивка – embroidered article, 32
ви́шити: ви́ши-ю, -єш *pf.* – embroider, 32
ви́шитий – embroidered, 32
ви́ще – higher, 31
ви́щий – taller, 30
вівто́рок, вівті́рка – Tuesday, 16
від *[+G]* – from, 18
відбува́тися: відбува́-ється, -ються – to happen, to take place, 27
відбу́тися: відбу́д-еться, -уться *pf.* – to happen, to take place, 27
ві́део *[indecl.]* – videoplayer, VCR, 17
відійти́: відійд-у́, -е́ш *pf.* – to depart *[on foot]*, 29
від'їжджа́ти: від'їжджа́-ю, -єш – to depart *[by vehicle]*, 27
від'ї́хати: від'ї́д-у, -еш *pf.* – to depart *[by vehicle]*, 27
ві́дповідь *[f]*, ві́дповіді – answer, 36
відповіда́ти: відповіда́-ю, -єш – to answer, to reply, 35
відпові́сти: відпові́-м, -си́ *pf.* – to answer, to reply, 35
відпочива́ти: відпочива́-ю, -єш – to rest, 22
відпочи́ти: відпочи́н-у, -еш *pf.* – to rest, 23
відсвяткува́ти: відсвятку́-ю, -єш *pf.* – to celebrate, 27
відсо́ток, відсо́тка – percent, 38
відхо́дити: відхо́джу, відхо́д-иш – to depart *[on foot]*, 29
відчини́ти: відчи́н-ю, -иш *pf.* – to open, 29
відчини́тися: відчи́н-иться, -яться – to be opened, 29
відчиня́ти: відчиня́-ю, -єш – to open, 29
відчиня́тися: відчиня́-ється, -ються – to be opened, 29
ві́дьма, *pl.* ві́дьми́, відьо́м – witch, 37
ві́за – visa, 18
візо́к, візка́, *pl.* візки́ – wagon, 34
вікно́, *pl.* ві́кна, ві́кон – window, 17
він – he, 2
ві́ник, -а – broom, 22
вінча́ння *[n]* – wedding ceremony, marriage, 27

вірити: вір-ю, -иш – to believe, 32
вірш, вірша – poem *[short]*, 36
вісім – eight, 19
вісімдеся́т – eighty, 19
вісімдеся́тий – eightieth, 27
вісімна́дцятий – eighteenth, 27
вісімна́дцять – eighteen, 19
вісімсо́т – eight hundred, 19
віта́льня, *g.pl.* віта́лень – living room, 14
ві́тер, ві́тру, *pl.* вітри́ – wind, 33
вітере́ць, вітерця́ – breeze, 33
вітри́льник, -а – sailboat, 25
вітри́на – showcase, display window, 14
ві́тряно – it's windy, 33
вія – eyelash, 31
віяти: ві-ю, -єш – to blow, 33
вкра́сти – (see укра́сти)
влі́тку – (see улі́тку)
вмива́ти – (see умива́ти)
вмира́ти – (see умира́ти)
вми́ти – (see уми́ти)
вмі́ти – (see умі́ти)
вниз – (see уни́з)
вночі́ – (see уночі́)
внук – grandson, 13
вну́ка – granddaughter, 13
внуча́ *[n]* – grandchild, 37
вода́, води́, *pl.* во́ди – water, 15
водій, водія́, *v.sg.* водію, *pl.* водії́ – driver, 12
водогра́й, водогра́ю – fountain, 25
водяні́ ли́жі – water skis, 34
возити: вожу́, во́з-иш *[it.]*
  – to haul, to transport, 10
волейбо́л, -у – volleyball *[game]*, 15
воло́сся *[n]* – hair, 28
вона́ – she, 2
вони́ – they, 2
воно́ – it, 2
восени́ – in the fall, 8
во́сьмий – eighth, 27
вра́нці – (see ура́нці)
все – (see усе́)
всі – (see усі́)
встава́ти – (see устава́ти)
всю́ди – (see усю́ди)
вті́шитися – (see уті́шитися)
вуж, вужа́, *pl.* вужі́ – snake, garter snake, 21

ву́жче – more narrowly, 31
ву́жчий – narrower, 30
вузьки́й – narrow, 30
ву́зько – narrowly, 31
ву́лиця – street, 14
вус, *pl.* ву́са і ву́си, *g.pl.* вус– mustache, 31
вуста́ *[pl]*, вуст – lips, 28
ву́хо – ear, 28
вчи́тель – (see учи́тель)
вчи́телька – (see учи́телька)
вчи́тися – (see учи́тися)
вчо́ра – (see учо́ра)
вхід, вхо́ду, *pl.* вхо́ди – entrance, 35
вхо́дити: вхо́джу, вхо́д-иш
  – to enter, to come into, 15
в'язни́ця – jail, 35

Г

газе́та – newspaper, 17
га́лстук, *-а* – necktie, tie, 20
галере́я – gallery, 35
гамане́ць, гаманця́, *pl.* гаманці́ – wallet, 18
гара́ж, -у – garage, 12
га́рний – nice, pretty, 26
гарні́ше – more beautifully, better, 31
гарні́ший – nicer, prettier, 30
га́рно – nicely, well, 31
ге́ній – genius, 11
герої́ня – heroine, 36
геро́й – hero, 36
гідра́нт, -а – hydrant, 35
гі́рше – worse, 4
гі́рший – worse, 30
гість, го́стя, *pl.* го́сті, госте́й, гі́стьми, го́стям, ... го́стях – guest *[m]*, 25
гіта́ра – guitar, 16
говори́ти: говор-ю́, -иш – to talk, to speak, 8
годи́на – hour, 29
годи́нник, -а – clock, watch, 17
го́йдалка – swing, 25
го́йдатися: го́йда-юся, -єшся
  – to rock, to swing, 34
го́кей, го́кею – hockey, 15
голи́ти: гол-ю́, -иш – to shave, 28
голи́тися: гол-ю́ся, -ишся – to shave oneself, 8
голова́, *pl.* го́лови, голі́в, ... голова́х
  – head, 31
голо́дний – hungry, 26

голодніше – more hungrily, 31
голодніший – hungrier, 30
гóлодно – hungrily, 31
голосніше – more loudly, 31
гóлосно – loudly, 5
голубéць, голубцá, *pl.* голубцí – cabbage roll, 19
гольф, гóльфу – golf, 15
горá, гори́, *pl.* гóри, гір – mountain, 21
горб, горбá, *pl.* горби́ – hill, 34
горíх, горíха, ... горíсі – nut, 19
гóрло, *g.pl.* гóрел і гóрлів – throat, 31
горня́тко – cup, 17
горóд, -у – garden, 30
горóдина *[sg]* – vegetables, 30
горóх *[sg]*, горóху, ... горóсі – peas, 30
гóстя, *pl.* (see гість) – guest *[f]*, 25
готéль, готéлю – hotel, 12
готíвка *[sg]* – cash, 18
готóвий – ready, prepared, 36
готувáти: готý-ю, -єш – to prepare, 15
гра, *pl.* íгри, íгор – game, 32
град, грáду – hail, 33
грани́ця – border *[of a country]*, 38
грáти: грá-ю, -єш – to play, 15
грéбінь, грéбеня – comb, 28
грек, грéка, *pl.* грéки – Greek *[m]*, 38
греки́ня – Greek *[f]*, 38
Грéція – Greece, 38
грéцький – Greek 38
гриб, грибá, *pl.* гриби́ – mushroom, 19
гримíти: грими́ть – to thunder, 33
громадя́нин, *pl.* громадя́ни, громадя́н – citizen *[m]*, 38
громадя́нка – citizen *[f]*, 38
грім, грóму – thunder, 33
грóші *[pl]*, грóшей, грíшми і грошима, грóшам, ... грóшах – money, 14
грýдень, грýдня – December, 16
грýди, *[pl]*, грудéй, грудьми́ і груди́ма, грýдям, ... грýдях, 31
грузови́к, *a* – truck, 35
грýша – pear, 30
грýшка – pear, 30
губá, *pl.* гýби, губ і губíв, ... гýбах – lip, 28
губи́ти: губ-лю́, -иш – to lose, 22
губнá помáда – lipstick, 28
гураґáн – hurricane, 33

Ґ

ґазéта – newspaper, 17
ґалерíя – gallery, 35
ґарáж, у – garage, 12
ґітáра – guitar, 16
ґольф, ґóльфу – golf, 15
ґýдзик, а – button, 22
ґýмка – eraser, 11

Д

давáти: да-ю́, -єш – to give, 20
данти́ст – dentist *[m]*, 24
данти́стка – dentist *[f]* 24
дáта – date *[calendar]*, 27
дáти: да-м, -си́ *pf.* – to give, 23
дáча – cottage, summer cottage, 25
два *[m,n]* – two, 19
двадця́тий – twentieth, 27
двáдцять – twenty, 19
дванáдцятий – twelfth, 27
дванáдцять – twelve, 19
двéрі *[pl]*, дверéй, дверми́ і двери́ма, двéрям, ... двéрях – door, 11
дві *[f]* – two, 19
двíсті – two hundred, 19
двір, дворá і двóру, *pl.* двори́ – yard, 21
де – where: in what place, 2
дев'ятдеся́т – ninety, 19
дев'ятдеся́тий – ninetieth, 27
дев'я́тий – ninth, 27
дев'ятнáдцятий – nineteenth, 27
дев'ятнáдцять – nineteen, 19
дев'янóстий – ninetieth, 27
дев'янóсто – ninety, 19
дéв'ятсóт – nine hundred, 19
дéв'ять – nine, 19
дезодорáнт, -а – deodorant, 28
денти́ст – dentist *[m]*, 24
денти́стка – dentist *[f]*, 24
день, дня – day, 16
день нарóдження *[n]* – birthday, 27
дéрево *[sg]* – wood, 32
дéрево, *pl.* дерéва – tree, 21
держáва – country, 38
десéрт, -у – dessert, 19
деся́тий – tenth, 27
дéсять – ten, 19

десь – somewhere: at some place, 7
детекти́в – detective, 36
детекти́вний – detective, 36
де́хто – some *[people]*, 6
деше́вий – inexpensive, cheap, 26
де́шево – cheaply, 31
деше́вше – more cheaply, 31
деше́вший – cheaper, 30
де́що – some *[things]*, 6
джем, *дже́му* – jam, 19
джи́нси *[pl]*, *джи́нсів, ... джи́нсах* – jeans, 20
джі́нси *[pl]*, джі́нсів, ... джі́нсах – jeans, 20
джіп, джі́па – jeep, 35
дзвони́ти: дзвон-ю́, -иш – to ring, 31
дзе́ркало, *pl.* дзеркала́, дзерка́л – mirror, 17
диви́тися: див-лю́ся, -ишся – to look at, 9
дивува́ти – to astonish someone, to amaze someone, to surprise someone, 33
дире́ктор – director *[m]*, 37
дире́кторка – director *[f]*, 37
дити́на, *pl.* ді́ти – child, 13
дитсадо́к, *дитсадка́* – kindergarten, 32
дитя́ *[n]* – baby, infant, 37
дия́вол, -а – devil, 37
дівча́та *[pl]*, дівча́т, ... дівча́тах – girls, 13
ді́вчина, *pl.* дівча́та – girl, 13
дід, *v.sg.* ді́ду! *pl.* діди́ – grandfather, 13
діду́сь – grandfather, 13
ді́дько, -а – devil, 37
діє́та – diet, 22
дім, до́му, *pl.* доми́ – home, 12
дістава́ти: діста-ю́, -є́ш – to get, 35
діста́ти: діста́н-у, -еш *pf.* – to get, 35
ді́ти *[pl]*, діте́й, дітьми, ді́тям, ... ді́тях – children, 13
для *[+G]* – for, 18
до *[+G]* – toward, 18
доба́ – twenty-four hour period, 29
до́бре – fine, well, 4
до́брий – good, 26
до́вгий – long, 26
до́вго – for a long time, 9
до́вше – for a longer time, 9
до́вший – longer, 30
догляда́ти: догляда́-ю, -єш – to look after, to take care of, 21
догля́нути: догля́н-у, -еш *pf.* – to look after, to take care of, 23

додо́му – home: towards home, 7
до́лар *[h]*, -а – dollar, 18
до́ляр *[h]*, -а – dollar, 18
до́ктор *[h]*, *pl.* доктори́ – doctor *[m]*, 12
до́кторка – doctor *[f]*, 12
до́повідь *[f]*, до́повіді – speech, 36
допомо́га – help, assistance, 36
доро́га, *pl.* доро́ги, дорі́г – road, 14
дороги́й – expensive, 26
до́рого – expensively, 31
доро́жче – more expensively, 31
доро́жчий – more expensive, 30
до́сить – enough, 19
дочка́, *pl.* до́чки, до́чок – daughter, 13
до́шка – chalkboard, 11
дощ, дощу́, *pl.* дощі́ – rain, 33
дощи́ти: дощи́ть – to rain: it's raining, 33
дощови́к, дощовика́, *pl.* дощовики́ – raincoat, 20
драби́на – ladder, 34
дру́гий – second, 27
дру́жба *[m]* – best man *[groom's attendant]*, 37
дру́жка, *pl.* дру́жки́, дру́жо́к,– bridesmaid, 37
дружи́на – wife, 13
ду́же – very, 4
ду́мати: ду́ма-ю, -єш – to think, 4
дурни́й – foolish, stupid, 26
дурні́ший – more foolish, 30
дурні́ше – more foolishly, more stupidly, 31
ду́рно – in vain; free of charge, 31
духи́ *[pl]*, духі́в, ... духа́х – perfume, 28
душ, ду́шу – shower, 28
душа́, *pl.* ду́ші, душ, ... ду́шах – soul, 37
ду́шно – it's hot, 33
дю́жина – dozen, 30
дя́дько, *pl.* дядьки́ – uncle, 13
дя́кувати: дя́ку-ю, -єш – to thank, 20

Е

Євро́па – Europe, 38
європе́єць, європе́йця – European *[m]*, 38
європе́йка – European *[f]*, 38
європе́йський – European, 38
екза́мен, -у – exam, 29
екску́рсія – excursion, outing, 25
експона́т, -а – artifact, 32

еле́ктрик – electrician, 24
електробри́тва – razor, 28
Еспанія – Spain, 38
еспа́нець, еспа́нця – Spaniard *[m]*, 38
еспа́нка – Spaniard *[f]*, 38
еспа́нський – Spanish, 38

Ж

жаке́т, а – jacket, 20
жартува́ти: жарту́-ю, -єш – to joke, 5
живі́т, живота́, *pl.* животи́ – abdomen, 31
живопліт, живопло́ту – hedge, 22
жи́ти: жив-у́, -е́ш – to live, 6
життя́ *[n]* – life, 36
жі́нка, *pl.* жінки́, жіно́к – woman, 11, wife, 13
жо́втень, жо́втня – October, 16
жо́втий – yellow, 26
жовті́ший – yellower, 30
жури́тися: жур-ю́ся, -ишся – to worry, 8
журна́л, журна́лу – magazine, 17
журналі́ст – journalist *[m]*, 24
журналі́стка – journalist *[f]*, 24

З

з (із, зі, зо) *[+G]* – from out of, 18
з (із, зі, зо) *[+I]* – with, along with, 21
за *[+I]* – behind, beyond, 21
за *[+A]* – for, 15; 18
за *[+A]* – in *[in time expressions]*, 29
заба́ва – formal dance, ball, 15
за́бавка, *pl.* забавки́, забаво́к – toy, 25
заблискати: забли́скає *pf.* – to lighten, to flash lightning, 33
заболі́ти: заболи́ть, заболя́ть – to ache, to hurt, 31
забува́ти: забува́-ю, -єш – to forget, 22
забу́ти: забу́д-у, -еш *pf.* – to forget, 23
завда́ння *[n]* – assignment, homework, 11
за́вжди – always, 3
завір'ю́ха – snowstorm, 33
заво́д, -у – factory, 35
завча́сно – too early, 29
загриміти: загрими́ть *pf.* – to thunder, 33
загуби́ти: загуб-лю́, -иш *pf.* – to lose, 23
зажу́рений – worried, 37
за́їзд, -у – driveway, 35

***зал**, за́лу* – hall, 29
за́ля – hall, 29
за́втра – tomorrow, 16
за́мість *[+G]* – instead of, in place of, 22
замо́вити: замо́в-лю, -иш *pf.* – to order, 23
замовля́ти: замовля́-ю, -єш – to order, 17
замовча́ти: замовч-у́, -и́ш *pf.* – to be silent, 23
заморо́зити: заморо́жу, заморо́з-иш *pf.*, 33
запам'ята́ти: запам'ята́-ю, -єш *pf.* – to remember, 23
запі́зно – too late, 29
запла́кати: запла́ч-у, -еш *pf.* – to cry, 23
заплати́ти: заплачу́, запла́т-иш *pf.* – to pay, 23
запра́вка – gasoline station, 35
запроси́ти: запрошу́, запро́с-иш *pf.* – to invite, 36
запро́шувати: запро́шу-ю, -єш – to invite, 36
зап'я́сток, зап'я́стка – wrist, 31
за́раз – right now, at this time, 5
зару́чуватися: зару́чу-юся, -єшся – to become engaged, 36
заручи́тися: заруч-у́ся, -ишся *pf.* – to become engaged, 36
засвиста́ти: засвищ-у́, -еш *pf.* – to whistle, 31
засі́дання *[n]* – meeting, 27
засмія́тися: засмі-ю́ся, -є́шся *pf.* – to laugh, 23
заспіва́ти: заспіва́-ю, -єш *pf.* – to sing, 23
застогна́ти: застогн-у́, -еш *pf.* – to groan, 23
за́хід, за́ходу – west, 16
захма́ритися: захма́риться *pf.* – to become cloudy, overcast, 33
захоті́ти: захо́ч-у, -еш *pf.* – to want, 23
заціка́вити: заціка́в-лю, -иш *pf.* – to be of interest to someone, 33
зачеса́ти: зачеш-у́, -еш *pf.* – to comb, 28
зачеса́тися: зачеш-у́ся, -ешся *pf.* – to comb oneself, 28
зачини́ти: зачин-ю́, -иш *pf.* – to close, 29
зачини́тися: зачи́н-иться, -яться *pf.* – to be closed, 29
зачиня́ти: зачиня́-ю, -єш – to close, 29
зачиня́тися: зачиня́-ється, -ються – to be closed, 29
за́чіска – hairdo, 28
зачі́сувати: зачі́су-ю, -єш – to comb, 28
зачі́суватися: зачі́су-юся, -єшся – to comb oneself, 28
збито́чний – mischievous, 32

збо́ри *[pl]*, збо́рів, ... збо́рах – meeting, 27
збудува́ти: збуду́-ю, -єш *pf.* – to build, 32
зва́жити: зва́ж-у, -иш *pf.* – to weigh, 23
звиха́ти: зви́ха́-ю, -єш – to sprain, 31
звихну́ти: звихн-у́, -е́ш *pf.* – to sprain, 31
звичайні́ше – more commonly, 31
звича́йно – usually, 3
зві́дки – from where, 9
зві́дси – from here, 9
зві́дти – from there, 9
звір *[h]*, звіра – animal *[wild], 25*
зготува́ти: зготу́-ю, -єш *pf.* – to prepare, 23
здава́тися: зда-є́ться, -ю́ться – to seem, 33
зда́тися: зда́-сться, зда-ду́ться *pf.* – to seem, 33
зда́ча *[sg]* – change *[money]*, 18
здивува́ти *pf.* – to astonish someone, to amaze someone, to surprise someone, 33
зді́бний – bright *[mentally]*, capable, 26
здібні́ше – more capably, 31
здібні́ший – brighter *[mentally]*, more capable, 30
зді́бно – capably, 31
здоро́вий – healthy, 26
здо́рово – healthily, 31
здоро́вше – more healthily, 31
здоро́вший – healthier, 30
зеле́ний – green, 26
зелені́ший – greener, 30
земля́, *pl.* зе́млі, земе́ль, ... зе́млях – earth, ground, 27
зе́ро – zero, 19
зима́, зими́, *pl.* зи́ми, зим – winter, 16
зимо́вий – winter, 33
зі́рка, зі́рки, *pl.* зірки́, зіро́к – star, 33
з'їзд, з'ї́зду – conference, convention, 27
з'ї́сти: з'ї-м, -си́ *pf.* – to eat, 23
зла́годити: зла́годжу, зла́год-иш *pf.* – to fix, repair, 23
злови́ти: злов-лю́, -иш *pf.* – to catch, 34
зло́дій, *pl.* злодії́ – thief *[m]*, 12
зло́дійка, *pl.* злоді́йки, злоді́йок – thief *[f]*, 12
зломи́ти: злом-лю́, -иш *pf.* – to break, 31
змага́ння *[n]* – contest, 34
зміни́ти: змін-ю́, -иш *pf.* – to change something, 33
зміни́тися: змін-ю́ся, -ишся *pf.* – to change oneself, 33
змі́нювати: змі́ню-ю, -єш – to change something, 33
змі́нюватися: змі́ню-юся, -єшся – to change oneself, 33
змогти́: змо́ж-у, -еш *pf.* – to be able, 23
зму́сити: зму́шу, зму́сиш *pf.* – to have to, 23
зму́чений – tired, exhausted, 37
знайо́мити: знайо́м-лю, -иш – to acquaint, 36
знайо́митися: знайо́м-люся, -ишся – to become acquainted, 36
знайти́: знайд-у́, -е́ш *pf.* – to find, 23
зна́ти: зна́-ю, -єш – to know, 4
знахо́дити: знахо́джу, знахо́д-иш – to find, 22
знов/зно́ву – again, 3
зо́всім не – not at all, 9
***зо́нтик**, -а* – umbrella, parasol, 18
зоопа́рк, -у – zoo, 25
зора́ти: зор-ю́, -еш *pf.* – to plough, 23
зо́шит, -а – notebook, 11
зроби́ти: зроб-лю́, -иш *pf.* – to do, 23
зрозумі́ти: зрозумі́-ю, -єш *pf.* – to understand, 23
зуб, зу́ба, *pl.* зу́би – tooth, 28
зубна́ па́ста – toothpaste, 28
зубна́ щі́тка – toothbrush, 28
зумі́ти: зумі́-ю, -єш *pf.* – to know how, 23
зу́па – soup, 19
зупи́нка – bus stop, 18
зустрі́нутися і зустрі́тися *pf.* зустрі́н-уся, -ешся – to meet, 35
зустріча́тися: зустріча́-юся -єшся – to meet, 35
зять, зя́тя, *pl.* зяті́ – son-in-law, 13

Й

його́ *[indecl.]* – his, its, 28

І

і/й – and, 3
і ... і – both ... and, 3
і́грашка – toy, 25
іко́на – icon, 32
ім'я́ *[n]*, *pl.* імена́ – name, personal name, 37
інді́єць, інді́йця – Indian *[m]*, 38
інді́йка – Indian *[f]*, 38
інді́йський – Indian, 38
І́ндія – India, 38
інжене́р *[h]* – engineer, 24
і́нколи – sometimes, 3
і́ноді – sometimes, 3

інститу́т, -у – institute, 35
інтерв'ю *[indecl.]* – interview, 37
і́нший – other, another, 36
ірля́ндець, ірля́ндця – Irishman, 38
Ірля́ндія – Ireland, 38
ірля́ндка – Irishwoman, 38
ірля́ндський – Irish, 38
і́спит, -у – exam, 29
істори́чний – historical, 36
italі́єць, італі́йця – Italian *[m]*, 38
італі́йка – Italian *[f]*, 38
італі́йський – Italian, 38
Іта́лія – Italy, 38
іти́: ід-у́, -е́ш *[dur.]* – to go/come *[on foot]*, 6

Ї

ї́да́льня, *g.pl.* їда́лень – dining room, 14
ї́здити: ї́жджу, ї́зд-иш *[it.]* – to go/come *[by vehicle]*, 10
її́ *[indecl.]* – her, hers, 28
ї́сти: їм, їси́, їсть, їмо́, їсте́, їдя́ть – to eat, 10
їх *[indecl.]* – their, theirs, 28
ї́хати: ї́д-у, -еш *[dur.]* – to go/come *[by vehicle]*, 7
ї́хній, ї́хня, ї́хнє, ї́хні – their, theirs, 28

К

кабіне́т , -у – office, 12
кабіне́т, -у – study, 14
ка́ва – coffee, 15
ка́вник, -а – coffee pot, percolator, 17
каза́ти: каж-у́, -еш – to say, 7
ка́зка, *pl.* казки́, казо́к – fairy tale, 36
календа́р *[s]*, календаря́, *pl.* календарі́ – calendar, 27
калі́ка *[m,f]* – cripple, 37
кало́рія – calorie, 22
калькуля́тор *[h]*, -а – calculator, 22
кальо́рія – calorie, 22
ка́мінь, ка́меня – stone, 22
Кана́да – Canada, 38
кана́дець, кана́дця; канаді́єць, канаді́йця – Canadian *[m]*, 38
кана́дка; канаді́йка – Canadian *[f]*, 38
кана́дський; канаді́йський – Canadian, 38
кана́па – couch, 14
кані́кули *[pl]*, кані́кул, ... кані́кулах – school holidays, 25
канцеля́рія – office, 12
капелю́х, капелю́ха, ... капелю́сі – hat, 20
ка́пець, ка́пця – slipper, 20
капу́ста *[sg]* – cabbage, 30
ка́рта – map, 35
ка́рти *[pl]*, карт – cards *[playing cards]*, 15
карти́на – painting, picture, 17
карто́пля *[sg]* – potatoes, 30
карусе́ля – merry-go-round, 34
карусе́ль *[f]*, *карусе́лі* – merry-go-round, 34
ка́са – cash register, 14
касе́та – cassette, 25
каси́р *[h]* – cashier *[m]*, 14
каси́рка – cashier *[f]*, 14
ката́тися: ката́-юся, -єшся – to engage in a leisure activity that involves movement on something, 34
кафете́рій – cafeteria, 12
кафете́рія – cafeteria, 12
ка́ша – porridge, 19
кварта́л, -у – block *[city block]*, 35
кварти́ра – apartment, 12
квасо́ля *[sg]* – beans, 30
квито́к, квитка́, *pl.* квитки́ – ticket, 15
кві́тень, кві́тня – April, 16
квітни́к, квітника́, *pl.* квітники́ – flower bed, 22
кві́тка, *pl.* квітки́, квіто́к – flower, 21
кед, ке́да – running shoe, gym shoe, 20
ке́пка – baseball cap, 20
кида́ти: кида́-ю, -єш – to throw, 34
ки́ли́м, -а, *pl.* килими́ – rug, 14
ки́нути: ки́н-у, -еш *pf.* – to throw, 34
кита́єць, кита́йця – Chinese *[m]*, 38
Кита́й – China, 38
кита́йка – Chinese *[f]*, 38
кита́йський – Chinese, 38
кише́ня – pocket, 22
кілогра́м, -а – kilogram, 19
кіломе́тр *[h]*, -а – kilometer, 34
кі́лька – several, some, a few, 19
кі́лькість *[f]*, кі́лькости – quantity, 36
кільце́ – ring, 28
кімна́та – room, 14
кіне́ць, кінця́, *pl.* кінці́ – end, 29
кіно́ *[indecl.]* – movies, movie theatre, 15
кінча́ти: кінча́-ю, -єш – to end, to finish, 29

кінча́тися: кінча́-ється, -ються
– to come to an end, 29
кінь, коня́ *pl.* ко́ні, ко́ней, кі́ньми, ко́ням,
... ко́нях – horse, 21
кіо́ск, -а – kiosk, 35
кі́стка, *pl.* кістки́, кісто́к – bone, 31
кі́сточка, *pl.* кісточки́, кісточо́к – ankle, 31
кістя́к, кістяка́, *pl.* кістяки́ – skeleton, 31
кіт, кота́, *pl.* коти́ – cat, 21
клас, кла́су – class, classroom, 11
кла́сти: клад-у́, -е́ш – to place, to put, 15
кли́кати: кли́ч-у, -еш – to call, to summon, 35
кліє́нт – client *[m]*, 24
кліє́нтка – client *[f]*, 24
клі́мат, -у – climate, 33
ключ, ключа́, *pl.* ключі́ – key, 18
кля́са, *g.pl.* кляс і кля́сів – class, classroom, 11
книга́рня, *g.pl.* книга́рень – bookstore, 14
кни́жка, *pl.* книжки́, книжо́к – book, 11
ковбаса́, *pl.* ковба́си – sausage, 19
ковбо́й – cowboy, 37
ко́вдра, *pl.* ко́вдри, ковдр і ко́вдер,
... ко́вдрах – quilt, 22
ковза́н, ковзана́, *pl.* ковзани́ – skate, 34
ко́взанка – skating rink, 34
ковзаня́р *[h]*, ковзаняра́, *pl.* ковзанярі́
– skater *[m]*, 34
ковзаня́рка – skater *[f]*, 34
ко́взатися: ко́вза-юся, -єшся – to skate, 34
ковта́ти: ковта́-ю, -єш – to swallow, 31
ковтну́ти: ковтн-у́, -е́ш – to swallow, 31
ко́жен/ко́жний – every, everyone, 32
кожу́х, кожу́ха, ... кожу́ху і ... кожу́сі
– fur coat, 20
кокте́йль, кокте́йлю – cocktail, 15
коли́ – when, 5
колі́но – knee, 31
ко́лір, ко́льору – colour, 32
ко́ло *[+G]* – beside, by, 18
кома́нда – team, 34
кома́р *[h]*, комара́, *n.pl.* комарі́ – mosquito, 21
комо́ра, *g.pl.* комо́р – pantry, storage room, 14
комп'ю́тер *[h]*, -а – computer, 11
конве́рт, -а – envelope, 18
конве́рта – envelope, 18
ко́нкурс, -у – competition, 32
конце́рт, конце́рту – concert, 15
кора́лі *[pl]*, кора́лів, ... кора́лях – coral beads, 28
кордо́н, -у – border *[of a country]*, 38
коре́єць, коре́йця – Korean *[m]*, 38
коре́йка – Korean *[f]*, 38
коре́йський – Korean, 38
Коре́я – Korea, 38
коридо́р *[h]*, -а – corridor, 11
кори́чневий – brown, 26
коро́бка, *pl.* коробки́, коробо́к – box, 25
коро́ва, *g.pl.* корі́в – cow, 21
коро́ткий – short, brief, 26
ко́ротко – briefly, 31
коро́тше – more briefly, 31
коро́тший – shorter, briefer, 30
коса́рка – lawn mower, 22
костю́м, -а – suit, 20
ко́тедж, -у – cottage, summer cottage, 25
котри́й – which, 26
коха́ти: коха́-ю, -єш – to love, to cherish, 36
ко́шик, -а – basket, 25
коштува́ти: кошту́-ю, -єш – to cost, 17
крава́тка – tie, 20
край, кра́ю, *pl.* краї́ – country, 38
краї́на – country, 38
краси́вий – beautiful, 26
крамни́ця – store, 14
кра́сти: крад-у́, -е́ш – to steal, 6
кра́ще – better, 4
кра́щий – better, 30
кра́яти: кра́-ю, -єш – to cut, to slice, 21
кре́йда *[sg]* – chalk, 11
крем, кре́му: крем для рук – hand lotion, 28
кри́жі *[pl]*, кри́жів, ... кри́жах
– back *[lower]*, 31
кри́кнути: кри́кн-у, -еш *pf.*
– to shout, to scream, 23
крича́ти: крич-у́, -и́ш – to shout, to scream, 8
крім *[+G]* – besides, except for, 22
крі́сло – chair, 12
кров *[f]*, кро́ви – blood, 36
ку́бик, -а – block *[child's toy]*, 32
куди́ – where: to what place, 7
куди́сь – somewhere: to some place, 7
кузе́н – cousin *[m]*, 13
кузи́на – cousin *[f]*, 13
кузи́нка – cousin *[f]*, 13
кукуру́дза *[sg]* – corn, 30
кула́к, кулака́, *pl.* кулаки́ – fist, 31
ку́льчик, -а – earring, 28

купáльник, -а – bathing suit, 20
купáти: купá-ю, -єш – to give a bath, 28
купáтися: купá-юся, -єшся – to bathe oneself, 5
купи́ти: куп-лю́, -иш *pf.* – to buy, 23
купувáти: купý-ю, -єш – to buy, 5
кури́ти: кур-ю́, -иш – to smoke, 8
кýртка – jacket, 20
кутóк, кутка́, *pl.* кутки́ – corner, 17
кýхар *[s]*, *pl.* кухарí – chef, cook, 24
кухáрка – chef, cook, 24
кýхня, *g.pl.* кýхонь – kitchen, 14
кущ, кущá, *pl.* кущí – bush, 21

Л

лабораторíя – laboratory, 22
лáва – bench, 21
лáвка – bench, 21
лáгодити: лáгоджу, лáгод-иш
– to fix, to repair, 21
лáзанка – jungle gym, 34
лáзити *[it.]*: лáжу, лáз-иш – to climb, to crawl, 34
лазни́чка – bathroom, 14
лáмпа – lamp, 17
легки́й – easy, light , 30
лéгко – easily, lightly , 31
лéгше – more easily, more lightly, 31
лéгший – easier, lighter , 30
лежáти: леж-ý, -и́ш – to be lying down, 8
лéкція – lesson, lecture, 11
летíти: лечý, лет-и́ш *[dur.]* – to fly, 9
летóвище – airport, 35
ли́жа – ski, 34
ли́жник – skier *[m]*, 34
ли́жниця – skier *[f]*, 34
лимóн, *-а* – lemon, 19
ли́пень, ли́пня – July, 16
лист, листá, *pl.* листи́ – letter, 18
листíвка – postcard, 18
листонóша *[m,f]* – letter carrier, 37
листопáд, -а – November, 16
лицé, лиця́, *pl.* ли́ця, лиц – face, 31
лицемíр *[h]* – hypocrite, 37
лишáти: лишá-ю, -єш – to leave, 22
лишé – only, 9
лиши́ти: лиш-ý, -иш *pf.* – to leave, 23
лівóруч – to the left, 6
лід, **льóду**, ... **льодý**, *pl.* **льоди́** – ice, 34
лíжко, *g.pl.* лíжок – bed, 14
лíзти *[dur.]*: лíз-у, -еш – to climb, to crawl, 34
лíкар *[s]*, *pl.* лікарí – doctor *[m]*, 12
лíкарка – doctor *[f]*, 12
лікáрня, *g.pl.* лікáрень – hospital, 12
лíки *[pl]*, лíків, ... лíках, – medicine, 31
лíкоть, лíктя – elbow, 31
лíпше – better, 4
лíпший – better, 30
ліс, лíсу, *pl.* ліси́, лісíв – forest, 21
літáк, літакá, *pl.* літаки́, літакíв – airplane, 18
літáти: літá-ю, -єш *[it.]* – to fly, 10
лíтній *[s]* – summer, 33
лíто – summer, 16
літр *[h]*, лíтра – litre, 30
лíфт, лíфта – elevator *[in a building]*, 35
ліхтáр *[s]*, ліхтаря́, *pl.* ліхтарí – street light, 35
ліхтáрик, -а – flashlight, 18
ліча́льник, -а – parking meter, 35
лови́ти: лов-лю́, -иш – to catch, 34
лóжечка, *pl.* ложечки́, ложечóк – teaspoon, 17
лóжка, *pl.* ложки́, ложóк – spoon, 17
ломи́ти: лом-лю́, -иш – to break, 31
лотерéя – lottery, 32
лошá *[n]* – colt, 37
люби́ти: люб-лю́, -иш – to love, to like, 9
любóв *[f]*, любóви – love, 36
лю́ди *[pl]*, людéй, людьми́, лю́дям, ... лю́дях
– people, 13
люди́на, *pl.* лю́ди – person, 13
лю́тий *[sub.]*, лю́того – February, 16
ляборатóрія – laboratory, 22
лягáти: лягá-ю, -єш – to lie down, 16
лягти́: ля́ж-у, -еш *pf.* – to lie down, 23
ля́лька, *pl.* ляльки́, ляльóк – doll, 32
ля́мпа – lamp, 17
льотерíя – lottery, 32

М

мáбуть – probably, 3
магази́н, *-у* – store, 14
майдáнчик, -а – playground, 25
мáйже – almost, 9
майнó *[sg]* – property, wealth, 38
малéнький – little, small, 26

мали́й – little, small, 26

ма́ло – little, not much, 4

малюва́ти: малю́-ю, -єш – to paint, 32

маля́р *[mx]*, маляра́, *pl.* малярі́ – painter, 24

маля́рка – painter *[f]*, 24

ма́ма, *pl.* мами́, мамі́в – mother, mom, 13

ма́па – map, 35

маргари́н, -у – margarine, 19

марґари́на – margarine, 19

ма́рка – stamp, postage stamp, 18

мармела́д, -у – marmalade, 19

мармеля́да – marmalade, 19

маршру́т, -у – itinerary, 29

ма́сло – butter, 19

ма́ти: ма́-ю, -єш – to have, 15

ма́ти *[f]*, ма́тері, *pl.* матері́ – mother, 36

маши́на – car, automobile, 12

ме́блі *[pl]*, ме́блів, ... ме́блях – furniture, 14

мед, ме́ду, *pl.* меди́ – honey, 19

меда́ля – medal, 34

меда́ль *[f]*, меда́лі – medal, 34

медбра́т, *pl.* медбрати́ – nurse *[m]*, 12

медсестра́, *pl.* медсе́стри, медсесте́р, медсе́страми, медсе́страм, ... медсе́страх – nurse *[f]*, 12

медо́вий мі́сяць – honeymoon, 36

ме́нше – less, 4

ме́нший – smaller, 30

меню́ *[indecl.]* – menu, 22

мер *[h]*, ме́ра – mayor, 37

мета́л, -у – metal, 32

мета́ль, -ю – metal, 32

мете́лик, -а – butterfly, 21

метро́ *[indecl.]* – subway, 29

меха́нік – mechanic, 12

мехіка́нець, мехіка́нця – Mexican *[m]*, 38

мехіка́нка – Mexican *[f]*, 38

мехіка́нський – Mexican, 38

Ме́хіко – Mexico, 38

ми – we, 2

мину́лий – past, 33

ми́ло – soap, 28

ми́ля – mile, 34

ми́ска, *pl.* миски́, мисо́к – bowl, soup bowl, 17

ми́тниця – customs *[at a border crossing]*, 38

ми́то – duty *[on imported goods]*, 38

між *[+I]* – among, between, 21

мій, моя́, моє́, мої́ – mine, my, 28

міліціоне́р *[h]* – police officer, 12

мі́нус – minus, 33

міну́та – minute, 29

міст, моста́ і мо́сту, *pl.* мости́ – bridge, 21

мі́сто, *pl.* міста́, міст – city, town, 12

мі́сце, *pl.* місця́, місці́в і місць – place, location, 11

мі́сяць, мі́сяця, *pl.* місяці́ – month, moon, 16

мітла́, мітли́, *pl.* мі́тли, мі́тел – broom, 22

міша́ти: міша́-ю, -єш – to stir, to mix, to shuffle, 21

міше́чок, міше́чка – bag, 25

мо́ва – language, 38

мовча́ти: мовч-у́, -и́ш – to be silent, 8

могти́: мо́ж-у, -еш – to be able, 6

мо́же – perhaps, maybe, 3

можли́во – perhaps, maybe, 3

мо́жна – it is possible, permitted, 9

молода́ *[sub.]*, молодо́ї – bride, 26

молоди́й *[sub.]*, молодо́го – bridegroom, 26

молоди́й – young, 26

мо́лодо – youthfully, 31

моло́дше – more youthfully, 31

моло́дший – younger, 30

молоко́, *pl.* моло́ка, моло́к – milk, 15

мо́ре, *pl.* моря́, морі́в – sea, 21

мо́рква *[sg]* – carrots, 30

моро́з, -у – frost, 33

моро́зиво – ice cream, 19

морози́льник, -а – deep freeze, freezer, 17

моро́зити: моро́жу, моро́з-иш – to freeze, 33

моте́ль, моте́лю – motel, 12

мотоса́ни *[pl]*, мотосане́й, мотосаньми́, ... мотоса́нях – snowmobile, 34

мотоци́кл, -а – motorcycle, 18

му́дрий – wise, smart, 26

мудрі́ше – more wisely, more smartly, 31

мудрі́ший – wiser, smarter, 30

му́дро – wisely, smartly, 31

муж, му́жа, *pl.* мужі́ – husband, 13

музе́й, музе́ю – museum, 11

му́зика – music, 32

музика́нт – musician *[m]*, 24

музика́нтка – musician *[f]*, 24

му́сити: му́шу, му́с-иш – to have to, 9

му́скул, -а – muscle, 31

му́ха – fly, 21

м'яз, м'я́за – muscle, 31
м'яса́рня, *g.pl.* м'яса́рень – meat market, 35
м'я́со – meat, 19
м'яч, м'яча́, *pl.* м'ячі́ – ball *[games, sports]*, 25

Н

на *[+L], [+A]* – on, at, 14
на *[+A]* – for, 15; 18
навесні́ – in the spring, 8
на́віть – even, 4
навчи́тися: навч-у́ся, -и́шся *pf.* – to learn, to study, 23
навшпи́ньки – on tiptoe, 34
нагоро́да – prize, 34
над *[+I]* – overhead, above, 21
надві́р – outdoors: to the outdoors, 7
надво́рі – outdoors: in the outdoors, 2
наді́ятися: наді́-юся, -єшся – to hope, 32
на́зва – name *[of book, object]*, 36
нали́сник, -а – crepe, nalysnyk, 19
намалюва́ти: намалю́-ю, єш *pf.* – to paint *[a picture]*, 32
нами́сто – necklace, 28
написа́ти: напиш-у́, -еш *pf.* – to write, 23
напле́чник, -а – knapsack, 11
нарече́на *[sub.]*, нарече́ної – fiancé, 36
нарече́ний *[sub.]*, нарече́ного – fiancée, 36
наро́д, -у – nation, 38
наро́джувати: наро́джу-ю, -єш – to give birth, 27
наро́джуватися: наро́джу-юся, -єшся – to be born, 27
народи́ти: народжу́, наро́д-иш *pf.* – to give birth, 27
народи́тися: народжу́ся, наро́д-ишся *pf.* – to be born, 27
насе́лення *[n]* – population, 38
насту́пний – following, next, 33
науко́вець, науко́вця – scientist, 24
на́ція – nation, 38
нача́льник – boss, manager *[m]*, 12
нача́льниця – boss, manager *[f]*, 12
наш, на́ша, на́ше, на́ші – our, ours, 28
не – not, 4
небага́то – not much, little, 4
не́бо, *pl.* небеса́ – heaven, sky, 27
неві́стка – daughter-in-law, 13
него́да – bad weather, 33
недале́ко *[+G]* – not far from, 22
неді́ля – Sunday, 16
недороги́й – inexpensive, cheap, 26
незаба́ром – soon, in a short time, 29
нема́/нема́є – there is no, there are no, 19
немовля́ *[n]* – baby, infant *[human]*, 37
ненадо́вго – for a short time, 29
неодру́жений – unmarried, 37
неприє́мний – unpleasant, 26
неро́ба *[m,f]* – lazybones, 37
несподі́ванка – surprise, 34
нести́: нес-у́, -е́ш *[dur.]* – to carry, 6
нетерпели́вий – impatient, 37
нечепу́ра *[m,f]* – slob, 37
нече́сний – dishonest, dishonourable, 37
нещасли́вий – unfortunate, unlucky, 26
неща́сний – miserable, unhappy, 26
ни́жче – lower, 33
ни́ні – today, 9
ні – no, 2
ні . . . ні – neither . . . nor, 3
ні́готь, ні́гтя – fingernail, toenail, 31
ніде́ – nowhere: at no place, 7
ніж – than, 30
ніж, ножа́, *pl.* ножі́ – knife, 17
ніко́ли – never, 7
ніку́ди – nowhere: to no place, 7
ніс, но́са, *pl.* носи́ – nose, 31
ніхто́ – no one, nobody, 6
Німе́ччина – Germany, 38
ні́мець, ні́мця – German *[m]*, 38
німе́цький – German, 38
ні́мка – German *[f]*, 38
німке́ня – German *[f]*, 38
ніч *[f]*, но́чі – night, 29
нічо́ – nothing, 6
нови́й – new, 26
новина́, *pl.* нови́ни – news item, 29
нови́нка – news item, 29
нові́ший – newer, 30
нога́, *pl.* но́ги, ніг – foot, 31
но́жиці *[pl]*, но́жиць, ... но́жицях – scissors, 17
носи́ти: ношу́, но́с-иш *[it.]* – to carry, to wear, 10
нудни́й – boring, 32

нуль, нуля́, *pl.* нулі́ – zero, 19
ня́ня – baby sitter, nanny, 25
ня́нька, *pl.* няньки́, няньо́к – baby sitter, nanny, 25

О

о/об *[+L]* – at *[in time expressions]*, 29
обі́д, -у – dinner, meal at noon, 15
обі́д: після обі́ду – in the afternoon, 8
обі́дати: обі́да-ю, -єш – to have dinner, 4
обли́ччя *[n], g.pl.* обли́ччів і обли́ч – face, 31
о́браз, -а, *pl.* образи́ – painting, picture, 17
обру́с, -а – tablecloth, 22
о́воч, -у – fruit, 30
***о́воч**, -у* – vegetable, 30
огіро́к, огірка́, *pl.* огірки́ – cucumber, 30
оголо́шення *[n]* – advertisement, 28
оде́ржувати: оде́ржу-ю, -єш – to receive, 22
оде́ржати: оде́рж-у, -иш – to receive, 23
оди́н *[m]* – one, 19
одина́дцятий – eleventh, 27
одина́дцять – eleven, 19
одна́ *[f]* – one, 19
одне́ *[n]* – one, 19
одру́жений – married, 37
одружи́тися: одру́ж-уся, -ишся *pf.* – to marry, to get married, 23
одру́жуватися: одру́жу-юся, -єшся – to marry, to get married, 5
о́дяг *[sg]*, -у – clothes, clothing, 20
одяга́ти: одяга́-ю, -єш, – to dress, 28
одяга́тися: одяга́-юся, -єшся, – to dress, 5
одягну́ти: одягн-у́, -еш *pf.* – to dress, 28
одягну́тися: одягн-у́ся, -ешся *pf.* – to dress oneself, 23
о́зеро, *pl.* озе́ра, озер і озір – lake, 21
о́ко, о́ка, ... о́ці, *pl.* о́чі, оче́й, очи́ма, очa̍м, ... оча́х – eye, 31
окулі́ст – oculist, optometrist, 24
окуля́ри *[pl]*, окуля́рів, ... окуля́рах – eyeglasses, 18
олíве́ць, олівця́, *pl.* олівці́ – pencil, 11
он – there, 2
ону́к – grandson, 13
ону́ка – granddaughter, 13
онуча́ *[n]* – grandchild, 37

о́пис, -у – description, 36
опі́вдні – at noon, 29
опі́вночі – at midnight, 29
оповіда́ння *[n]* – short story, 36
оптимі́ст – optimist *[m]*, 32
оптимі́стка – optimist *[f]*, 32
ора́нжевий – orange, 26
ора́ти: ор-ю́, -еш – to plough, 7
Організа́ція Об'є́днаних На́цій (ООН) – United Nations (UN), 38
***орке́стр** [h], -у* – orchestra, 16
орке́стра – orchestra, 16
осе́ля – summer camp, camp, 25
осі́нній *[s]* – fall, 33
о́сінь *[f]*, о́сени – autumn, fall, 16
оста́нній *[s]* – last, 33
ось – here, 2
офіціа́нт – waiter, 13
офіція́нт – waiter, 13
офіціа́нтка – waitress, 13
офіція́нтка – waitress, 13

П

па́дати: па́да-ю, -єш – to fall, 22
паку́нок, паку́нка – parcel, 18
па́лець, па́льця – finger, 28
па́лець на нозі́ – toe, 31
пальто́ *pl.* па́льта – coat *[winter]*, 20
пампу́шка – doughnut, 30
па́м'ятник, -а – monument, 21
пам'ята́ти: пам'ята́-ю, -єш – to remember, 4
пан, па́на, *pl.* пани́, *v.pl.* пано́ве – Mr., sir, 13
па́ні *[indecl.]* – Mrs., madam, 13
па́нна, *pl.* панни́, панні́в – Miss, 13
панчо́ха, *g.pl.* панчі́х – stocking, 20
папі́р *[h]*, папе́ру – paper, 32
парасо́ля – umbrella, parasol, 18
***парасо́ль**, -я* – umbrella, parasol, 18
парк, па́рку – park, 21
па́рка – parka, 20
парка́н, паркана́, *pl.* паркани́ – fence, 21
па́рно – it's sultry, 33
пасо́к, паска́, *pl.* паски́ – belt, 20
па́спорт, -а – passport, 18
паціє́нт – patient *[m]*, 12
паціє́нтка – patient *[f]*, 12

па́хощі *[pl]*, па́хощі, па́хощів, ... па́хощах – perfume, 28

па́чка, *pl.* пачки́, пачо́к – package, carton, 18

пе́вен/пе́вний – sure, certain, 32

пе́кар *[s]* – baker *[m]*, 24

пе́карка – baker *[f]*, 24

пека́рня – bakery, 35

пе́кло – hell, 27

пекти́: печ-у́, -е́ш – to bake, 32

пе́ред *[+I]* – in front of, before, 21

пере́клад, -у – translation, 36

переклада́ти: перекладá-ю, -єш – to translate, 36

перекладá́ч – translator *[m]*, 36

перекладá́чка – translator *[f]*, 36

перекла́сти: переклад-у́, -е́ш *pf.* – to translate, 36

пере́куска – snack, light lunch, 15

перехі́д, перехо́ду – crosswalk, 35

перехре́стя *[n]* – intersection, 12

перо́, *pl.* пе́ра – pen, 11

пе́рсик, -а – peach, 30

пе́рстінь, пе́рстеня, *pl.* пе́рстені – ring, 28

перука́р *[s]* – hair stylist, hairdresser *[m]*, 24

перука́рка – hair stylist, hairdresser *[f]*, 24

перука́рня – hair salon, 35

пе́рший – first, 27

пес, пса, *pl.* пси – dog, 21

песимі́ст – pessimist *[m]*, 32

песимі́стка – pessimist *[f]*, 32

пе́чиво *[sg]* – baked goods, pastry, 30

п'є́са – play, 36

пивни́ця – basement, 14

пи́во – beer, 15

пилосмо́к, -а – vacuum cleaner, 17

пилосо́с, -а – vacuum cleaner, 17

пирі́г, пирога́, *pl.* пироги́ – dumpling, varenyk, perogy, 19

пи́санка, *pl.* писанки́, писано́к – pysanka, Easter egg, 32

писа́ти: пиш-у́, -еш – to write, 7

письме́нник – writer *[m]*, 36

письме́нниця – writer *[f]*, 36

пита́ння *[n]* – question, 36

пита́ти: пита́-ю, -єш – to ask, to inquire, 4

пи́ти: п'-ю, -єш – to drink, 5

піані́но *[indecl.]* – piano, 16

пів – half, 29

півгоди́ни – half an hour, 29

пі́вдень, пі́вдня – noon, south, 16

пі́вніч *[f]*, пі́вночі – midnight, north, 16

пігу́лка – pill, 31

під *[+I]* – under, beneath, 21

підборі́ддя *[n]*, *g.pl.* підборі́дь і підборі́ддів – chin, 31

підва́л, -у – basement, 14

підзе́мка – subway, 29

підло́га, *g.pl.* підло́г – floor, 14

підру́чник, -а – textbook, 11

піжа́ма *[sg]* – pyjamas, 20

пі́зній *[s]* – late, 33

пізні́ше – later, 10

пі́зно – late, 5

пікні́к, пікні́ка́, *pl.* пікніки́ – picnic, 21

піло́т – pilot, 24

пілю́ля – pill, 31

пі́сля *[+G]* – after, 18

післяза́втра – day after tomorrow, 16

пі́сля обі́ду – in the afternoon, 8

пісо́к, піску́, *pl.* піски́ – sand, 25

пі́сня, *pl.* пісні́, пісе́нь – song, 32

піти́: під-у́, -е́ш *pf.* – to go, to walk, 23

пі́шки – on foot, 34

піч *[f]*, печі́ – oven, 36

піяні́но – piano, 16

пла́вати: пла́ва-ю, -єш *[it.]* – to swim, 10

пла́кати: пла́ч-у, -еш – to cry, 7

пласти́нка – record *[music]*, 25

плати́ти: плачу́, пла́т-иш – to pay, 9

платі́вка – record *[music]*, 25

платня́ – salary, wages, 37

пла́ття *[n]* – dress, 20

плащ, плаща́, *pl.* плащі́ – coat *[spring, fall]*, 20

племі́нник – nephew, 13

племі́нниця – niece, 13

плече́, *pl.* пле́чі, плече́й, плечи́ма, пле́чам, ... пле́чах – shoulder, 31

плисти́: плив-у́, -е́ш *[dur.]* – to swim, 6

плюс – plus, 33

пляж, пля́жу – beach, 21

пля́ма – spot, stain, 22

пля́шка, *pl.* пляшки́, пляшо́к – bottle, 30

по *[+A]*; *[+L]* – for, 22; all over, about, 34

поба́витися: поба́в-люся, -ишся *pf.* – to play, 34

поба́чення *[n]* – appointment, date, 29

поба́чити: поба́ч-у, -иш *pf.* – to see, 23
побі́гти: побіж-у́, -и́ш *pf.* – to run, 23
поборо́тися: побор-ю́ся, -ешся *pf.* – to fight, 23
повезти́: повез-у́, -е́ш *pf.* – to haul, to transport, 23
поверну́ти: поверн-у́, -еш *pf.*
– to give back, to return, 29
поверну́тися: поверн-у́ся, -ешся *pf.*
– to come back, to return, 29
поверта́ти: поверта́-ю, -єш
– to give back, to return, 29
поверта́тися: поверта́-юся, -єшся
– to come back, to return, 29
повече́ряти: повече́ря-ю, -єш *pf.*
– to have supper, 23
пови́дло – jam, 19
пови́нен/пови́нний – ought, should, 32
пові́льний – slow, 32
пові́льно – slowly, 5
повільні́ше – more slowly, 31
по́вінь *[f]*, по́вені – flood, 36
пові́рити: пові́р-ю, -иш *pf.* – to believe, 32
по́вість *[f]*, по́вісті, повісте́й – novelette, 36
пові́яти: пові́-ю, -єш *pf.* – to blow, 33
пово́лі – slowly, 5
повто́рювати: повто́рю-ю, -єш
і **повторя́ти**: повторя́-ю, -єш – to repeat, 35
повтори́ти: повтор-ю́, -иш *pf.* – to repeat, 35
пога́ний – bad, 26
пога́но – badly, poorly, 4
поговори́ти: поговор-ю́, -иш *pf.* – to talk, 23
пого́да – weather, 33
пого́йдатися: пого́йда-юся, -єшся *pf.*
– to rock, to swing, 34
поголи́ти: погол-ю́, -иш *pf.* – to shave, 28
поголи́тися: погол-ю́ся, -ишся *pf.*
– to shave oneself, 23
погра́ти: погра́-ю, -єш *pf.* – to play, 23
подару́нок, подару́нка – gift, present, 18
пода́ток, пода́тку – tax, 38
подзвони́ти: подзвон-ю́, -иш – to ring, 31
подиви́тися: подив-лю́ся, -ишся *pf.*
– to look at, 23
поді́бний – similar, 36
подо́батися: подо́ба-юся, -єшся – to appeal, 33
по́дорож *[f]*, по́дорожі – trip, 36
поду́мати: поду́ма-ю, -єш *pf.* – to think, 23
по́душка, *pl.* по́ду́шки, по́ду́шок – pillow, 22
подя́кувати: подя́ку-ю, -єш *pf.* – to thank, 23
пое́ма – poem *[long]*, 36

пое́т – poet *[m]*, 36
поете́са – poet *[f]*, 36
пое́зія – poetry, 36
пожартува́ти: пожарту́-ю, -єш *pf.* – to joke, 23
поже́жна маши́на – fire truck, 35
поже́жник – fire fighter, 35
пожи́ти: пожив-у́, -е́ш *pf.* – to live, 23
пожури́тися: пожур-ю́ся, -ишся *pf.*
– to worry, 23
позавчо́ра – day before yesterday, 16
позича́ти: позича́-ю, -єш
– to lend, to borrow, 20
пози́чити: пози́ч-у, -иш *pf.*
– to lend, to borrow, 23
по́зичка – loan, 37
познайо́мити: познайо́м-лю, -иш *pf.*
– to acquaint, 36
познайо́митися: познайо́м-люся, -ишся *pf.*
– to become acquainted, 36
по́їзд, -а, *pl.* поїзди́ – train, 18
пої́хати: пої́д-у, -еш *pf.*
– to go by vehicle, to ride, 23
показа́ти: покаж-у́, -еш *pf.* – to show, 31
пока́зувати: пока́зу-ю, -єш – to show, 31
поката́тися: поката́-юся, -єшся *pf.*
– to engage in a leisure activity that involves movement on something, 34
покла́сти: поклад-у́, -еш *pf.*
– to place, to put, 23
покли́кати: покли́ч-у, -еш *pf.*
– to call, to summon, 35
поко́взатися: поко́вза-юся, -єшся *pf.*
– to skate, 34
покоха́ти: покоха́-ю, -єш – to love, to cherish, 36
покра́яти: покра́-ю, -єш *pf.* – to cut, 23
покупе́ць, покупця́, *pl.* покупці́
– customer *[m]*, 14
поку́пка – purchase, purchased item, 30
покупни́ця – customer *[f]*, 14
покури́ти: покур-ю́, -иш *pf.* – to smoke, 23
по́ле, *pl.* поля́, піль і полі́в – field, 21
поле́жати: поле́ж-у, -иш *pf.*
– to be lying down, 23
полеті́ти: полечу́, полет-и́ш *pf.* – to fly, 23
поли́ця – shelf, 14
поліца́й – police officer, 12
полі́зти: полі́з-у, -еш *pf.* – to climb, to crawl, 34
полуни́ця – strawberry, 30

полюби́ти: полюб-лю́, -иш *pf.*
– to love, to like, 23

поля́к, поляка́, *pl.* поляки́ – Pole *[m]*, 38

по́лька – Pole *[f]*, 38

по́льський – Polish, 38

По́льща – Poland, 38

помага́ти: помага́-ю, -єш – to help, to assist, 20

пома́лу – slowly, 5

помалюва́ти: помалю́-ю, -єш *pf.*
– to paint (a building, etc.), 32

помара́нча – orange, 15

помара́нчовий – orange, 26

поме́рти: помр-у́, -е́ш – to die, 27

поме́шкання *[n]* – apartment, 12

помідо́р *[h]*, -а – tomato, 30

по́міч *[f]*, по́мочі – assistance, help, 36

поміша́ти: поміша́-ю, -єш *pf.*
– to stir, to mix, to shuffle, 23

помогти́: помо́ж-у́, -еш *pf.* – to help, to assist, 23

понеді́лок, понеді́лка – Monday, 16

понести́: понес-у́, -е́ш *pf.* – to carry, 23

поноси́ти: поношу́, поно́с-иш *pf.* – to wear, 23

пообі́дати: пообі́да-ю, -єш *pf.*
– to have dinner, 23

поплисти́: поплив-у́, -е́ш *pf.* – to swim, 23

попо́лудні – in the afternoon, 8

попрацюва́ти: попрацю́-ю, -єш *pf.*
– to work, 23

попроси́ти: попрошу́, попро́с-иш *pf.*
– to request, to plead, 23

пора́ – season, time, 16

пора́дити: пора́джу, пора́д-иш *pf.*
– to advise, to give advice, 35

порозмовля́ти: порозмовля́-ю, -єш *pf.*
– to converse, to speak, 23

портфе́ль, -я – briefcase, 11

посвіти́ти: посвічу́, посві́т-иш *pf.*
– to shine for a while, 33

поси́діти: поси́джу, поси́д-иш *pf.*
– to be sitting, 23

посила́ти: посила́-ю, -єш – to send, 20

поска́ржитися: поска́рж-уся, -ишся *pf.*
– to complain, 23

посла́ти: пошл-ю́, -еш *pf.* – to send, 23

послу́хати: послу́ха-ю, -єш *pf.* – to listen, 23

посміти: посмі́-ю, -єш *pf.* – to dare, 36

поснідати: посні́да-ю, -єш *pf.*
– to have breakfast, 23

посо́л, посла́, *pl.* посли́ – ambassador, 38

посо́льство – embassy, 38

поспа́ти: посп-лю́, -и́ш *pf.* – to sleep, 23

поспіши́ти: поспіш-у́, -и́ш *pf.* – to hurry, 23

посто́яти: посто́-ю, -їш *pf.*
– to stand, to be standing, 23

по́суд *[sg]*, -у – dishes, 17

посудоми́йка, *g.pl.* посудоми́йок
– dishwasher, 17

потанцюва́ти: потанцю́-ю, -єш *pf.*
– to dance, 23

потелефонува́ти: потелефону́-ю, -єш *pf.*
– to telephone, 23

по́тім – afterwards, then, 5

потрі́бен/потрі́бний – needed, necessary, 33

потрі́бно – it is needed, it is necessary, 20

по́тяг, -у – train, 18

похвали́ти: похвал-ю́, -иш *pf.* – to praise, 29

похвали́тся: похвал-ю́ся, -ишся *pf.*
– to boast, to brag, 29

похова́ти: похова́-ю, -єш *pf.* – to bury, 27

по́хорон, -у – funeral, 27

поцілува́ти: поцілу́-ю, -єш *pf.* – to kiss, 32

поча́ти: почн-у́, -е́ш *pf.* – to begin, 29

поча́тися: почн-е́ться, -у́ться *pf.* – to begin, 29

поча́ток, поча́тку – beginning, 29

почека́ти: почека́-ю, -єш *pf.* – to wait, 23

почина́ти: почина́-ю, -єш – to begin, 29

почина́тися: почина́-ється, -жться
– to begin, 29

почи́стити: почи́щу, почи́ст-иш *pf.*
– to clean, 23

почу́ти: почу́-ю, -єш *pf.* – to hear, 23

поши́ти: поши́-ю, -єш *pf.* – to sew, 26

по́шта – post office, 18

пошто́ва скри́нька – mailbox, 35

пошука́ти: пошука́-ю, -єш *pf.*
– to look for, to search, 23

поясни́ти: поясн-ю́, -и́ш *pf.* – to explain, 35

поя́снювати: поя́сню-ю, -єш – to explain, 35

праба́ба – great grandmother, 13

пра́внук – great grandson, 13

пра́внука – great granddaughter, 13

право́руч – to the right, 6

пра́дід – great grandfather, 13

прасува́ти: прасу́ю-ю, -єш – to iron, 26

пра́ти: пер-у́, -е́ш – to launder, 26

працівни́к, працівника́ *pl.* працівники́
– worker *[m]*, employee *[m]*, 12

працівни́ця – worker *[f]*, employee *[f]*, 12
працюва́ти: працю́-ю, -єш – to work, 5
пра́ця – work, 29
президе́нт – president, 38
прекра́сний – beautiful, 26
прекра́сно – excellently, 4
прига́дувати: прига́ду-ю, -єш
– to recall, to remind, 32
пригада́ти: пригада́-ю, -єш *pf.*
– to recall, to remind, 32
приго́да, *pl.* приго́ди, приго́д – adventure, 36
приго́дницькикй – adventureful, 36
пригріва́ти: пригріва́-ю, -єш – to warm, 33
пригрі́ти: пригрі́-ю, -єш *pf.* – to warm, 33
прие́мний – pleasant, 26
приємні́ше – more pleasantly, 31
приємні́ший – more pleasant, 30
прие́мно – pleasantly, 31
прийма́ти: прийма́-ю, -єш
– to accept, to welcome, 28
прийня́ти: (future) прийм-у́, -е́ш *pf.*
(past) прийня́-в ,-ла́, -ло́- ли́
– to accept, to welcome, 28
прийти́: прийд-у́, -е́ш *pf.* – to arrive *[on foot]*, 29
приїжджа́ти: приїжджа́-ю. -єш
– to arrive *[by vehicle]*, 27
приї́хати: приї́д-у, -еш *pf.*
– to arrive *[by vehicle]*, 27
присни́тися: присн-ю́ся, -и́шся *pf.*
– to appear to someone in a dream, 33
прихо́дити: прихо́джу, прихо́д-иш
– to arrive *[on foot]*, 29
приче́па *[m,f]* – nuisance *[of a person]*, 37
приз, *при́зу*, *pl.* *призи́* – prize, 34
прі́звище – surname, 11
про *[+A]* – about, 15
прові́нція – province, 38
прогно́з, -у: прогно́з пого́ди
– weather forecast, 33
програва́ти: програ-ю́, -є́ш
– to lose *[opp. of to win]*, 32
програ́ти: програ́-ю, -єш *pf.*
– to lose *[opp. of to win]*, 32
прогу́лянка – walk, 25
продава́ти: прода-ю́, -є́ш – to sell, 5
продаве́ць, продавця́, *pl.* продавці́
– salesclerk *[m]*, 14
продавни́ця – salesclerk *[f]*, 14
продавщи́ця – salesclerk *[f]*, 14
прода́ти: прода́-м, -си́ *pf.* – to sell, 23
про́за – prose, 36
проси́ти: прошу́, про́с-иш
– to request, to plead, 9
про́ти *[+G]* – across from, against, 22
профе́сор *[h]*, *pl.* профе́сори́ – professor, 11
прохі́д, прохо́ду – walk, 25
проце́нт, -а – percent, 38
прочита́ти: прочита́-ю, -єш *pf.* – to read, 23
про́шу – please, 9
пря́мо – straight ahead, 6
психіа́тр *[h]* – psychiatrist, 24
психія́тр *[h]* – psychiatrist, 24
психо́лог – psychologist, 24
птах, птаха́, *pl.* птахи́ – bird *[big]*, 21
пта́шка, *pl.* пташки́, пташо́к – bird *[small]*, 21
пу́динг, *-у* – pudding, 19
пу́диґ, -у – pudding, 19
пуло́вер *[h]*, -а – pullover, 20
пуля́ре́с, -а – purse, 18
пунш, пу́ншу – punch *[drink]*, 15
пурпу́рний – purple, 26
пурпуро́вий – purple, 26
п'яни́ця *[m,f]* – drunkard, 37
п'ята́, *pl.* п'яти́, п'ят – heel, 31
п'ятдеся́т – fifty, 19
п'ятдеся́тий – fiftieth, 27
п'я́тий – fifth, 27
п'ятна́дцятий – fifteenth, 27
п'ятна́дцять – fifteen, 19
п'я́тниця – Friday, 16
п'ятсо́т – five hundred, 19
п'ять – five, 19

Р

ра́да – council, 37
ра́дити: ра́джу, ра́д-иш
– to advise, to give advice, 35
ра́діо *[indecl.]* – radio, 17
радіопереда́ча – radio program, 29
ра́зом – together, 5
рай, ра́ю – paradise, 27
раме́но́, рамена́, *pl.* раме́на, раме́н
– shoulder, 31
рані́ше – earlier, 10
ра́нній *[s]* – early, 33
ра́но – early, 5

ра́нок, ра́нку – morning, 29
ра́туша – city hall, 35
реда́ктор *[h]* – editor *[m]*, 24
реда́кторка – editor *[f]*, 24
рекла́ма – advertisement, 28
рекля́ма – advertisement, 28
ре́мінь, ре́меня – belt, 20
рестора́н – restaurant, 12
ри́ба – fish, 19
ри́нок, ри́нку – market, 35
рі́дко – seldom, rarely, 3
рі́дний – native, 38
рідня́ – family *[extended]*, 13
рі́дше – less frequently, less often, 31
різьба́ – carving, carved artifact, 32
рік, ро́ку, ... ро́ці, *pl.* роки́ – year, 16
ріка́, *pl.* ріки – river, 21
річ *[f]*, ре́чі – thing, 36
роби́ти: роб-лю́, -иш – to do, 9
робітни́к, робітника́, *pl.* робітники́ – labourer *[m]*, 12
робітни́ця – labourer *[f]*, 12
робо́та – work, 29
роди́на – family *[immediate]*, 13
ро́дич – relative *[m]*, 13
ро́дичі *[pl]*, *g.pl.* ро́дичів – relatives, parents, 13
ро́дичка – relative *[f]*, 13
роже́вий – pink, 26
розі́гравка – raffle, 32
розмовля́ти: розмовля́-ю, -єш – to converse, to speak, 4
розта́нути: розта́не *pf.*– to thaw, 33
розумі́ти: розумі́-ю, -єш – to understand, 4
розу́мний – intelligent, 26
розумні́ше – more intelligently, 31
розумні́ший – more intelligent, 30
розу́мно – intelligently, 31
ро́лик, -а – roller skate, 34
рома́н, -у – novel, 36
росі́йський – Russian, 38
росія́нин, *pl.* росія́ни, росія́н – Russian *[m]*, 38
росія́нка – Russian *[f]*, 38
Росі́я – Russia, 38
росли́на – plant *[in general]* 25
рости́: рост-у́, -е́ш – to grow, 6
рот, ро́та, *pl.* роти́, – mouth, 31
рука́, *pl.* ру́ки, рук – hand, arm 28
рукави́ця – mitt, mitten, 20
рукави́чка – glove, 20
руса́лка – mermaid, 37
рух, ру́ху (ву́личний рух) – traffic, 35
ру́чка – pen, 11
рушни́к, рушника́, *pl.* рушники́ – towel, 28
***рюкза́к**, рюкзака́, pl. рюкзаки́* – knapsack, 11

С

сад, са́ду, ... саду́ і са́ді, *pl.* сади́ – orchard, 30
садовина́ *[sg]* – fruit, 30
садо́чок, садо́чка – kindergarten, 32
***сала́т**, -у* – lettuce, salad, 19
сала́та – lettuce, salad, 19
сам/сами́й – alone, oneself, 38
санда́ля – sandal, 20
са́ндвіч, -а – sandwich, 19
са́нки́ *[pl]*, са́но́к – sled, 34
санте́хнік – plumber, 24
све́кор *[h]*, све́кра – father-in-law *[woman's]*, 13
свекру́ха – mother-in-law *[woman's]*, 13
све́тер *[h]*, све́тра – sweater, cardigan, 20
***светр** [h], све́тра* – sweater, cardigan, 20
свиста́ти: свищ-у́, -еш – to whistle, 31
свій, своя́, своє́, свої́ – one's own, 28
світ, сві́ту, *pl.* світи́ – world, 27
світи́ти: свічу́, сві́т-иш – to shine, 33
світлофо́р *[h]*, -а – traffic lights, 18
сві́чка *pl.* свічки́, свічо́к – candle, 32
свічни́к, свічника́, *pl.* свічники́ – candlestick, 32
святкува́ти: святку́-ю, -єш – to celebrate, 27
свя́то – holiday, feast day, 27
свяще́ник – priest, 24
себе́ – oneself, 22
секрета́р *[s]*, секретаря́, *pl.* секретарі́ – secretary *[m]*, 12
секрета́рка – secretary *[f]*, 12
секу́нда – second *[time]*, 29
селе́ра *[sg]* – celery, 30
село́, *pl.* се́ла, сіл – village, small town, 12
селяни́н, *pl.* селя́ни, селя́н – peasant *[m]*, 38
селя́нка – peasant *[f]*, 38
серве́тка – serviette, 22
се́ред *[+G]* – among, in the middle of, 22
середа́ – Wednesday, 16
сере́жка – earring, 28

серйо́зний – serious, 36
се́рпень, се́рпня – August, 16
се́рце, *pl.* серця́, серде́ць – heart, 31
сестра́, *pl.* се́стри, сесте́р, се́страми, се́страм, ... се́страх – sister, 13
сиві́ший – greyer *[of hair]*, 30
си́вий – grey *[of hair]*, 26
сиді́ти: сиджу́, сид-и́ш – to be sitting, 9
си́льний – strong, 26
сильні́ше – more strongly, 31
сильні́ший – stronger, 30
си́льно – strongly, 31
син, *v.sg.* си́ну!, *pl.* сини́ – son, 13
си́ній *[s]* – blue, 26
сині́ше – more bluely, 31
сині́ший – bluer, 30
си́ньо – bluely, 31
сир *[h]*, си́ру, *pl.* сири́ – cheese, 19
сире́на – siren, 35
сирота́ *[m,f]* – orphan, 37
сіда́ти: сіда́-ю, -єш – to sit down, 16
сік, со́ку, *pl.* со́ки – juice, 15
сіль *[f]*, со́ли – salt, 36
сім – seven, 19
сімдеся́т – seventy, 19
сімдеся́тий – seventieth, 27
сімсо́т – seven hundred, 19
сім'я́, сім'ї́, сім'є́ю; *pl.* сі́м'ї, сіме́й і сі́м'їв, сі́м'ями – family *[immediate]*, 13
сімна́дцятий – seventeenth, 27
сі́рий – grey, 26
сірі́ший – greyer, 30
сі́сти: ся́д-у, -еш *pf.* to sit down, 23
сі́чень, сі́чня – January, 16
сказа́ти: скаж-у́, -еш *pf.* – to say, 23
скака́лка – skipping rope, 34
скака́ти: скач-у́, -еш – to jump, to leap, 34
ска́ржитися: ска́рж-уся, -ишся – to complain, 8
скатерти́на – tablecloth, 22
скейт, -у – skateboard, 34
скеле́т, -а – skeleton, 31
скі́льки – how much, 4
скінчи́ти: скінч-у́, -и́ш *pf.* – to finish, to end, 29
скінчи́тися: скінч-и́ться, -а́ться *pf.* – to come to an end, 29
склеп, скле́пу – store, 14
скло – glass, 32
скля́нка, *pl.* склянки́, склянóк – glass *[for drinking]*, 17
ско́чити: ско́ч-у, -иш *pf.* – to jump, to leap, 34
скри́ня – trunk, chest, 32
скри́пка, *pl.* скрипки́, скрипо́к – violin, 16
скупа́р *[s]*, скупаря́, *pl.* скупарі́ – miser, 37
скупа́ти: скупа́-ю, -є́ш *pf.* – to give a bath, 28
скупа́тися: скупа́-юся, -є́шся *pf.* – to bathe oneself, 23
сли́ва – plum, 30
сли́вка – plum, 30
словни́к, словника́, *pl.* словники́ – dictionary, 11
сло́во, *pl.* слова́, слів – word, 27
слов'яни́н, *pl.* слов'я́ни, слов'я́н – Slav *[m]*, 38
слов'я́нка – Slav *[f]*, 38
сло́їк, -а – jar, 30
слу́хати: слу́ха-ю, -єш – to listen, 4
сльоза́, *pl.* сльо́зи, сліз – tear, 31
сльота́ – rainy weather, 33
смачни́й – tasty, 30
смачні́ше – more tastily, 31
смачні́ший – tastier, 30
сма́чно – tastily, 31
смерть *[f]*, сме́рти – death, 36
смета́на – cream *[sour]*, 19
смі́ти: смі́-ю, -єш – to dare, 36
смітни́к, смітника́, *pl.* смітники́ – garbage can, 35
смішни́й – funny, 36
сни́тися: сн-ю́ся, -ишся – to appear to someone in a dream, 33
сніг, сні́гу, *pl.* сніги́ – snow, 33
снігова́ ба́ба – snowman, 34
снігови́й дід – snowman, 34
smія́тися: смі-ю́ся, -є́шся – to laugh, 5
сніда́нок, сніда́нку – breakfast, 15
сні́дати: сні́да-ю, -єш – to have breakfast, 4
сніжи́ти: сніжи́ть – to snow: it's snowing, 33
сні́жка – snowball, 34
соло́дкий – sweet, 30
со́лодко – sweetly, 31
соло́дше – more sweetly, 31
соло́дший – sweeter, 30
солони́на – bacon, 19
соло́ма – straw, 32
со́нце, *pl.* со́нця, со́не́ць і со́нців – sun, 33

со́нячно – it's sunny, 33
сопі́лка – sopilka, 16
со́рок – forty, 19
сороко́вий – fortieth, 27
соро́чка, *pl.* сорочки́, сорочо́к – shirt, 20
со́тий – hundredth, 27
спа́льня, *g.pl.* спа́лень – bedroom, 14
спа́ти: сп-лю, -иш – to sleep, 9
спе́ка – heatwave, 33
спекти́: спеч-у́, -е́ш *pf.* – to bake, 32
спи́на – back *[upper]*, 31
спита́ти: спита́-ю, -єш *pf.* – to ask, to inquire, 23
співа́к, співака́, *pl.* співаки́ – singer *[m]*, 24
співа́ти: співа́-ю, -єш – to sing, 4
співа́чка – singer *[f]*, 24
спідни́ця – skirt, 20
спізни́тися: спізн-ю́ся, -ишся *pf.* – to be late, 35
спі́знюватися: спі́зню-юся, -єшся – to be late, 35
спіши́ти: спіш-у́, -и́ш – to hurry, 8
сподо́батися: сподо́ба-юся, -єшся *pf.* – to appeal, 33
Сполу́чені Шта́ти Аме́рики (США) – United States of America (USA)
спорт, спо́рту – sport, 34
спуска́лка – slide, 25
стадіо́н, -у – stadium, 15
ста́йня, *pl.* ста́йні, ста́єнь – barn, 21
ста́нція – station *[train]*, 29
стари́й – old, 26
ста́роста *[m]* – match-maker, starosta, 37
ста́рший – older, 30
сте́жка, *pl.* стежки́, стежо́к – path, 21
сте́рео *[indecl.]* – stereo, 17
стіл, стола́, *pl.* столи́ – table, 12
стіле́ць, стільця́, *pl.* стільці́ – chair, 12
сті́льки – so much, so many, 19
стіна́, стіни́, *pl.* сті́ни – wall, 14
сто – hundred, 19
стогна́ти: сто́гн-у, -еш – to groan, 7
стодо́ла – barn, 21
сто́лик, -а – coffee table, end table, 17
столі́ття *[n]* – century, 27
сто́млений – tired, exhausted, 37
сторі́нка, *pl.* сторі́нки́, сторі́но́к – page, 27
сторі́ччя *[n]* – century, 27
сто́рож, *pl.* сторожі́, сторожі́в – janitor, 24
сто́янка – parking lot, 35
стоя́ти: сто-ю́, -ї́ш – to stand, to be standing, 9
студе́нт – student *[m]*, 11
студе́нтка – student *[f]*, 11
сту́кати: сту́ка-ю, -єш – to knock, 31
сту́кнути: сту́кн-у, -еш *pf.* – to knock, 31
субо́та – Saturday, 16
сувені́р *[h]*, -а – souvenir, 18
судця́ *[m]* – judge, 37
суке́нка – dress, 20
суко́нка – dress, 20
су́мка – purse, 18
сумни́й – sad, 26
сумні́ше – more sadly, 31
сумні́ший – sader, 30
су́мно – sadly, 31
суни́ця – strawberry, 30
***суп**, су́пу*, *pl.* *супи́* – soup, 19
сусі́д – neighbour *[m]*, 25
сусі́дка – neighbour *[f]*, 25
сфотографува́ти: сфотографу́-ю, -єш *pf.* – to photograph, 23
схід, схо́ду – east, 16
схова́ти: схова́-ю, -єш – to hide, 27
схова́тися: схова́-юся, -єшся – to hide, conceal oneself, 27
схоті́ти: схо́ч-у, -еш *pf.* – to want, 23
схоті́тися: схо́четься *pf.* – to feel an urge to do something, 33
схо́ди *[pl]*, схо́дів, ... схо́дах – stairs, 11
сюди́ – here: to this place, 7
***сюрпри́з**, -у* – surprise, 34
сього́дні – today, 9
сього́дні вве́чері – tonight, this evening, 9
сього́дні вве́чорі – tonight, this evening, 9
сього́дні вра́нці – this morning, 9
сьо́мий – seventh, 27

Т

та́ – and, 11
та́бір *[h]*, та́бору – summer camp, camp, 25
табле́тка – pill, 31
табли́ця – chalkboard, 11
так – yes, 2
так – in such a manner, so, 8

такóж – too, also, 2
таксí *[indecl.]* – taxi, cab, 12
таксíвка – taxi, cab, 12
талановúтий – talented, 30
талановúто – talentedly, 31
там – there, 2
тáнець, тáнцю, *pl.* тáнці – dance, 32
тáнути: тáне – to thaw, to melt, 33
танцювáти: танцю́-ю, -єш – to dance, 5
танцюрúст – dancer *[m]*, 24
танцюрúстка – dancer *[f]*, 24
тарíлка, *pl.* тарілкú, тарілóк – plate, 17
тáто, *v.sg.* тáту! – dad, 13
тварúна – animal *[in general]*, 25
твій, твоя́, твоє́, твої́ – your *[s]*, yours *[s]*, 28
теáтр *[h]*, -у – theatre, 15
теж – too, also, 2
телевíзор *[h]*, -а – television set, 17
телепередáча – television program, 29
телефóн, -у – telephone, 17
телефóн-автомáт (автомáт, -а)
– pay telephone, 35
телефонíст – telephone operator *[m]*, 24
телефонíстка – telephone operator *[f]*, 24
телефóнна бу́дка – telephone booth, 35
телефонувáти: телефону́-ю, -єш
– to telephone, 5
теля́ *[n]* – calf, 37
тéмний – dark, 33
температу́ра – temperature, 33
тéніс, -у – tennis, 15
тенісíвка – running shoe, gym shoe, 20
тéніска – T-shirt, 20
тепéр – now, 2
тéплий – warm, 33
тéпло – it's warm, 33
термóметр, -а – thermometer, 33
терпелúвий – patient, 37
тéсля *[m]* – carpenter, 37
тесть, тéстя, *pl.* тéсті – father-in-law *[man's]*, 13
течка – briefcase, 11
тéща – mother-in-law *[man's]*, 13
ти – you, 2
тúсяча – one thousand, 19
тúждень, тúжня – week, 16
тúхо – quietly, 5
тúхше – more quietly, 31
тíло, *pl.* тілá, тіл – body, 31
тíльки – only, 9
тíстечко – cookie, 19
тíсто – dough *[for bread, etc.]*, 32
тíтка, *pl.* тіткú, тітóк – aunt, 13
тíшити: тíш-у, -иш
– to make someone happy, 28
тíшитися: тíш-уся, -ишся
– to be delighted, glad, happy, 8
тканúна – fabric, 32
то – that, 11
тобóґан – toboggan, 34
товáр *[h]*, -у – goods, merchandise, 38
товáриш, *pl.* товаришí – friend *[m]*, 11
товáришка, *pl.* товаришкú – friend *[f]*, 11
тодí – then, at that time, 5
той, та, те, ті – that, 27
тому́ що – because, 6
торбúнка – purse, 18; bag, 25
торнáдо – tornado, 33
торт, тóрта, *pl.* тортú – cake, 19
травá, травú, *pl.* трáви – grass, 21
трáвень, трáвня – May, 16
травнúк, траникá, *pl.* травникú – lawn, 22
трáктор *[h]*, -а, *pl.* тракторú – tractor, 25
трамвáй, трамвáя – streetcar, 29
трамплíн, -а – trampoline, 34
трéба – it is necessary, 9
трéтій *[s]* – third, 26
три – three, 19
тридця́тий – thirtieth, 27
триколíсник, -а – tricycle, 34
тринáдцятий – thirteenth, 27
трúдцять – thirty, 19
тринáдцять – thirteen, 19
трúста – three hundred, 19
тролéйбус, -а – trolley bus, 29
тротуáр *[h], -у* – sidewalk, 14
трофéй, трофéя – trophy, 34
трóхи – not much, a little bit, 19
труднúй – difficult, 32
туалéт, *-у* – bathroom, 14
тудú – there: to that place, 7
тумáн, -у – fog, 33
тумáнно – it's foggy, 33

туне́ль, туне́лю – tunnel, 35
тури́ст – tourist *[m]*, 12
тури́стка – tourist *[f]*, 12
тут – here: in this place, 2
ту́фля – shoe, 20
тюрма́ – jail, 35
тяжки́й – heavy, 29
тя́жчий – heavier, 30

У

у/в *[+G]* – at, 18
у/в *[+L], [+A]* – in, 14; into, 15
уве́сь, уся́, усе́, усі́ – all, 28
уве́чері/вве́чері – in the evening, 8
уве́чорі/вве́чорі – in the evening, 8
увійти́/ввійти́: увійд-у́, -е́ш *pf.* – to enter, to come into, 23
угóру/вгóру – up, upwards, 6
удéнь/вдень – during the day, in the daytime, 8
удоли́ну/вдоли́ну – down, downwards, 6
удóма/вдóма – at home, 2
ужé/вже – already, 2
ужива́ти: ужива́-ю, -єш – to use, 28
ужи́ти: ужив-у́, -е́ш *pf.* – to use, 28
узи́мку/взи́мку – in the winter, 8
узя́ти/взя́ти: візьм-у́, -еш *pf.* – to take, 23
Украї́на – Ukraine, 38
украї́нець, украї́нця – Ukrainian *[m]*, 38
украї́нка – Ukrainian *[f]*, 38
украї́нський – Ukrainian, 38
укра́сти/вкра́сти: украд-у́, -е́ш *pf.* – to steal, 23
улі́тку/влі́тку – in the summer, 8
улю́блене заня́ття *[n]* – hobby, 32
улю́блений – favorite, 32
уме́рти: умр-у́, -е́ш *pf.* – to die, 27
умива́льня, *g.pl.* умива́лень – bathroom, 14
умива́ти: умива́-ю, -єш – to wash, 28
умива́тися: умива́-юся, -єшся – to wash oneself, 28
умира́ти: умира́-ю, -єш – to die, 27
уми́ти: уми́-ю, -єш *pf.* – to wash, 28
уми́тися: уми́-юся, -єшся *pf.* – to wash oneself, 28
умі́ти/вмі́ти: умі́-ю, -єш – to know how, 4
уни́з/вниз – down, downwards, 6
університе́т, -у – university, 11
уночі́/вночі́ – at night, 8
упа́сти: упад-у́, -е́ш *pf.* – to fall, 23
урага́н, *-у* – hurricane, 33
ура́нці/вра́нці – in the morning, 8
уро́дини *[pl]*, уро́дин, ... уро́динах – birthday, 27
уро́к, -у– lesson, 11
у́ряд, -у – government, 38
усé/все – everything, 6
усí/всі – everyone, everybody, 6
усміха́тися: усміха́-юся, -єшся – to smile, 31
усміхну́тися: усміхн-у́ся, -е́шся *pf.* – to smile, 31
у́спіх, -у – success, 34
уста́ *[pl]*, уст, ... уста́х – lips, 28
устава́ти/встава́ти: уста-ю́, -є́ш – to get up, 5
уста́ти/вста́ти: уста́н-у, -еш *pf.* – to get up, 23
усю́ди/всю́ди – everywhere, 7
уті́шити/вті́шити: уті́ш-у, -иш *pf.* – to make someone happy, 28
уті́шитися/вті́шитися: уті́ш-уся, -ишся *pf.* – to be delighted/glad/happy, 23
учени́ця – pupil *[f]*, 11
у́чень, у́чня – pupil *[m]*, 11
учи́тель/вчи́тель, *pl.* учителі́ – teacher *[m]*, 11
учи́телька/вчи́телька, *pl.* учительки́, учительо́к – teacher *[f]*, 11
учи́тися/вчи́тися: уч-у́ся, -ишся – to learn, to study, 8
учóра/вчóра – yesterday, 16

Ф

фа́брика – factory, 35
фа́рба – paint, 32
фа́рма – farm, 13
фа́рмер *[h]* – farmer *[m]*, 13
фа́рмерка – farmer *[f]*, 13
фасо́ля *[sg]* – beans, 30
фе́рма – farm, 13
фе́рмер *[h]* – farmer *[m]*, 13
фе́рмерка – farmer *[f]*, 13
фе́я – fairy, 37
фільм, фі́льму, *pl.* фі́льми – film, 32
фіра́нка – curtain, 17
фонта́н, -а – fountain, 25

фóто *[indecl.]* – photograph, 18
фотоапарáт, -а – camera, 18
фотóграф – photographer, 24
фотогрáфія – photograph, 18
фотографувáти: фотографу́-ю, -єш
– to photograph, 21
Фрáнція – France, 38
францу́женка – Frenchwoman, 38
францу́з – Frenchman, 38
францу́зький – French, 38
фри́збі *[indecl.]* – frizbee, 34
фрукт, *фру́кта*, *pl.* *фру́кти* – fruit, 30
фунт, фу́нта, *pl.* фунти́ – pound, 30
футбóл, -у – football *[game]*, 15
футбóлка – T-shirt, 20

Х

хáта, *pl.* хати́, хат і **хатíв** – house, 12
хвали́ти: хвал-ю́, -иш – to praise, 29
хвали́тися: хвал-ю́ся, -ишся
– to boast, to brag, 29
хвили́на – minute, 29
хви́ля – wave, 34
хвóрий – ill, sick, 26
хворíший – more ill, sicker, 30
хемчи́стка – drycleaning shop, 28
хідни́к, хідникá, *pl.* хідники́ – sidewalk, 14
хімчи́стка – drycleaning shop, 28
хіру́рг – surgeon, 24
хліб, хлíба, *pl.* хліби́ – bread, 19
хліби́на – loaf of bread, 30
хлóпець, хлóпця – boy, 13
хмáра – cloud, 33
хмáритися: хмáриться
– to become cloudy, overcast, 33
хмáрно – it's cloudy, 33
ховáти: ховá-ю, -єш
– to bury; to hide, to conceal, 27
ховáтися: ховá-юся, -єшся
– to hide oneself, to conceal oneself, 27
ходи́ти: ходжу́, хóд-иш *[it.]*
– to go/come *[on foot]*, 10
хокéй, *хокéю* – hockey, 15
холоди́льник, -а – refrigerator, fridge, 17
холóдний – cold, 33
хóлодно – it's cold, 33
хорóший – nice, pretty, 26
хотíти: хóч-у, -еш – to want, 7
хотíтися: хóчеться
– to feel an urge to do something, 33
хребéт, хребтá, *pl.* хребти́ – spine, 31
хрест, хрестá, *pl.* хрести́ – cross, 32
христи́ни *[pl]*, христи́н, ... христи́нах
– baptism, christening, 27
християни́н, *pl.* христия́ни, христия́н
– Christian *[m]*, 38
христия́нка – Christian *[f]*, 38
хто – who, 3
хтонéбудь – anyone, anybody, 6
хтось – someone, 6
худóжник – artist *[m]*, 24
худóжниця – artist *[f]*, 24
ху́стка, *pl.* хустки́, хустóк – kerchief, 20
ху́тро, *g.pl.* хутр і ху́тер – fur coat, 20

Ц

це – this, 11
цей, ця, це, ці – this, 27
цент, цéнта – penny, cent, 18
цéрква, *pl.* церкви́, церкóв – church, 18
цибу́ля *[sg]* – onions, 30
цимбáли *[pl]*, цимбáлів, ... цимбáлах
– tsymbaly, dulcimer, 16
цитри́на – lemon, 19
цікáвий – interesting, 32
цікáвити: цікáв-ю, -иш
– to be of interest to someone, 33
цілувáти: ціл́у-ю, -єш – to kiss, 32
цукéрка – candy, sweets, 30
цукéрок, цукéрка – candy, sweets, 30
цу́кор *[h]*, цу́кру – sugar, 19

Ч

чай, чáю, *pl.* чаї́– tea, 15
чáйник, -а – teapot; kettle, 17
час, чáсу, *pl.* часи́ – time, 29
часни́к *[sg]*, часнику́ – garlic, 30
чáсом – sometimes, 3
чáсто – often, frequently, 3

ча́сто: як ча́сто – how often, 10
часті́ше – oftener, more frequently, 31
ча́шка, *pl.* чашки́, чашо́к – cup, 17
чверть *[f]*, чве́рти – one-fourth, quarter, 29
чека́ти: чека́-ю, -єш – to wait, 4
че́мний – obedient, polite, 32
чемода́н, *-а* – suitcase, valise, 18
че́рвень, че́рвня – June, 16
черво́ний – red, 26
червоні́ший – redder, 30
че́рга – line-up, queue, 35
череви́к, -а – shoe, 20
че́рево, *pl.* чере́ва, чере́в – abdomen, 31
че́рез *[+A]* – across, through, because of, 22
че́рез *[+A]* – in *[in time expressions]*, 29
че́сний – honest, honourable, 37
четве́р *[h]*, четверга́ – Thursday, 16
четве́ртий – fourth, 27
чи – or, 3; if, whether (conj.), 8
чий, чия́, чиє́, чиї́ – whose, 28
числі́вник, -а – numeral, 27
число́, *pl.* чи́сла, чи́сел – date *[calendar]*, 27
чи́стий – clean, 26
чи́стити: чи́щу, чи́ст-иш – to clean, 22
чисті́ше – more cleanly, 31
чисті́ший – cleaner, 30
чи́сто – cleanly, 31
чита́ти: чита́-ю, -єш – to read, 4
чо́біт, чо́бота, *pl.* чо́боти, чобі́т, чобітьми́, ... чо́ботах – boot, 20
чо́вен, човна́, *pl.* човни́ – boat, 21
чолові́к – man, 11; husband, 13
чому́ – why, 6
чо́рний – black, 26
чорні́ший – blacker, 30
чорт, чо́рта, *pl.* чорти́ – devil, 37
чоти́ри – four, 19
чоти́риста – four hundred, 19
чотирна́дцятий – fourteenth, 27
чотирна́дцять – fourteen, 19
чужи́й – foreign, 38
чужи́нець, чужи́нця – foreigner *[m]*, 38
чужи́нка – foreigner *[f]*, 38
чу́ти: чу́-ю, -єш – to hear, 4

Ш

ша́лик, -а – scarf, 20
шампу́нь, щампу́ню – shampoo, 28
ша́пка, *pl.* шапки́, шапо́к – cap; baseball cap, 20
шатро́, *pl.* ша́тра, ша́тер – tent, 25
ша́фа, *pl.* шафи́, шафі́в – cupboard, closet, 14
ша́хи *[pl]*, ша́хів, ... ша́хах – chess, 15
ша́шки *[pl]*, ша́шок, ... ша́шках – checkers, 15
швидка́ допомо́га – ambulance, 35
швидки́й – fast, 30
шви́дко – quickly, 5
шви́дше – more quickly, 31
шви́дший – faster, 30
шепта́ти: шепч-у́, -еш – to whisper, 7
шепну́ти: шепн-у́, -е́ш *pf.* – to whisper, 23
ши́нка – ham, 19
широ́кий – wide, 30
ши́роко – widely, 31
ши́рше – more widely, 31
ши́рший – wider, 30
ши́ти: ши́-ю, -єш – sew, 26
ши́я – neck, 28
шістдеся́т – sixty, 19
шістдеся́тий – sixtieth, 27
шістна́дцятий – sixteenth, 27
шістна́дцять – sixteen, 19
шістсо́т – six hundred, 19
шість – six, 19
шкарпе́тка – sock, 20
шкі́ра – skin, 31
шко́ла, *g.pl.* шкіл – school, 11
школя́р *[mx]*, школяра́ *pl.* школярі́ – pupil *[m]*, 11
школя́рка – pupil *[f]*, 11
шлу́нок, шлу́нку – stomach, 31
шлюб, шлю́бу – wedding ceremony, marriage, 27
шокола́дка – chocolate bar, 30
шоколя́дка – chocolate bar, 30
шо́рти *[pl]*, шо́ртів, ... шо́ртах – shorts, 20
шосе́ *[indecl.]* – highway, 35
шо́стий – sixth, 27
шотля́ндець, шотля́ндця – Scot *[m]*, 38
Шотля́ндія – Scotland
шотля́ндка – Scot *[f]*, 38

шотля́ндський – Scottish, 38
шофе́р *[h]* – chauffeur, 12
шпита́ль, шпита́лю – hospital, 12
штани́*[pl]*, штанів, ... штана́х – pants, 20
шу́ба – fur coat, 20
шука́ти: шука́-ю, -єш
– to look for, to search for, 18
шухля́да – drawer, 14

Щ

щасли́вий – fortunate, lucky, 26
щасливі́ше – more fortunately, 31
шасливі́ший – more fortunate, luckier, 30
щасли́во – fortunately, luckily, 31
ще – still, yet, 2
ще ні – not yet, 3
щі́тка, *pl.* щітки́, щіто́к – brush, 28
що – what, 3; that (conj.), 8
щоб – so that, 35
щове́чора – every evening, 10
щогоди́ни – every hour, 10
щодня́ – every day, 10
щока́, *pl.* що́ки, щік – cheek, 31
щомі́сяця – every month, 10
щоне́будь – anything, 6
щоно́чі – every night, 10
щора́нку – every morning, 10
щоро́ку – every year, 10
щось – something, 6
щоти́жня – every week, 10
щохвили́ни – every minute, 10

Ю

ювіле́й, ювіле́ю – anniversary, 27
юри́ст – lawyer, 24
ю́шка, *pl.* юшки́, юшо́к – soup, 19

Я

я – I, 2
я́блуко – apple, 15
я́года – berry, 30
язи́к, язика́, *pl.* язики́ – tongue, 31
яйце́, *pl.* я́йця, яє́ць – egg, 19
як – how, 4; as, like, than, 30
яки́й – what (kind), 26
я́кість *[f]*, я́кости – quality, 36
як ча́сто – how often, 10
япо́нець, япо́нця – Japanese *[m]*, 38
Япо́нія – Japan, 38
япо́нка – Japanese *[f]*, 38
япо́нський – Japanese, 38
ярина́ *[sg]* – vegetables, 30
я́сно – it's clear, 33

ENGLISH-UKRAINIAN VOCABULARY

A

abdomen – живі́т, живота́, *pl.* животи́; че́рево, *pl.* чере́ва, чере́в, 31

able, to be – могти́: мо́ж-у, -еш, 6
pf. змоти́: змо́ж-у, -еш, 23

about – про *[+A]*, 15; по *[+L]*, 34

above – над *[+I]*, 21

accept – прийма́ти: прийма́-ю, -єш
pf. прийня́ти: (future) прийм-у́, -е́ш
(past) прийня́-в, -ла́, -ло́- ли́, 28

accident – ава́рія; ви́падок, ви́падку, 29

accordion – акордіо́н, -а; акордео́н, -а, 16

accountant – бухга́льтер *[h]*; *бухга́лтер [h]*, 24

ache – біль *[f]*, бо́лю, 31

ache – болі́ти: боли́ть, боля́ть, 31
pf. заболі́ти: заболи́ть, заболя́ть, 31

acquaint – знайо́мити: знайо́м-лю, -иш
pf. познайо́мити: познайо́м-лю, -иш, 36

acquaint: to become acquainted
– знайо́митися: знайо́м-люся, -ишся
pf. познайо́митися:
познайо́м-люся, -ишся, 36

across – че́рез *[+A]*, 22

across from – про́ти *[+G]*, 22

actor – акто́р *[h]*, 24

actress – акто́рка; *актри́са*, 24

address – адре́са, 18

adventure – приго́да, *pl.* приго́ди, приго́д, 36

adventureful – приго́дницький, 36

advertisement – оголо́шення *[n]*; рекля́ма; *рекла́ма*, 28

advise – ра́дити: ра́джу, ра́д-иш
pf. пора́дити: пора́джу, пора́д-иш, 35

a few – кі́лька, 19

after – пі́сля *[+G]*, 18

afternoon: in the afternoon – пі́сля обі́ду, 8

afterwards – по́тім, 5

again – знов/зно́ву, 3

against – про́ти *[+G]*, 22

airplane – літа́к, літака́, *pl.* літаки́, 18

airport – летовище; *аеродро́м;, -у, аеропо́рт, -у*, 35

alarm clock – буди́льник, -а, 29

a little bit – тро́хи, 19

all, everyone, everything
– уве́сь, уся́, усе́, усі́, 6, 29

all over – по *[+L]*, 34

almost – ма́йже, 9

alone – сам/сами́й, 38

along with – з (із, зі, зо) *[+I]*, 21

a lot – бага́то, 4

already – уже́/вже, 2

also – тако́ж; теж, 2

always – за́вжди, 3

amaze – дивува́ти: диву́-ю, -єш, 33
pf. здивува́ти: здиву́-ю, -єш, 33

ambassador – посо́л, посла́, *pl.* посли́; амбаса́дор *[h]*, 38

ambulance – швидка́ допомо́га, 35

America (USA) – Аме́рика (США)

American – америка́нський, 38

American *[f]* – америка́нка, 38

American *[m]* – америка́нець, америка́нця, 38

among – між *[+I]*, 21; се́ред *[+G]*, 22

and – і/й, а, 3; та, 11

angel – а́нгел, 37

animal *[in general]* – твари́на, 25

animal *[wild]* – звір, звíра *[h]*, 25

ankle – кі́сточка, *pl.* кісточки́, кісточо́к, 31

anniversary – ювіле́й, ювіле́ю, 27

another – і́нший, 36

answer – ві́дповідь *[f]*, ві́дповіді, 36

answer – відповіда́ти: відповіда́-ю, -єш
pf. відповí́сти: відпові́-м, -си́, 35

anybody – хтоне́будь, 6

anyone – хтоне́будь, 6

anything – щоне́будь, 6

apartment – поме́шкання *[n]*; *кварти́ра*, 12

appeal – подо́батися: подо́ба-юся, -єшся
pf. сподо́батися: сподо́ба-юся, -єшся, 33

appear in a dream to someone
– сни́тися: сн-ю́ся, -и́шся,
pf. присни́тися: присн-ю́ся, -и́шся, 33

apple – я́блуко, 15

appointment – поба́чення *[n]*, 29

April – кві́тень, кві́тня, 16

apricot – абрико́са, 30

architect – архіте́кт; архіте́ктор *[h]*, 24

arm – рука́, руки́, *pl.* ру́ки, рук, 28

arrive *[by vehicle]*
– приї́жджа́ти: приї́жджа́-ю. -єш
pf. приї́хати: приї́д-у, -еш, 27

arrive *[on foot]*
– прихóдити: прихóджу, прихóд-иш
pf. прийти́: прийд-ý, -éш, 29
artifact – експонáт, -а, 32
artist *[f]* – худóжниця, 24
artist *[m]* – худóжник, 24
as – як, 30
ask – питáти: питá-ю, -єш, 4
pf. спитáти: спитá-ю, -єш, 23
assignment – завдáння *[n]*, 11
assist – помагáти: помагá-ю, -єш, 20
pf. помогти́: помож-ý, -еш, 23
assistance – пóміч *[f]*, пóмочі; допомóга, 36
assistant *[f]* – асистéнтка, 22
assistant *[m]* – асистéнт, 22
astonish – дивувáти: дивý-ю, -єш,
pf. здивувáти: здивý-ю, -єш, 33
at *[in time expressions]* – о/об *[+L]*, 29
at – на *[+L]*, *[+A]*, 14
at home – удóма/вдóма, 2
at midnight – опíвночі, 29
at night – уночí/вночí, 8
at noon – опíвдні, 29
at that time – тодí, 5
at this moment – зáраз, 5
auditorium – авдитóрія; *аудитóрія*, 35
August – сéрпень, сéрпня, 16
aunt – тíтка, *pl.* тітки́, тітóк, 13
Australia – Австрáлія, 38
Australian – австралíйський, 38
Australian *[f]* – австралíйка, 38
Australian *[m]* – австралíєць, австралíйця, 38
autumn – óсінь *[f]*, óсени, 16

B

baby *[human]* – дитя́ *[n]*, немовля́ *[n]*, 37
baby sitter – ня́ня; ня́нька, 24
back *[lower]* – кри́жі *[pl]*, кри́жів,... кри́жах, 31
back *[upper]* – спи́на, 31
bacon – солони́на; *бекóн, -у*, 19
bad – погáний, 26
badly – погáно, 4
bad weather – негóда, 33
bag – торби́нка; мішéчок, мішечка, 25
baggage – багáж, -ý, 25
bake – пекти́: печ-ý, -éш
pf. спекти́: спеч-ý, -éш, 32
baked goods – пéчиво *[sg]*, 30
baker *[f]* – пéкарка, 24
baker *[m]* – пéкар *[s]*, 24
bakery – пекáрня, 35
balcony – балькóн, -а; балкóн, -а, 14
ball *[formal dance]* – забáва; баль, бáлю, *pl.* балí, 15
ball *[games, sports]* – м'яч, м'ячá, *pl.* м'ячí, 25
ballet – балéт, -у, 36
banana – банáн, -а, 15
band *[musical]* – бáнда; ансáмбль,
ансáмбля, 16
bandage – бандáж, бандажá, *pl.* бандажí, 31
bandura – бандýра, 16
bank *[building]* – банк, бáнку, 14
bank *[of a river]* – бéрег, бéрега, ... бéрегові і
... бéрезі, *pl.* береги́, 21
banquet – бенкéт, -у, 22
baptism – христи́ни *[pl]*, христи́н,
... христи́нах, 27
barn – стáйня, *pl.* стáйні, стáєнь; стодóла, 21
baseball *[game]* – бейсбóл, -у, 15
baseball cap – шáпка; *кéпка*, 20
basement – пивни́ця; підвáл, -у, 14
basket – кóшик, -а, 24
basketball *[game]* – баскетбóл, -у, 15
bathe: to give a bath – купáти: купá-ю, -єш, 27
pf. скупáти: скупá-ю, -єш, 27
bathe oneself – купáтися: купá-юся, -єшся, 5
pf. скупáтися: скупá-юся, -єшся, 23
bathing suit – купáльник, -а, 20
bathroom – лазни́чка; умивáльня; *туалéт, -у*, 14
bathtub – вáнна, 28
battery – батарéйка, 32
be – бýти: я є, ти є, 2
be able – могти́: мóж-у, -еш, 6
pf. змогти́: змóж-у, -еш, 23
beach – пляж, пля́жу, 21
beans – квасóля *[sg]*; фасóля *[sg]*, 30
beard – бородá, *pl.* бóроди́, борíд, 31
beautiful – прекрáсний; *краси́вий*, 26
be blameable – ви́нен/ви́нний, 32
be born – нарóджуватися: нарóджу-юся, -єшся
pf. народи́тися: нарóджуся, нарóд-ишся, 27
because – бо; томý що, 6
because of – чéрез *[+A]*, 22
become acquainted
– знайóмитися: знайóм-люся, -ишся
pf. познайóмитися: познайóм-люся,
-ишся, 35

become cloudy – хмáритися: хмáриться
pf. захмáритися: захмáриться, 33

become engaged
– зарýчуватися: зарýчу-юся, -єшся
pf. заручи́тися: зарýч-уся, -ишся, 36

bed – лíжко, *g.pl.* лíжок, 14

be delighted – тíшитися: тíш-уся, -ишся, 8
pf. утíшитися: утíш-уся, -ишся, 23

bedroom – спáльня, *g.pl.* спáлень, 14

bee – бджолá, *pl.* бджóли, бджіл, 21

beer – пи́во *[sg]*, 15

beet – буря́к, -а, 30

before – пéред *[+I]*, 21

be frightened – боя́тися: бо-ю́ся, -ї́шся, 9

begin – починáти: починá-ю, -єш
pf. почáти: почн-ý, -éш, 29

begin – починáтися: починá-ється, -ються
pf. почáтися: почн-éться, -ýться, 29

beginning – почáток, почáтку, 29

be glad – тíшитися: тíш-уся, -ишся, 8
pf. утíшитися: утíш-уся, -ишся, 23

behind – за *[+I]*, 21

belt – пасóк, паскá, *pl.* паски́;
рéмінь, рéменя, 20

be late – спíзнюватися: спíзню-юся, -єшся
pf. спізни́тися: спізн-ю́ся, -и́шся, 35

believe – вíрити: вíр-ю, -иш
pf. повíрити: повíр-ю, -иш, 32

be lying down – лежáти: леж-ý, -и́ш, 8
pf. полéжати: полéж-у, -иш, 23

bench – лáва; лáвка, 21

beneath – під *[+I]*, 21

berry – я́года, 30

beside – бíля *[+G]*; кóло *[+G]*, 18

besides – крім *[+G]*, 22

be silent – мовчáти: мовч-ý, -и́ш, 8
pf. замовчáти: замовч-ý, -и́ш, 23

be sitting – сидíти: сиджý, сид-и́ш, 9
pf. поси́діти: поси́джу, поси́д-иш, 23

be standing – стоя́ти: сто-ю́, -ї́ш, 9
pf. постóяти: постó-ю, -їш, 23

best man *[groom's attendant]* – дрýжба *[m]*, 37

better – крáще; лíпше, 4

better – крáщий; лíпший, 30

between – між *[+I]*, 21

beyond – за *[+I]*, 21

bicycle – велосипéд, -а, 18

big – вели́кий, 26

bigger – бíльший, 30

bike – велосипéд, -а, 18

bird *[big]* – птах, птáха, *pl.* птахи́, 21

bird *[small]* – птáшка, *pl.* пташки́, пташóк, 21

birth: to give birth
– нарóджувати: нарóджу-ю, -єш
pf. народи́ти: народжý, нарóд-иш, 27

birthday – день нарóдження *[n]*;
урóдини *[pl]*, урóдин, ... урóдинах, 27

black – чóрний, 26

blacker – чорнíший, 30

block *[child's toy]* – кýбик, -а, 32

block *[city block]* – квартáл, -у, 35

blood – кров *[f]*, крóви, 36

blouse – блю́зка, *pl.* блюзки́, блюзóк; *блýзка, pl. блузки́, блузóк*, 20

blow – вíяти: вí-ю, вí-єш
pf. повíяти: повí-ю, -єш, 33

blue – си́ній *[s]*, 26

bluer – синíший, 30

boat – чóвен, човн-á, *pl.* човни́, 21

boast – хвали́тися: хвал-ю́ся, -ишся
pf. похвали́тся: похвал-ю́ся, -ишся, 29

body – тíло, *pl.* тілá, тіл, 31

bone – кíстка, *pl.* кістки́, кістóк, 31

bonfire – вáтра, *g.pl.* вáтер, 25

book – кни́жка, *pl.* книжки́, книжóк, 11

bookstore – книгáрня, *g.pl.* книгáрень, 14

boot – чóбіт, чóбота, *pl.* чóботи, чобíт,
чобітьми́, ... чóботах, 20

border *[of a country]* – грани́ця; кордóн, -у, 38

boring – нудни́й, 32

borrow – позичáти: позичá-ю, -єш, 20
pf. пози́чити: пози́ч-у, -иш, 23

borshch – борщ, борщý, *pl.* борщí, 19

boss *[f]* – начáльниця, 12

boss *[m]* – начáльник, 12

both ... and – і ... і, 3

bottle – пля́шка, *pl.* пляшки́, пляшóк, 30

bouquet – букéт, -а, 22

bowl – ми́ска, *pl.* миски́, мисóк, 17

box – корóбка, *pl.* коробки́, корóбóк, 25

boy – хлóпець, хлóпця, 13

bracelet – браслéт, -а, 28

brag – хвали́тися: хвал-ю́ся, -ишся
pf. похвали́тся: похвал-ю́ся, -ишся, 29

bread – хліб, хлíба, *pl.* хлібú, 19

break – ломи́ти: лом-лю́, -иш
pf. зломи́ти: злом-лю́, -иш, 31

breakfast – снідáнок, снідáнку, 15

breakfast: to have breakfast
– снíдати: снíда-ю, -єш, 4
pf. поснíдати: поснíда-ю, -єш, 23
breast – грýди *[pl]*, грудéй, грудьмú
і грудúма, ... грýдях, 31
breeze – вітерéць, вітерця́, 33
bride – молодá *[sub.]*, молодóї, 26
bridegroom – молодúй *[sub.]*, молодóго, 26
bridesmaid – дрýжка, *pl.* дрýжкú, дрýжóк, 37
bridge – міст, мостá і мóсту, *pl.* мостú, 21
brief – корóткий, 26
briefcase – тéчка; *портфéль, портфéля,* 11
briefer – корóтший, 30
bright *[mentally]* – здíбний, 26
brighter *[mentally]* – здібнíший, 30
broom – мітлá, *pl.* мíтли, мíтел; вíник, -а, 22
brother – брат, брáта, *pl.* братú, 13
brown – корúчневий, 26
brush – щíтка, *pl.* щіткú, щітóк, 28
build – будувáти: будý-ю, -єш
pf. збудувáти: збудý-ю, -єш, 32
builder – будівнúк, будівникá, *pl.* будівникú;
будівéльник, 24
building – будúнок, будúнка і будúнку, 12
bun – бýлочка, 19
bury – ховáти: ховá-ю, -єш
pf. поховáти: поховá-ю,-єш, 27
bush – кущ, кущá, *pl.* кущí, 21
bus – автóбус, -а, 18
bus stop – зупúнка, 18
but – а; алé, 3
butter – мáсло, 19
butterfly – метéлик, -а, 21
button – ґýдзик, -а, 22
buy – купувáти: купý-ю, -єш, 5
pf. купúти: куп-лю́, -иш, 23
by – бíля *[+G]*; кóло *[+G]*, 18

C

cab – таксíвка; таксí *[indecl.]*, 12
cabbage – капýста *[sg]*, 30
cabbage roll – голубéць, голубця́, *pl.* голубцí, 19
cafeteria – кафетéрія; кафетéрій, 12
cake – торт, тóрта, *pl.* тортú, 19
calculator – калькуля́тор *[h]*, -а, 22
calendar – календáр *[s]*, календаря́,
pl. календарí, 27
calf *[cow's offspring]* – теля́ *[n]*, 37

call – клúкати: клúч-у, -еш
pf. поклúкати: поклúч-у, -еш, 35
calorie – кальóрія, *калóрія,* 22
camera – фотоапарáт, -а, 18
camp – тáбір *[h]*, тáбору; осéля *g.pl.* осéль, 25
can – бляшáнка; *бáнка*, 30
Canada – Канáда, 38
Canadian – канáдський; канадíйський, 38
Canadian *[f]* – канáдка; канадíйка, 38
Canadian *[m]* – канáдець, канáдця;
канадíєць, канадíйця, 38
candle – свíчка, *pl.* свічкú, свічóк, 32
candlestick – свічнúк, свічникá,
pl. свічникú, 32
candy – цукéрка; цукéрок, цукéрка, 30
cap – шáпка, *pl.* шапкú, шапóк: *кéпка*, 20
capable – здíбний, 26
capable: more capable – здібнíший, 30
capably – здíбно, 31
capably: more capably – здібнíше, 31
car – áвто; *машúна*, 12
cardigan – свéтер *[h]*, свéтра; *светр [h]*,
свéтра, 20
cards *[playing cards]* – кáрти *[pl]*, карт,
... кáртах, 15
carpenter – тéсля *[m]*, 36
carrots – мóрква *[sg]*, 30
carry – нестú: нес-ý, -éш *[dur.]*, 6
pf. понестú: понес-ý, -éш, 23
carry – носúти: ношý, нóс-иш *[it.]*, 10
pf. понестú: понес-ý, -еш, 23
carton – пáчка, *pl.* пачкú, пачóк, 18
carved artifact – різьбá, 32
carving – різьбá, 32
cash – готíвка *[sg]*, 18
cashier *[f]* – касúрка, 14
cashier *[m]* – касúр *[h]*, 14
cash register – кáса, 14
cassette – касéта, 25
cat – кіт, котá, *pl.* котú, 21
catch – ловúти: лов-лю́, -иш
pf. зловúти: злов-лю́, -иш, 34
celebrate – святкувáти: святкý-ю, -єш
pf. відсвяткувáти: відсвяткý-ю, -єш, 27
celery *[sg]* – селéра, 30
cent – цент, цéнта, 18
century – сторíччя *[n]*; столíття *[n]*, 27
certain – пéвен/пéвний, 32
chair – крíсло; стілéць, стільця́, *pl.* стільцí, 12

chalk – кре́йда *[sg]*, 11
chalkboard – табли́ця; *до́шка*, 11
change *[money]* – зда́ча *[sg]*, 18
change – змі́нювати: змі́ню-ю, -єш
pf. зміни́ти: змін-ю́, -иш, 33
change oneself
– змі́нюватися: змі́ню-юся, -єшся
pf. зміни́тися: змін-ю́ся -ишся, 33
chauffeur – шофе́р *[h]*, 12
cheap – деше́вий; недороги́й, 26
cheaper – деше́вший, 30
cheaply – де́шево; недо́рого, 31
cheaply: more cheaply – деше́вше, 31
checkers – ша́шки *[pl]*, ша́шок, ... ша́шках,15
cheek – щока́, щоки́, *pl.* що́ки, щік, 31
cheese – сир *[h]*, си́ру, *pl.* сири́, 19
chef *[f]* – куха́рка, 24
chef *[m]* – ку́хар *[s]*, *pl.* кухарі́, 24
cherish – коха́ти: коха́-ю, -єш
pf. покоха́ти: покоха́-ю, -єш, 36
chess – ша́хи *[pl]*, ша́хів, ... ша́хах, 15
chest *[body]* – гру́ди *[pl]*, груде́й, грудьми́
і грудима, ... гру́дях, 31
chest *[trunk]* – скри́ня, 32
child – дити́на, *pl.* ді́ти, 13
children – ді́ти, діте́й, ді́тьми, ді́тям,
... ді́тях, 13
chin – підборі́ддя *[n]*, *g.pl.* підборідь і
підборі́ддів, 31
China – Кита́й, 38
Chinese – кита́йський, 38
Chinese *[f]* – кита́йка, 38
Chinese *[m]* – кита́єць, кита́йця, 38
chocolate bar – шоколя́дка; *шокола́дка* , 30
choose – вибира́ти: вибира́-ю, -єш, 17
pf. ви́брати: ви́бер-у, -еш, 23
christening – христи́ни *[pl]*, христи́н,
... христи́нах, 27
Christian *[f]* – христия́нка, 38
Christian *[m]* – християни́н, *pl.* христия́ни,
христия́н, 38
church – це́рква, *pl.* церкви́, церко́в, 18
citizen *[f]* – громадя́нка, 38
citizen *[m]* – громадя́нин, *pl.* громадя́ни,
громадя́н, 38
city – мі́сто, *pl.* міста́, міст, 12
city block – кварта́л, -у, 35
city hall – ра́туша, 35
class – кля́са, *g.pl.* кляс і кля́сів; *клас, -у*, 11
classroom – кля́са, *g.pl.* кляс і кля́сів;
клас, -у, 11
clean – чи́стий, 26
clean – чи́стити: чи́щу, чи́ст-иш, 22
pf. почи́стити: почи́щу, почи́ст-иш, 23
cleaner – чисті́ший, 30
cleanly – чи́сто, 31
cleanly: more cleanly – чисті́ше, 31
clear: it's clear – я́сно, 22
client *[f]* – клі́єнтка, 24
client *[m]* – клі́єнт, 24
climate – клі́мат, -у, 33
climb – ла́зити *[it.]*: ла́жу, ла́з-иш
лі́зти *[dur.]*: лі́з-у, -еш
pf. полі́зти: полі́з-у, -еш, 34
clock – годи́нник, -а, 17
close – зачиня́ти: зачиня́-ю, -єш
pf. зачини́ти: зачи́н-ю, -иш, 29
close (shut) oneself in
– зачиня́тися: зачиня́-юся, -єшся
pf. зачини́тися: зачи́н-юся, -ишся, 29
closet – ша́фа, *pl.* шафи́, шафі́в, 14
close to – бли́зько *[+G]*, 22
clothes – о́дяг *[sg]*, -у, 20
clothing – о́дяг *[sg]*, -у, 20
cloud – хма́ра, 33
cloudy: it's cloudy – хма́рно, 33
coat *[spring, fall]* – плащ, плаща́, *pl.* плащі́, 20
coat *[winter]* – пальто́, *pl.* па́льта, 20
cocktail – кокте́йль, кокте́йлю, 15
coffee – ка́ва, 15
coffee table – сто́лик, -а, 17
coffee pot – ка́вник, -а, 17
cold – холо́дний, 33
cold: it's cold – хо́лодно, 33
colour – ко́лір, ко́льору, 32
colt – лоша́ *[n]*, 37
comb – гре́бінь, гре́беня, 28
comb – зачі́сувати: зачі́су-ю, -єш
pf. зачеса́ти: зачеш-у́, -еш, 28
comb oneself – зачі́суватися: зачі́су-юся, -єшся
pf. зачеса́тися: зачеш-у́ся, -ешся, 28
come *[by vehicle]* – ї́здити: ї́жджу, ї́зд-иш *[it.]*, 10
pf. пої́хати: пої́д-у, -еш, 23
come *[by vehicle]* – ї́хати: ї́д-у, -еш *[dur.]*, 7
pf. пої́хати: пої́д-у, -еш, 23
come *[on foot]* – іти́: ід-у́, -е́ш *[dur.]*, 6
pf. піти́: під-у́, -е́ш, 23

come *[on foot]* – ходи́ти: ходжу́, хо́д-иш *[it.]*, 10
pf. піти́: під-у́, -е́ш, 23
come back – поверта́тися: поверта́-юся, -єшся
pf. поверну́тися: поверн-у́ся, -ешся, 29
come into – вхо́дити: вхо́джу, вхо́д-иш, 15
pf. увійти́: увійд-у́, -е́ш, 23
come out of
– вихо́дити: вихо́джу, вихо́д-иш, 18
pf. ви́йти: ви́йд-у, -еш, 23
commonly: more commonly – звичайні́ше, 31
competition – ко́нкурс, -у, 32
complain – ска́ржитися: ска́рж-уся, -ишся, 8
pf. поска́ржитися: поска́рж-уся, -ишся, 23
computer – комп'ю́тер *[h]*, -а, 11
conceal – хова́ти: хова́-ю, -єш
pf. захова́ти: захова́-ю, -єш, 27
conceal oneself – хова́тися: хова́-юся, -єшся
pf. схова́тися: схова́-юся, -єшся, 27
concert – конце́рт, -у, 15
conference – з'їзд, з'ї́зду, 27
construction worker – будіве́льник; будівни́к, будівника́, *pl.* будівники́, 24
contest – змага́ння *[n]*, 34
convention – з'їзд, з'ї́зду, 27
converse – розмовля́ти: розмовля́-ю, -єш, 4
pf. порозмовля́ти: порозмовля́-ю, -єш, 23
cook *[f]* – куха́рка, 24
cook *[m]* – ку́хар*[s]*, *pl.* кухарі́, 24
cookie – ті́стечко, 19
coral beads – кора́лі *[pl]*, кора́лів, ... кора́лях, 28
corn – кукуру́дза *[sg]*, 30
corner – куто́к, кутка́, *pl.* кутки́, 17
corridor – коридо́р *[h]*, -а, 11
cost – коштува́ти: кошту́-ю, -єш, 17
cottage – ко́тедж, -у; *да́ча* , 25
couch – кана́па, 14
council – ра́да, 37
country – край, кра́ю, *pl.* краї́; краї́на; держа́ва, 38
cousin *[f]* – кузи́на; кузи́нка, 13
cousin *[m]* – кузе́н, 13
cow – коро́ва, *g.pl.* корі́в, 21
coward – боягу́з, 37
cowboy – ковбо́й, 37
crawl – ла́зити *[it.]*: ла́жу, ла́з-иш
лі́зти *[dur.]*: лі́з-у, -еш
pf. полі́зти: полі́з-у, -еш, 34
cream *[sour]* – смета́на, 19
cream *[sweet]* – вершки́ *[pl]*, вершкі́в, ... вершка́х, 19
crepe – нали́сник, -а, 19
cripple – калі́ка *[m,f]*, 37
cross – хрест, хреста́, *pl.* хрести́, 32
crosswalk – перехі́д, перехо́ду, 35
cry – пла́кати: пла́ч-у, -еш, 7
pf. запла́кати: запла́ч-у, -еш, 23
cucumber – огіро́к, огірка́, *pl.* огірки́, 30
cup – горня́тко; ча́шка, *pl.* чашки́, чашо́к, 17
cupboard – ша́фа, *pl.* шафи́, шафі́в, 14
curtain – фіра́нка, 17
customer *[f]* – покупни́ця, 14
customer *[m]* – покупе́ць, покупця́, *pl.* покупці́, 14
customs *[at a border crossing]* – ми́тниця, 38
cut – кра́яти: кра́-ю, -єш, 21
pf. покра́яти: покра́-ю, -єш, 23

D

dad – та́то, *v.sg.* та́ту!, 13
dance *[formal]* – заба́ва; баль, ба́лю, *pl.* балі́, 15
dance – та́нець, та́нцю, *pl.* та́нці, 32
dance – танцюва́ти: танцю́-ю, -єш, 5
pf. потанцюва́ти: потанцю́-ю, -єш, 23
dancer *[f]* – танцюри́стка, 24
dancer *[m]* – танцюри́ст, 24
dare – smі́ти: смі́-ю, -єш,
pf. посмі́ти: посмі́-ю, -єш, 36
dark – те́мний, 33
date – поба́чення *[n]*, 29
date *[calendar]* – да́та; число́, *pl.* чи́сла, чи́сел, 27
daughter – дочка́, *pl.* до́чки, до́чок, 13
daughter-in-law – неві́стка, *pl.* неві́стки́, неві́сто́к, 13
day – день, дня, 16
day after tomorrow – післяза́втра, 16
day before yesterday – позавчо́ра, 16
day: every day – щодня́, 10
day: during the day – уде́нь/вдень, 8
daytime: in the daytime – уде́нь/вдень, 8
death – смерть *[f]*, сме́рти, 36
debt – борг, бо́ргу, ... боргу́, *pl.* борги́, 37
December – гру́день, гру́дня, 16
deep freeze – морози́льник, -а, 17
delighted: to be – ті́шитися: ті́ш-уся, -ишся, 8
pf. уті́шитися: уті́ш-уся, -ишся, 23

dentist *[f]* – денти́стка; *данти́стка*, 24

dentist *[m]* – денти́ст; *данти́ст* , 24

deodorant – дезодора́нт, -а, 28

depart *[by vehicle]*
– від'їжджа́ти: від'їжджа́-ю, -єш
pf. від'ї́хати: від'ї́д-у, -еш, 27

depart *[on foot]*
– відхо́дити: відхо́джу, відхо́д-иш
pf. віді́йти́: віді́йд-у́, -е́ш, 29

description – о́пис, -у, 36

dessert – десе́рт, -у, 19

detective – детекти́в, 36

detective – детекти́вний, 36

devil – дия́вол; ді́дько; чорт, чо́рта,
pl. чорти́; біс, бі́са, *pl.* біси́

dictionary – словни́к, словника́,
pl. словники́, 11

die – умира́ти: умира́-ю, -єш
pf. у/по/ме́рти: у/по/мр-у́, -е́ш, 27

diet – дiє́та, 22

difficult – трудни́й, 32

dining room – ї́да́льня, *g.pl.* ї́да́лень, 14

dinner *[meal at noon]* – обі́д, -у, 15

dinner *[evening meal]* – вече́ря, 15

dinner: to have dinner
– обі́дати: обі́да-ю, -єш, 4
pf. пообі́дати: пообі́да-ю, -єш, 23

director*[f]* – дире́кторка , 37

director*[m]* – дире́ктор *[h]*, 37

dirtier – брудні́ший, 30

dirtily – бру́дно, 31

dirtily: more dirtily – брудні́ше, 31

dirty – брудни́й, 26

dishes – по́суд *[sg]*, -у, 17

dishonest – нече́сний, 37

dishonourable – нече́сний, 37

dishwasher – посудоми́йка,
g.pl. посудоми́йок, 17

display window – вітри́на, 14

do – роби́ти: роб-лю́, -иш, 9
pf. зроби́ти: зроб-лю́, -иш, 23

doctor *[f]* – лі́карка; до́кторка, 12

doctor *[m]* – лі́кар *[s]*, *pl.* лікарі́; до́ктор *[h]*,
pl. доктори́, 12

dog – пес, пса, *pl.* пси, 21

doll – ля́лька, 32

dollar – до́ляр *[h]*, -а; до́лар *[h]*, -а, 18

door – две́рі *[pl]*, двере́й, двiрми́ і двери́ма,
две́рям, ... две́рях, 11

dough *[for bread, etc.]* – ті́сто, 32

doughnut – пампу́шка, 30

down – уни́з/вниз, удоли́ну/вдоли́ну, 6

downwards – уни́з/вниз, удоли́ну/вдоли́ну, 6

dozen – дю́жина, 30

drawer – шухля́да, 14

dress – суке́нка; суко́нка; *пла́ття*, 20

dress oneself – одяга́тися: одяга́ю-ся, -єшся, 5
pf. одягну́тися: одягн-у́ся, -ешся, 23

dress – одяга́ти: одяга́-ю, -єш
pf. одягну́ти: одя́гн-у, -еш, 28

drink – пи́ти: п'-ю, -єш, 5
pf. ви́пити: ви́п'-ю, -єш, 23

drive *[by vehicle]* – ї́хати: ї́д-у, -еш *[dur.]*, 7
pf. пої́хати: пої́д-у, -еш, 23

drive *[by vehicle]* – ї́здити: ї́жджу, ї́зд-иш *[it.]*, 10
pf. пої́хати: пої́д-у, -еш, 23

driver – воді́й, водія́, *v.sg.*водíю, *pl.* водії́, 12

driveway – за́ї́зд, -у, 35

druggist *[f]* – апте́карка, 24

druggist *[m]* – апте́кар *[s]*, 24

drugstore – апте́ка, 28

drum – бараба́н, -а, 16

drunkard – п'яни́ця*[m,f]*, 37

drycleaning shop – хемчи́стка; *хімчи́стка*, 28

dry – витира́ти: витира́-ю, -єш
pf. ви́терти: ви́тр-у, -еш, 28

dry oneself – витира́тися: витира́-юся, -єшся
pf. ви́тертися: ви́тр-уся, -ешся, 28

dulcimer – цимба́ли *[pl]*, цимба́лів,
... цимба́лах, 16

dumpling – варе́ник; пирі́г, пирога́,
pl. пироги́, 19

during the day – уде́нь/вдень, 8

duty *[tax on imported goods]* – мито́, 38

E

ear – ву́хо, 28

earlier – рані́ше, 10

early – ра́но, 5

early – ра́нній *[s]*, 33

earring – ку́льчик, -а; сере́жка, 28

earth – земля́, *pl.* зе́млі, земе́ль,
... зе́млях, 27

east – схід, схо́ду, 16

Easter egg – пи́санка, *pl.* писанки́,
писано́к, 32

easier – ле́гший, 30

easily – ле́гко, 31

easily: more easily – ле́гше, 31
easy – легки́й, 30
eat – ї́сти: їм, їси́, їсть, їмо́, їсте́, їдя́ть, 10
pf. з'ї́сти: з'ї-м, -си́, 23
editor *[f]* – реда́кторка, 24
editor *[m]* – реда́ктор *[h]*, 24
egg – яйце́, *pl.* я́йця, яє́ць, 19
eight – ві́сім, 19
eighteen – вісімна́дцять, 19
eighteenth – вісімна́дцятий, 27
eighth – во́сьмий, 27
eight hundred – вісімсо́т, 19
eightieth – вісімдеся́тий, 27
eighty – вісімдеся́т, 19
either ... or – або́ ... або́, 3
elbow – лі́коть, лі́ктя, 31
electrician – еле́ктрик, 24
elevator *[in a building]* – ліфт, лі́фта, 35
eleven – одина́дцять, 19
eleventh – одина́дцятий, 27
embassy – посо́льство; амбаса́да, 38
embroider – вишива́ти: вишива́-ю, -єш
pf. ви́шити: ви́ши-ю, -єш, 32
embroidered – ви́шитий, 32
embroidered article – ви́шивка, 32
employee *[f]* – працівни́ця, 20
employee *[m]* – працівни́к, працівника́, *pl.* працівники́, 20
end – кіне́ць, кінця́, *pl.* кінці́, 29
end – кінча́ти: кінча́-ю, -єш
pf. скінчи́ти: скінч-у́, -и́ш, 29
end: to come to an end
– кінча́тися: кінча́-ється, -ються
pf. скінчи́тися: скінч-и́ться, -а́ться, 29
end table – сто́лик, -а, 17
engage in a leisure activity that involves movement on something
– ката́тися: ката́-юся, -єшся
pf. поката́тися: поката́-юся,-єшся, 34
engage: to become engaged
– зару́чуватися: зару́чу-юся, -єшся
pf. заручи́тися: заруч-у́ся, -ишся, 36
engineer – інжене́р *[h]*, 24
England – А́нглія, 38
English – англі́йський, 38
Englishman – англі́єць, англі́йця, 38
Englishwoman – англі́йка, 38
enough – до́сить, 19
enter, – вхо́дити: вхо́джу, вхо́д-иш, 15
pf. увійти́: увійд-у́, -е́ш, 23
entrance – вхід, вхо́ду, *pl.* вхо́ди, 35
envelope – конве́рта; конве́рт, -а, 18
eraser – ґу́мка, 11
Europe – Євро́па, 38
European – европе́йський, 38
European *[f]* – европе́йка, 38
European *[m]* – европе́єць, европе́йця, 38
even – на́віть, 4
evening – ве́чір *[h]*, ве́чора, *pl.* вечори́, 29
evening: every evening – щове́чора, 10
evening: in the evening – уве́чорі/вве́чорі, уве́чері/вве́чері, 8
evening meal – вече́ря, 15
evening social – вечі́рка, 15
evening: this evening
– сього́дні вве́чорі; сього́дні вве́чері, 9
every – ко́жен/ко́жний, 32
everybody – усі́/всі, 6
every day – щодня́, 10
every evening – щове́чора, 10
every hour – щогоди́ни, 10
every minute – щохвили́ни, 10
every month – щомі́сяця, 10
every morning – щора́нку, 10
every night – щоно́чі, 10
everyone – усі́/всі, 6
every one – ко́жен/ко́жний, 32
everything – усе́/все, 6
every week – щоти́жня, 10
everywhere – усю́ди/всю́ди, 7
every year – щоро́ку, 10
exam – і́спит, -у; екза́мен, -у, 29
excellently – прекра́сно, 4
except for – крім *[+G]*, 22
excursion – екску́рсія, 25
exhausted – сто́млений; зму́чений, 37
exhibition – ви́ставка, 32
exit – вихо́дити: вихо́джу, вихо́д-иш, 18
pf. ви́йти: ви́йд-у, -еш, 22
exit – ви́хід, ви́ходу, *pl.* ви́ходи, 35
expensive – дороги́й, 26
expensive: more expensive – доро́жчий, 30
expensively – до́рого, 31
expensively: more expensively – доро́жче, 31

explain – поя́снювати: поя́сню-ю, -єш,
pf. поясни́ти: поясн-ю́, -и́ш, 35
eye – о́ко, ... о́ці, *pl.* о́чі, оче́й, очи́ма, оча́м, ... оча́х, 31
eyebrow – брова́, *pl.* бро́ви, брів, 31
eyelash – вія, 31
eyeglasses – окуля́ри *[pl]*, окуля́рів, ... окуля́рах, 18

F

fable – ба́йка, *pl.* байки, байо́к, 36
fabric – ткани́на, 32
face – лице́, *pl.* ли́ця, лиць; обли́ччя *[n]*, *g.pl.* обли́ч і обли́ччів, 31
factory – фа́брика; *заво́д, -у*, 35
fairy – фе́я, 37
fairy tale – ка́зка, *pl.* казки́, казо́к, 36
fall – осі́нній *[s]*, 16
fall – о́сінь *[f]*, о́сени, 16
fall – па́дати: па́да-ю, -єш, 22
pf. упа́сти: упад-у́, -е́ш, 23
fall: in the fall – восени́, 8
family *[extended]* – рідня́ *[sg]*, 13
family *[immediate]* – роди́на; сім'я́, сім'ї́, сім'є́ю; сі́м'ї, сі́мей і сі́м'їв, сі́м'ями, ... сі́м'ях, 13
fan *[enthusiatic supporter]* – болі́льник, 34
farm – фа́рма, *фе́рма*, 13
farmer *[f]* – фа́рмерка; *фе́рмерка* , 13
farmer *[m]* – фа́рмер *[h]*; *фе́рмер [h]*, 13
fast – швидки́й, 30
faster – шви́дший, 30
father – ба́тько, *pl.* батьки́, 13
father-in-law *[man's]* – тесть, те́стя, *pl.* те́сті, 13
father-in-law *[woman's]* – све́кор *[h]*, све́кра, *pl.* све́кри, 13
fault: to be at fault – ви́нен/ви́нний, 32
favorite – улю́блений, 32
fear – боя́тися: бо-ю́ся, -ї́шся, 9
feast day – свя́то, 27
February – лю́тий *[sub.]*, лю́того, 16
feel like doing something – хоті́тися: хо́четься
pf. схоті́тися: схо́четься, 33
fence – парка́н, паркана́, *pl.* паркани́, 21
few – кі́лька, 19
fiancé – нарече́ний *[sub.]*, нарече́ної, 36
fiancée – нарече́на *[sub.]*, нарече́ного, 36
field – по́ле, *pl.* поля́, піль і полі́в, 21
fifteen – п'ятна́дцять, 19
fifteenth – п'ятна́дцятий, 27
fifth – п'я́тий, 27
fiftieth – п'ятдеся́тий, 27
fifty – п'ятдеся́т, 19
fight – боро́тися: бор-ю́ся, -ешся, 7
pf. поборо́тися: побор-ю́ся, -ешся, 23
film – фільм, фі́льму, *pl.* фі́льми, 32
find – знахо́дити: знахо́джу, знахо́д-иш, 22
pf. знайти́: знайд-у́, -е́ш, 23
fine – до́бре, 4
finger – па́лець, па́льця, *pl.* па́льці, 28
fingernail – ні́готь, ні́гтя, *pl.* ні́гті, 31
finish – кінча́ти: кінча́-ю, -єш
pf. скінчи́ти: скінч-у́, -и́ш, 29
finish: to be finished
– кінча́тися: кінча́-ється, -ються,
pf. скінчи́тися: скінч-и́ться, -а́ться, 29
fire fighter – поже́жник, 35
fire truck – поже́жна маши́на, 35
first – пе́рший, 27
fish – ри́ба, 19
fist – кула́к, кулака́, *pl.* кулаки́, 31
five – п'ять, 19
five hundred – п'ятсо́т, 19
fix – ла́годити: ла́годжу, ла́год-иш, 21
pf. зла́годити: зла́годжу, зла́год-иш, 23
flashlight – ліхта́рик, -а, 18
flash of lightning – бли́скавка, 33
flash lightning – бли́скати: бли́скає, 33
pf. забли́скати: забли́скає
flood – по́вінь *[f]*, по́вені, 36
floor – підло́га, *g.pl.* підло́г, 14
flower – кві́тка, *pl.* квітки́, квіто́к, 21
flower bed – квітни́к, квітниа́, *pl.* квітни́й, 22
fly – леті́ти: лечу́, лет-и́ш *[dur.]*, 9
pf. полеті́ти: полечу́, полет-и́ш, 23
fly – літа́ти: літа́-ю, -єш *[it.]*, 10
pf. полеті́ти: полечу́, полет-и́ш, 23
fly – му́ха, 21
fog – тума́н, -у, 33
foggy: it's foggy – тума́нно, 33
following – насту́пний, 33
foolish – дурни́й, 26
foolish: more foolish – дурні́ший, 26
foot – нога́, *pl.* но́ги, ніг, 31
football *[game]* – футбо́л, -у, 15
for – за *[+A]*; на *[+A]*, 15; для *[+G]*, 18; по *[+A]*, 22
for a long time – до́вго, 9

for a longer time – до́вше, 9
for a short time – ненадо́вго, 29
foreign – чужи́й; інозе́мний, 38
foreigner *[f]* – чужи́нка; інозе́мка, 38
foreigner *[m]* – чужи́нець, чужи́нця; інозе́мець, інозе́мця, 38
forest – ліс, лі́су, *pl.* ліси́, 21
forget – забува́ти: забува́-ю, -єш, 22
pf. забу́ти: забу́д-у, -еш, 23
fork – виде́лка, 17
formal dance – заба́ва; баль, ба́лю, *pl.* балі́, 15
former – бу́вший, 33
for nothing – ду́рно, 31
fortieth – сороко́вий, 27
fortunate – щасли́вий, 26
fortunate: more fortunate – щасливі́ший, 30
fortunately – щасли́во, 31
fortunately: more fortunately – щасливі́ше, 31
forty – со́рок, 19
fountain – водогра́й, водогра́ю; фонта́н, -у, 21
four – чоти́ри, 19
four hundred – чоти́риста, 19
fourteen – чотирна́дцять, 19
fourteenth – чотирна́дцятий, 27
fourth – четве́ртий, 27
France – Фра́нція, 38
freeze – моро́зити: моро́жу, моро́з-иш,
pf. заморо́зити: заморо́жу, заморо́з-иш, 33
freezer – морози́льник, -а, 17
French – францу́зький, 38
Frenchman – францу́з, 38
Frenchwoman – францу́женка, 38
frequently – ча́сто, 3
frequently: more frequently – частíше, 31
Friday – п'я́тниця, 16
fridge – холоди́льник, -а, 17
friend *[f]* – това́ришка, *pl.* товаришки́, товаришо́к, 11
friend *[m]* – това́риш, *pl.* товариші́, 11
frightened, to be – боя́тися: бо-ю́ся, -ї́шся, 9
frizbee – фри́збі *[indecl.]*, 34
from – від *[+G]*, 18
from here – звíдси, 9
from out of – з *[+G]*, 18
from there – звíдти, 9
from where – звíдки, 9
frost – моро́з, -у, 33
fruit – садовина́ *[sg]*; о́воч, -у; *фрукт, фру́кта, pl. фру́кти*, 30
funeral – по́хорон, -у, 27
funny – смішни́й, 36
fur coat – ху́тро, *g.pl.* хутр і ху́тер; кожу́х, кожу́ха, ... кожу́ху і ... кожу́сі; *шу́ба*, 20
furniture – ме́блі *[pl]*, ме́блів, ... ме́блях, 14

G

gallery – ґалері́я, *галере́я*, 35
game – гра *pl.* і́гри, і́гор, 32
garage – ґара́ж, -у; гара́ж, -у, 12
garbage can – смітни́к, смітника́, *pl.* смітники́, 35
garden – горо́д, -у, 30
garlic – часни́к *[sg]*, часнику́, 30
garter snake – вуж, вужа́, *pl.* вужі́, 21
genius – ге́ній, 11
gasoline – бензи́на, *бензи́н,-у*, 35
gas station – запра́вка, 35
German – німе́цький, 38
German *[f]* – німке́ня; ні́мка, 38
German *[m]* – ні́мець, ні́мця, 38
Germany – Німе́ччина, 38
get – діставá́ти: діста-ю́, -є́ш
pf. діста́ти: діста́н-у, -еш, 35
get married
– одру́жуватися: одру́жу-юся, -єшся, 5
pf. одружи́тися: одру́ж-уся, -ишся, 23
get up – устава́ти/встава́ти: уста-ю́, -є́ш, 5
pf. уста́ти/вста́ти: уста́н-у, -еш, 23
gift – подару́нок, подару́нка, 18
girl – ді́вчина, *pl.* дівча́та, 13
give – дава́ти; да-ю́, -є́ш, 20
pf. да́ти: да-м, -си́, 23
give advice – ра́дити: ра́джу, ра́д-иш
pf. пора́дити: пора́джу, пора́д-иш, 35
give back – поверта́ти: поверта́-ю, -єш
pf. поверну́ти: поверн-у́, -еш, 29
give birth – наро́джувати: наро́джу-ю, -єш,
народи́ти: надо́джу, наро́д-иш, 27
glad: to be glad – ті́шитися: ті́ш-уся, -ишся, 8
pf. уті́шитися: уті́ш-уся, -ишся, 23
gladden someone – ті́шити: ті́ш-у, -иш,
pf. уті́шити: уті́ш-у, -иш, 28
glass – скло, 32
glass *[for drinking]* – скля́нка, *pl.* склянки́, склянóк, 17

glove – рукави́чка, 20
go *[by vehicle]* – ї́хати: ї́д-у, -еш *[dur.]*, 7
pf. пої́хати: пої́д-у, -еш, 23
go *[by vehicle]* – ї́здити: ї́жджу, ї́зд-иш *[it.]*, 10
pf. пої́хати: пої́д-у, -еш, 23
go *[on foot]* – іти́: ід-у́, -е́ш *[dur.]* , 6
pf. піти́: під-у́, -е́ш, 23
go *[on foot]* – ходи́ти: ходжу́, хо́д-иш *[it.]*, 10
pf. піти́: під-у́, -е́ш, 23
God – Бог, Бо́га, *v.sg.* Бо́же! *pl.* боги́, 37
golf – ґольф, -у; *гольф, -у*, 15
good – до́брий, 26
goods – това́р *[h]*, това́ру, 38
government – у́ряд, -у, 38
grandchild – онуча́ *[n]*, внуча́ *[n]*, 37
granddaughter – ону́ка; вну́ка, 13
grandfather – дід, *v.sg.* ді́ду!
pl. діди́; діду́сь, 13
grandmother – ба́ба, *pl.* баби́, бабі́в; бабу́ся, 13
grandpa – дід, *v.sg.* ді́ду! *pl.* діди́; діду́сь, 13
grandson – ону́к; внук, вну́ка, 13
granny – ба́ба, *pl.* баби́, бабі́в; бабу́ся, 13
grapes – виногра́д *[sg]*, -у, 30
grass – трава́, трави́, *pl.* тра́ви, 21
great – вели́кий, 26
greater – бі́льший, 30
great granddaughter – пра́внука, 13
great grandfather – пра́дід, *v.sg.* пра́діду!
pl. пра́діди, 13
great grandmother – праба́ба, 13
great grandson – пра́внук, 13
Greece – Гре́ція, 38
Greek – гре́цький, 38
Greek *[f]* – греки́ня, 38
Greek *[m]* – грек, гре́ка, *pl.* гре́ки, 38
green – зеле́ний, 26
greener – зелені́ший, 30
grey – сі́рий; си́вий *[of hair]*, 26
greyer – сірі́ший; сиві́ший *[of hair]*, 30
groan – стогна́ти: сто́гн-у, -еш, 7
pf. застогна́ти: застогн-у́, -еш, 23
ground – земля́, 27
grow – рости́: рост-у́, -е́ш, 6
pf. ви́рости: ви́рост-у, -еш, 23
guest *[f]* – го́стя, *pl.* (see гість), 25
guest *[m]* – гість, го́стя, *pl.* го́сті, госте́й
гі́стьми, го́стям, ... го́стях, 25
guilty – ви́нен/ви́нний, 32
guitar – ґіта́ра; *гіта́ра*, 16
gym shoe – тенісі́вка: *кед, ке́да*, 20

H

hail – град, гра́ду, 33
hair – воло́сся *[n]*, 28
hairdo – за́чіска, 28
hairdresser *[f]* – перука́рка, 24
hairdresser *[m]* – перука́р *[h]*, 24
hair salon – перука́рня, 35
hair stylist *[f]* – перука́рка, 24
hair stylist *[m]* – перука́р *[h]*, 24
half – пів, 29
half an hour – півгоди́ни, 29
hall – за́ля; *зал, за́лу*, 29
ham – ши́нка, 19
hand – рука́, *pl.* ру́ки, рук, 28
hand lotion – крем, -у: крем для рук, 28
happen – відбува́тися: відбува́-ється, -ються, 27
pf. відбу́тися: відбу́д-еться, -уться
happier – веселі́ший, 30
happily – ве́село, 31
happily: more happily – веселі́ше, 31
happy – весе́лий, 26
hat – капелю́х, капелю́ха, ... капелю́сі, 20
haul – везти́: вез-у́, -е́ш *[dur.]* , 6
pf. повезти́: повез-у́, -е́ш, 23
haul – вози́ти: вожу́, во́з-иш *[it.]*, 10
pf. повезти́: повез-у́, -е́ш, 23
have – ма́ти: ма́-ю, -єш, 15
have breakfast – сні́дати: сні́да-ю, -єш, 4
pf. посні́дати: посні́да-ю, -єш, 23
have dinner – обі́дати: обі́да-ю, -єш, 4
pf. пообі́дати: пообі́да-ю, -єш, 23
have supper – вече́ряти: вече́ря-ю, -єш, 4
pf. повече́ряти: повече́ря-ю, -єш, 23
have to – му́сити: му́шу, му́с-иш, 9
pf. змусити: зму́шу, зму́с-иш, 23
he – він, 2
head – голова́, *pl.* го́лови, голі́в,
... голова́х, 31
healthier – здоро́вший, 30
healthily – здо́рово, 31
healthily: more healthily – здоро́вше, 31
healthy – здоро́вий, 26
hear – чу́ти: чу́-ю, -єш, 4
pf. почу́ти: почу́-ю, -єш, 23
heart – се́рце, *pl.* серця́, серде́ць, 31
heatwave – спе́ка, 33
heaven – не́бо, *pl.* небеса́, 27
heavier – тя́жчий, 30
heavily – тя́жко, 31

heavily: more heavily – тя́жче, 31
heavy – тяжки́й, 30
hedge – живоплі́т, живопло́ту, 22
heel – п'ята́, п'яти́, *pl.* п'я́ти, п'ят, 31
helicopter – вертолі́т, вертольо́та, 35
hell – пе́кло, 27
help – по́міч *[f]*, по́мочі; допомо́га, 36
help – помага́ти: помага́-ю, -єш, 20
pf. помогти́: помо́ж-у́, -еш, 23
her – її́ *[indecl.]*, 28
here: from here – зві́дси, 9
here: in this place – тут, 2
here, – ось, 2
here: to this place – сюди́, 7
hero – геро́й, 36
heroine – геро́їня, 36
hers – її́ *[indecl.]*, 28
hide – хова́ти: хова́-ю, -єш
pf. схова́ти: схова́-ю, -єш, 27
hide oneself – хова́тися: хова́-юся, -єшся, 27
pf. схова́тися: схова́-юся, -єшся
high – висо́кий, 26
higher – ви́щий, 30
highly – ви́соко, 31
highly: more highly – ви́ще, 31
highway – шосе́ *[indecl.]*; автостра́да, 35
hill – горб, горба́, *pl.* горби́, 34
his – його́ *[indecl.]*, 28
historical – істори́чний, 36
hobby – улю́блене заня́ття *[n]*, 32
hockey – го́кей, го́кею; *хоке́й, хоке́ю*, 15
holiday – свя́то, 27
holidays – вака́ції *[pl]*, вака́цій, ... вака́ціях, 25
home – дім, до́му, *pl.* доми́, 12
home: at home – удо́ма/вдо́ма, 2
home: to a home, homewards – додо́му, 7
homewards – додо́му, 7
homework – завда́ння *[n]*, 11
honest – че́сний, 37
honey – мед, ме́ду, *pl.* меди́, 19
honeymoon – медо́вий мі́сяць, 36
honourable – че́сний, 37
hope – наді́ятися: наді́-юся, -єшся, 32
horse – кінь, коня́, *pl.* ко́ні, коне́й, кі́ньми,
ко́ням, ко́нях, 21
horseback rider *[f]* – ве́ршниця, 34
horseback rider *[m]* – ве́ршник, 34
hospital – ліка́рня, *g.pl.* ліка́рень; шпита́ль,
шпита́лю, 12

hot: it's hot – ду́шно, 33
hotel – готе́ль, готе́лю, 12
hour – годи́на, 29
hour: every hour – щогоди́ни, 10
house – ха́та, *pl.* хати́, хат і хаті́в; *буди́нок,
буди́нка і буди́нку*, 12
house plant – вазо́нок, вазо́нка, 17
how – як, 4
how much – скі́льки, 4
how often – як ча́сто, 10
hundred – сто, 19
hundredth – со́тий, 27
hungrier – голодні́ший, 30
hungrily – го́лодно, 31
hungrily: more hungrily – голодні́ше, 31
hungry – голо́дний, 26
hurricane – гураґа́н, -у; *ураган, -у*, 33
hurry – спіши́ти: спіш-у́, -и́ш, 8
pf. поспіши́ти: поспіш-у́, -и́ш, 23
hurt – болі́ти: боли́ть, боля́ть
pf. заболі́ти: заболи́ть, заболя́ть
husband – чолові́к; муж, му́жа, *pl.* мужі́, 13
hydrant – гідра́нт, -а, 35
hypocrite – лицемі́р *[h]*, 37

I

I – я, 2
ice – лід, льо́ду, ... льоду́, *pl.* льоди́, 34
ice cream – моро́зиво, 19
icon – іко́на, 32
idler – неро́ба *[m,f]*, 37
if – чи, 8
ill – хво́рий, 26
ill: more ill – хворі́ший, 30
impatient – нетерпели́вий, 37
important – важли́вий, 32
in *[in time expressions]* – за *[+A]* , че́рез *[+A]*, 29
in – у/в *[+L]* , *[+A]* , *[+G]*, 14
in a short time – незаба́ром, 29
India – І́ндія, 38
Indian – інді́йський, 38
Indian *[f]* – інді́йка, 38
Indian *[m]* – інді́єць, інді́йця, 38
inexpensive – деше́вий, недороги́й, 26
inexpensive: more inexpensive – деше́вший, 30
inexpensively – де́шево, 31

inexpensively: more inexpensively – дешéвше, 31
infant – дитя́ *[n]*, немовля́ *[n]*, 37
in front of – пéред *[+I]*, 21
in place of – зáмість *[+G]*, 22
inquire – питáти: питá-ю, -єш, 4
pf. спитáти: спитá-ю, -єш, 23
instead of – зáмість *[+G]*, 22
institute – інститýт, -у, 35
in such a manner – так, 8
intelligent – розýмний, 26
intelligent: more intelligent – розумні́ший, 30
intelligently – розýмно, 31
intelligently: more intelligently – розумні́ше, 31
interest: to be of interest to someone
– цікáвити: цікáв-лю, -иш
pf. зацікáвити: зацікáв-лю, -иш, 33
interesting – цікáвий, 32
intersection – перехрéстя *[n]*, 12
interview – інтерв'ю́ *[indecl.]*, 37
in the afternoon – попóлудні, після обíду, 8
in the daytime – удéнь/вдень, 8
in the evening
– увéчорі/ввéчорі; увéчері/ввéчері, 8
in the fall – восени́, 8
in the middle of – сéред *[+G]*, 22
in the morning – урáнці/врáнці, 8
in the spring – навеснí, 8
in the summer – улíтку/влíтку, 8
in the winter – узи́мку/взи́мку, 8
into – у/в *[+A]* , 15
invite – запрóшувати: запрóшу-ю, -єш
pf. запроси́ти: запрошý, запрóс-иш, 36
Ireland – Ірля́ндія, 38
Irish – ірля́ндський, 38
Irishman – ірля́ндець, ірля́ндця, 38
Irishwoman – ірля́ндка, 38
iron – прасувáти: прасý-ю, -єш
pf. ви́прасувати: ви́прасу-ю, -єш, 26
it – вонó, 2
Italy – Íталія, 38
Italian – італíйський, 38
Italian *[f]* – італíйка, 38
Italian *[m]* – італíєць, італі́йця, 38
itinerary – маршрýт, -у, 29
its – йогó *[indecl.]*, 28

J

jacket – жакéт, -а; кýртка, 20
jail – тюрмá; в'язни́ця, 35
jam – пови́дло; *джем, джéму*, 19
janitor – стóрож, стóрожа, *pl.* сторожí, 24
January – сíчень, сíчня, 16
Japan – Япóнія, 38
Japanese – япóнський, 38
Japanese *[f]* – япóнка, 38
Japanese *[m]* – япóнець, япóнця, 38
jar – слóїк, -а; *бáнка*, 30
jeans – джíнси *[pl]*, джíнсів, ... джíнсах;
джи́нси, джи́нсів, ... джи́нсах, 20
jeep – джіп, джíпа, 35
joke – жартувáти: жартý-ю, -єш, 5
pf. пожартувáти: пожартý-ю, -єш, 23
journal – журнáл, -у, 17
journalist *[f]* – журналíстка, 24
journalist *[m]* – журналíст, 24
judge – суддя́ *[m]*, 37
juice – сік, сóку, *pl.* сóки, 15
July – ли́пень, ли́пня, 16
jump – скакáти: скач-ý, -еш
pf. скóчити: скóч-у, -иш, 34
June – чéрвень, чéрвня, 16
jungle gym – лáзанка, 34

K

kerchief – хýстка, *pl.* хустки́, хустóк, 20
kettle – чáйник, -а, 17
key – ключ, ключá, *pl.* ключí, 18
kilogram – кілогрáм, -а, 19
kilometer – кіломéтр, -а, 34
kindergarten – садóчок, садóчка; *дитсадóк, дитсадкá*, 32
kiosk – кіóск, -а, 35
kiss – цілувáти: цілý-ю, -єш
pf. поцілувáти: поцілý-ю, -єш, 32
kitchen – кýхня, *g.pl.* кýхонь, 14
knapsack – наплéчник, -а; *рюкзáк, рюкзакá, pl. рюкзаки́*, 11
knee – колíно, 31
knife – ніж, ножá, *pl.* ножí, 17
knock – стýкати: стýка-ю, -єш
pf. стýкнути: стýкн-у, -еш, 31
know – знáти: знá-ю, -єш, 4

know how – умíти/вмíти: умí-ю, -єш, 4
pf. зумíти: зумí-ю, -єш, 23
Korea – Корéя, 38
Korean – корéйський, 38
Korean *[f]* – корéйка, 38
Korean *[m]* – корéєць, корéйця, 38
kylym – ки́ли́м, -а, *pl.* килими́, 14

L

laboratory – лябораторія; *лабораторія*, 22
labourer *[f]* – робітни́ця, 12
labourer *[m]* – робітни́к, робітникá, *pl.* робітники́, 12
ladder – драби́на, 34
lake – óзеро, *pl.* озéра, озéр і озір, 21
lamp – ля́мпа; *лáмпа*, 17
language – мóва, 38
last – остáнній *[s]*, 33
late – пізній *[s]*, 33
late – пізно, 5
late: to be late
– спізнюватися: спізню-юся, -єшся
pf. спізни́тися: спíзн-юся, -ишся, 35
later – пізніше, 10
laugh – смія́тися: смі-ю́ся, -є́шся, 5
pf. засмія́тися: засмі-ю́ся, -є́шся, 23
launder – прáти: пер-ý, -éш
pf. ви́прати: ви́пер-у, -еш, 26
lawn – травни́к, травникá, *pl.* травники́, 22
lawn mower – косáрка, 22
lawyer – адвокáт; юри́ст, 24
lay oneself down – лягáти: лягáю, -єш, 16
pf. лягти́: ля́ж-у, -еш, 23
lazybones – нерóба *[m,f]*, 37
leap – скакáти: скач-ý, -еш
pf. скóчити: скóч-у, -иш, 34
learn – учи́тися/вчи́тися: уч-ýся, -ишся, 8
pf. навчи́тися: навч-ýся, -и́шся, 23
leave – лишáти: лишá-ю, -єш, 22
pf. лиши́ти: лиш-ý, -иш, 23
lecture – лéкція, 11
left: to the left – ліврóуч, 6
lemon – цитри́на; *лимóн, -а*, 19
lend – позичáти: позичá-ю, -єш, 20
pf. пози́чити: пози́ч-у, -иш, 23
less – мéнше, 4
lesson – лéкція; *урóк, -у*, 11
letter – лист, листá, *pl.* листи́, 18
letter carrier – листонóша *[m,f]*, 37
lettuce – салáта; *салáт, -у*, 19
librarian *[f]* – бібліотéкарка, 12
librarian *[m]* – бібліотéкар *[s]*, 12
library – бібліотéка, 12
lie down – лягáти: лягá-ю, -єш, 16
pf. лягти́: ля́ж-у, -еш, 23
lie: to be lying down – лежáти: леж-ý, -и́ш, 8
pf. полéжати: полéж-у, -иш, 23
lie: to tell a lie – брехáти: бреш-ý, -еш, 7
pf. брéхнути: брехн-ý, -éш, 23
life – життя́ *[n]*, 36
light – лéгкий, 30
lighten – бли́скати: бли́скає,
pf. забли́скати: забли́скає, 33
lighter – лéгший, 30
light lunch – перéкуска, 15
lightly – лéгко, 31
lightly: more lightly – лéгше, 31
lightning – бли́скавка, 33
like – ніж; як, 29
like – люби́ти: люб-лю́, -иш, 9
pf. полюби́ти: полюб-лю́, -иш, 23
line-up – чéргá, чéргй, *pl.* чéрги, 35
lip – губá, губи́, *pl.* гýби, губíв, ... гýбах; устá/вустá *[pl]*, уст/вуст, 28
lipstick – губнá помáда, 28
listen – слýхати: слýха-ю, -єш, 4
pf. послýхати: послýха-ю, -єш, 23
litre – літр *[h]*, лíтра, 30
little – мали́й; малéнький, 26
little – мáло; небагáто, 4
live – жи́ти: жив-ý, -éш, 6
pf. пожи́ти: пожив-ý, -éш, 23
living room – вітáльня, *g.pl.* вітáлень, 14
loaf of bread – хлібúна, 30
loan – пóзичка, 37
location – мíсце, *pl.* місця́, місців і місць, 11
long – дóвгий, 26
long: for a long time – дóвго, 9
longer – дóвший, 30
longer: for a longer time, 9 – дóвше
look after – доглядáти: доглядá-ю, -єш, 21
pf. догля́нути: догля́н-у, -еш, 23
look at – диви́тися: див-лю́ся, -ишся, 9
pf. подиви́тися: подив-лю́ся, -ишся, 23
look for – шукáти: шукá-ю, -єш, 18
pf. пошукáти: пошукá-ю, -єш, 23

lose – губи́ти: губ-лю́, -иш, 22
pf. загуби́ти: загуб-лю́, -иш, 23
lose *[opp. of to win]* – програва́ти: програ-ю́, -є́ш
pf. програ́ти: програ́-ю, -єш, 32
lot: a lot – бага́то, 4
lottery – льотері́я, *лотере́я*, 32
loudly – го́лосно, 5
loudly: more loudly – голосні́ше, 31
love – любо́в *[f]*, любо́ви, 36
love – люби́ти: люб-лю́, -иш, 9
pf. полюби́ти: полюб-лю́, -иш, 23
lower – ни́жче, 31
luckier – щасливі́ше, 30
luckily – щасли́во, 31
luckily: more luckily – щасливі́ше, 31
lucky – щасли́вий, 28
lunch *[meal at noon]* – обі́д, -у, 15
lunch *[light lunch]* – пере́куска, 15
lying down, to be – лежа́ти: леж-у́, -и́ш, 5
pf. поле́жати: поле́ж-у, -иш, 23

M

madam – па́ні *[indecl.]*, 13
magazine – журна́л, -у, 17
mailbox – пошто́ва скри́нька, 35
man – чолові́к, 11
manager *[f]* – нача́льниця, 12
manager *[m]* – нача́льник, 12
manner: in such a manner – так, 8
map – ма́па; ка́рта, 35
March – бе́резень, бе́резня, 16
margarine – марґари́на; *маргари́н, -у*, 19
market – база́р *[h]*; ри́нок, ри́нку, 35
marmalade – мармеля́да; *мармела́д, -у*, 19
marriage – вінча́ння *[n]*; шлюб, шлю́бу, 27
married – одру́жений, 37
marry: get married
– одру́жуватися: одру́жу-юся, -єшся, 5
pf. одружи́тися: одруж-у́ся, -ишся, 23
match-maker – ста́роста *[m]*, 37
May – тра́вень, тра́вня, 16
maybe – мо́же; можли́во, 3
mayor – мер, ме́ра, 36
meal at noon – обі́д, -у, 15
meat – м'я́со, 19
meat market – м'яса́рня, 35
mechanic – меха́нік, 12
medal – меда́ля; *меда́ль [f]*, *меда́лі*, 34
medicine – лі́ки *[pl]*, лі́ків, ... лі́ках, 31
meet – зустріча́тися: зустріча́-юся, -єшся
pf. зустрі́нутися і зустрі́тися:
зустрі́н-уся, -ешся, 35
meeting – збо́ри *[pl]*, збо́рів, ... збо́рах;
засі́дання *[n]*, 27
melt – та́нути: та́не
pf. роста́нути: роста́не, 33
menu – меню́ *[indecl.]*, 22
merchandise – това́р, -у, 38
mermaid – руса́лка, 37
merry-go-round – карусе́ля; *карусе́ль [f]*,
карусе́лі, 34
metal – мета́ль, мета́лю; мета́л, -у, 32
Mexican – мехіка́нський, 38
Mexican *[f]* – мехіка́нка, 38
Mexican *[m]* – мехіка́нець, мехіка́нця, 38
Mexico – Ме́хіко, 38
midnight – пі́вніч *[f]*, пі́вночі, 16
mile – ми́ля, 34
milk – молоко́, *pl.* моло́ка, моло́к, 15
mine – мій, моя́, моє́, мої́, 28
minute – хвили́на; міну́та, 29
minute: every minute – щохвили́ни, 10
mirror – дзе́ркало, *pl.* дзеркала́, дзерка́л, 17
mischievous – збито́чний, 32
miser – скупа́р *[s]*, скупаря́, *pl.* скупарі́, 27
miserable – неща́сний, 26
Miss – па́нна, *pl.* панни́, панні́в, 13
mitt – рукави́ця, 20
mitten – рукави́ця, 20
mix – міша́ти: міша́-ю, -єш, 21
pf. поміша́ти: поміша́-ю, -єш, 23
mom – ма́ма, *pl.* мами́, мамі́в, 13
Monday – понеді́лок, понеді́лка, 16
money – гро́ші *[pl]*, гро́шей, грі́шми і
гроши́ма, гро́шам, ... гро́шах, 14
month – мі́сяць, мі́сяця, *pl.* місяці́, 16
month: every month – щомі́сяця, 10
monument – па́м'ятник, -а, 21
moon – мі́сяць, мі́сяця, *pl.* місяці́, 16
more – бі́льше, 4
morning – ра́нок, ра́нку, 29
morning: every morning – щора́нку, 10
morning: in the morning – ура́нці/вра́нці, 8
morning: this morning – сього́дні вра́нці, 9
mosquito – кома́р *[h]*, комара́, *n.pl.* комарі́, 21

motel – мотéль, мотéлю, 12
mother – мáма, *pl.* мами́, мамíв, 13
mother – мáти *[f]*, мáтері, *pl.* матері́, 36
mother-in-law *[man's]* – тéща, 13
mother-in-law *[woman's]* – свекру́ха, 13
motorcycle – мотоци́кл, -а, 18
mountain – горá, *pl.* гóри, гір, 21
mouth – рот, рóта, *pl.* роти́, 31
movies – кінó *[indecl.]*, 15
movie theatre – кінó *[indecl.]*, кінотеáтр, -у, 15
Mr. – пан, пáна, *pl.* пани́, *v.pl.* панóве, 13
Mrs. – пáні *[indecl.]*, 13
much – багáто, 4
much: how much – скíльки, 4
much: not much – небагáто; мáло, 4
muscle – му́скул, -у; м'яз, м'я́за, 31
museum – музéй, музéю, 11
mushroom – гриб, грибá, *pl.* гриби́, 19
music – му́зика, 32
musician *[f]* – музикáнтка, 24
musician *[m]* – музикáнт, 24
mustache – вус, *pl.* ву́са і ву́си, *g.pl.* вус, 31
my – мій, моя́, моє́, мої́, 28

N

nalysnyk – нали́сник, -а, 19
name *[personal name]* – ім'я́ *[n]*, *pl.* іменá, 37
name *[of book, object]* – нáзва, 36
nanny – ня́ня; ня́нька, *pl.* няньки́, няньóк, 25
narrow – вузьки́й, 30
narrower – ву́жчий, 30
narrowly – ву́зько, 31
narrowly: more narrowly – ву́жче, 31
nation – нáція; нарóд, -у, 38
native – рíдний, 38
near – бли́зько *[+G]*, 22
necessary – потрíбен/потрíбний, 33
necessary: it's necessary – потрíбно, 20
neck – ши́я, 28
necklace – нами́сто, 28
necktie – кравáтка; *гáлстук, -а*, 20
needed – потрíбен/потрíбний, 33
neighbour *[f]* – сусíдка, 25
neighbour *[m]* – сусíд, 25
neither ... nor – ні ... ні, 3
nephew – племíнник, 13
never – нікóли, 7
new – нови́й, 26
newer – новíший, 30
news item – нови́нка; новинá, *pl.* нови́ни, 29
newspaper – газéта, 17
next – насту́пний, 33
nice – гáрний, хорóший, 26
nicely – гáрно, 31
nicely: more nicely – гарнíше, 31
nicer – гарнíший, 30
niece – племíнниця, 13
night – ніч *[f]*, нóчі, 29
night: at night – уночí/вночí, 8
night: every night – щонóчі, 10
nine – дéв'ять, 19
nine hundred – дéв'ятсóт, 19
nineteen – дев'ятнáдцять, 19
nineteenth – дев'ятнáдцятий, 27
ninetieth – дев'ятдеся́тий; *дев'янóстий*, 27
ninety – дев'ятдеся́т; *дев'янóсто*, 19
ninth – дев'я́тий, 27
no – ні, 2
nobody – ніхтó, 6
noon – пíвдень, пíвдня, 16
no one – ніхтó, 6
north – пíвніч *[f]*, пíвночі, 16
nose – ніс, нóса, *pl.* носи́, 31
not – не, 4
not at all – зóвсім не, 9
notebook – зóшит, -а, 11
not far from – недалéко *[+G]*, 22
nothing – нíщó, 6
not much – небагáто; мáло, 4
not much – трóхи, 19
not yet – ще ні, 3
novelette – пóвість *[f]*, пóвісті, повістéй, 36
novel – ромáн, -у, 36
November – листопáд, -а, 16
now – тепéр, 2
now: right now, at this time – зáраз, 5
nowhere: at no place – нідé, 7
nowhere: to no place – ніку́ди, 7
nuisance *[of a person]* – причéпа *[m,f]*, 37
numeral – числíвник, -а, 27
nurse *[f]* – медсестрá, *pl.* медсéстри, медсестéр, медсéстрам, медсéстрами, ... медсéстрах, 12
nurse *[m]* – медбрáт, *pl.* медбрати́, 12
nut – горíх, горíха, ... горíсі, 19

O

obedient – че́мний, 32
October – жо́втень, жо́втня, 16
oculist – окулі́ст, 24
office – канцеля́рія; *кабіне́т, -у*, 12
often – ча́сто, 3
often: how often – як ча́сто, 10
old – стари́й, 26
older – ста́рший, 30
on, at – на, 14
one – оди́н, одна́, одне́, 19
one-fourth – чверть *[f]*, чве́рти, 29
oneself – себе́, 22
oneself – сам/сами́й, 38
one's own – свій, своя́, своє́, свої́, 28
on foot – пі́шки, 34
on horseback – ве́рхи, 34
onions – цибу́ля *[sg]*, 30
only – ті́льки; лише́, 9
on tiptoe – навшпи́ньки, 34
open – відчиня́ти: відчиня́-ю, -єш
pf. відчини́ти: відчин-ю́, -иш, 29
open: to be opened
– відчиня́тися: відчиня́-ється, -ються
pf. відчини́тися: відчи́н-иться, -яться, 29
optimist*[f]* – оптимі́стка, 32
optimist*[m]* – оптимі́ст, 32
optometrist – окулі́ст, 24
or – або́; чи, 3
orange – помара́нча; *апельси́н, -а*, 15
orange – помара́нчовий; *ора́нжевий*, 26
orchard – сад, са́ду, ... саду́ і̲ са́ді, *pl.* сади́, 30
orchestra – орке́стра; *орке́стр [h], -у*, 16
order – замовля́ти: замовля́-ю, -єш, 17
pf. замо́вити: замо́в-лю, -иш, 23
orphan – сирота́ *[m,f]*, 37
other – і́нший, 36
ought – пови́нен/пови́нний, 32
our – наш, на́ша, на́ше, на́ші, 28
ours – наш, на́ша, на́ше, на́ші, 28
outdoors – надво́рі, 2
outdoors: to the outdoors – надвір, 7
outing – екску́рсія, 25
outside – надво́рі, 2
oven – піч *[f]*, печі́, 36
overcast – хма́ритися: хма́риться
pf. захма́ритися: захма́риться, 33
overcoat – пальто́, *pl.* па́льта, 20
overhead – над *[+I]*, 21
owe: to owe something – ви́нен/ви́нний, 32

P

package – па́чка, *pl.* пачки́, пачо́к, 18
page – сторі́нка, *pl.* сторінки́, сторіно́к, 27
pain – біль, бо́лю, 31
paint – фа́рба, 32
paint – малюва́ти: малю́-ю, -єш
pf. (a picture) намалюва́ти: намалю́-ю, -єш
pf. (a building, etc.) помалюва́ти:
помалю́-ю, -єш, 32
painter *[f]* – маля́рка, 24
painter *[m]* – маля́р *[mx]*, маляра́, *pl.* малярі́, 24
painting – карти́на; о́браз, -а, *pl.* образи́, 17
pantry – комо́ра, *g.pl.* комо́р, 14
pants – штани́ *[pl]*, штані́в, ... штана́х і̲ шта́нях, 20
paper – папі́р *[h]*, папе́ру, 32
paradise – рай, ра́ю, 27
parasol – парасо́ля; *парасо́ль, -я; зо́нтик, -а*, 18
parcel – паку́нок, паку́нка, 18
parents – батьки́ *[pl]*, батькі́в; ро́дичі *[pl]*, ро́дичів, 13
park – парк, па́рку, 21
parka – па́рка, 20
parking lot – автоста́вка; *стоя́нка*, 35
parking meter – лічи́льник, -а, 35
party – вечі́рка, 15
passport – па́спорт, -а, 18
past – мину́лий, 33
pastry – пе́чиво *[sg]*, 30
path – сте́жка, *pl.* стежки́, стежо́к, 21
patient – терпели́вий, 37
patient *[f]* – паціє́нтка, 12
patient *[m]* – паціє́нт, 12
pay – плати́ти: плачу́, пла́т-иш, 9
pf. заплати́ти: заплачу́, запла́т-иш, 23
pay telephone – телефо́н-автома́т
(телефон, -у; автомат, -а), 35
peach – пе́рсик, -а, 30
pear – гру́ша, гру́шка, 30
peas – горо́х *[sg]*, горо́ху, ... горо́сі, 30
peasant *[m]* – селя́нин, *pl.* селя́ни, селя́н, 38
peasant *[f]* – селя́нка, 38
pen – перо́, *pl.* пе́ра; *ру́чка*, 11
penny – цент, це́нта, 18
pencil – олíве́ць, олівця́, *pl.* олівці́, 11
people – лю́ди *[pl]*, люде́й, людьми́, лю́дям, ... лю́дях, 13
percent – проце́нт, -а; відсо́ток, відсо́тка, 38

percolator – ка́вник, -а, 17
perfume – па́хощі *[pl]*, па́хощів, па́хощах; духи́ *[pl]*, духі́в, ... duха́х, 28
perhaps – мо́же; можли́во, 3
perogy – варе́ник, -а; пирі́г, пирога́, *pl.* пироги́, 19
person – люди́на, *pl.* лю́ди, люде́й, 13
personal name – ім'я́ *[n]*, *pl.* імена́, 37
pessimist *[f]* – песимі́стка, 32
pessimist *[m]* – песимі́ст, 32
pharmacist *[f]* – апте́карка, 24
pharmacist *[m]* – апте́кар *[s]*, 24
pharmacy – апте́ка, 28
photo – фотогра́фія; фо́то *[indecl.]*, 18
photograph – фотогра́фія; фо́то *[indecl.]*, 18
photograph – фотографува́ти: фотографу́-ю, -єш, 21
pf. сфотографува́ти: сфотографу́-ю, -єш, 23
photographer – фото́граф, 24
piano – піяні́но; *піані́но [indecl.]*, 16
picnic – пікні́к, пікніка́, *pl.* пікніки́, 21
picture – карти́на; о́браз, -а, *pl.* образи́, 17
pill – табле́тка; піґу́лка; *пілю́ля*, 30
pillow – по́душка, *pl.* поду́шки, поду́шок, 22
pilot – піло́т, 24
pink – роже́вий, 26
place – мі́сце, *pl.* місця́, місці́в і місць, 11
place – кла́сти: клад-у́, -е́ш, 15
pf. покла́сти: поклад-у́, -е́ш, 23
plant *[in general]* – росли́на, 25
plant *[potted]* – вазо́нок, вазо́нка, 17
plate – тарі́лка, *pl.* тарілки́, таріло́к, 17
play – п'є́са, 36
play – ба́витися: ба́в-люся, -ишся
pf. поба́витися: поба́в-люся, -ишся, 34
play – гра́ти: гра́-ю, -єш, 15
pf. пограти: погра́-ю, -єш, 23
playground – майда́нчик, -а, 25
plead – проси́ти: прошу́, про́с-иш, 9
pf. попроси́ти: попрошу́, попро́с-иш, 23
pleasant – прии́мний, 26
pleasanter – приємні́ший, 30
pleasantly – прии́мно, 31
pleasantly: more pleasantly – приємні́ше, 31
plough – ора́ти: ор-ю́, -еш, 7
pf. зора́ти: зор-ю́, -еш, 23
plum – сли́ва; сли́вка, 30
plumber – санте́хнік, 24
pocket – кише́ня, 22
poem *[long]* – пое́ма, 36
poem *[short]* – вірш, ві́рша, 36
poet *[f]* – поете́са, 36
poet *[m]* – пое́т, 36
poetry – пое́зія, 36
Poland – По́льща, 38
police officer – поліца́й; *міліціоне́р [h]*, 12
Polish – по́льський, 38
Polish *[f]* – по́лька, 38
Polish *[m]* – поля́к, поляка́, *pl.* поляки́, 38
polite – че́мний, 32
poor – бі́дний, 26
poorer – бідні́ший, 30
poorly – пога́но, 4; бі́дно, 31
poorly: more poorly – погані́ше; бідні́ше, 31
population – насе́лення *[n]*, 38
porridge – ка́ша, 19
postcard – листі́вка, 18
poster – афі́ша, 11
postage stamp – ма́рка, 18
post office – по́шта, 18
potatoes – карто́пля *[sg]*, 30
pound – фунт, фу́нта, *pl.* фу́нти, фу́нтів, 30
praise – хвали́ти: хвал-ю́, -иш
pf. похвали́ти: похвал-ю́, -иш, 29
prepare – готува́ти: готу́-ю, -єш, 15
pf. зготува́ти: зготу́-ю, -єш, 23
prepared – гото́вий, 36
present – подару́нок, подару́нка, 18
president – президе́нт, 38
pretty – га́рний, 26
prettier – гарні́ший, *хоро́ший*, 30
priest – свяще́ник, 24
prize – нагоро́да; *приз, при́зу, pl. призи́*, 34
probably – ма́буть, 3
professor – профе́сор *[h]*, *pl.* професори́, 11
property – майно́ *[sg]*, 38
prose – про́за, 36
province – провінція, 38
psychiatrist – психія́тр *[h]*; *психіа́тр [h]*, 24
psychologist – психо́лог, 24
public display – ви́ставка, 32
pudding – пу́динґ-у; *пу́динг, -у*, 19
pullover – пуло́вер *[h]*, -а, 20
punch *[drink]* – пунш, -у, 15
pupil *[f]* – учени́ця; школя́рка, 11

pupil *[m]* – у́чень, у́чня; школя́р *[mx]*, школяра́, *pl.* школярі́, 11
purchase – поку́пка, 30
purchased item – поку́пка, 30
purple – пурпуро́вий; *пурпу́рний*, 26
purse – торби́нка; пуля́ре́с, -а; *су́мка*, 18
put – кла́сти: клад-у́, -е́ш, 15
pf. покла́сти: поклад-у́, -е́ш, 23
pyjamas – піжа́ма *[sg]*, 20
pysanka – пи́санка, *pl.* писанки́, писано́к, 32

Q

quality – я́кість *[f]*, я́кости, 36
quantity – кі́лькість *[f]*, кі́лькости, 36
quarter – чверть *[f]*, чве́рти, 29
question – пита́ння *[n]*, 36
queue – че́рга́, черги́, *pl.* че́рги, 35
quickly – шви́дко, 5
quickly: more quickly – шви́дше, 31
quietly – ти́хо, 5
quietly: more quietly – ти́хше, 31
quilt – ко́вдра, *pl.* ковдр і ко́вдер, 22

R

radio – ра́діо *[indecl.]*, 17
radio program – радіопереда́ча, 29
raffle – розі́гравка, 32
rain – дощ, дощу́, *pl.* дощі́, 33
rain: to rain – дощи́ти: дощи́ть, 33
rainbow – весе́лка, 33
raincoat – дощови́к, дощовика́, *pl.* дощовики́, 20
rainy weather – сльота́, 33
rarely – рі́дко, 3
rarely: more rarely – рі́дше, 31
razor – бри́тва; електробри́тва, 28
read – чита́ти: чита́-ю, -єш, 4
pf. прочита́ти: прочита́-ю, -єш, 23
ready – гото́вий, 36
recall – прига́дувати: прига́ду-ю, -єш
pf. пригада́ти: пригада́-ю, -єш, 32
receive – оде́ржувати: оде́ржу-ю, -єш, 22
оде́ржати: оде́рж-у, -иш, 23
record *[music]* – платі́вка; *пласти́нка*, 25
red – черво́ний, 26
redder – червоні́ший, 30
refrigerator – холоди́льник, -а, 17
relative *[f]* – ро́дичка, 13
relative *[m]* – ро́дич, 13
remember – пам'ята́ти: пам'ята́-ю, -єш, 4
pf. запам'ята́ти: запам'ята́-ю, -єш, 23
remind – прига́дувати: прига́ду-ю, -єш
pf. пригада́ти: пригада́-ю, -єш, 32
request – проси́ти: прошу́, про́с-иш, 9
pf. попроси́ти: попрошу́, попро́с-иш, 23
repair – ла́годити: ла́годжу, ла́год-иш, 21
pf. зла́годити: зла́годжу, зла́год-иш, 23
repeat – повто́рювати: повто́рю-ю, -єш
і повторя́ти: повторя́-ю, -єш
pf. повтори́ти: повто́р-ю, -иш, 35
reply – відповіда́ти: відповіда́-ю, -єш
pf. відповісти: відпові́-м, -си́, 35
reply – ві́дповідь *[f]*, ві́дповіді, 36
rest – відпочива́ти: відпочива́-ю, -єш, 22
pf. відпочи́ти: відпочи́н-у, -еш, 23
restaurant – рестора́н, -у, 12
return – поверта́тися: поверта́-юся, -єшся
pf. поверну́тися: поверн-у́ся, -ешся, 29
return – поверта́ти: поверта́-ю, -єш
pf. поверну́ти: поверн-у́, -еш, 29
rich – бага́тий, 26
richer – бага́тший, 30
ride *[by vehicle]* – ї́хати: ї́д-у, -еш *[dur.]*, 7
pf. пої́хати: пої́д-у, -еш, 23
ride *[by vehicle]* – ї́здити: ї́жджу, ї́зд-иш *[it.]*, 10
pf. пої́хати: пої́д-у, -еш, 23
right now – за́раз, 5
right: to the right – право́руч, 6
ring – пе́рстінь, пе́рстеня, *pl.* пе́рстені; кільце́, 28
ring – дзвони́ти: дзвон-ю́, -иш
pf. подзвони́ти: подзвон-ю́, -иш, 31
river – ріка́, *pl.* рі́ки, 21
road – доро́га, *pl.* доро́ги, дорі́г, 14
rock – го́йдатися: го́йда-юся, -єшся
pf. пого́йдатися: пого́йда-юся, -єшся, 34
roller skate – ро́лик, -а, 34
room – кімна́та, 14
rug – ки́ли́м, -а, *pl.* килими́, 14
run – бі́гти: біж -у́, -и́ш *[dur.]*, 8
pf. побі́гти: побіж-у́, -и́ш, 23
run – бі́гати: бі́га-ю, -єш *[it.]*, 10
pf. побі́гти: побіж-у́, -и́ш, 23
running shoe – тенісі́вка; *кед, ке́да*, 20
Russia – Росі́я, 38
Russian – росі́йський, 38
Russian *[f]* – росія́нка, 38
Russian *[m]* – росія́нин, *pl.* росія́ни, росія́н, 38

S

sad – сумни́й, 26
sader – сумні́ший, 30
sadly – су́мно, 31
sadly: more sadly – сумні́ше, 31
sailboat – вітри́льник, -а, 25
salad – сала́та; *сала́т, -у*, 19
salary – платня́, 37
salesclerk *[f]* – продавни́ця; *продавщи́ця*, 14
salesclerk *[m]* – продаве́ць, продавця́, *pl.* продавці́, 14
salt – сіль *[f]*, со́ли, 36
sand – пісо́к, піску́, *pl.* піски́, 25
sandal – босоні́жка; санда́ля, 20
sandwich – са́ндвіч. -а, 19
Saturday – субо́та, 16
sausage – ковбаса́, *pl.* ковба́си, 19
say – каза́ти: каж-у́, -еш, 7
pf. сказа́ти: скаж-у́, -еш, 23
scarf – ша́лик, -а, 20
school – шко́ла, *pl.* шко́ли, шкіл, 11
school holidays – кані́кули *[pl]*, кані́кул, ... кані́кулах, 25
scientist – науко́вець, науко́вця, 24
scissors – но́жиці *[pl]*, но́жиць, ... но́жицях, 17
Scot*[f]* – шотля́ндка, 38
Scotland – Шотля́ндія, 38
Scot*[m]* – шотля́ндець, шотля́ндця, 38
Scottish – шотля́ндський, 38
scream – кrича́ти: крич-у́, -и́ш, 8
pf. кри́кнути: кри́кн-у, -еш, 23
sea – мо́ре, *pl.* моря́, морі́в, ... моря́х, 21
search – шука́ти: шука́-ю, -єш, 18
pf. пошука́ти: пошука́-ю, -єш, 23
season – пора́, 16
second – дру́гий, 27
second *[time]* – секу́нда, 29
secretary *[f]* – секрета́рка, 12
secretary *[m]* – секрета́р *[s]*, секретаря́, *pl.* секретарі́, 12
see – ба́чити: ба́ч-у, -иш, 8
pf. поба́чити: поба́ч-у, -иш, 23
seem – здава́тися: зда-є́ться, -ю́ться
pf. зда́тися: зда́-сться, -ду́ться, 33
seldom – рі́дко, 3
seldom: more seldom – рі́дше, 31
select – вибира́ти: вибира́-ю, -єш, 17
pf. ви́брати: ви́бер-у, -еш, 23
sell – продава́ти: прода-ю́, -є́ш, 5
pf. прода́ти: прода́-м, -си́, 23
send – посила́ти: посила́-ю, -єш, 20
pf. посла́ти: пошл-ю́, -е́ш, 23
September – ве́ресень, ве́ресня, 16
serious – серйо́зний, 36
serviette – серве́тка, 22
seven – сім, 19
seven hundred – сімсо́т, 19
seventeen – сімна́дцять, 19
seventeenth – сімна́дцятий, 27
seventh – сьо́мий, 27
seventieth – сімдеся́тий, 27
seventy – сімдеся́т, 19
several – кі́лька, 19
sew – ши́ти: ши́-ю, -єш
pf. поши́ти: поши́-ю, -єш, 26
shampoo – шампу́нь, шампу́ню, 28
shave oneself – голи́тися: гол-ю́ся, -ишся, 8
pf. поголи́тися: погол-ю́ся, -ишся, 23
shaver – бри́тва; електробри́тва, 28
shave someone – голи́ти: гол-ю́, -иш, 28
pf. поголи́ти: погол-ю́, -иш, 27
she – вона́, 2
shelf – поли́ця, 14
shine – світи́ти: свічу́, сві́т-иш
pf. посвіти́ти: посвічу́, посві́т-иш, 33
shirt – соро́чка, *pl.* сорочки́, сорочо́к, 20
shoe – череви́к, -а; ту́фля, 20
shore – бе́рег, бе́рега ... бе́регові і ... бе́резі, *pl.* береги́, 21
short – коро́ткий, 26
shorter – коро́тший, 30
shortly – ко́ротко, 31
shortly: more shortly – коро́тше, 31
shorts – шо́рти *[pl]*, шо́ртів, ... шо́ртах, 20
short story – опові́дання *[n]*, 36
should – пови́нен/пови́нний, 32
shoulder – раме́но; плече́, *pl.* пле́чі, плече́й і пліч, плечи́ма, ... пле́чах, 31
shout – крича́ти: крич-у́, -и́ш, 8
pf. кри́кнути: кри́кн-у, -еш, 23
show – пока́зувати: пока́зу-ю, -єш
pf. показа́ти: покаж-у́, -еш, 31
showcase – вітри́на, 14
shower – душ, ду́шу, 28
shuffle – міша́ти: міша́-ю, -єш, 21
pf. поміша́ти: поміша́-ю, -єш, 23
sick – хво́рий, 26

sicker – хворíший, 30
sidewalk – хідни́к, хідника́, *pl.* хідники́; *тротуа́р [h], -у*, 14
silent, to be: – мовча́ти: мовчу́, -и́ш, 8
pf. замовча́ти: замовч-у́, -и́ш, 23
similar – поді́бний, 36
sing – співа́ти: співа́-ю, -єш, 4
pf. заспіва́ти: заспіва́-ю, -єш, 23
singer *[f]* – співа́чка, 24
singer *[m]* – співа́к, співака́, *pl.* співаки́, 24
Sir – пан, *pl.* пани́, *v.pl.* пано́ве, 13
siren – сире́на, 35
sister – сестра́, *pl.* се́стри, сесте́р, се́страми, се́страм, ... се́страх, 13
sit: to be sitting – сиді́ти: сиджу́, сид-и́ш, 9
pf. поси́діти: поси́джу, поси́д-иш, 23
sit down – сіда́ти: сіда́-ю, -єш, 16
pf. сі́сти: ся́д-у, -еш, 23
six – шість, 19
six hundred – шістсо́т, 19
ixteen – шістна́дцять, 19
sixteenth – шістна́дцятий, 27
sixth – шо́стий, 27
sixtieth – шістдеся́тий, 27
sixty – шістдеся́т, 19
skate – ковза́н, козана́, *pl.* ковсани́, 34
skate – ко́взатися: ко́вза-юся, -єшся
pf. поко́взатися: поко́вза-юся, -єшся, 34
skateboard – скейт, -у, 34
skater *[f]* – ковзаня́рка, 34
skater *[m]* – ковзаня́р *[h]*, ковзаняра́, *pl.* ковзанярі́, 34
skating rink – ко́взанка, 34
skeleton – скеле́т, -а; кістя́к, кістька́, *pl.* кістяки́, 31
ski – ли́жа, 34
skier *[f]* – ли́жниця, 34
skier *[m]* – ли́жник, 34
skin – шкі́ра, 31
skipping rope – скака́лка, 34
skirt – спідни́ця, 20
sky – не́бо, *pl.* небеса́, небе́с, 27
slacks – штани́ *[pl]*, штані́в, ... штана́х, 20
Slav *[f]* – слов'я́нка, 38
Slav *[m]* – слов'яни́н, слов'я́ни, слов'я́н, 38
sled – са́нки́ *[pl]*, са́но́к, 34
sleep – спа́ти: сп-лю, -иш, 9
pf. поспа́ти: посп-лю́, -и́ш, 23
slice – кра́яти: кра́-ю, -єш
pf. покра́яти: покра́-ю, -єш
slide – спуска́лка, 25
slipper – ка́пець, ка́пц-ю, 20
slob – нечепу́ра *[m,f]*, 37
slow – пові́льний, 32
slowly – пові́льно; пово́лі; пома́лу, 5
slowly: more slowly – повільні́ше, 31
small – мали́й; мале́нький, 26
smaller – ме́нший, 30
small town – село́, 12
smart – му́дрий, 26
smarter – мудрі́ший, 30
smartly – му́дро, 31
smartly: more smartly – мудрі́ше, 31
smile – усміха́тися: усміха́-юся, -єшся
pf. усміхну́тися: усміхн-у́ся,-е́шся, 31
smoke – кури́ти: кур-ю́, -иш, 8
pf. покури́ти: покур-ю́, -иш, 23
snack – пере́куска, 15
snake *[garter snake]* – вуж, вужа́, *pl.* вужі́, 21
snow – сніг, сні́гу, *pl.* снігй, 33
snow: to snow – сніжи́ти: сніжи́ть, 33
snowball – сні́жка, 34
snow man – снігови́й дід, снігова́ ба́ба, 34
snowmobile – мотоса́ни *[pl]*, мотосане́й; мотосаньми́, ... мотоса́нях; автоса́ни *[pl]*, автосане́й, автосаньми́, ... автоса́нях, 34
snowstorm – завір'ю́ха, 33
so – так, 8
soap – ми́ло, 28
soccer – футбо́л, -у, 15
sock – шкарпе́тка, 20
so many – сті́льки, 19
some *[people]* – де́хто, 6
some *[things]* – де́що, 6
some – кі́лька, 19
somebody – хтось, 6
someone – хтось, 6
someplace: at someplace – десь, 7
someplace: to someplace – куди́сь, 7
something – щось, 6
sometimes – і́ноді; і́нколи; ча́сом, 3
somewhere: at some place – десь, 7
somewhere: to some place – куди́сь, 7
so much – сті́льки, 19
son – син, *v.sg.* си́ну!, *pl.* сини́, 13
song – пі́сня, 32

son-in-law – зять, з'я́тя, *pl.* з'яті́, 13
soon – незаба́ром, 29
sopilka – сопі́лка, 16
so that – щоб, 35
soul – душа́, *pl.* ду́ші, душ, ... ду́шах, 37
soup – ю́шка, *pl.* юшки́, юшо́к; зу́па; *суп, су́пу, pl. супи́*, 19
soup bowl – ми́ска, *pl.* миски́, мисо́к, 17
south – пі́вдень, пі́вдня, 16
souvenir – сувені́р *[h]*, -а, 18
Spain – Éспа́нія, 38
Spaniard *[f]* – еспа́нка, 38
Spaniard *[m]* – еспа́нець, еспа́нця, 38
Spanish – еспа́нський, 38
speak – говори́ти: говор-ю́, -иш, 8
pf. поговори́ти: поговор-ю́, -иш, 23
speech – до́повідь *[f]*, до́повіді, 36
spine – хребе́т, хребта́, *pl.* хребти́, 31
spoon – ло́жка, *pl.* ложки́, ложо́к, 17
sport – спорт, спо́рту, 34
spot – пля́ма, 22
sprain – звиха́ти: звиха́-ю, -єш
pf. звихну́ти: звихну́, -е́ш, 31
spring – весна́, 16
spring – весня́ний, 33
spring: in the spring – навесні́, 8
stadium – стадіо́н, -у, 15
stain – пля́ма, 22
stairs – схо́ди *[pl]*, схо́дів, ... схо́дах, 11
stamp *[postage stamp]* – ма́рка, 18
stand: to be standing – стоя́ти: сто-ю́, -ї́ш, 9
pf. посто́яти: посто́-ю, -їш, 23
star – зі́рка, *pl.* зірки́, зіро́к, 33
starosta – ста́роста, 37
station *[train]* – ста́нція, 29
steal, кра́сти: крад-у́, -е́ш, 6
pf. укра́сти: украд-у́, -е́ш, 23
stereo – сте́рео *[indecl.]*, 17
still – ще, 2
stir – міша́ти: міша́-ю, -єш, 21
pf. поміша́ти: поміша́-ю, -єш, 23
stocking – панчо́ха, *g.pl.* панчі́х, 20
stomach – шлу́нок, шлу́нку, 31
stone – ка́мінь, ка́меня, 22
storage room – комо́ра, *g.pl.* комо́р, 14
store – крамни́ця; склеп, скле́пу; *магази́н, -у*, 14
storm – бу́ря, 33
straight ahead – пря́мо, 6
straw – соло́ма, 32
strawberry – суни́ця; полуни́ця, 30
street – ву́лиця, 14
streetcar – трамва́й, трамва́я, 29
street light – ліхта́р, ліхтаря́ *pl.* ліхтарі́, 35
strong – си́льний, 26
stronger – сильні́ший, 30
strongly – си́льно, 31
strongly: more strongly – сильні́ше, 31
struggle – боро́тися: бор-ю́ся, -ешся, 7
pf. поборо́тися: побор-ю́ся, -ешся, 23
student *[f]* – студе́нтка, 11
student *[m]* – студе́нт, 11
study – кабіне́т, -у, 14
study – учи́тися/вчи́тися: уч-у́ся, -ишся, 8
pf. навчи́тися: навч-у́ся, -ишся, 23
stupid – дурни́й, 26
stupid: more stupid – дурні́ший, 30
subway – підзе́мка; метро́ *[indecl.]*, 29
success – у́спіх, -у, 34
sugar – цу́кор *[h]*, цу́кру, 19
suit – костю́м, -а, 20
suitcase – валі́зка; *чемода́н, -а*, 18
sultry: it's sultry – па́рно, 33
summer – лі́то, 16
summer – лі́тній *[s]*, 33
summer camp – та́бір *[h]*, та́бору; осе́ля *g.pl.* осе́ль, 25
summer cottage – ко́тедж, -у; *да́ча* , 25
summer: in the summer – улі́тку/влі́тку, 8
summon – кли́кати: кли́ч-у, -иш
pf. покли́кати: покли́ч-у, -еш, 35
sure – пе́вен/пе́вний, 32,
surgeon – хіру́рг, 24
surname – прі́звище, 11
surprise – дивува́ти: диву́-ю, -єш, 33
pf. здивува́ти: здиву́-ю, -єш, 33
surprise – несподі́ванка; *сюрпри́з, -у*, 34
sun – со́нце, *pl.* со́нця, со́нець і со́нців, 33
Sunday – неді́ля, 16
sunny: it's sunny – со́нячно, 33
supper *[evening meal]* – вече́ря, 15
supper: to have supper
– вече́ряти: вече́ря-ю, -єш, 4
pf. повече́ряти: повече́ря-ю, -єш, 23
swallow – ковта́ти: ковта́-ю, -єш
pf. ковтну́ти: ковтну́, -е́ш, 31
sweater – све́тер *[h]*, све́тра; *светр [h], све́тра*, 20
sweet – соло́дкий, 30

sweeter – солóдший, 30
sweetly – сóлодко, 31
sweetly:more sweetly – солóдше, 31
sweets – цукéрка; цукéрок, цукéрка, 30
swim – плисти́: плив-ý, -éш *[dur.]*, 6
pf. поплисти́: поплив-ý, -éш, 23
swim – плáвати: плáва-ю, -єш *[it.]*, 10
pf. поплисти́: поплив-ý, -éш, 23
swimming pool – басéйн, -у, 25
swing – гóйдалка, 25
swing – гóйдатися: гóйда-юся, -єшся
pf. погóйдатися: погóйда-юся, -єшся, 34

T

table – стіл, столá, *pl.* столи́, 12
tablecloth – обрýс, -а; скатерти́на, 22
take – брáти: бер-ý, -éш, 7
pf. взя́ти: візьм-ý, -éш, 23
take care of – доглядáти: доглядá-ю, -єш, 21
pf. догля́нути: догля́н-у, -еш, 23
take place – відбувáтися: відбувá-ється, -ються
pf. відбýтися: відбýд-еться, -уться, 27
tale – бáйка, 36
talk – говори́ти: говор-ю́, -иш, 8
pf. поговори́ти: поговор-ю́, -иш, 23
tall – висóкий, 26
taller – ви́щий, 30
talented – таланови́тий, 30
talentedly – таланови́то, 31
tapestry – ки́ли́м, -а, *pl.* килими́, 14
tastier – смачні́ший, 30
tastily – смáчно, 31
tastily: more tastily – смачні́ше, 31
tasty – смачни́й, 30
tax – подáток, подáтку, 38
taxi – таксíвка; таксі *[indecl.]*, 12
tea – чай, чáю, *pl.* чаї́, 15
teacher *[f]* – учи́телька, *pl.* учительки́, учительóк, 11
teacher *[m]* – учи́тель, *pl.* учителí, 11
team – комáнда, 34
teapot – чáйник, -а, 17
tear – сльозá, *pl.* сльóзи, сліз, 31
teaspoon – лóжечка, *pl.* ложечки́, ложечóк, 17
teddy bear – ведмéдик, -а, 32
telephone – телефóн, -у, 17
telephone – телефонувáти: телефонý-ю, -єш, 5
pf. потелефонувáти: потелефонý-ю, -єш, 23
telephone booth – телефóнна бýдка, 35
telephone operator *[f]* – телефоні́стка, 24
telephone operator *[m]* – телефоні́ст, 24
television program – телепередáча, 29
television set – телеві́зор *[h]*, -а, 17
tell a lie – брехáти: бреш-ý, -еш, 7
pf. брехнýти: брехн-ý, éш, 23
temperature – температýра, 33
ten – дéсять, 19
tennis – тéніс, -у, 15
tent – шатрó, *pl.* шáтра, шáтер, 25
tenth – деся́тий, 27
textbook – підрýчник, -а, 11
than – як; ніж, 30
thank – дя́кувати: дя́ку-ю, -єш, 20
pf. подя́кувати: подя́ку-ю, -єш, 23
that – то, 11
that – той, та, те, ті, 27
that (conj.) – що, 8
thaw – тáнути: тáне,
pf. розтáнути: розтáне, 33
theatre – теáтр *[h]*, -у; кінотеáтр, -у, 15
theatre: movie theatre – кіно *[indecl.]*, 15
their – ї́хній, ї́хня, ї́хнє, ї́хні; їх *[indecl.]*, 28
theirs – ї́хній, ї́хня, ї́хнє, ї́хні; їх *[indecl.]*, 28
then: afterwards – пóтім, 5
then: at that time – тоді́, 5
there are no – немá/немáє, 19
there is no – немá/немáє, 19
there: from there – звíдти, 9
there: in that place – там; он, 2
there: to that place – туди́, 7
thermometer – термóметр, -а, 33
they – вони́, 2
thief *[f]* – злóдійка, *pl.* злоді́йки, злоді́йок, 12
thief *[m]* – злóдій, *pl.* злодії́ , 12
thing – річ *[f]*, рéчі, 36
think – дýмати: дýма-ю, -єш, 4
pf. подýмати: подýма-ю, -єш, 23
third – трéтій *[s]*, 27
thirteen – тринáдцять, 19
thirteenth – тринáдцятий, 27
thirtieth – тридця́тий, 27
thirty – три́дцять, 19
this – це, 11
this – цей, ця, це, ці, 27
this evening – сьогóдні ввéчорі; сьогóдні ввéчері, 9

this morning – сьогóдні врáнці, 9
thousand – ти́сяча, 19
three – три, 19
three hundred – три́ста, 19
throat – гóрло, *g.pl.* горéл і горлі́в, 31
through – чéрез *[+A]*, 22
throw – кидáти: кидá-ю, -єш
pf. ки́нути: ки́н-у, -еш, 34
thunder – гримі́ти: грими́ть
pf. загримі́ти: загрими́ть, 33
thunder – грім, грóму, 33
Thursday – четвéр *[h]*, четвергá, 16
ticket – квитóк, квиткá, *pl.* квитки́, 15
tie – кравáтка; *гáлстук, -а*, 20
time – час, чáсу, *pl.* часи́, 29
time: at that time – тоді́, 5
time: at this time, right now – зáраз, 5
time: for a long time – дóвго, 9
time: for a longer time – дóвше, 9
tin – бляшáнка; *бáнка*, 30
tired – стóмлений; змýчений, 37
toboggan – тобóґан, -а, 34
today – сьогóдні, ни́ні, 9
toe – пáлець на нозі́ (пáльця), 31
toenail – ні́готь, ні́гтя, 31
together – рáзом, 5
tomato – помідóр *[h]*, -а, 30
tomorrow – зáвтра, 16
tomorrow: day after tomorrow – післязáвтра, 16
tongue – язи́к, язикá, *pl.* язики́, 31
tonight – сьогóдні ввéчорі, сьогóдні ввéчері, 9
too – такóж; теж, 2
too early – завчáсно, 29
too late – запі́зно, 29
tooth – зуб, зýба, *pl.* зýби, 28
tooth brush – зубнá щі́тка, 28
toothpaste – зубнá пáста, 28
tornado – торнáдо, 33
to the left – лівóруч, 6
to the right – праворуч, 6
tourist *[f]* – тури́стка, 12
tourist *[m]* – тури́ст, 12
toward – до, 18
towel – рушни́к, рушникá, *pl.* рушники́, 28
town – мі́сто, *pl.* містá, 12
town: small town – селó, *pl.* сéла, сіл, 12
toy – зáбавка, *pl.* забавки́, забавóк; *і́грашка*, 25

tractor – трáктор *[h]*, -а, *pl.* трактори́, 25
traffic – рух, рýху (вýличний рух), 35
traffic light – світлофóр *[h]*, -а, 18
train – пóїзд, -а, *pl.* поїзди́; пóтяг, -а, 18
trampoline – трамплі́н, -а, 34
translate – перекладáти: перекладá-ю, -єш
pf. переклáсти: переклад-ý, -éш, 36
translation – перéклад, -у, 36
translator *[f]* – перекладáчка, 36
translator *[m]* – перекладáч, 36
transport – везти́: вез-ý, -éш *[dur.]*, 6
pf. повезти́: повез-ý, -éш, 23
transport – вози́ти: вожý, вóз-иш *[it.]*, 10
pf. повезти́: повез-ý, -éш, 23
tree – дéрево, *pl.* дерéва, 21
tricycle – триколі́сник, -а, 34
trip – пóдорож *[f]*, пóдорожі, 36
trolley bus – тролéйбус, -а, 29
trophy – трофéй, трофéя, 34
truck – вантáжка, *грузови́к,- а*, 35
trunk – скри́ня, 32
trunk *[of a car]* – багáжник, -а, 25
T-shirt – тéніска; *футбóлка*, 20
tsymbaly – цимбáли *[pl]*, цимбáлів,
... цимбáлах, 16
Tuesday – вівтóрок, вівті́рка, 16
tunnel – тунéль, тунéлю, 35
TV – телеві́зор *[h]*, -а, 17
twelfth – дванáдцятий, 27
twelve – дванáдцять, 19
twentieth – двадця́тий, 27
twenty – двáдцять, 19
twenty-four hour period – добá, 29
two – два; дві, 19
two hundred – дві́сті, 19

U

Ukrainian – украї́нський, 38
Ukrainian *[f]* – украї́нка, 38
Ukrainian *[m]* – украї́нець, украї́нця, 38
Ukraine – Украї́на, 38
umbrella – парасóля; *парасоль, -я*;
збнтик, -а, 18
uncle – дя́дько, *pl.* дядьки́, 13
under – під *[+I]*, 21
understand – розумі́ти: розумі́-ю, -єш, 4
pf. зрозумі́ти: зрозумі́-ю, -єш, 23

unfortunate – нещасли́вий, 26
unhappy – неща́сний, 26
United Nations (UN)
– Організа́ція Об'є́днаних На́цій (ООН), 38
United States of America (USA)
– Сполу́чені Шта́ти Аме́рики (США), 38
university – університе́т, -у, 11
unlucky – нещасли́вий, 26
unmarried – неодру́жений, 37
unpleasant – неприє́мний, 26
up – угóру/вгóру, 6
upwards – угóру/вгóру, 6
use – ужива́ти: ужива́-ю, -єш
pf. ужи́ти: ужив-у́, -е́ш, 28
usually – звича́йно, 3

V

vacation – вака́ції *[pl]*, вака́цій, ... вака́ціях, 25
vacuum cleaner – пилосмóк, -а; пилосóс, -а, 17
valise – валі́зка; *чемода́н, -а*, 18
varenyk – варе́ник, -а; пирі́г, пирога́,
pl. пироги́, 19
vase – ва́за, 17
VCR – ві́део *[indecl.]*, 17
vegetables – горóдина *[sg]*; ярина́ *[sg]*; *óвочі*, 30
veranda – вера́нда, 14
very – ду́же, 4
videoplayer – ві́део *[indecl.]*, 17
village – селó, *pl.* се́ла, сіл, 12
violin – скри́пка, *pl.* скрипки́, скрипóк, 16
visa – ві́за, 18
volleyball *[game]* – волейбóл, -у, 15

W

wages – платня́, 37
wagon – візóк, візка́, *pl.* візки́, 34
wait – чека́ти: чека́-ю, -єш, 4
pf. почека́ти: почека́-ю. -єш, 23
waiter – офіція́нт; *офіціа́нт*, 13
waitress – офіція́нтка; *офіціа́нтка*, 13
walk – прогу́лянка; прóхід, прохóду, 25
wall – стіна́, стіни́, *pl.* сті́ни, стін, 14
wallet – гамане́ць, гаманця́, *pl.* гаманці́, 13
want – хоті́ти: хóч-у, -еш, 7
pf. с/за/хоті́ти: с/за/хóч-у, -еш, 23
warm – те́плий, 33
warm – пригріва́ти: пригріва́-ю, -єш
pf. пригрі́ти: пригрі́-ю, -єш, 33
warm: it's warm – те́пло, 33
wash – умива́ти: умива́-ю, -єш
pf. уми́ти: уми́-ю, -єш, 28
wash oneself – умива́тися: умива́-юся, -єшся
pf. уми́тися: уми́-юся, -єшся, 28
watch – годи́нник, -а, 17
water – вода́, води́, *pl.* вóди, 15
water skis – водяні́ ли́жі, 34
wave *[of water]* – хви́ля, 34
we – ми, 2
wealth – майнó *[sg]*, 38
wear – носи́ти: ношу́, нóс-иш, 10
(carry) *pf.* понести́: понес-у́, -е́ш, 23
(wear) *pf.* поноси́ти: поношу́, понóс-иш, 23
weather – погóда, 33
weather forecast – прогнóз, -у:
прогнóз погóди, 33
wedding ceremony – вінча́ння *[n]*; шлюб, -у, 27
wedding reception – весі́лля *[n]*, 27
Wednesday – середа́, 16
weed – бур'я́н, бур'яну́, *pl.* бур'яни́, 21
week – ти́ждень, ти́жня, 16
week: every week – щоти́жня, 10
weigh – ва́жити: ва́ж-у, -иш, 8
pf. зва́жити: зва́ж-у, -иш, 23
welcome – прийма́ти: прийма́-ю, -єш
pf. прийня́ти: (future) прийм-у́, -е́ш
(past) прийня́-в, -ла́, -лó -ли́, 28
well – дóбре, 4
west – за́хід, за́ходу, 16
what – що, 3
what kind – яки́й, 26
when – коли́, 5
where: from where – зві́дки, 9
where: in what place – де, 2
where: to what place – куди́, 7
whether – чи, 8
which – котри́й, 26
whistle – свиста́ти: свищ-у́, -еш
pf. сви́снути: сви́сн-у, -еш, 31
whisper – шепта́ти: шепч-у́, -еш, 7
pf. ше́пнути: шепн-у́, -е́ш, 23
white – бі́лий, 26
whiter – білі́ший, 30
who – хто, 3
whose – чий, чия́, чиє́, чиї́, 28
why – чому́, 6

wide – широ́кий, 30
widely – ши́ро́ко, 31
widely: more widely – ши́рше, 31
wider – ши́ркий, 30
wife – дружи́на; жі́нка, *pl.* жінки́, жіно́к, 13
win – вигравáти: вигра-ю́, -є́ш
pf. ви́грати: ви́гра-ю, -єш, 32
wind – ві́тер, ві́тру, *pl.* вітри́, 33
windy: it's windy – ві́тряно, 33
window – вікно́, *pl.* ві́кна, ві́кон, 17
window: display window – вітри́на, 14
wine – вино́, 15
winter – зимá, *pl.* зими́, зим, 16
winter – зимо́вий, 33
winter: in the winter – узи́мку/взи́мку, 8
wise – му́дрий, 26
wisely – му́дро, 31
wisely: more wisely – мудрі́ше, 31
wiser – мудрі́ший, 30
witch – ві́дьма, *g.pl.* ві́дьо́м, 37
with – з *[+I]*, 21
without – без *[+G]*, 18
woman – жі́нка, *pl.* жінки́, жіно́к, 11
wood – де́рево, 32
word – сло́во, *pl.* словá, слів, 27
work – прáця; робо́та, 29
work – працювáти: працю́-ю, -єш, 5
pf. попрацювáти: попрацю́-ю, -єш, 23
worker *[f]* – праці́вни́ця, 12
worker *[m]* – працівни́к, працівникá,
pl. працівники́, 12
world – світ, сві́ту, *pl.* світи́, 27
worried – зажу́рений, 37
worry – жури́тися: жур-ю́ся, -ишся, 8
pf. пожури́тися: пожур-ю́ся, -ишся, 23
worse – гі́рше, 4
worse – гі́рший, 30
wrist – зап'я́сток, зап'я́стка, 31
write – писáти: пиш-у́, -еш, 7
pf. написáти: напиш-у́, -еш, 23
writer *[f]* – письме́нниця, 36
writer *[m]* – письме́нник, 36

Y

yard – двір, дворá і дво́ру, *pl.* двори́ 21
year – рік, ро́ку, *pl.* роки́, 16
year: every year – щоро́ку, 10
yellow – жо́втий, 26
yellower – жовті́ший, 30
yes – так, 2
yesterday – учо́ра/вчо́ра, 16
yesterday: day before yesterday – позавчо́ра, 16
yet – ще, 3
you – ти; ви, 2
young – молоди́й, 26
younger – моло́дший, 30
your *[p]* – ваш, вáша, вáше, вáші, 28
your *[s]* – твій, твоя́, твоє́, твої́, 28
yours *[p]* – ваш, вáша, вáше, вáші, 28
yours *[s]* – твій, твоя́, твоє́, твої́, 28
youthfully – мо́лодо, 31
youthfully: more youthfully – моло́дше, 31

Z

zero – зе́ро; нуль, нуля́, *pl.* нулі́, 19
zoo – зоопáрк, -у, 25

A BRIEF INDEX

PRONOUNS

VERBS